HUMAN
GEOGRAPHY
SPATIAL DESIGN IN WORLD SOCIETY

McGRAW-HILL SERIES IN GEOGRAPHY

EDWARD J. TAAFFE AND JOHN W. WEBB, *Consulting Editors*

HUMAN GEOGRAPHY
SPATIAL DESIGN IN WORLD SOCIETY

John F. Kolars
John D. Nystuen

Professors of Geography
University of Michigan

Drawings by
Derwin Bell

Department of Geology
University of Michigan

McGRAW-HILL BOOK COMPANY

New York   St. Louis   San Francisco   Düsseldorf   Johannesburg
Kuala Lumpur   London   Mexico   Montreal   New Delhi   Panama
Paris   São Paulo   Singapore   Sydney   Tokyo   Toronto

Cover Illustration:
From **Metamorphose**, *M. C. Escher, Escher Foundation*
Collection Haags, Gemeentemuseum, The Hague.

Front Matter Illustrations:
From **Double Planetoid**, *M. C. Escher, Escher Foundation Collection*
Haags, Gemeentemuseum, The Hague.

From **Tower of Babel**, *M. C. Escher, Escher Foundation Collection*
Haags, Gemeentemuseum, The Hague.

This book was set in Palatino by Black Dot, Inc.
The editors were Stephen D. Dragin, Janis M. Yates, and Helen Greenberg;
the designer was J. E. O'Connor;
the production supervisor was Joe Campanella.
The printer was Federated Lithographers-Printers, Inc.;
the binder, The Book Press, Inc.

HUMAN GEOGRAPHY
SPATIAL DESIGN IN WORLD SOCIETY

1 2 3 4 5 6 7 8 9 0 F L B P 7 9 8 7 6 5 4

LIBRARY OF CONGRESS CATALOGING IN PUBLICATION DATA

Kolars, John F
  Human Geography: spatial design in world society.

  (McGraw-Hill series in geography)
  Includes bibliographical references.
  1. Anthropo-geography.   2. Cities and towns.
3. Human ecology.   I. Title.
GF41.K66   301.36'1   74-6351
ISBN 0-07-035327-1

To
Jeffrey,
Leslie,
and Christine

CONTENTS

Contents

Contents

Contents

PREFACE

"We shape our buildings and afterwards our buildings shape us."
Winston Churchill

Humans, like hermit crabs, inherit the abandoned homes of others, or, corallike, constantly create additions to their cities. Urban-directed creatures, we depend upon man-made environments as well as natural ones, and find our lives increasingly focused upon major metropolitan areas. In order to understand these patterns of new growth in world society, geographers examine the spatial organization which sustains it.

Human Geography: Spatial Design in World Society is the offspring of our basic introductory text, *Geography: The Study of Location, Culture, and Environment.* In the preface to the original text we express our purpose:

> . . . to introduce modern geography to students with no previous knowledge of the subject and to demonstrate how a geographic point of view can enhance our understanding of the world around us. To do this, we discuss social and physical systems and the interaction between them in terms of their spatial attributes, including their dimensions, densities, scale relationships, associations, and patterns. In this way, we come to our definition of geography as *the study of man-environment systems from the viewpoint of spatial relationships and spatial processes.*

While we recommend the original, integrated text as being representative of the full spectrum of geography, many people have expressed interest in shorter texts emphasizing either locational analysis or environmental systems. To meet these requests, we have divided the original text into its two main parts and present this volume as the first of two which will cover the same materials as our longer work.

This volume is not simply one-half the original text between new covers. Approximately 20 percent more textual material has been added, along with a proportionate amount of new figures and tabular data. Detailed discussions have been provided for more complex subjects, including the role of scale in determining indices of segregation, a method of operationalizing the mean information field, and a detailed case study of the spatial structuring of a nationwide business. In addition, the historical development of transportation networks, urban areas, and urban-industrial regions have all received special attention.

In this book we emphasize the importance of locational analysis as a means of further understanding world society. Chapter by chapter, increasingly complex ideas are presented. These include spatial hierarchies, region building, and spatial optimization. We also consider important geographic theories of human behavior, including Christaller's ideas of the central place hierarchy, Thünen's model of agricultural land use, and Hägerstrand's insights into spatial diffusion. We also treat the role of communication in considerable detail in Chapters 6 and 7. Recognition of communication as the catalyst for human activity represents something of a departure from existing geography texts, but we are confident of the growing interest in such materials.

This volume emphasizes urbanism as a global life-style of enormous consequence which can be better appreciated from a geographic point of view. To quote again from the preface to the original text:

> We make no claim that geography offers the only valid view of man and nature. But geography does provide an important and basic approach to such matters. We hope that this book will present insights into spatial behavior and that the ideas elaborated in the case studies can be transferred to situations relevant to you. At the same time, we try not to present any simple world view as the correct and only one. Phrasing this in the vocabulary of the geographer, we do not try to point the way; we only try to help you find out where you are. You must choose your own goals, your own destinations. Our only word of caution is that human activities invariably take place in an environmental framework and have environmental consequences.

We have less to say in this book about the environmental consequences of worldwide urbanization, but that subject is treated fully in the second half of our basic text as well as in *Environmental Geography,* the forthcoming companion to this volume. Our main concern here is to present the urbanizing earth in a spatial framework. We hope that this will lead our readers to investigate for themselves the complete picture of man in his environmental context.

In writing a textbook, the first thing the authors learn is that the task can be accomplished only with the help of many others. We first wish to thank the students at the University of Michigan who have taken the introductory courses upon which our effort is based. The constant challenge of their critical and inquiring minds has been a spur to our ambitions. Equally important to us have been the advice and criticism of our consulting editor, Arthur Getis, who has successfully alternated as devil's advocate and staunch friend. The actual presentation of the subject matter in graphic form could not have been done without the advice and help of Waldo R. Tobler, whose new *Hyperelliptical Map Projection* was especially created to serve as the base for the world maps throughout most of the text.* Many of the other base maps have also been provided by Waldo Tobler, whose knowledge and ability in computerized mapping have allowed flexibility in our choice of map projections. In the same manner, we feel that the illustrations and maps prepared by Derwin Bell will long survive the words that accompany them. Finally, we wish to thank our many able assistants at the university, as well as the staff at McGraw-Hill, who have provided support, advice, and encouragement above and beyond the call of duty. If errors, omissions, or oversights vex our critics, only the authors are to blame.

John F. Kolars
John D. Nystuen

*W. R. Tobler, "The Hyperelliptical and Other New Pseudo Cylindrical Equal Area Map Projections," *Journal of Geophysical Research,* v. 78, No. 11, April 1973, pp. 1753–1759.

HUMAN GEOGRAPHY
SPATIAL DESIGN
IN WORLD SOCIETY

1 | LOCATION AND ENVIRONMENT: A GEOGRAPHIC POINT OF VIEW

This book emphasizes cities and the urban life-style associated with them. At the same time, we introduce a series of increasingly complex spatial insights which represent geography's special contribution to both the social and physical sciences. Chapter by chapter we build a spatial picture of human activity.

To accomplish this we rely both upon factual descriptions of reality and upon models which simplify real world relationships. One of the great advantages of the human mind is its ability to symbolize and abstract the avalanche of sensations and perceptions with which it is confronted. Model building is a formal and systematic way of doing this, and by means of it reality can be simplified for basic understanding. By beginning with the simplest of models which barely approximate reality we can little by little complicate them in a controlled manner until what was once confusing becomes clear.

We begin our model building with very simple assumptions about human behavior in space. To accomplish this, we reduce the natural world to a featureless plain. Once we have gained some insight into human behavior, we are able to reintroduce the complexities of nature in order to see what changes result from their presence. Thus, we begin with simple models of reality and proceed to more factual descriptions of the complex whole. We hope in this manner to show how a *geographic point of view* increases and enriches our understanding of the world in which we live.

Numbers Without Dimensions

In order to understand the expression *a geographic point of view*, let us consider the following list of numbers:

49 72 34 31 31 74 69 39 60 44 56 67

This sequence might represent many things: the age of participants in a panel discussion, the number of houses in a sample of Chinese hamlets, or the distance traveled daily by commuters to Wall Street. These numbers are, in fact, average monthly temperatures in a mid-latitude, or temperate, location. No discernible progression appears associated with them. Yet the list as set down is a sequence, in this case ordered by alphabetizing the months of the year. How much more logical to arrange the numbers as they occur chronologically (Figure 1-1), for the temporal arrangement carries with it additional infor-

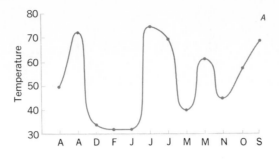

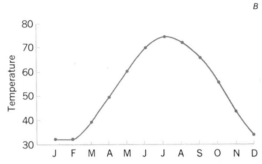

Figure 1-1 Average monthly temperature *(A)*
Monthly temperature arranged alphabetically by
month. (*B*) Monthly temparature arranged
chronologically by month.

mation about the seasonal values of the figures.

In the same way, many lists are ordered alphabetically which might better have some other arrangement. This is particularly true of things relating to the earth-space in which we live. Census tables showing population and other characteristics of various political units often list Alaska next to Alabama and Ethiopia after England. Geographers find this practice no more logical than alphabetizing the months of the year. Examples showing the importance of the location of things in space, just as in time, are found everywhere. The clustering of the poor in "poverty pockets" and of minority groups in "ghettos," and the congregation of major industries within a small portion of the world's nations, as well as the fact that we recognize areas by such regional phrases as "the Corn Belt" and "the Holy Land," immediately suggest that spatial ordering has taken place in the real world. The problems of Alabama and

the problems of Alaska are very different although their juxtaposition in alphabetized lists falsely suggests some type of continuity nonexistent in reality. Alabama and Georgia, Alaska and British Columbia, England and Scotland, and Ethiopia and the Sudan are all more logically paired than any alphabetically associated countries.

Another example of the need to identify places by location, as well as by name, occurs when international data are presented. Table 1–1 shows the per capita income for selected European countries. On the left, the values are arranged by listing the countries alphabetically with names designated through common English usage. The same values are listed on the right, but the list has been alphabetized using the official names which each country chooses to use for itself. Which alphabetical listing is correct? By whose criteria should information be compiled?

Still another example of this problem will occur if you travel to Europe next summer. At that time will you stay in Cologne or Köln, Florence or Firenze? The latter names are locally correct; the former are, at best, rather poor English transliterations.

Cross-cultural confusion like this can be overcome by locating cities, countries, and other places using spatial coordinates such as latitude and longitude. While a number of geographic techniques exist for recording, storing, and analyzing information through the use of coordinates, maps are the most familiar way in which this is done. The figures given in Table 1–1 have been plotted in Figure 1–2. Notice that in addition to overcoming the language difficulties inherent in the alphabetical lists, the distribution of per capita income on the map of Europe suggests additional information that the lists conceal. Per capita incomes are highest in northwest Europe and diminish to the east and south with surprising regularity. In the same way, per capita incomes for all the countries of the world show a distinct spatial ordering (Figure 1–3).

Now compare the world per capita income map with the one showing population growth rates throughout the world (Figure 1–4). The

*Human
Geography:
Spatial
Design
in World
Society*

4

Table 1–1 Per Capita National Income for Europe (U.S.$)*

Common English Name		Official Name as Designated by Each Country	
Country	Income	Country	Income
Albania	400	Bundesrepublik Deutschland	1,970
Austria	1,320	Československá Socialĭstická	1,240
Belgium	1,810	Deutsche Demokratische Republik	1,430
Bulgaria	770	Éire	980
Czechoslovakia	1,240	Estado Español	730
Denmark	2,070	Federativna Socijalistička Republika	
Finland	1,720	Jugoslavija	510
France	2,130	Kongeriget Danmark	2,070
Germany (Dem. Republic)	1,430	Kongeriket Norge	2,000
Germany (Fed. Republic)	1,970	Koninkrijk der Nederlanden	1,620
Greece	740	Konungariket Sverige	2,620
Hungary	980	Llydveldid Island	1,680
Iceland	1,680	Magyar Nepköztársaság	980
Ireland	980	Narodna Republika Bulgaria	770
Italy	1,230	Polska Rzeczpospolita Ludowa	880
Netherlands	1,620	Repubblica Italiana	1,230
Norway	2,000	Republica Popullore E Shipërisë	400
Poland	880	República Portuguesa	460
Portugal	460	Republica Socialista România	780
Romania	780	Republik Österrich	1,320
Spain	730	Republique Française	2,130
Sweden	2,620	Royaume de Belgique/Koninkrijk België	1,810
Switzerland	2,490	Schweiz/Suisse/Svizzera	2,490
Turkey	310	Soyuz Sovyetskikh Sotsialisticheskikh	
United Kingdom	1,790	Respublik	1,110
U.S.S.R.	1,110	Suomen Tasavalta	1,720
Yugoslavia	510	Türkiye Cumhuriyeti	310
		United Kingdom	1,790
		Vasileion Tis Ellados	740

*National income –value of the nation's output of goods and services, including balance
of income from abroad.
Source: *Statesman's Yearbook, 1967*; Population Reference Bureau, 1971

corresponding patterns on these two maps indicate a strong correlation in geographic space between high growth rates and low incomes. In the same manner the average consumption of proteins and calories shown on the world nutrition map (Figure 1–5) indicates greatest need in the developing nations of the world. The grouping of problems such as these in specific areas suggests that it would be useful to study the patterns formed by various geographic distributions. However, map patterns are not always simple or easy to understand. Figure 1–6 demonstrates world variations in population densities. Large numbers of people live in some areas, while other places are empty, or nearly so. But notice that both the rich nations and the poor nations have areas of sparse as well as dense population. Variations such as these complicate our understanding of the distribution of the world's problems.

Spatial patterns, like those revealed to us on the accompanying maps, attract the geographer's attention. Almost all phenomena,

*Location
and
Environment*

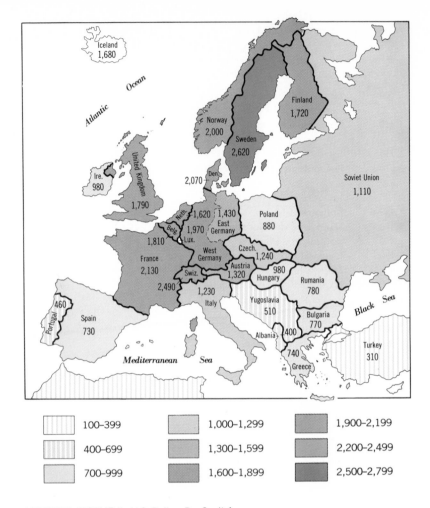

NATIONAL INCOME (In U.S. Dollars Per Capita)

Figure 1-2 European per capita national income in U.S. dollars, 1968
(Population Reference Bureau, 1971; based on 1968 data supplied by the
International Bank for Reconstruction and Development)

Figure 1-3 World per capita national income in U.S. dollars, 1968 (Op. cit., Figure 1-2)

Figure 1-4 Annual rate of population increase, 1971 The darker the area, the greater the birthrate. If the annual birthrate remained at a constant value of 2.0, it would take thirty-five years for the population to double. At a constant rate of 3.0, the population would double in twenty-three years.

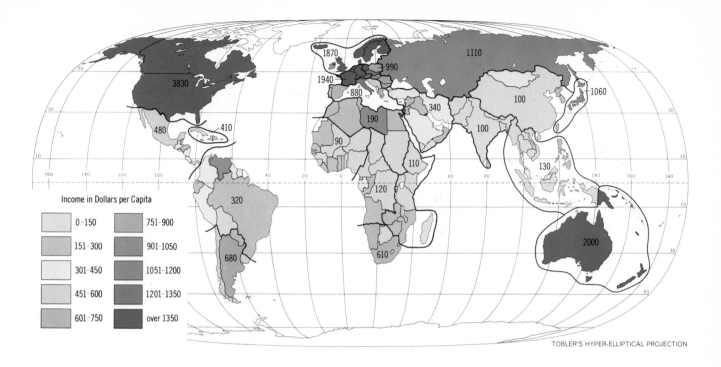

Income in Dollars per Capita

0–150	751–900
151–300	901–1050
301–450	1051–1200
451–600	1201–1350
601–750	over 1350

3830

1870
1940
990
880
1940
90
190
340
100
100
1060
480
410
320
110
120
130
610
680
2000

TOBLER'S HYPER-ELLIPTICAL PROJECTION

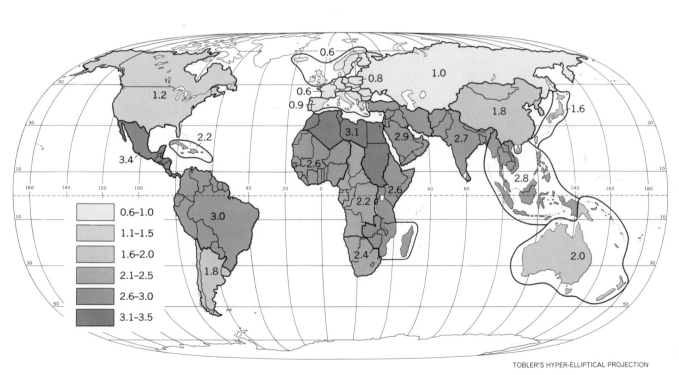

0.6
0.8
1.0
0.6
0.9
1.2
2.2
3.4
3.1
2.9
2.7
1.8
1.6
2.6
2.8
2.6
2.2
3.0
2.6
2.4
1.8
2.0

	0.6–1.0
	1.1–1.5
	1.6–2.0
	2.1–2.5
	2.6–3.0
	3.1–3.5

TOBLER'S HYPER-ELLIPTICAL PROJECTION

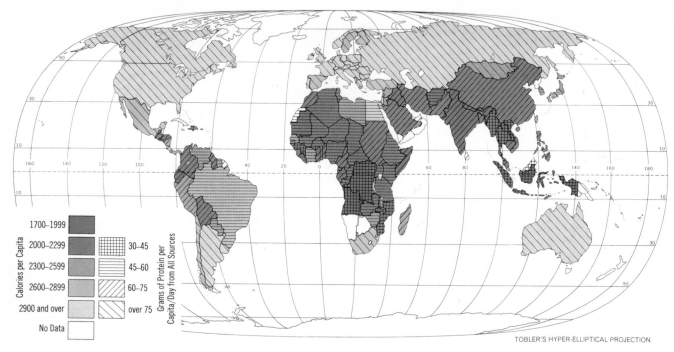

Calories per Capita
- 1700–1999
- 2000–2299
- 2300–2599
- 2600–2899
- 2900 and over
- No Data

Grams of Protein per Capita/Day from All Sources
- 30–45
- 45–60
- 60–75
- over 75

TOBLER'S HYPER-ELLIPTICAL PROJECTION

Figure 1-5 World food supply (net food supplies per capita at retail level) Statistics on food consumption are for the latest year available, mainly from 1960 to 1970. They are not uniformly reliable, since they generally reflect over- rather than underestimates. They are also averages by country; great variations exist in almost every country, so that even in countries which have average surplus consumption there are undernourished people. (Prepared from data in *UN Statistical Abstract 1970*, Table 161)

from the level of nutrition to population densities, cultures, and political ideologies, can be better understood when considered in a spatial context. Most of the problems facing mankind have a spatial character, an analysis of which will help with their solution. The *analytical techniques* referred to later in this book are useful in understanding complicated spatial relationships, but mastery of techniques is only one part of problem solving. It is also necessary to have available the *facts* which relate to the problems. Equally important are *theories* to suggest how the facts should be arranged and which analytical techniques are most appropriate. The combination of geographic facts, techniques, and theories presented in this book establishes a *geographic point of view*, particularly useful for under-

standing the kaleidoscopic world in which we live.

Nominal versus geographic locations

The first insight associated with the geographic point of view is a simple but important one. We must distinguish between words implying places as nominal classifications and words referring to specific locations. Place terms used in nominal or nonspatial classifications cannot be located on maps. Phrases like

the rural and urban sectors of the economy
the developed and developing worlds
Western civilization
black America
suburbia

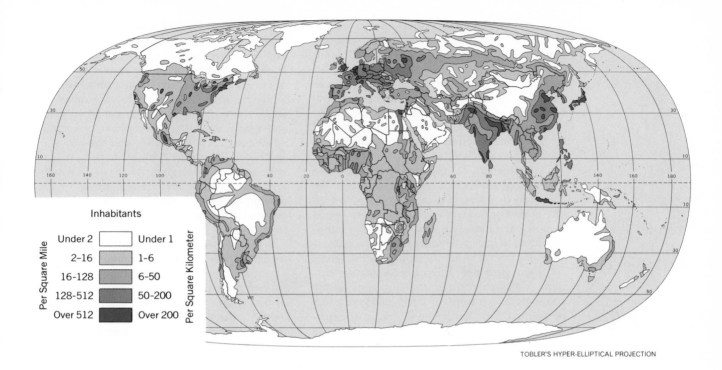

Figure 1-6 World population density.

TOBLER'S HYPER-ELLIPTICAL PROJECTION

Inhabitants

Per Square Mile		Per Square Kilometer
Under 2		Under 1
2–16		1–6
16–128		6–50
128–512		50–200
Over 512		Over 200

use place terms nominally. Obviously, these words indicate different sorts of environments, but beyond this distinction what do such words tell us? Where are the *rural and urban sectors* of the economy located? Are the country-dwelling commuters of Connecticut and Michigan who travel each day to offices and factories in the city better assigned to rural or urban America? How many factories must a nation have to be located in the *developed* rather than the *developing* world? Why do courses in *Western civilization* include Mesopotamia, Egypt, and sometimes Persia, but not Sub-Saharan Africa? What happens when *black America* wants to become part of suburbia?

The use of place words in this manner presents an abstract division of data. There is nothing wrong in using words this way, but it is important to remember that abstract words often have as many connotations as

there are people using them. Distinguishing place terms with real locations from place terms used nominally is one way of clarifying our thinking. Trying to define the geographic locations of place terms used nominally gives us additional insight and information—even if we find the real locations of certain nominal terms as elusive as *the end of the rainbow*. On the other hand, learning to think about real space in abstract terms is an important step in understanding spatial theories and analytical techniques, which, in turn, lead us to new insights about the real world.

Dimensional Primitives: A Way of Looking at the World

We all use words referring to location in our everyday speech. Proper nouns like *New York* and common nouns like *country* and *city*, as well as adjectives like *near* and *far*, occur in

*Location
and
Environment*

nearly every sentence. We also use a variety of spatial words with strong emotional overtones. The umpire shouts, "You're out," meaning the player must leave the field. He is literally sent out of the area of action. To be *on the in* is to be well-informed. In medieval Europe, to *sit below the salt* was to be placed in a menial position at a lord's table. *Right* and *left* have strong political connotations which we read about every day.

The problem in dealing with terms like those above is to make them exact. In this task, we may turn to mathematicians for help. We do not intend to assign numbers to the world around us; rather, we shall consider mathematicians in their role as logicians and philosophers. In considering the nature of the world and their attempts to describe it, mathematicians long ago realized that for consistency and logic every word in every theorem must be defined. This led to the dilemma of defining every word of the definitions defining the words. Since this exercise could go on and on like the ever-diminishing images in two barber shop mirrors, a solution to the problem of ultimate definitions was needed.

The practical solution found for this problem was to agree that the meaning of certain terms should be accepted intuitively. These undefined terms, upon which the subsequent logical structures of mathematics are built, are called *primitives*. In like manner, certain basic statements which describe the fundamental conditions held to be constant throughout any sequence of mathematical reasoning are called *axioms* and are composed of *primitives*. In these axioms, each word is required for a complete description but does not duplicate the meaning of the other words; that is, each word is necessary and independent. Having been given this start, and carefully staying within the original limits of the axioms, we can evolve elaborate systems of logic from such terms.

In much the same way it is possible to describe the world in all its geographic complexity and yet to begin with only a limited number of dimensional *primitives* arranged to form a small set of *basic spatial concepts*. Con-

sider Figure 1–7, "Cities with Over 2 Million Population." At the scale[1] of this map the entire world can be depicted on a single page. The cities which interest us appear as a series of dots or points when drawn at this scale. But in reality they cover many square miles and are of various shapes. On this map, city area and shape are not considered important. The number of very large cities and their location are the data the map is meant to present, so it is sufficient to designate each city as a point without size or shape. Here, then, is the first of the primitives with which our geographic viewpoint can be created: A *point* is considered to be a dimensionless location.

Beginning with the concept of a point, we may then derive two additional elements so essential to geography that they can be considered primitives in their own right. A series of points arranged one after another creates a *line*. A collection of adjacent points arranged in a nonlinear fashion, or a line which closes upon itself, defines an *area*. Imagine a plain, smooth tabletop. If one grain of salt is placed on this surface and viewed from a distance, it will, for all practical purposes, appear as a dimensionless point. A row of salt grains viewed from the same distance will appear as a line. A dense sprinkling of salt, one grain in depth, when viewed from across the room will define an area on the tabletop; when seen from only a few inches or feet away, this same area will visually decompose into individual grains or points.

Point, *line*, and *area* concepts are important to geographers for several reasons. Not only do they form the basic or primitive elements in various systems of geometry and topology, but they may be used to describe all manner of things in the real world. In Figure 1–7, the *points* marking the cities represent foci of human activity and wealth, as well as concentrations of people. *Lines* on maps represent everything from transportation routes to national boundaries. *Areas* stand for nations, regions, forests, oceans and continents, and every other feature extending in two dimen-

[1]An expression which we must accept without definition until Chapter 2.

sions. We can think of cities as *points* linked by transportation *lines* to each other and to farming *areas*. There is another dimensional primitive with which we will be concerned as our discussion unfolds. *Volume* follows logically after area. However, we will limit our present argument to points, lines, and areas, for those are the spatial elements upon which map making relies. Later in this book we will talk about spatial variation in the distribution of many things, such as income and population. Such distributions can be shown on two-dimensional maps, just as we can depict plains, contoured surfaces, hills, and mountains. Two-dimensional, or flat, distributions are plotted along two axes designated x and y. The third dimension is plotted on a third, or z, axis.

The most direct linear value that can be shown on the z axis is elevation. Measures of vertical values, such as for building heights, are thus shown on the z axis. Very often the value plotted on the z axis represents an abstraction: for example, population density. On the other hand, geographic locations in the form of points, lines, and areas always are shown by x and y coordinates.

An orderly view of relations between dimensional primitives

The most common of everyday things can be viewed spatially. Consider the campus where you are now studying. You and your fellow students can be thought of as concentrations of biotic energy endowed with the desire to learn. At a map scale suitable for showing the entire campus, people appear as points. On good days, two things may happen: the sun will shine, and your professors will give bril-

Figure 1-7 Cities with over 2 million population.   Notice that although there is a concentration of very large cities in the Eastern United States and Western Europe, there is actually a greater total in the non-western world. Even so, these many large cities contain a much smaller proportion of the total population of the non-western world, which is still largely rural. (1970 data.)

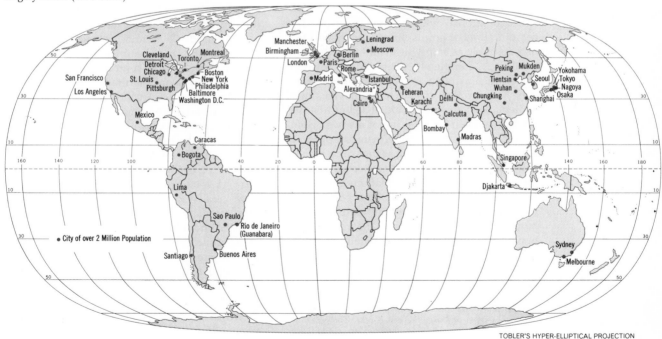

TOBLER'S HYPER-ELLIPTICAL PROJECTION

liant lectures. From a geographical point of view the difference between lecturing professors and sunshine is that the professors are *punctiform*, or pointlike, while sunlight washes in upon the earth as an areal phenomenon. That is, for our purposes sunlight cannot be separated into individual points of light but equally covers the entire area of the campus. A lecture is generated at a point, the professor's head. When students wish to enjoy the sun, the geographical relationship can be described essentially as one of point to area, since they will disperse across the lawns in a fairly even distribution in order to sun themselves. If you attend a lecture, the spatial patterning is one of many points clustered around a single point.

In summary, points may be thought of as concentrations, or foci. Lines represent a double function as either paths of movement or boundaries. Areas show the extent of things and represent distributions or dispersals. Another way of looking at areas is that they are used to generalize and classify the world around us. This is the campus; that is the town; beyond is the countryside.

Now let us consider Figure 1–8, "Dimensional Relations," which shows all the possible combinations of points, lines, and areas. One-half the table is empty; it would be redundant to fill it in completely.[2] The various relationships are illustrated by selected urban examples. The number of such examples is almost endless; each reader should develop his own conceptual skills by thinking of his own examples. Note that these relationships appear in the world of nature as well as the world of man.

In the upper-left-hand corner is the cell representing point–point relationships. While we have already discussed one point–point example—the lecturer and his audience—urban examples are plentiful. The relationship between a wholesale establishment, such as a bakery, and its retail outlets can be thought of as points relating to points. An example of point–line relationships would be the prob-

[2]Any such array as this is often referred to as a *matrix*. Individual squares or boxes are called *cells*. The horizontal lines are called *rows*, and the vertical ones are called *columns*.

lem of locating bus stops along a bus route. Should they be stationed at every block, which would make the trip very slow, or should the stops be far apart, which would allow quick trips but be inconvenient for the people walking to the bus stops? A similar problem would be to find the best locations for several ice cream vendors on a boardwalk. Point–area relationships are illustrated by the problem of the optimal location of television stations. The transmitter is located at a point but broadcasts over a more or less continuous area. (Viewers within that area may be thought of as points, which opens up the possibility of interpreting problems in several ways.) Ideally, television stations should be located at the center of the most dense concentration of population. But high population densities mean high land values and taxes, which might make the station unprofitable. These factors must be taken into account in finding the best location.

At the intersection of the second row and second column the line–line relationships that interest city dwellers include the problem of interchanges where superhighways cross each other. Other examples would include the problem of bridge building where canals and streets intermingle. Line–area examples immediately call to mind all manner of traffic problems. Anyone who has been caught in the five o'clock rush as the central business district empties out along limited-access highways into the suburbs can vouch for the frustrations of inadequate line–area relationships.

The complexity of area–area relationships stems from the inherent difficulties of defining areas in terms of logical sets of variables as well as of defining their extent and boundaries. A relatively straightforward example of area–area relationships which results in complex interactions is the city of Berlin (Figure 1–9). Although the entire prewar city originally functioned as a single urban entity, subsequent political differences have separated the two parts. Their zone of contact is the infamous Berlin Wall. Other urban examples of area–area relationships are the ways in which major cities divide the space intervening between themselves and their neigh-

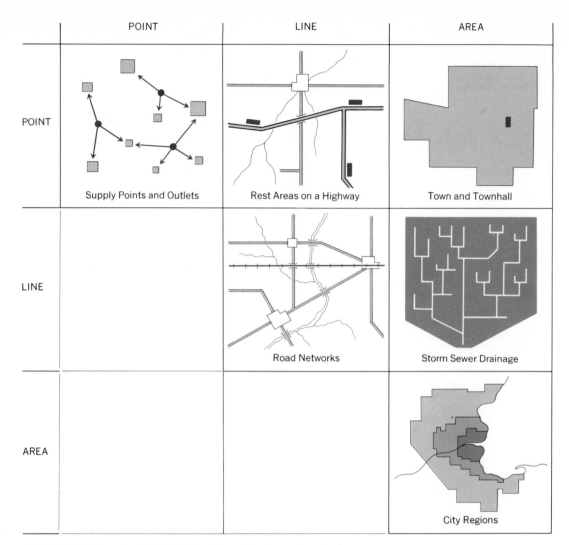

	POINT	LINE	AREA
POINT	Supply Points and Outlets	Rest Areas on a Highway	Town and Townhall
LINE		Road Networks	Storm Sewer Drainage
AREA			City Regions

Figure 1-8 Dimensional relations All spatial phenomena can be characterized by their spatial dimensions. When spatial elements interact, the dimensions involved will influence the geographical pattern that results. The table shows point–point, point–line, point–area, and other kinds of elements in some type of association. The classifications could also be extended to include volumetric relationships by the addition of a row and a column to the table. For example, air pollution problems could be considered a point-to-volume or a line-to-volume interaction depending upon the dimension of the pollution sources.

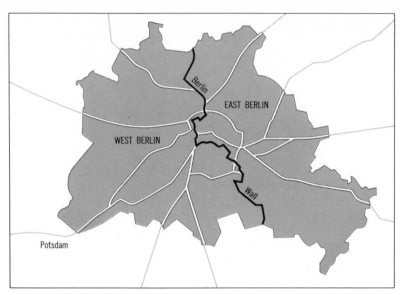

Figure 1-9 The Berlin Wall West Berlin is a spatially separated enclave of West Germany in East German territory as a consequence of the termination of World War II. Germany was divided into two parts by Western and Communist powers; Berlin, the former capital, also was divided. In the following years, thousands of East Germans fled Communist control by crossing into West Berlin despite efforts to halt them. Eventually the East German regime erected a solid, fortified, and patrolled wall between the two halves of the city in order to prevent the escapes. The wall remains a real and symbolic barrier between the two Germanys. The unusual geographical circumstance is a major factor in the political tension generated by this situation.

Figure 1-10 Peutinger map (*E. Tabula Peutingeriana*) The map shows routes across Asia Minor in classical times. It contains information about the route network or connections but none about true distances or directions. (*Journal of a Tour in Asia Minor*, William Martin Leake, London: John Murray, 1824)

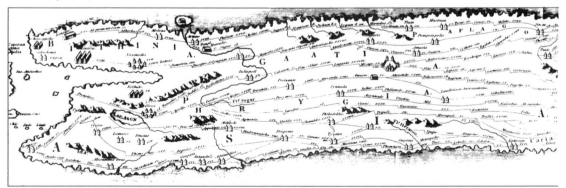

bors, thus dividing their customers, water supplies, and room for expansion. On still another level, the maintenance of gang territories, or "turfs," within major cities results in street violence and even deaths when rival groups attempt to extend the areas under their control.

Some Basic Spatial Concepts

Once we have learned to think about the world in terms of its point, line, and area characteristics, these dimensional primitives can be used to define basic spatial concepts or axiomatic statements. When geographers talk about space, they do not mean astronomical space. The exploration of interplanetary and interstellar space is the work of astronomers and engineers, not of geographers. Geographers also do not consider space as an object or condition which exists of itself. The space which concerns us is defined functionally by the relationship between things. It is the nature of this geometric and topological relationship that forms the basis for the study of geographic space.

Let us take a simple example to show some geographic concepts. Imagine a large room, either a ballroom or a gymnasium. The empty room provides no clues or directions on how a crowd might behave if gathered there. Now imagine that a dance is to be held in the room. Musicians enter and choose a position at random along one of the walls. Once they have

established themselves, the crowd which has come to listen and dance does not behave randomly, but arranges itself in a very determinate fashion. Nearest the music are those people who want to watch the musicians. In order to see as well as hear, this group will form a semicircle around the orchestra. Before the semicircle is complete, a second rank of listeners may build up near the center, rather than remain too far toward the side. In this area the people will be packed closely together.

Beyond the watchers will be couples more interested in each other and in dancing. They will tend to remain in an area beyond people who are just listening, but within easy range of the music. Here every couple will need a larger space in order to dance, but the total area—while filled with fewer people—will be completely appropriated. Finally, in the areas along the walls and farthest from the musicians will be small groups of people talking or waiting to dance. In this last area there may be empty, unused floor space, as well as clusters of people.

What, then, are the spatial concepts which relate to this scene? First, directional orientation. There is a directional quality to the orchestra. Those spectators interested in the music not only will crowd as close to the musicians as possible, but will also face them. The musicians, in turn, will orient themselves toward the crowd. The human form has a natural orientation—a front and a back—which defines a line of sight. A location or a point

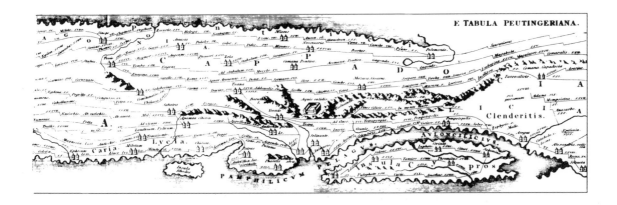

and a line of sight or ray are necessary and sufficient to define orientation. Thus, *direction* is of critical importance in understanding the spatial organization of the scene we are considering.

Distance is another important spatial quality. The sound of the music varies with distance. If the musicians are thought of as communicating to the crowd, they speak most directly to the semicircle of listeners, and somewhat less directly to the dancers beyond, who also are distracted by their own interests. Finally, on the edges of the scene, where the music is soft enough to allow conversation, the people are less directly involved with the musicians.

Intensity of communication falling off continuously with distance is a property shared by many, but not all, phenomena. An example of the opposite effect of distance is a transportation cost which normally rises with distance. Other phenomena are invariant with distance —at least within some range. Legal jurisdiction is as binding at the borders of a state as at its center.

Despite variations in behavior within the room, all the people are there because of the musicians' presence. If the orchestra leaves, the spatial patterning of the people within the room dissolves, for the functional associations which brought them there no longer exist at that place. The room will soon become empty. This relationship between the people and the musicians may be spoken of as a *functional association.*

There is a special type of functional associa-tion specifically spatial in character which is referred to as *connectivity.* By this we mean a special relation which objects in space have to each other. Look at Figures 2–3 and 1–10: one is taken from a railroad time schedule; the other is a twelfth-century copy of a third-century A.D. Roman road map. In both maps, although they were drawn seventeen centuries apart, certain spatial qualities are present, just as other spatial qualities are absent. The first shows the Green Bay and Western Railroad which connects Lake Michigan with the Minneapolis–St. Paul area, and the second shows roads in Asia Minor. In both maps, cities and routes are of major interest. In both maps, true proportional distances are lacking. In both maps, true directions or map orientation are also absent. And yet both maps contain significant amounts of information and provide keys to successful travel between the towns they show. Although true portrayals of distance and direction are absent, each shows the correct relative position or adjacency between cities. The *connectivity* of their space has been maintained. No matter how distorted their portrayal of the world, a traveler could find his way from city to city using these maps, for each city maintains its connectivity with its neighbors.

These, then, are the first three spatial concepts with which we are concerned: *distance*, *direction*, and *connectivity*. They will appear again and again in the following chapters. In combination with point, line, and area dimensional concepts, this provides a beginning for all kinds of geographic analysis.

2 | CITY SPACE — CONCEPTS OF SCALE

The Importance of Scale in Human Affairs

Suppose a spaceship operated by alien creatures visits Earth, their mission to seek intelligent life on the planet. While in orbit they remain too high to observe detail on the ground. During the landing phase of the journey, heat-shield problems prevent their monitoring the surface. Once on the ground they immediately find life, but detect only creatures of low intelligence having a simple form of social organization. The alien creatures are tiny; their ship, no bigger than an acorn, has landed in a grassy meadow, and those ant-sized explorers have indeed discovered ants. Upon leaving the earth they record that the planet lacks a developed civilization. They never see humans, and so they are unable to judge what mankind has achieved.

Their scale of observation has been inappropriate. If they had been able to look from their portholes at certain elevations during the descent, they might have noted human figures and the geometric forms of man-made structures. But even then they might not have noticed us, for their own technology might produce a landscape composed of curved forms and irregular elements. In such a case, they would not recognize the crystallike and geometric structures characteristic of our settlement patterns as the products of intelligent life or life at all. Their mission might fail

because of two types of problems: one related to the scale of observation and the other to pattern recognition.

Surprisingly, all humans are like those alien creatures. Earth phenomena, both physical and cultural, often occur at scales vastly different from the range within which our unaided senses function. Thus, we frequently fail to make accurate observations of the world in which we live. Sometimes instruments allow us to change our scale of observation and to broaden the range of signals we can monitor. For example, telescopes allow us to see long distances into the hugeness of the universe, while microscopes let us probe into the world of microbes and molecules. Nevertheless, we run the risk of failing to observe the phenomena which interest us most because we may choose the wrong scales of observation. We also may not perceive a pattern when we see one if we fail to recognize that a particular form or arrangement has significance. Finally, patterns may be so obscured by unwanted information that we may need special devices to filter out all but the critical data.

Instruments for changing the scale of observation

Telescopes and microscopes are familiar scientific instruments which change the scale of observation. At the scale at which geographers

Figure 2-1 (A) Apollo VI space photograph of the Dallas–Fort Worth, Texas, area Large roadways are only partially visible. The photograph is an example of a geographical data display in which distance and direction are close to being correctly represented, whereas connectivity is uncertain and fragmented. Other notable features are the light areas, which are devoted mainly to commercial and residential land uses, and the dark areas, which are agricultural fields and groves of trees. Notice how the area between the two cities is built up with urban land uses. This is a physical reflection of the interaction which exists between the two cities.

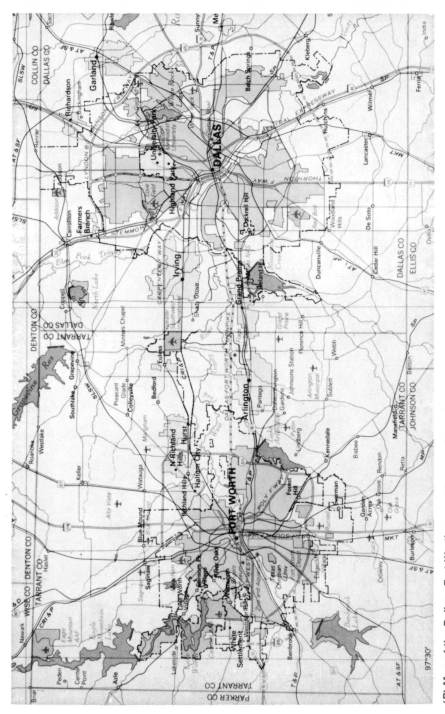

(B) Map of the Dallas–Fort Worth area   The map shows the same area as the space photograph above. Notice the similarities, but also notice that additional sets of data have been added to the map; to name a few: political boundaries, railroads, airfields, and place names. Connectivity of transport lines is much more complete, compared to the space shot. The photograph, on the other hand contains information not on the map: for example, the texture, or mosaic, of land uses present and the grid pattern of the roads, which are best seen in the upper-right-hand corner. (Photo by permission of the National Aeronautics and Space Administration; map from *National Atlas of the United States of America*, U.S. Dept. of the Interior, Geological Survey, Washington, D.C., 1970)

observe things, air photographs and maps are similar instruments of observation. Both maps and photos allow us to record very large areas of the earth's surface. Maps much more than air photographs, however, are selective filters which can be used to enhance important elements and to diminish or eliminate unimportant ones. Figure 2–1*A* and *B* shows a satellite photo and a highway map of the Dallas–Fort Worth area of Texas. Notice how each presents a large but different set of information.

Space, when portrayed on maps, may also be stretched and transformed in a controlled manner. Such controlled distortions of map space are called *map transformations*. Figures 2–2 and 2–3 show familiar types of map transformations: one, a Bostonian's view of the United States; and the other, the area served by a particular railroad company. In each case, the area most important to the map maker has been enlarged at the expense of other places. While these illustrate subjective map transformations, Figure 2–4 shows a map which emphasizes southern Michigan according to a

Figure 2-2 *A* **Bostonian's view of the United States** (Daniel K. Wallingford, Columbia University Bookstore, New York)

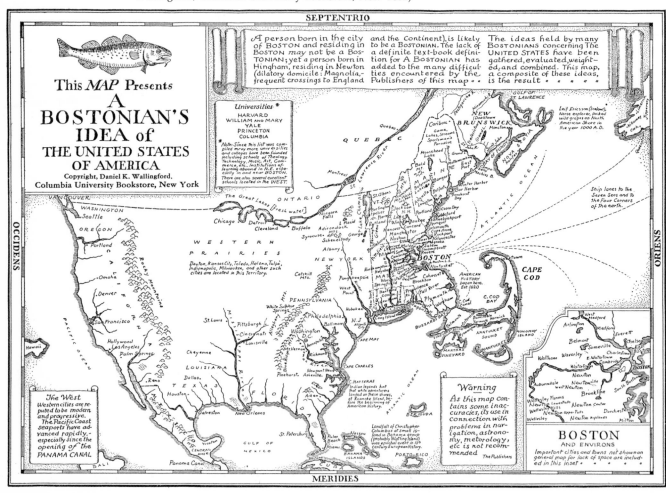

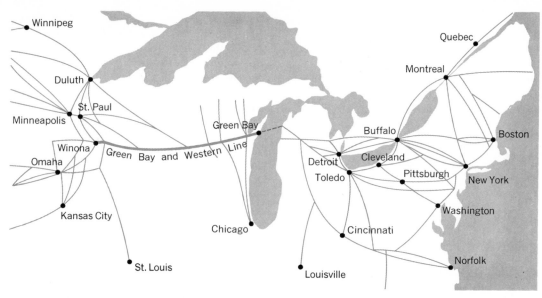

Figure 2-3 The Green Bay and Western Railroad Distances, direction, and area are distorted on this map, but connections are correct. The purpose of the map is to show the connectivity of the railroad company's rail network. (By permission of the Green Bay and Western Railroad Company, Green Bay, Wisconsin)

mathematical formula. Conversely, inappropriate choice of transformations can obscure meaningful patterns. Thus, the Bostonian's map would not serve the needs of a traveling salesman.

Any collection of information recorded by areal units may be considered an instrument of spatial observation. The United States Census Bureau reports information by census tracts, which are small areas within which the number of houses, the number of people by age distribution, and many other facts are listed. Information is also sometimes presented in city, county, state, or national units. For cities of more than 50,000, "block statistics," which describe the units defined by intersecting streets (i.e., city blocks), are also available.

There are many similarities between mechanical instruments, such as cameras, and the charts and tables produced by census enumerators and social scientists. Just as you may place a filter over the camera lens to re-

move unwanted wavelengths of light, census enumerators may choose to list only certain kinds of phenomena. The photographer may use other optical devices to enhance the edges of photographic images; the choice of enumeration categories may similarly enhance or delete particular census data. For example, businesses below a certain size may be omitted from an enumeration; or census tracts which have a few nonfarm families but which are still mainly used for farming may be counted as completely agricultural for some purposes.

Limitations on scale change as an analytical procedure

Just as both optical and census instruments perform transformations on data, each instrument has its own peculiar limitations which distort the information transmitted. For example, data about a city are often reported only for the area within the city limits. Although city boundaries define the legal jurisdiction

Figure 2-4 Map emphasizing southeastern Michigan In this map projection centered on the state of Michigan, distance from the center is plotted as the square root of actual distance. The effect is to enlarge the center of the map at the expense of its edges.

of the municipality, the city as a unified place of settlement may extend far beyond its limited political jurisdiction. Data reported for the political unit alone—that is, the municipality —may be incomplete in terms of the city as a regional entity with far-reaching functions. The nature of the census unit is just as important as the speed of a camera lens, and one must be very aware of the characteristics and capabilities of the statistical instruments used in order to avoid errors of observation.

In the motion picture *Blow Up*, the story line centered on a photographer who took a picture of two people in a park. Later he discovered the real story in the picture—the image of what appeared to be a body lying in some bushes in the background. The size of the body was very small relative to the field of vision. Because of this, and to learn if there really was a body in the picture, the photographer enlarged the photograph in order to see more clearly the segment which had attracted his attention. The first enlargement he made was more enticing, but still the picture was too small for him to be certain that a body

was truly shown in the photograph. Eventually, however, he enlarged the part of the photo showing the body so many times that, just as the information he sought was within his grasp, the grains of the photo emulsion and the other optical and technical characteristics of the instruments he used for enlarging and processing blurred the picture into a random pattern of gray tones. In other words, just as his choice of scale was about to reveal the truth, the ratio of unwanted to needed information became too great to retain the pattern. At the movie's end the photographer still was uncertain about what he had photographed and was unable to learn whether a crime really had been committed.

This scenario reveals the necessity for establishing upper and lower bounds on what we wish to observe. If a subject is too small a part of the total picture, it will be lost in an overwhelming flow of useless information. If it is too large, only one small portion of the whole will dominate the entire picture. The end result will be like the blind men and the elephant, each of whom could describe the elephant only in terms of the one part he could touch. In the same way, maps and other instruments used to record and display facts are heavily dependent on their inherent limitations as well as on the perceptions of the researcher using them. To have confidence in facts, one must be sure of the methods employed to gather and present them.

Site and Situation as Changes in Scale

Spatial observations involve both positional control and identification of local values or intensities. Positional control means keeping track of the location of each observation relative to other observations or to some fixed delineation of earth-space. Knowing the location of each observation allows preservation of spatial order, the importance of which was discussed in Chapter 1. The major reference system for knowing where things are in the world is the latitude and longitude coordinate grid, which uses the equator and the prime meridian as its reference bases. But it is not always necessary to know the latitude and longitude of a place to maintain positional control. All that is needed is information about the relative locations of elements under study.

The situation and site of cities as a problem of scale

To speak of the relative location or situation of things is to comment on the properties of the space in which they are found. Spatial properties need not be constant. In one context we may be concerned only with linear distance; in another, travel time may be the best way to measure functional distances. Other attributes of the space, such as direction and connection, may also be involved. With good locational control one can speak of the shape or pattern of spatial systems. Without such control only intensity measures at given sites remain. Geographers distinguish relative location and intensities at specific places by referring to *situation* and *site* characteristics.

The character of a site is also obtained by observation. Site data include the quantity and type of all manner of things found at a given location. For example, such data might include the number of people living in a house, the ethnic character of those same people, their income, and many other attributes. Site observations may also include the number of houses in a city, the energy produced at a given place, the total built-up area of a city or region, or the proportion of multistory buildings to single-story structures. That is, any identifying characteristics can be used to describe a site. The choice of what is described depends upon the needs of the observer and the problems he wishes to solve. When measuring site characteristics, there is no concern for positional control. The important feature is the quality or intensity of the thing observed.

In summary, geographers speak of site and situation. Observations of site refer to the qualities or attributes of a place; observations of situation refer to the position or location of a place relative to other places. A site is best thought of as an area with particular attributes.

If the same place is thought of in relation to other places, it is best considered as a point location. This involves a change of scale. Figure 2–5 illustrates such a transition from point to area. At a scale of 1:500,000 the town of Gettysburg, Pennsylvania, appears as a point connected by lines (roads) to other settlements also shown as points. At a larger scale, 1:130,000, the town appears as an undifferentiated built-up area with roads radiating from it. At still larger scales it is seen as a heterogeneous area composed of streets, houses, public buildings, and parks.

Characteristics of site and situation

Site and situation characteristics can be both good and bad. Cities may prosper from being well situated and from having pleasing site conditions. They may also encounter difficulties from being poorly situated or from having negative site characteristics. Calcutta, India, for example, is located in a swamp, a poor site. Because of its site, clean drinking water is scarce, waste disposal is difficult, and special precautions must be taken with the foundations of buildings lest they crack or sink into the soft ground. The situation of Calcutta, on the other hand, is a good one. The city is located at tidewater and can be reached by oceangoing vessels. Upstream from the city are the Ganges–Brahmaputra river system and the Gangetic Plain, populated by millions. Thus, Calcutta's situation is a good one, allowing it to serve as the major commercial gateway between a large population and the rest of the world.

Other places which are important because of their location come easily to mind. The barren, steep-sided Rock of Gibraltar is a poor site for normal activities. At the same time, its location at the entrance to the Mediterranean Sea gives it great strategic value and makes it well suited to serve as a fortress. Similar rocky eminences in remote deserts and along open, empty shores have no situational value and are avoided because of their difficult site properties. But like Gibraltar, the port of Aden, located at an inhospitable site, is occupied

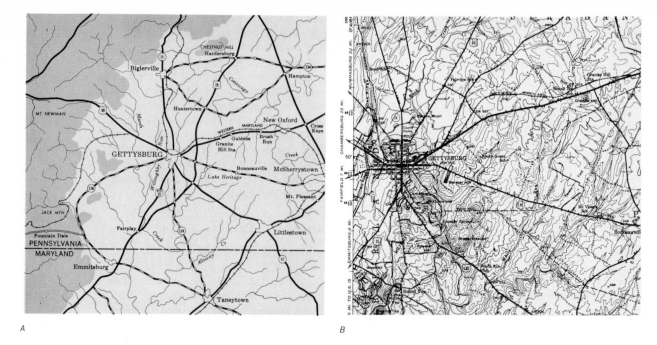

A

B

because of its position at the entrance to the Red Sea.

Some places have good sites but poor locations. A familiar example is beautiful Rio de Janeiro with Sugar Loaf Mountain rising above its curving beaches. But Rio de Janeiro is badly located with respect to the rest of Brazil. It is on the eastern coastal periphery, cut off from the interior by a difficult mountain range. To counteract these qualities and to promote the development of the interior, the capital of Brazil has been moved from Rio de Janeiro well inland to Brazilia. Situation, not site qualities, led to this move.

In any investigation, the classification of phenomena according to site or situation depends upon the scale of observation. If the internal pattern of Calcutta is to be considered, a large-scale map is necessary. This choice of scale would allow a close inspection of Calcutta and would reveal the city as a heterogeneous set of areas constituting business districts, caste neighborhoods, and transportation networks, all of which have either high or low population densities with people who can be described as rich or poor.

A further enlargement of a given district within the city would reveal the location of individual buildings or activities. A particular hotel might be the one used most by foreign visitors. This could be explained either by the quality of service available—a site attribute —or by the convenience of its location relative to points of interest within the city—a situational attribute.

Knowing the character and location of all the parts of the city has little meaning in discussing the role of the city in world affairs. At such a scale Calcutta is better considered a point, well located with respect to world trade and the pattern of population distribution in India.

Indices of segregation as a problem in the choice of scale

The preceding discussion may seem very esoteric; "What good will it do me?" is a fair question for the student to ask. In reply, it must be said that the scales at which things happen affect us all. For example, indices of segregation have been widely employed in

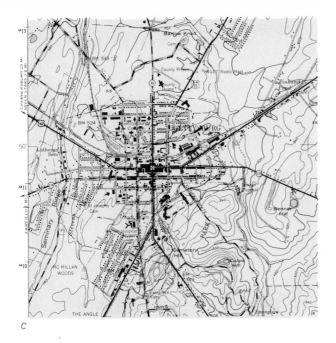

C

Figure 2-5 Scale transition from a point to an area Gettysburg, Pennsylvania, at three different map scales: (A) 1:500,000, (B) 1:130,000, and (C) 1:48,000. Notice that the total area covered gets smaller as the scale of the map enlarges. Large-scale maps are close-up views. Small-scale maps are distant views. (U.S. Geological Survey topographic maps)

urban studies to allow a comparison of the degree of racial segregation within and among cities. Such indices are often unwieldy and inaccurate because they do not maintain positional control of their data, nor do they pay strict attention to site definitions; that is, the scale at which the accumulation of internal differences occurs is overlooked. The result may be a false impression of the amount of segregation in a given neighborhood or city. In much the same way, the spatial definition of poverty, industrialization, and political preferences depends upon the scale of observation.

A critical analysis of segregation indices

American cities are characterized by residential separation of the races—a fact which few people would deny. People studying this condition have attempted to describe the degree of segregation by using quantitative indices which make it possible to rank cities according to the racial homogeneity of each subunit within them. Many indices have been devised, but none work well. To work well means that

the index which is based on real data gathered and analyzed by an empirical procedure corresponds with our theoretical notion of segregation. Moreover, changes in the index from one census period to the next should reflect real changes in the degree of segregation. The phrase "residential segregation" is open to several interpretations. We offer the following definition: Residential segregation means that the races live in separate parts of a town, and that in any given block or neighborhood the households are all of one race.

How segregation indices are computed

Segregation indices are ways of quantifying the above conditions. A high index number should mean significant segregation, while a low value should mean little or no racial segregation. A typical index, shown in Figure 2–6, compares two ratios for every subregion of the city. The first ratio is the population of a given minority group in a subregion of a city as a proportion of the total number of that group in the city as a whole. The second ratio is similar and shows the proportion of the ma-

City Space—Concepts of Scale

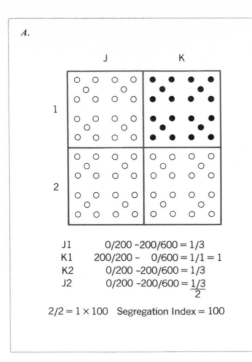

A.

	J	K
J1		0/200 –200/600 = 1/3
K1		200/200 – 0/600 = 1/1 = 1
K2		0/200 –200/600 = 1/3
J2		0/200 –200/600 = 1/3

$\frac{}{2}$

2/2 = 1 × 100   Segregation Index = 100

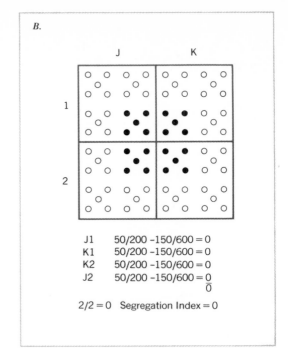

B.

	J	K
J1		50/200 –150/600 = 0
K1		50/200 –150/600 = 0
K2		50/200 –150/600 = 0
J2		50/200 –150/600 = 0

$\overline{0}$

2/2 = 0   Segregation Index = 0

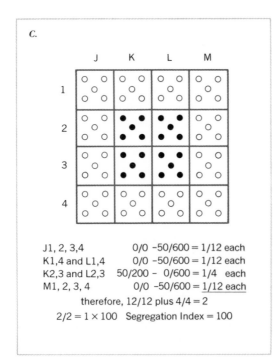

C.

J1, 2, 3, 4   0/0 –50/600 = 1/12 each
K1,4 and L1,4   0/0 –50/600 = 1/12 each
K2,3 and L2,3   50/200 – 0/600 = 1/4   each
M1, 2, 3, 4   0/0 –50/600 = 1/12 each

therefore, 12/12 plus 4/4 = 2

2/2 = 1 × 100   Segregation Index = 100

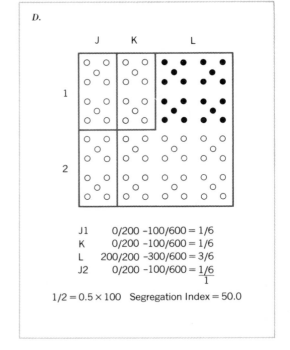

D.

	J	K	L
J1			0/200 –100/600 = 1/6
K			0/200 –100/600 = 1/6
L			200/200 –300/600 = 3/6
J2			0/200 –100/600 = 1/6

$\frac{}{1}$

1/2 = 0.5 × 100   Segregation Index = 50.0

jority group in each subregion to the total of the majority in the entire city. If the two ratios in a given subregion are equal and if this is true for all the subregions, then the city is totally integrated because every subregion has the same share of minority people. There is a rational basis for this index. Suppose that in a city the population is 10 percent Negro. Then, in a perfectly integrated city, one in every ten households in every neighborhood of the city should be Negro. The index ranges from 0 to 100. Using this form (0–100), the value of the index for Birmingham, Alabama, is 92.8. One way to look at this is to say that 92.8 percent of all the Negro families are located in blocks with an above-average proportion of Negro residences. In order to have the index go to zero for Birmingham, 92.8 percent of the Negroes would have to exchange houses with whites located in districts that are disproportionately white. A glance at Table 2–1 will show that the segregation index values range in the 70s and 80s for a sample of American cities. Thus, the original statement that segregated residential patterns are quite prevalent in American cities is substantiated.

Segregation indices from a geographic point of view

In order to appreciate this method of analysis from a geographic viewpoint and to gain

Table 2–1 Segregation Index Values for Sample American Cities

Detroit	84.5
Chicago	92.6
Jackson, Mich.	89.3
Los Angeles	81.8
Daytona Beach	96.7
Phoenix	85.6
Atlanta, Ga.	93.6
New Orleans	86.3

Source: Karl E. Taueber and Alma F. Taeuber, *Negroes in Cities*, Aldine, Chicago, 1965.

further insight into the way in which the choice of scale affects it, let us now review the procedure for obtaining the index with particular emphasis upon the spatial conditions which are involved. Figure 2–6 shows four examples of a hypothetical city which has uniform population densities in all of its parts, but which is 100 percent segregated. That is, all the black citizens live in a single cluster which contains no white residences. In each case visual inspection confirms the segregated character of the city. However, the real world is obviously much more complicated than these diagrams and cannot be analyzed by simple inspection. For this reason, segregation indices are used as instruments to interpret the world in understandable terms. The problem is that even with very simple examples

Figure 2-6 Four variations in segregation indices of a hypothetical city   Segregation Index (Also called Disimilarity Index)

$$D = \tfrac{1}{2} \left[\text{Sum of absolute values of } \frac{B_i}{B_{\text{total}}} - \frac{W_i}{W_{\text{total}}} \right] \times 100$$

B_i = Number of black households in ith cell
W_i = Number of white households in ith cell
B_{total} and W_{total} are total black and total white households, respectively, in city
Index value of *0* indicates no segregation
Index value of *100* indicates complete segregation
All examples assume population of 200 black households and 600 white households. Cells (residential tracts) identified by marginal coordinates.
      ● = 10 black households   ○ = 10 white households

Actual spatial segregation remains the same in each example, but the index varies from 0 to 100 dependsing upon size and arrangement of residential tracts.

our methods can be misleading. An examination of the examples in Figure 2–6 reveals that results can differ depending upon the size of the census unit used and also upon where the boundaries of census units are drawn.

A word of caution on the choice of scale

Figure 2–7 shows what might be called the population distribution in an ideal hypothetical city. Here our minority is evenly distributed throughout the city in the same proportion as it exists in the city as a whole. Both sizes of census units used in our previous example reveal the same amount of segregation or integration (Examples 1 and 2). But if an even smaller filter is used, perhaps drawn on the basis of individual households, every group becomes isolated within its own census unit, and again the segregation index climbs to 100 (Example 3). In other words, there are not only upper limits on the sizes at which we should observe things, but lower limits as well. It all depends upon the goals of the observer. In this example residential segregation is a social issue operating at the neighborhood scale. Reducing the scale of observation to individual households is like not being able to see the forest for the trees.

What about the study of individual behavior? It has been said that "The proper study of mankind is man." This advice may contain a spatial as well as a philosophical truth: Humanity, overwhelming when seen en masse, is still composed of individuals. Certainly, mold seen with the naked eye may seem ugly but when viewed through a microscope separates itself into individual organisms of great beauty. Whatever the frustrations of mass society, we should never lose sight of its individual components.

The Scale at Which Things Happen

Scale considerations are important in two ways. We have seen that the scales with which we choose to observe the world influence our interpretations of it. In much the same way, the behavior of an individual can vary significantly from that of the group or population to which he belongs. What a person says as an individual may not match what he does as the elected chairman of a committee; what he does as chairman of a committee may not match how he votes as the member of a political party; how he acts as the member of a political party may be different from his response as a loyal citizen to international conditions. Such changes in behavior do not mean that this person is inconsistent or hypocritical, but rather that different types of events take place at different scales or levels of organization and his responses to those events may vary accordingly. What may be appropriate at one level can be inconsistent at the next. An appreciation of the different scales at which things happen can be useful in understanding the nature of the world.

Personal space

The analysis of the personal space in which individuals function is of interest to anthropologists and sociologists as well as geographers, and is sometimes referred to as the study of *proxemics*. Each one of us surrounds himself with a small territory which he feels to be his own. We have all experienced the feeling of uneasiness when we suddenly find our elbow in competition with that of some stranger for the same armrest in a theater. This "bubble" of personal space is very important to us. We prefer that strangers "keep their distance," although friends may come closer. In American society, the only people whom we readily welcome within touching distance are our close relatives and loved ones. The next time you attend a ball game or movie, observe the way in which the crowd shares the limited space which it occupies. Dates and married couples may hold hands or walk with their arms touching, but strangers will attempt to preserve their own personal spaces, although the distances which separate them may be reduced to a few inches or less. In order to do this and to minimize the flood of sensation that accompanies any crowd, people will take evasive action. Their movements will become restricted; they walk with short steps and keep

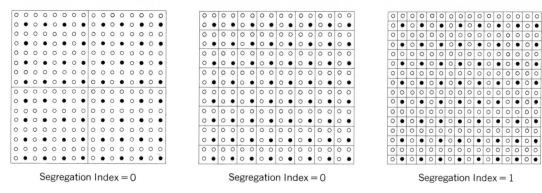

Segregation Index = 0   Segregation Index = 0   Segregation Index = 1

All Examples Are Based on a Population 25% Black and 75% White.

Figure 2-7 Three segregation indices in a hypothetical city with even distribution of minority population.

their arms close to their sides. If inadvertently touched by someone, they will draw back as sharply as the confined space allows. Conversely, within the limits of this most intimate of personal spaces nothing is more pleasant than the awareness of the touch and perhaps even the aroma and warmth of someone you love.

Living or work space

Beyond the more intimate limits of each person's space are the areas or territories within which we live our daily lives. The classroom and the dormitory, as well as the office and the rooms of your own home, represent another and larger type of space which has special meaning. Within this living or work space, distances are measured from about two to three feet for conversations between casual acquaintances, to perhaps tens of feet for lectures, group activities, and parties. Conversations are carried on in normal tones, and individuals respect each others' personal "bubbles" of territory; office workers can exchange information, meetings are carried out across conference tables, and students and counselors interact comfortably at these distances. We are able to focus our gaze upon the facial expressions of the people with whom we are communicating. Slight movements and changes in the tone of a person's voice give

clues to the way in which he is reacting to the situation. Living spaces are controlled by the construction of soundproof walls and doors that can close off rooms for greater privacy. Under these conditions members of a family may choose to come together to share their feelings, such as on Christmas when presents are opened around the tree. At other times, an individual will feel a need to be alone and may lock the door of his room to ensure privacy.

These units of personal, working, and living space are the indivisible building blocks which society uses to organize the areas which it occupies. Be sure to keep them in mind as you consider how larger spaces such as urban areas are organized.

House and neighborhood space

A group of houses upon their individual lots or several apartment buildings and other structures along a street constitute still another type of space, which might also include large lecture halls, auditoriums, gardens, and small parks. Distances here may range from 100 to perhaps 1,000 feet, the outer limit often being the limits of line-of-sight recognition. Where living units are concerned, territories of this size are often thought of as neighborhoods. Larger groups of people can meet under these circumstances. Usually an individual will not know all the other persons gathered nearby but will share some common purpose with them. A speaker can be recognized from a distance, but friends may become lost in the crowd. Communication becomes more difficult; sound amplifying devices become necessary for public meetings. If you wish to talk with someone, you may have to walk within speaking range, and often we telephone our friends next door rather than visit them. Under these conditions contacts between people become more specialized and less casual. We designate certain places for meetings, others for private domiciles, still others for parks and playgrounds. In this way, spatial specialization exerts an increasing control on human communication. Symbols such as the standardized shape of traffic markers often supplant lettered signs, and messages are more often directed from one person to many listeners rather than on a person-to-person basis. The neighborhood may become an important feature of city life within these distances, and the distribution of minority groups can often be mapped at this scale.

City-hinterland space

The scale of change between neighborhood and city marks a transition where the study of face-to-face behavior, sometimes called *proxemics*, gives way to more specifically geographic spatial considerations. A city consists of many neighborhoods and specialized areas which function together in a manner different from that of a cluster of households. In addition, the city occupies a central focus within a region or hinterland which it serves and which in turn is dependent upon the urban center. The extent of the city and its hinterland is fixed in large part by the distance which commuters will travel to and from work. Research has shown that the average American commuter will travel no farther than about 60 minutes either going to or coming from work. Depending upon road and traffic conditions, this means that the linear commuting distances traveled in and near a city vary from 4 to 40 miles. Beyond this distance communication becomes more difficult, and it is within this

range that local news media, radio and television, daily newspapers, and urban institutions—such as local and metropolitan governments—are effective. Crowding, traffic congestion, and possible bottlenecks in communication must be overcome by routine channelization. Superhighways, one-way street systems, Federal Communications Commission regulations, and many other devices are used to expedite the movement of people, goods, and information under these conditions.

Regional-national space

Nations can be thought of as clusters of cities and the regions which they represent. The distances at which humans interact in terms of regional and national systems vary from a few hundred miles to several thousand. In order to tie such vast areas together, news media—such as nationwide broadcasting and television networks—must be organized. In the same way, political parties need not only "grass roots" organizations but also nationally organized superstructures to coordinate the efforts of the thousands of local groups. Nations need carefully designed chains of administrative command and clearly defined relationships between local and national governments in order to function effectively. Highways physically bind the nation together. A strong constitution and legal system, which clarify and standardize numberless individual differences in human behavior, are other means of communication within the nation. Thus, the type of human activities served at this level can be thought of as nationwide transportation, political, legal, and economic systems, to name a few of the possibilities.

Global space

Finally, individual nations and international blocs relate to each other on a global scale. The world itself is the limit of the distances involved, with 12,000 miles the farthest that one point can be from another on the surface of the globe. World affairs of all kinds are carried on at this scale. Trade agreements and cultural exchanges are the alternatives to misunderstandings and warfare. In this case, international communications systems, including satellite relay stations and transoceanic cables, facilitate the exchange of information. Translation from one language to another is essential, and international organizations like the United Nations and the International Red Cross help coordinate the efforts of individual countries. In the same way, trade and customs barriers, as well as visa and passport requirements, can restrict travel and the flow of goods and ideas. The ever-increasing improvement in transportation and communication technology draws the world together, but the subsequent sense of crowding and the urgency of instantaneous news coverage may unnecessarily magnify the problems of organization at a global scale.

representative fraction

Table 2–2 shows the relationship of these scales of human activity to each other. It should be recognized that the transition from one scale to another is continuous and that all of the indicated scales are ranked along a continuum rather than existing in reality as discrete pigeonholes or quanta. Special attention should be given to the column labeled "representative fraction." This term is used particularly by cartographers on the maps which they prepare. It is a way of accurately indicating the relationship between the real world and its graphic representation. The numerator, the number which appears before the colon, indicates one unit of *linear* measure (inches, centimeters, etc.) on the map; the second number, the denominator, represents the number of inches or centimeters (or whatever *linear* unit is specified) of the real world indicated by one map unit. Thus, if we were to draw a life-sized picture of a man, 1 inch on the paper would represent 1 inch of the man's actual measurements. If his nose were 2 inches long in reality, it would appear 2 inches long in the drawing. This would be indicated by a representative fraction 1:1, or 1/1. If we were to draw a very

large map of a room in which everything appeared one-fourth actual size (e.g., a table 4 feet square would appear as a rectangle 12 by 12 inches on the paper), the representative fraction would be 1:4, or 1/4. Maps of manageable size must be quite small regardless of the areas they represent. Thus, most representative fractions are very small by the above standards. Maps which show 1 mile represented by 1 inch on paper have an R.F. (the common abbreviation for representative fraction) of 1:63,360. The range of representative fractions shown in the table suggests the scale of the maps which could be used to plot the corresponding activities. Maps of personal space are seldom if ever made, but in order to complete the table, an R.F. of 1:1 has been included.

How Scale Changes Operate in Human Affairs

Many of the problems which human beings must solve pertain to the scales at which various processes operate. We quickly learn not to trim our fingernails with dressmaking shears—there are smaller scissors designed to do the job. The difference between the two types of tools is a matter of scale, and the problems encountered when we use the wrong-sized tool for the job are occasioned by a lack of fit.

After recognizing that human activities proceed at different scales, we are faced with trying to understand how communication across scales works. Communication is often not very successful because the media involved do not match the job to be done.

Advertising: An economic example

Many activities demand a proper fit between the processes and equipment involved. One example of this is the problem faced by firms wishing to advertise through magazine ads. A large metropolitan bank may wish to gain the prestige of advertising in a nationally recognized magazine. Such publications may have circulations in the millions and distribute copies in all fifty states as well as throughout

Table 2-2 Relationship of Population Groups, Types of Activities, and Scales of Interaction

Type of Space	Spatial Range	Characteristics of Interaction				
	Radius from person (representative fraction)	Primary modes of interaction	Selected controls	Type of function	Number of people involved	
Personal space	Arm's length 1:1	Voice, touch, taste, smell	Evasive movement	Intimate contact	1, 2, 3, . . .	
Living or working space (private space)	10–50 feet 1:50	Audio and visual (sharp focus on facial expression and slight movement or tonal changes	Impervious walls, doors	Effective personal conversation, 1-to-1 exchanges	. . . 50–400 . . .	
House and neighborhood space	100–1,000 feet (line of sight) 1:500	Audio-visual (sound amplification)	Spatial specialization	Impersonal interactions symbol recognition, many-to-one exchanges	. . . 100–1,000 . .	
		Limit of Proxemic Interaction				
City–hinterland space	4 to 40 miles (60-minute one-way commute) 1:50.000 1:63.630 = 1 inch = 1 mile	Local news media, TV, urban institutions, commuter systems	Routine channelization	Mean information field, daily contact space	. . . 50,000–10 million	
Regional–national space	200–3,000 miles 1:500,000	National network of news media, national organizations, common language desirable	Hierarchies	Legal-economic-political systems	200+ million	
Global space	12,000 miles 1:50,000,000	International communication networks, translator services, world organizations, international blocs	Travel restrictions, trade barriers and trade agreements	War, trade, cultural exchanges	3+ billion	

the world. Page rates for advertising in these magazines are predicated on very large audiences and are extremely expensive. In fact, banks seeking customers in only one city or one metropolitan area may find such costs prohibitive. When national-level magazines first began to be published, very few local firms could justify the expense of advertising in their pages. And yet this source of income

was desirable for the publishers, just as the prestige of their pages was desirable to potential advertisers. The problem was a lack of fit in the scales at which the two institutions functioned. In recent years this problem has been largely overcome by publishing regional editions of national magazines. Thus, the major news stories, feature articles, and fiction appear in the copies printed and bound in every region in which they are sold, but the advertising is solicited locally as well as nationally. Special pages are inserted in editions meant to be distributed within restricted areas. In this way a metropolitan bank may place an advertisement which will reach only those customers within range of the bank's services. At the same time, larger companies selling automobiles or soap on a national basis will also place advertising in the same issue. Rates are adjusted according to the estimated customer potential for each type, and all the parties benefit from the adjustment in scale which has been made.

Metropolitan versus local city government: A political example

A second example illustrating this point relates to the problems of local and regional government. In years past, central cities such as St. Louis and Chicago were largely self-sufficient in terms of the services which they provided for their inhabitants and the local tax base which met the expenses of city government. This was particularly true in the period before mass transportation and the automobile. At that time, most people who worked in the city shopped there and took advantage of its streets, parks, schools, and playgrounds, and also lived within the legal limits of the town. The taxes they paid were directly available as payment for the services they received. Moreover, the population represented a cross section of the settlement's economy. The rich, the poor, and the middle class, as well as businesses, factories, and residential areas, were found within the city boundaries.

Recent developments have greatly changed the situation just described. As city populations have increased, more and more of the wealthy and middle class have moved to the suburbs and now commute to work. This has had a multiple effect upon the central city. New suburban towns are growing up on the perimeters of the cities. Such settlements frequently incorporate and became legally independent communities with the power to levy taxes on their inhabitants. The central city thus loses suburban taxpayers as a source of revenue, particularly with regard to property taxes. At the same time, because the suburbs have become legally independent, the city is no longer able to expand outward and incorporate recently settled areas. There is an absolute outward limit placed upon the city's growth as a legal entity. However, many suburbanites continue to travel to the city for employment. Ever-increasing numbers of automobiles necessitate new access highways and terminal facilities such as parking structures. The central city is strangling in crowds of cars and clouds of exhaust fumes. Funds to pay for the new roads and parking structures and for the upkeep on the overburdened pavements must be provided by the central city government—not by the commuters, who are taxed at their places of residence in the independent suburbs. Many factories and businesses which in turn wish to expand seek the congestion-free suburbs with their lower land values and tax rates, and another source of revenue is denied the central city. Finally, new migrants to the city generally come from poor rural areas. Many of these newcomers are from culturally disadvantaged groups which present the inner-city schools with an additional educational burden. Suburban schools often offer higher salaries and better working conditions which in turn lure teachers away from the city.

As the inner city and its government groan under this collection of woes, new solutions to the problem are sought. One suggestion has been the idea of metropolitan governments. Such governments would be organized much like that of the federal government of the United States. That is, while maintaining local independence in many things, the suburban city governments would unite with the central city to form an overall governing body which could levy certain taxes and redistribute resources for the good of the entire community both within and without the central city limits. This in essence constitutes a scale change in the approach to urban problems. Metropolitan governments as such, however, have until

City Space— Concepts of Scale

very recently met with no success in their formation. (In Canada, metropolitan Toronto seems to be a successful exception to this observation.) The people of the suburbs have been unwilling either to share their taxes with the inner city or in turn to accept responsibility for the special problems found at the core of the urban region.

As the white flight to the suburbs continues, the proportion of poor black residents increases within the central city. Where once this group represented a minority, the roles of white and black are being reversed and some cities are now electing black mayors for the first time. In other cities councilmen and high officials are being chosen from minority groups.

Parallel to this latest set of changes is the growth of a new attitude toward metropolitan government. Where once nonwhite groups constituted an unrepresented minority, they now are a major political force within the central city. The formation of metropolitan governments would allow suburban candidates the chance to win office and to control the inner city, once more placing the black minority at a disadvantage. In this way, the scale change from small local governments to larger units not only offers potential aid to the central city but also threatens the role of inner-city residents in representative government. Thus, black leaders of the core areas are now being faced with a new set of political problems which further demonstrate how the many parts of an urban area are mutually interdependent.

Politics, planning, and survival all relate to the size, shape, and growth patterns of urban areas. If we are to survive as urban dwellers and urban neighbors, we must understand as much as possible about the growth and function of cities. Inevitably, three questions must be answered about urban places whenever we attempt to understand how they prosper or decline. Where do urban people come from? What forces help to create the general character of cities? What tangible shapes do cities take, and are such shapes clues to the processes underlying city growth? The concern of this chapter is largely the third question, although the first two are dealt with briefly.

Sources of Urban Growth

The growth of urban population has already been discussed in Chapter 1. Let us only remind ourselves of the general origins of urban people and of the magnitude of urban population growth, particularly in America. Cities increase in two ways—through migration and through natural increase. At present, natural increase accounts for the greater part of urban population growth, but in earlier decades and in the eighteenth and nineteenth centuries migration was more important. Such migration consisted of two types: the movement of rural people into cities and the mass movement of urban and rural populations from one region or country to another as the result of political, economic, and other pressures.

Typical of this latter type is the migration to the United States of more than 34 million immigrants between 1841 and 1930. More than 80 percent of these migrants come from Europe (Table 3–1).

Earlier migrations had peopled the thirteen colonies with smaller groups of white and black people, but no other population movement in history can compare with that great journey from the Old World to the New at the end of the nineteenth and the beginning of the twentieth centuries. Two out of three foreign-born residents of the United States chose city homes in 1900, although the nation as a whole at that time was only 40 percent urban. By 1950, 64 percent of our population was urbanized and 36 percent rural. At the same time in 1950 about 80 percent of all foreign-born Americans lived in the nation's cities.

For the present discussion of city space, we need only be aware of the numbers of people who arrived and that they came to America to live primarily in its cities. This international migration temporarily eased Europe's population crisis. Such relief was short-lived, however, and later internal migration from farms to

Table 3-1 Immigration to the United States, 1820-1968

Period	Europe	Asia	America	Oceania	Africa	Total
1820	7,691	5	387		1	8,084
1821-1830	98,817	10	11,564		16	110,407
1831-1840	495,688	48	33,424		54	529,214
1841-1850	1,597,501	82	62,469		55	1,660,107
1851-1860	2,452,660	41,455	74,720		210	2,569,045
1861-1870	2,065,270	64,630	166,607	36	312	2,296,855
1871-1880	2,272,262	123,823	404,044	10,914	358	2,811,401
1881-1890	4,737,046	68,380	426,967	12,574	857	5,245,824
1891-1900	3,558,978	71,236	38,972	3,965	350	3,673,501
1901-1910	8,136,016	243,567	361,888	13,024	7,368	8,761,863
1911-1920	4,376,564	192,559	1,143,671	13,427	8,443	5,734,664
1921-1930	2,477,853	97,400	1,516,716	8,726	6,286	4,106,981
1931-1940	348,289	15,344	160,037	3,011	1,750	528,431
1941-1950	621,704	31,780	354,804	19,242	7,367	1,034,897
1951-1960	1,328,293	147,453	996,944	16,204	14,092	2,502,986
1961-1968	904,965	255,289	1,390,603	15,900	17,395	2,584,152
Total	35,479,597	1,356,061	7,143,817	117,023	64,914	44,161,412

Does not include 269,321 "Not Specified" immigrants for the years 1820-1968.
Source: *Annual Report*, U.S. Immigration and Naturalization Service, 1968.

factories had the same result in Europe as in America. Everywhere towns and cities expanded at an astonishing rate.

Processes of Urban Growth

It is risky to describe the physical growth of a single city or single type of settlement and to say with confidence that the pattern described fits more than a few real examples. On the other hand, we need a general description of the development of American cities to serve as a background for more abstract theories of city growth. The following characterization of urban development in America is intended not so much as a complete picture, but rather as a frame for the theories which conclude the chapter.

Cities at the beginning of the Industrial Revolution

In accordance with our ideas of point, line, and area relationships, cities may be thought of as being tied together by routes along which

move people, supplies, products, and messages. At the beginning of the Industrial Revolution, water transport predominated, and the carriers on such routes were oceangoing ships, riverboats, and canal barges. River and canal towns as well as seaports were of great importance, and their core areas grew up within easy reach of good docking facilities. When railroads appeared somewhat later in the nineteenth century, the first engines were underpowered, and trains had to seek out the lowest mountain passes, the flattest land, and the gentlest slopes. This meant that the tracks often followed the rivers or coastlines and entered settlements at points near existing port facilities. In other settlements lacking water transport, railroads also kept to the lowest ground and avoided hills and steep grades. Factories, warehouses, and businesses which depended upon rail and water transportation for raw materials and the shipment of finished goods were located along the waterfronts and near the railroads. Businesses also were concentrated near the docks and rail lines. As a result, business districts were often pointlike clusters or linear in form, following transportation lines. These historic core areas were often noisy, dirty, and unhealthy, with fevers and poor drinking water adding to the problems of the inhabitants, the more fortunate of whom moved to higher ground and commuted to work by horse and buggy. The poorer working class, with little or no public transportation, had to live within walking distance of the factories. Thus, the idea of the "other side of the tracks" or the "poor in the hollow and the rich on the hill" became an established fact in early industrial society.

Other nineteenth century urban characteristics

Coal-burning steam engines were another factor contributing to location of the working population in nineteenth century cities. These steam engines were used to turn drive shafts, which in turn were connected by means of moving belts to individual looms, drill presses, sewing machines, and all other types of factory equipment. Such belt-driven mechanisms presented particular problems to the designers of factories. If the belt-drives were too long, they sagged and either dragged on the ground or had to be held up by auxiliary rollers. In either case much power was lost. A better design was to run the main belt-drives vertically from an engine in the factory basement to machines and equipment located directly overhead. Factories were stacked vertically floor above floor, with the source of power in the basement. Raw materials had to be lifted to the upper floors, while semifinished and finished goods were lowered to waiting transport at ground level. This constituted an inefficient system which constantly fought the pull of gravity. When new sources of power became available, this style was rapidly abandoned, but in many older American cities multistoried red-brick factory buildings dating from the nineteenth century can still be found near the railroad tracks and along the waterfronts.

All these conditions resulted in cities at the beginning of the nineteenth century which were constricted and crowded. Clusters of vertical, belt-drive factories, located in low-lying areas along transportation routes, were surrounded by the densely packed dwellings of factory workers, who could travel no farther to work than they could walk at the end of a long, hard day. Better neighborhoods, which accommodated the wealthy, were removed from the original factory and business districts and often located on higher ground. Under such crowded conditions, population growth forced the cities to expand outward from their historic cores. Such expansion depended in turn upon new developments in the technology of manufacturing and transportation.

Late nineteenth and early twentieth century cities

The distances mechanical energy could be transmitted and workers could travel to their jobs were severely limited at the beginning of the Industrial Revolution. New inventions in the century that followed rapidly changed the internal design of factories and the commuting patterns of their employees. Knowledge of how to produce, transport, and use electricity became important. Centrally located plants, dependent upon falling water or burning coal, made available electric power which could be transported along cables or overhead wires. This in turn allowed a new form of mass transportation to develop; the electric interurban train and the electric trolley soon changed the American city landscape. Commuter lines extended outward from the original city centers along lengthening radial lines. As Figure 3–1 shows, small suburbs sprang up along these electric interurban lines, and cities grew outward in response to the new means of transportation. Electricity also meant that machines no longer needed to be attached to steam engines by unwieldy belt-driven mechanisms. Instead, machines powered by electricity could be located wherever their owners wished. It became a simple matter to lead power to the machine by means of an insulated cable. This meant in turn that factories no longer had to be stacked floor on

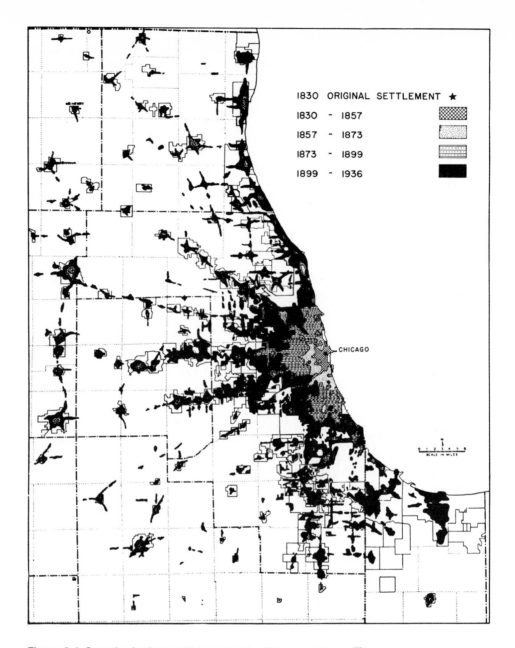

Figure 3-1 Growth of urban settlement in the Chicago region The concentric rings of growth are clearly visible. Also apparent is the heavier growth along the lake shore to the north. The linear development radiating from the center is the effect on suburban land use of the electric interurban railways and, later, of the United States highway system.
(*The Structure and Growth of Residential Neighborhoods in American Cities*, Homer Hoyt, Federal Housing Administration, U.S. Govt. Printing Office, Washington, D.C., 1939, p. 98)

floor above steam engines. Gravity became much less of an enemy as factories went horizontal, with products moving from point to point on the assembly line along moving tracks. Thus, the familiar one-story industrial plant filling many acres of land became a working reality. However, the construction of such buildings required large tracts of cheap land, unavailable in the crowded cities. In addition, taxes were increasingly levied by larger cities to pay for improvements in transportation and social services demanded by a better organized and educated labor force. The suburbs offered not only land in sufficient quantities but sometimes tax advantages as inducements for luring new business their way.

The twentieth century city

The movement of industry and business to the suburbs might not have been possible but for parallel improvements in transportation. By 1910 the internal combustion engine was developed to the point where the private automobile became practical. Parallel developments in petroleum refining and road building helped create a new urban environment characterized by increasing numbers of automobiles. After World War II, lighter, stronger steel alloys, aluminum, and other modern metals replaced heavy, brittle cast iron; synthetic rubber reduced the price of tires. The price of cars went down relative to the income-earning ability of the workers who produced them. The electric interurban train had lost popularity and streetcar tracks were torn up as private autos and public trolleybuses carried more and more of the public to work, market, and play. Eventually, the interurban lines were replaced with high-speed limited-access highways which also radiated outward from the central parts of cities.

In interurban times, once the commuter arrived at his suburban station, he had to find his way home on foot or by horse and buggy. Suburban towns, as a result, were restricted to areas very near the electric train tracks. This meant that as the radiating rail lines pushed farther and farther from the cities,

the distances between the various branches increased. More and more inaccessible farmland remained between the lengthening spokes of the wheel-shaped network of facilities. Since the advent of the auto, the commuter no longer has been restricted at the homeward end of his trip from the city. After leaving the expressway, he simply drives a few miles farther into the previously inaccessible land near the centers of the pie-shaped sectors between the major highways. The unused farmlands away from major routes have already begun to fill up, and today cities spread outward in all directions from their cores. Factories once located outside of urban areas are now far behind the advancing built-up edges of the cities. Workers commute by automobile laterally around metropolitan perimeters as well as along radial routes leading to and from city centers.

The inefficient factories of the nineteenth century are largely abandoned and often torn down, and the tenements near the center of the cities no longer house immigrants from Europe. Now a new wave of poor people, both black and white, often rural and largely from the South, or Spanish Americans from the Southwest and Puerto Rico, have arrived. The workers' tenements of yesterday have become slums and black ghettoes, while the children and grandchildren of poor first-generation Irish, Italian, and Polish immigrant workers now are substantial middle-class suburbanites. But the city as a dynamic ever-changing entity continues to expand.

A Simple Model of City Growth

This thumbnail sketch of urban events in America over the last 1½ centuries scarcely indicates the complexities of the changes that have occurred. Geographic theories help us to order and then interpret the kaleidoscopic urban world. In this way we come to the third set of questions posed at the beginning of this chapter. How does a spatial point of view enlarge our understanding of city processes?

City Space— Models of City Growth

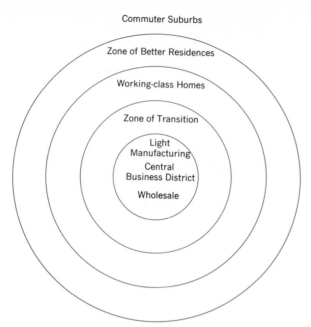

Commuter Suburbs

Zone of Better Residences

Working-class Homes

Zone of Transition

Light Manufacturing

Central Business District

Wholesale

Figure 3-2 The concentric ring model of city growth (After Ernest Burgess, "Growth of the City," *Proceedings of the American Sociological Society*, vol. 18, 1923, 85–89.)

The concentric ring theory

Just as we can tell the age and fortunes of a tree by looking at its rings, cities also have telltale patterns by which they reveal themselves to us. In fact, a "concentric ring" theory of city growth was suggested by Ernest Burgess in the 1920s (Figure 3–2). Burgess and his colleagues at the University of Chicago conducted a number of studies of their city. Their conclusions reflect the particular nature of Chicago and its surroundings, but also provide a useful, if undetailed, model of city growth. Chicago is located on the southwestern shore of Lake Michigan on a level lake plain. Expansion away from the original settlement core near the lakeshore is limited only to the east by the lake itself. In all other directions the level plain offers few barriers to urban expansion, and according to Burgess's model of city growth, cities should grow outward evenly in all directions from a central

nucleus or core. Over a long enough period of time, and given several successive stages of growth, the city will develop a series of concentric rings or zones surrounding the central business district (often referred to as the CBD). In the CBD are found the major retail functions and government services associated with large cities. Department stores, good restaurants, and specialty shops will cluster there along with government buildings, courts of law, hotels, museums, and theaters. According to Burgess a mixture of light manufacturing establishments and wholesale businesses is found immediately surrounding the CBD. These two sets of establishments in combination are the ones most able to pay the high rents characteristic of the city center. In turn, all these establishments depend upon the centrality of their location and their easy accessibility to large numbers of potential customers.

At an early period in the history of the city, the zone ringing the central core was occupied by workers with residents of higher economic class just beyond. Cities, however, constantly grow and change, and additional firms seeking the locational advantages of the city center have only two choices. The CBD can expand vertically to accommodate new businesses in skyscrapers, or it can expand horizontally, encroaching upon the residential areas surrounding it. In Burgess's concentric ring model, emphasis is placed upon outward horizontal growth. As a result the compound core, or CBD, is ringed by a *zone of transition*. Private homes become rooming houses; businesses exert more and more pressure for land; and residential blight characterizes the area. It is in this zone that the ills of the city are most evident. Disease and poor health accompany tenements and slums, while illiteracy, unemployment, and crime go hand in hand. In this home for recent immigrants is one of America's critical problem areas, for which various "treatments" such as *urban renewal* and the *model cities* programs have been suggested.

If we were to travel directly away from the center of Burgess's hypothetical city, the next ring beyond the zone of transition would contain working-class homes of increasingly good quality. Signs of urban blight would give way to lower-middle-class respectability. The quality and cost of homes would continue to increase with distance from the center and would be matched by a decrease in residential density. Next, a zone of better residences would ring that of the established working class. Finally, on the edges of the city the commuter suburbs would present an incompletely built up area with small satellite towns and intervening empty fields.

Density and density surfaces

One way in which to think of what the Burgess model tells us about cities is to consider the distribution of people within a growing settlement in a succession of time periods. Figure 3–3 shows population densities at increasing distances from the CBD. In this case, the definition of density is the number of people counted at their place of residence and living on a given unit of land. This can be represented as a number of points located within a given area. This could be measured, for example, in terms of hundreds of people per city block, but since city blocks vary in size, we most often refer to the number of people per square mile. (In any case, this represents a *point–area* relationship like those discussed in Chapter 1.)

Line t_1 in Figure 3–3 shows the distribution of people within the original settlement. When the town was first founded, everyone lived within walking distance of its center. Even then central locations had added value, although in general there was plenty of room for all. Latecomers, the poor, and full- or part-time farmers were most likely to live farthest away. In any event most of the population lived close to the center; their numbers diminished regularly with increasing distance.

A somewhat later period is shown by line t_2.[1] The city has continued to grow both in

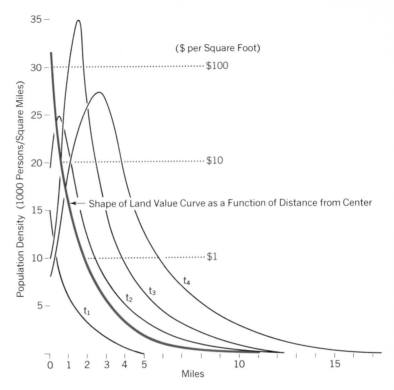

Figure 3-3 Urban population density radially from city center at different time periods in growth process The family of curves represents a hypothetical change in residential density as the city grows through time periods t, t_1, etc. The decline in population density at the center is caused by displacement of residences by business and industrial uses. These curves may be described by varying parameters of a mathematical expression relating population density to distance from the center of the city. This expression is the gamma distribution $d_r = ar^b e^{-er} + d_o$, where d_r is population density at radius r; d_o is central population density; and a, b, and c are parameters. A central crater is formed when $b > o$. See S. Angel and G. M. Hyman, "Urban Spatial Interaction," *Environment and Planning*, vol. 4, 1972, p. 107.

[1]*Technical note*: The use of a small t with a numerical subscript (read: "t sub one, t sub two . . .") is a standard way of indicating successive periods of time or stages.

population and in area. The center is filling with nonresidential uses. Increasing rents and competition for land have forced residents to seek homes farther from the CBD, and population densities are increasing rapidly at the edges. Line t_3 shows population density and

City Space— Models of City Growth

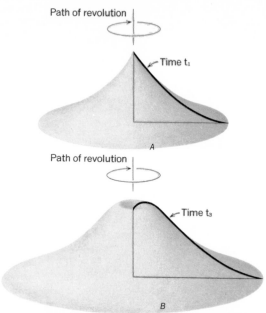

Figure 3-4 Urban population density surfaces
(*A*) Density surface at time t_1. (*B*) Density surface at time t_3. These surfaces are three-dimensional representations of two of the curves shows in Figure 3-3. They are formed by rotating the curves in a complete circle around the center of the city.

distance relationships still later. The town is becoming a city, and the characteristic rings described by Burgess are beginning to appear in a more complete form. The outer edge of the city continues to grow, and population densities there continue to increase in a regular manner. Nearer the center, the *zone of transition* with its packed tenements and slums accounts for the crest of population densities somewhat away from the actual center. The CBD is shown by lower density values. This is because the office buildings and shops at the very center of the city allow fewer apartment buildings and other residences. Line t_4 represents the contemporary city with a relatively empty CBD, a ring of slum housing just beyond, and steadily diminishing residential densities stretching out to the remoter suburbs. Urban expansion can thus be imagined as a wave of population

density moving outward from some central point.

In this two-dimensional graph the area beneath the line represents the total number of people found along one radius leading directly outward from the center of the city. Although a line has no width but only length, we assume that the area on the graph is one unit wide, since measures of density are in points per square unit. This diagram can be thought of in three dimensions if the area defined by the abscissa and one of the lines t_1, t_2, t_3, etc., is revolved around the vertical axis, or ordinate.[2] A cone-shaped volume, or witch's hat, results from this revolution (Figure 3-4). The volume of the space beneath the surface of the cone will be equal to the total population of the city.

Note how the less densely populated CBD at period t_3 forms a hole in the center (Figure 3-4). This does not mean that land has grown less valuable at that point. Non-residential activities are able to pay more for use of centrally located land than can households. If we were to measure land value, the line showing this in dollars per unit area would have its highest point at the very center. This is represented in Figure 3-3 by the red line measured on its own vertical axis in dollars per square foot.

Obviously, the real world varies enormously from the orderly picture presented by Burgess, and the concentric ring model has been criticized for its failure to describe the true complexity of modern cities. It should be remembered, though, that simple models have advantages as well as drawbacks. In this case, the model recognizes the desirability of a central location and the historical realities of city growth. Establishments which can afford to pay the highest rent command the most central positions. Residents and smaller

[2] *A useful suggestion*: In all graphs the two lines at right angles to each other are referred to as the *y*, or vertical, coordinate, and the *x*, or horizontal, coordinate. These lines are also called the *ordinate* and the *abscissa*. Nearly everyone has trouble remembering which is which. If you remember that your lips form a vertical "O" shape when you say ordinate, and a thin, flat line when you say abscissa, the distinction can be easily remembered.

businesses must seek locations on the edges. As the city grows, land use changes occur with some lapse of time between one major use and another. For example, abandoned higher-class residences may eventually be torn down to provide space for office buildings, but meanwhile poorer immigrants find shelter in the former mansions of the rich just as hermit crabs live in the castoff shells of other sea creatures.

The Burgess model assumes city growth unhindered by variations in the physical environment in which the city exists. Thus Burgess's model is symmetrical in all directions. This symmetry is the result of two qualities. The first is the assumption that all building sites are exactly alike. This results in a *homogeneous surface* having everywhere the same *site characteristics* such as soils and drainage. The second quality refers to uniform ease of transportation in all directions at every point. A surface with this quality is called an *isotropic surface* or *isotropic plain*. This condition would cease to exist if transportation were improved in one direction but not in others—for example, by building a north-south road but not an east-west one.

Models of City Growth More Closely Approximating Reality

By ignoring the complexities of the real world, isotropic surfaces allow us to concentrate on simple processes of city growth. Other models more complex than that of Burgess consider the environments in which cities exist. Let us now examine some of these additional ideas of city growth which more closely approximate the real world.

As cities grow, their several functions become separated by greater and greater distances and the role of high-speed transportation becomes more important. Today access highways link suburban homes with downtown offices. Access provided by these routes is not everywhere equally available, and some parts of the city will be better served than others. The first modification of the isotropic plain upon which our model city

Atlanta's central business district. This view looks north along Peach Tree Street, the main street of Atlanta, Georgia. As with other central cities, building heights and land values decline with distance from the center of the city.

stands is therefore a simple one. Transportation will be cheaper and better along some routes leading from the center than along others. Further complications might also include the presence of steep slopes, bodies of water, and other physical barriers to expansion. However, if only differences in transport are considered, the concentric ring pattern will be drawn out along major routes until the city pattern becomes more star-shaped. This is shown in Figure 3–5, which continues to resemble Burgess's model because of its symmetry around a central point.

The radial sector theory

In 1939 Homer Hoyt suggested a variation of the earlier symmetrical models of city growth. Hoyt was employed by the Federal Housing Administration to learn more about the areal distribution of home mortgage risks within expanding cities. Using large quan-

Figure 3-5 (A) Concentric zone model Under the assumption of equal transport costs in all directions, the ideal concentric ring pattern is deduced.

(B) Concentric zone model modified by radial transport routes Transport costs along the six evenly spaced radial routes is assumed to be less than in other radial directions. The resulting land use pattern is extended along these routes.

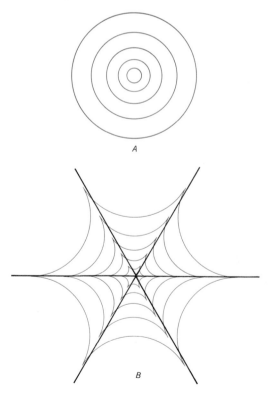

A

B

44

tities of *block census data* he determined that high-value residential neighborhoods tended to grow outward from the city center within limited wedge-shaped sectors along radial transport lines. In other words, while a concentric ring pattern does occur, there is at a given distance from the CBD considerable lateral variation within any zone. Figure 3–6 shows the variation found by Hoyt in the distribution of high-rent neighborhoods for a number of cities. It should be noted that the value of land, or rent, grades downward in all directions from the most valuable sectors.

It is important to remember that the theories and models of city growth which we create may best represent conditions for a particular time or place. Both the zone and sector theories thus far discussed seem to fit earlier periods of city growth better than the present one. Some cities have now reached such giant sizes and are so complex that simple models are no longer adequate. The next three theories of city growth more nearly match the conditions and problems inherent in Megalopolis (see Figure 3–7) and other major conurbations.

The multiple nuclei theory

Modern cities have grown so large that they have absorbed or captured many of their smaller neighbors. At the same time, distances from the CBD to outlying areas are often too great for casual shopping trips. Factories and businesses located at suburban sites generate new need for local services. These and other factors help to create a new type of city with not one but several core areas. These multiple centers of activity are tied together by superhighways and serve a far-flung urban population. Many residents of modern cities may visit the main or central business district only on special occasions. This results in a city with not one but many nuclei around which growth occurs.

Chauncy Harris and Edward Ullman first described this type of city in 1945. They recognized an urban land use pattern with several discrete nuclei which develop for different reasons (Figure 3–8). Some parts of their model city grow because of specialized facilities. These might include the waterfront district, specializing in shipping, or the main CBD, which possesses the advantage of greatest accessibility. Other places through historical accident accumulate many businesses of the same kind and offer customers a wide selection of similar goods and services. These focal points within the city attract customers by having many similar or related offerings and can provide a wider range of goods and services at lower prices than more isolated facilities. Still other types of urban activities are detrimental to each other and seek to locate maximum distances apart. For example, factories and better-class retail shops are seldom if ever found close together. Finally, certain activities can afford to pay high rents while others must seek the cheapest land possible. High-rise office buildings occupy valuable land near the center of urban areas, while used car lots, which require large amounts of relatively cheap land, must seek peripheral locations.

This idea of the *multiple nuclei city* describes large modern settlements more accurately than do the models of Hoyt and Burgess. However, none of these models completely meets the needs of city planners or informed citizens who must make decisions about the urban environments in which they live. The Burgess and Hoyt models have the advantage of simplicity, but they fail to describe reality sufficiently. The model of Ullman and Harris describes the land use pattern in modern cities but does not suggest any spatial order to the process which might allow us to predict future conditions beyond a simple extension of the existing pattern. We have yet to consider urban models which can help us to anticipate future needs in terms of not only quantity but also location. For example, we may be quite certain that the city in which we live is growing outward from its center in a complex way, but in ten years or twenty how many more schools and shopping centers will be needed and just where should we put them?

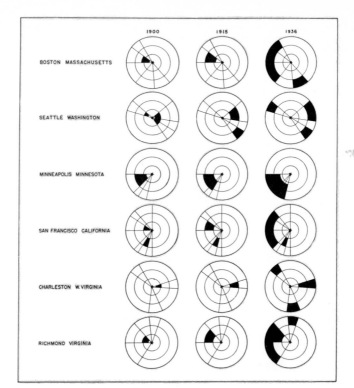

Figure 3-6 The radial sector theory of Homer Hoyt Shifts in location of fashionable residential areas in six American cities, 1900 to 1936. Fashionable residential areas are indicated by solid black. (Op. cit., Figure 3-1, p. 115)

Population densities and processes of city growth

In order to answer the above questions it becomes necessary to carefully reexamine the *processes* of city growth. One way to do this is to consider the basic spatial concepts which are involved. Among such concepts the idea of population density plays an especially important part. Density has been defined as the number of points per given area. Population density is the number of people per given area. Figure 3–9*A* and *B* shows two areas within urban Detroit. Part *B* depicts the distribution of households in an older, built-up portion of the city. It is easy to see

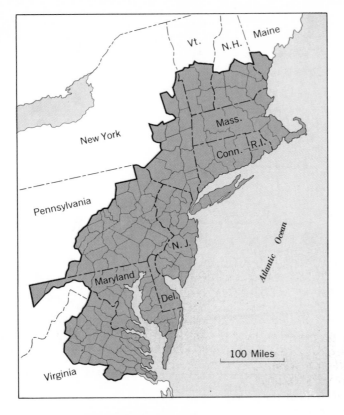

that densities are everywhere great and relatively uniform. Part *A* shows an area 10 miles farther from the center of Detroit, where the city is penetrating rural areas. Such great variation in density is typical of large cities. All cities show unequal distributions of people. If we understand such variations, we will have made a step toward understanding the processes of city growth.

Figure 3–10*A* and *B* shows population densities within the entire Detroit metropolitan

Figure 3-7 The original Megalopolis Professor Jean Gottmann defines a nearly continuous built-up area on the Eastern seaboard of the United States as *Megalopolis*, a new urban form of coalesced metropolitan areas. The areal units used to identify Megalopolis are counties which meet certain criteria of urbanism, such as a low percent of the work force in agriculture, high population densities, etc. This does not mean that the region is a solid mass of people and urban facilities. There are considerable areas of farms, forests, and empty land in Megalopolis. Gottmann has defined an urban region of great complexity and interaction. He argues that it is useful to consider it a single entity for many purposes. (After Jean Gottmann, *Megalopolis*, The Twentieth Century Fund, New York, 1961)

3-8 Urban land use pattern showing several discrete nuclei (After C. D. Harris and E. L. Ullman, "The Nature of Cities," *Annals of the American Academy of Political and Social Science* CCXLII, Nov. 1945, part of figure 5.)

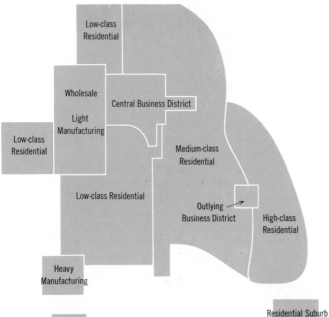

Figure 3.9 (*A*) Distribution of households in the expanding suburban edge of the Detroit metropolitan region At the suburban edge of the metropolitan region, housing developments often can be distinguished by their curving street patterns. Areas of low housing densities and curving streets contain high-income housing. A scattering of housing is found along the square section line roads in the open land to the west.

(*B*) Distribution of households in an older, built-up portion of Detroit, Michigan Household density is uniformly high in solidly built-up areas of Detroit. The density declines with distance from the central business district, which is off the map to the southeast. The empty spaces are given to nonresidential land uses, such as industrial and commercial sites and parks.

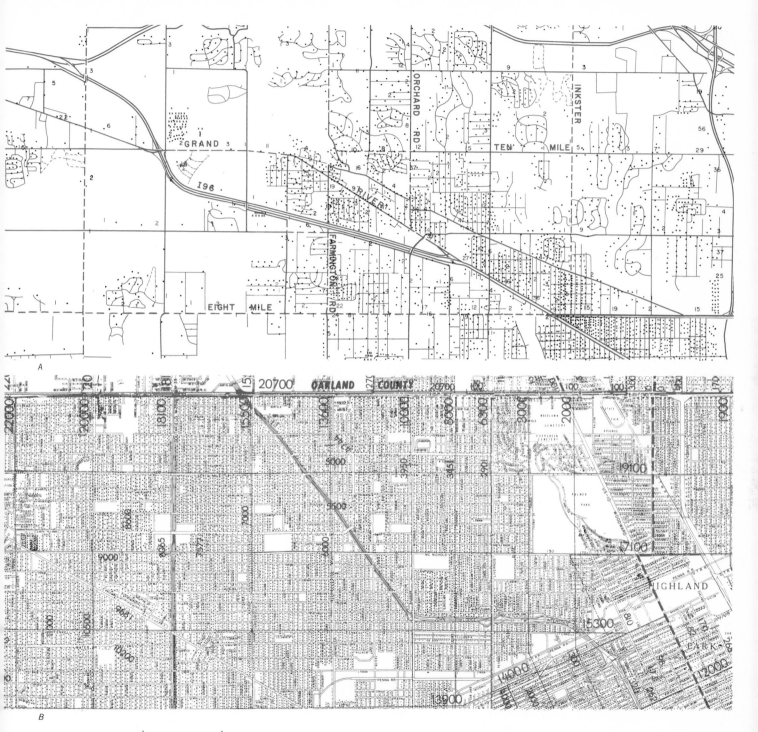

A

B

| 1 Mile

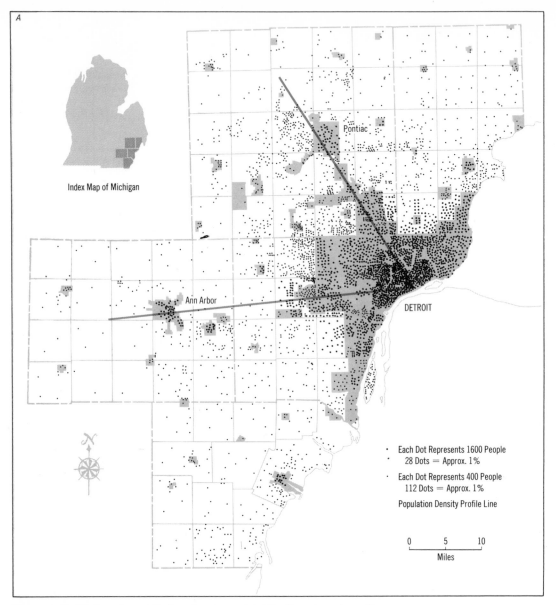

Index Map of Michigan

Pontiac

Ann Arbor

DETROIT

· Each Dot Represents 1600 People
  28 Dots = Approx. 1%

· Each Dot Represents 400 People
  112 Dots = Approx. 1%

Population Density Profile Line

0   5   10
    Miles

Figure 3-10 (A) Detroit population density, 1960 The Detroit metropolitan region extends into a five-county area in southeastern Michigan. The population density is greatly variable, with a high peak in the center of Detroit and lower peaks centered on satellite cities in the suburbs. The pattern is typical of American cities.

(B) Profile of Detroit population density (*Opposite page.*) Population density levels along two lines shown on the map in part *A*. The lines extend through two satellite cities (p. 45). (Donald R. Deskins, "Settlement Patterns for the Detroit Metropolitan Area 1930–1970," paper for the Metropolitan Community Research Project and Department of Geography, University of Michigan, Ann Arbor, June 1963, graph pages 80–81 and map series, map 5.)

area. The two lines of Figure 3–10*B* represent density profiles plotted from the CBD to the suburbs. Both lines have a shape similar to the curve illustrated by line t_2 in Figure 3–3. In terms of actual types of housing and numbers of people, we find that near the center of the city multistory apartment buildings create population densities of 25,000 people per square mile. Beyond the ring of apartment buildings come individual houses on small lots with nearly 10,000 inhabitants on each square mile of urban land. This would be similar to the densities shown in Figure 3–9*A*. Finally, suburban population density drops to less than 500 people per square mile in some places but rises again to minor peaks in the vicinity of satellite cities. These profiles confirm the observations of Harris and Ullman about multicored metropolitan areas.

The exponential decay function

The above relationship of residential densities to distance from the city center can also be conveniently expressed by a mathematical formula suggested by Colin Clark:

$$y = ae^{-bx}$$

which can also be written

$$\log y = \log a - bx$$

In this formula y equals the density of residential population, x equals the distance from the city center, and a and b are constants which must be defined in terms of the particular urban system for which the formula is being used. A line representing this formula resembles the slope of the cone in Figure 3–4*A* but differs from the schematic representation in Figure 3–4*B* in that it does not include the "backslope" or hole in the donut indicating the lower population density in the central business district. Slightly more complicated functions could be used to describe this condition as well as to add the effects of satellite cities. While some readers may wish to further explore the mathematical implications of these expressions, it is only

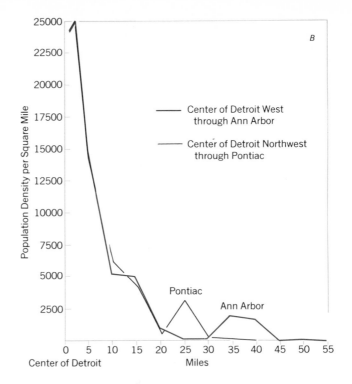

necessary for us to emphasize two things with regard to Clark's idea. First, the distribution of residential densities can be described mathematically. Land values, rents, the amounts invested in buildings, and other variables are similarly distributed. Second, these generalized distributional patterns are symmetrical with respect to the city center.

An important thing to remember about the application of the exponential decay function to urban models is that curves described by the function always represent *average* conditions. At any given distance from the center, the height and slope of a line in Figure 3–3 will be the average of all the lateral sectors in a given ring such as is shown in Hoyt's diagrams. Although such averages cannot tell us what to expect to find at a specific location, they offer insights into the nature of American cities. We can expect curves similar to the one shown for almost every large settlement whether its population is 500,000 or 5,000,000.

City Space— Models of City Growth

49

The law of allometric growth

We note that regardless of size, all large cities in a particular economic and cultural system have the same general characteristics. All their parts or functional areas share relatively fixed proportions of the total area of each city. For example, in the United States, regardless of city size, the total area devoted to commercial activities occupies about 3 to 4 percent of the entire built-up area. Single-family dwellings use up about 40 percent of the entire city space, while streets and highways account for approximately another 28 percent. The total allotment of various land uses by area is shown in Table 3–2. These figures may seem strange and may not match our views of reality. For example, the CBD in a large metropolis may not be large enough to account for 3 percent of the area of the city. However, if the areas of all the outlying shopping centers and small neighborhood business districts are added to that of the CBD, the estimate will be approximately correct. This means that even the multiple nuclei model of city growth can be described in a regular or mathematical manner if it is viewed as a set of aggregate conditions.

This principle can be better understood by drawing an analogy with biologic growth. For example, when a child is about two years old, parents can tell what its mature height will be by doubling its height at that time. Moreover, if the child is normal and healthy,

all its parts will continue to share approximately the same proportion of its total stature and weight no matter how large an adult it becomes. This rule is generally true for animals of the same species and is called the *law of allometric growth*. Swedish farmers measure the chest circumference of cows in order to estimate the amount of edible meat which the animal will produce. It does not matter whether the cow is large or small: the proportion between chest girth and the final weight of butchered meat will remain constant. By the same token, paleontologists can reconstruct the general appearance of prehistoric men from a few bones or teeth. All that is necessary is that the organic proportions and the size limits of a particular species be known.

To summarize we can say that, within a given species, if the size of one part is known, it is possible to predict the size of the entire individual or of its other parts. If the total size is known, it is possible to predict the size or proportion of one or more of its parts.

Stig Nordbeck has applied this law of allometric growth to many inanimate things, including volcanoes and large cities. His reasoning is that while a city grows and maintains its same general shape and function, the various parts within it will retain the same proportion to each other regardless of city size. It follows that if the size or rate of growth of one type of land use is known, it is possible to predict the total size of the city or the size of the various areas devoted to other land-using activities. Conversely, if a city planner has an estimate of the future population of the city, he can also estimate the total increment of streets, shopping centers, sewers, and residential areas which must be added to accommodate that future population.

Applications of the law of allometric growth

There are many interesting applications of the idea of allometric growth. Geographers have shown that for every settlement there is a regular relationship between the size of

Table 3–2 Land Use in American Cities as a Proportion of Total City Space

Residential	39.6
Streets	28.2
Public-Semipublic	11.0
Parks, playgrounds	6.7
Commercial	3.3
Heavy and light industry	6.4
Railroads	4.8
Total	100.0

Source: Harland Bartholomew, *Land Use in American Cities*, Harvard, Cambridge, Mass., 1965, from table 3, app. C.

the built-up area and its population. Although most cities are irregular in shape, this relationship can be thought of more clearly if we assume that settlements are all shaped like perfect circles and let the size of the circle be proportional to the total area of the city we wish to consider. In this case, the circle representing the city would be proportional to both the size of the built-up area and the population living in the built-up area. The radius of such a circle can be expressed by the formula

$$r = aP^b$$

P is the population, and r is the radius, while a, the maximum density, and b, the rate that density declines with distance, are coefficients based on empirical observations of the particular cities being considered. If the area of the city is known and we wish to estimate the population, the same formula can be written

$$P = \left(\frac{r}{a}\right)^{1/b}$$

Waldo Tobler has demonstrated this application of the law of allometric growth for the cities of Fort Worth and Dallas, Texas. Using an Apollo VI photograph of the two cities (Figure 2–1) he estimated their built-up areas, which appear as lighter shades of gray on the photograph. Coefficients a and b were supplied by previous studies of American cities. It took only 15 minutes to estimate a total population of 668,000. This number is within 2 percent of the 1960 census figure! Since people constantly come and go from large cities, and since the census itself has some margin for error, this figure estimated by Tobler is as reasonable or accurate as that compiled over many weeks by hundreds of census workers. The implications of this are important because it means that in the near future it will be possible to take gross census measures of city populations simply by repeating Tobler's method of analysis using low-cost satellite photographs of every part of the world.

The disadvantage of predictions based on Nordbeck's model of city growth is that his is in no way a positional theory. By this we mean that it does not allow us to specify locations for the component parts of the city but deals only in total values. A projection of future needs in terms of shopping centers can show that 10 million additional square feet will be needed by 1980 in a particular city, but not where to locate the new shopping facilities, or whether there should be one large center or several smaller ones. This is particularly true when we consider Ullman and Harris's observations about modern cities. The more multinucleated a city becomes, the more scattered and divided will be its functioning parts. Another note of caution is that if a city undergoes an important cultural or technological change, its patterns of growth may suddenly begin moving along a new and unexpected path. The invention of the internal combustion engine and the automobile caused such a dislocation in earlier patterns of city growth. Though we know much less about the significance of cultural changes, it is likely that as one subculture replaces another within a city, changes in the basic system may make prediction by use of the allometric model difficult. However, deviations from a predicted growth pattern may be used to identify significant cultural shifts.

Urbanization Defined

To further understand the environment in which we live, we must consider the themes of urbanization and population growth as cultural processes. By urbanization we mean the manner in which populations change from rural life patterns to those of city dwellers. From our geographical point of view, urbanization may be described as the process by which humanity gathers into point locations or urban clusters rather than remaining thinly distributed across agricultural areas. As Kingsley Davis points out, a careful distinction should be made between the absolute growth of cities and the process of urbani-

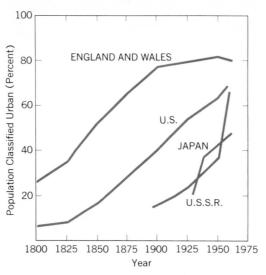

zation. In an urbanizing society, the proportion of city dwellers within the total population increases steadily, sometimes dramatically. Countries which have already gone through this process can no longer be said to be urbanizing. Such populations are urbanized. In this case, the proportion of city to rural population remains constant, and the nation is predominantly urban. For example, 80 percent of the population of England and Wales lives in urban agglomerations of 100,000 or more, a proportion which has remained almost constant for the last 25 years. England is thus urban, no longer urbanizing.

In countries which have already been urbanized, cities can continue to grow in absolute size along with overall population growth. This does not mean that the population is becoming proportionately more urban. Figure 3–11 shows the rates of urbanization for four countries: Japan, the Union of Soviet Socialist Republics, the United States, and England and Wales. Note that the percentage of urban population in England and Wales in recent years has remained nearly constant. Japan's urban population is increasing most rapidly relative to its total size. The United States and the Soviet Union are increasing their urban populations at about the same rate, although in absolute terms the United States is more urbanized.

England is typical of the distinction between urbanization and absolute city growth. For example, the constancy of urban population within the British population is in sharp contrast with the growth of the London region. Within this region, defined as an area within 40 miles of Piccadilly Circus, population grew by 800,000 in the period 1951–1961. It is estimated that in the next 20 years the population of the same area will increase by 1,900,000. At the same time, England's urban-rural population ratio may actually decrease.

The adjustment of people to the geographical space in which they live reflects their economic activities, life-styles, and total numbers. The transition from rural to urban ways of life has already brought about significant changes for much of the world's population. As cities increase in number and size, they coalesce to form urban areas which may become as large as some agricultural regions. Thus, as shown in Figure 3–12, the spatial form of the dominant life-style on earth has changed from *farm areas* with scattered punctiform settlements to contemporary cities serving as major foci for human activities. In the foreseeable future, the dominant life-style will be found in vast *urban areas*.

The two processes, urbanization and the growth of very large cities, create overlapping

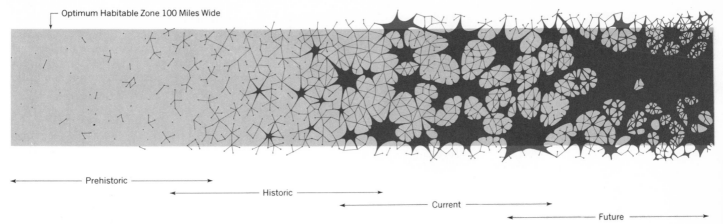

Optimum Habitable Zone 100 Miles Wide

◄──────── Prehistoric ────────►

◄──────── Historic ────────►

◄──────── Current ────────►

◄──────── Future ────────►

Figure 3-12 Evolution of urban form This is an abstract representation of the change in human organization of space through time. The organization proceeds from scattered punctiform settlements in prehistoric times to a predominantly rural agricultural landscape organized by a network of transport lines and urban points. Currently, the urban landscape is expanding in large areas. In the future, the dominant life-style and spatial organization may be urban. The figure is meant to show settlement in a 100-mile zone best suited for habitation. In the future, even with a greatly increased population expected, the world will have vast areas with inhospitable conditions nearly empty of people. The implication is that future populations will have to extend the urban order into the poor resource areas to some extent.

sets of problems. Urbanization is associated with questions of migration and changes in life-style. Very large cities create problems of access, high densities, and overburdening of the environment. These two sets of problems will be examined in many ways in the following chapters. Let us first review the nature of world population growth, which is closely associated with them.

The explosion that isn't

Perhaps the most common term used by social scientists with grim predictions for the future is the expression *the population explosion.* The cataclysmic overtones of that phrase nevertheless hold out nuances of hope. Surely after the catastrophe, some lucky survivors will pull themselves from the ruins, dust themselves off, and start over again. To a human observer far enough away to be safe,

A farmhouse in a mountainous region of Colombia, South America. The house was built by the owner-occupant twenty-five years ago. It is surrounded by vegetable and tree crops, which provide most of the food the family consumes.

A squatter settlement in Bombay, India. These houses were illegally built in an area subject to floods in the monsoon season. The building in the left foreground is a small store. Notice the people sleeping on the public pathway. This is a common practice among the poor of Bombay, where there is a tropical climate. The housing density and lack of security preclude any food growing around the houses.

Public housing in Hong Kong, 1970. Hong Kong has absorbed hundreds of thousands of refugees from mainland China in the past twenty-five years. At first, many found homes in squatter settlements similar to those in Bombay. In recent years the Hong Kong government has attempted to solve the housing problem with housing projects, of which these structures are a part. Space is very scarce in Hong Kong, and they have chosen to build many high-rise apartment buildings. Such structures and the necessary transportation facilities accompanying them have been financially possible in Hong Kong because of the relatively high average income, compared to other developing economies, which has been achieved by its fast-growing commercial and industrial economy.

a conventional explosion displays maximum violence simultaneously with the triggering action, and thereafter the force of the blast rapidly depletes itself. In other words, if you and the structure you're in survive the initial destruction, you are among the survivors— you are alive.

This is simply not an accurate analogy for the growth of world population. The sequence of events taking place around us, and to which we contribute by our own presence, is actually the reverse of any known explosion. An explosion rapidly dissipates its energy and loses its potential for further damage or further growth; world population increases daily, and every increase magnifies its potential for disaster.

The upward sweep of the world population curve, shown in Figure 3–13, is familiar to most readers. While world population growth estimates vary according to the viewpoint and techniques employed by various demographers, the story is always much the same. Ten thousand years ago, at the time the domestication of plants and animals was first taking place, the world was inhabited by perhaps 5 million people. By the beginning of the first millennium A.D., more certain supplies of food, improved technologies, and more efficient forms of political and urban organization had helped increase world population to perhaps as much as 275 million, although other estimates for this period are as low as 133 million. For the next ten centuries, until A.D. 1000, the total population of the world scarcely varied. Deficits in some places were countered by local surges of population in others, but the overall pattern was one of relative stagnation. Thereafter, from A.D. 1000 to about 1650, world population doubled in size, but it was only in the nineteenth century that the 1 billion mark was passed. Sometime between 1930 and 1940, population had again doubled. By 1970, more than 3.5 billion people were alive, and all of you who read this book may expect to share planet Earth with more than 6 billion neighbors if you survive until the year 2000.

This spectacular and ominous increase in

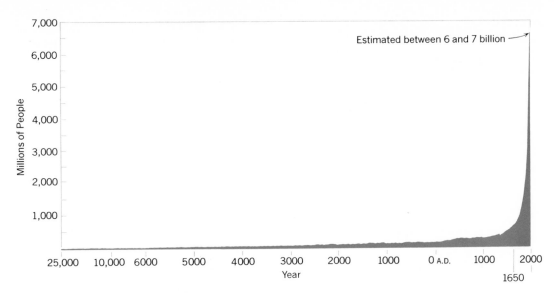

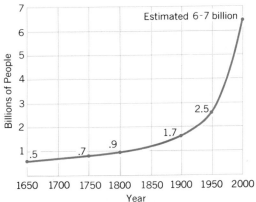

Figure 3-13 World population growth The long-time view of world population growth emphasises how unusual current conditions are. The current rate of growth has no precedence, and it cannot continue very long. On a different scale, the smaller graph shows changes in the past three centuries with a forecast to the year 2000. (References: William Petersen, *Population*, 2d ed., Macmillan, New York, 1969; Glenn T. Trewartha, *A Geography of Population: World Patterns*, Wiley, New York, 1969; Edward S. Deevey, Jr., "The Human Population," *Scientific American*, vol. 203, September, 1960; John D. Durrand, "A Long-Range View of World Population Growth," *Annals of the American Academy of Political and Social Science*, vol. 367, 1967; *U.N. Demographic Yearbook 1970*)

population can be better appreciated in terms of the survival rates of various groups of people throughout history. Figure 3–14 shows the longevity, or average life expectancy, of eleven human groups in ancient and modern times. Illness, warfare, malnutrition, and famine were everyday occurrences for all our ancestors. The selection process was brutal and only the strongest survived.

Contrast the longevity of preindustrial societies with that of Americans in recent times. The results of the Industrial and Scientific Revolutions of the nineteenth century are demonstrated here. Improvements not only

in the means of production but also in the fields of agriculture, transportation, banking, trade, communications, and medicine all serve to extend the life-span.

One important element of these examples must not be overlooked. Just as the growth of world population has been sporadic through time until the last few centuries, so has the average length of life and the increase in numbers of people varied from place to place at any given period in history. This is illustrated in part by the variations in life expectancy at birth, as shown in Figure 3–15. We must also remember that local variations are

*City Space—
Models of
City
Growth*

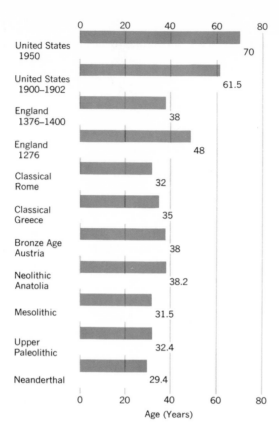

Figure 3-14 Longevity in ancient and modern times Longevity, or average life expectancy, is a useful population statistic established by means of life tables. Life tables include records of the number of people alive in each age bracket, the age-specific death rate, and other data. The average number of years of expected life at birth may be derived from these data. Life insurance companies use them to determine life insurance risk rates. Longevity is usually calculated at birth. One of the main reasons for the longer life expectancy in modern times, compared with earlier periods, is the reduction in infant deaths. Considerable data are needed to calculate accurate life expectancy rates. Since these data clearly are not available for ancient times, the rates quoted in the graph must be taken as gross approximations. (Edward S. Deevey, Jr., "The Human Population," *Scientific American,* September 1960, copyright © 1960 by Scientific American, Inc. All rights reserved.)

hidden within data compiled for large political or census units. The survival rate in Appalachia is not the same as in New England.

The distribution of urbanization

In the same way that we may subdivide the world into geographical regions for which we show survival rates and other demographic characteristics, we may also want to talk about populations in terms of their urban and rural qualities. People, in changing their life-styles, also change their geographical locations. American cities have, in the last 70 years, sheltered a larger and larger proportion of the American population. In 1890 approximately 18 percent of the total inhabitants of the United States lived in its cities; by 1900, 40 percent; by 1930, the urban segment had increased to 56.2 percent; while in 1970, 69.9 percent were classified by the census as urban dwellers. The same trend is found everywhere in the world. Table 3–3 gives some indication of the magnitude of this change from rural to urban modes of life.

An example from the non-Western world illustrates these startling trends in the redistribution of population. During the 10 years from 1941 to 1951, more than 9 million people in India moved to the cities. Their destinations were the larger urban places; their origins, the poor and isolated hamlets and villages scattered across the countryside. This was approximately 3 percent of the 1941 rural population which generated the move and 20 percent of the original urban population in the same year.

Urbanization has become one of the most important issues of the last 150 years. World population in that time increased about 3.5 times, from 960 million in 1800 to 3.6 billion in 1970. During the same period, the total population of cities and urbanized areas with more than 100,000 inhabitants grew nearly 43 times, from 15.6 to 669.0 million. The distribution of urbanization by world regions is shown in Table 3–4 and Figure 3–16. The

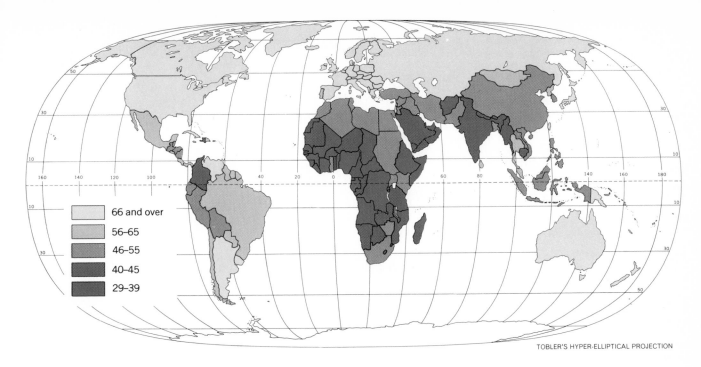

TOBLER'S HYPER-ELLIPTICAL PROJECTION

Figure 3-15 Life expectancy at birth, by nation, 1970 The values shown
on this map are subject to the measurement errors described in the text and
in the caption of Figure 3-14. Nevertheless, a clear spatial pattern is
observable. Life expectancy is generally less in the underdeveloped countries
of the world. The darkest areas indicate places where infant and child
mortality rates are high. In these societies, the commonplace loss of children
through death is in great contrast to the experience of people in more
advanced economies.

Table 3-3 Development of Urbanism

Region	% of Total Regional Population in Cities over 100,000			
	1850	1900	1950	1970
Africa	0.2	1.1	5.2	10.2
America	3.0	12.8	22.6	24.7
Asia	1.7	2.1	7.5	10.1
Europe and U.S.S.R.	4.9	11.9	19.9	27.1
Oceania		21.7	39.2	44.6

Source: 1850 to 1950: Gerald Breese, *Urbanization in Newly Developing Countries*, Prentice-
Hall, Englewood Cliffs, N.J., 1966, p. 22. 1970 data: *U.N. Demographic Yearbook 1970*,
U.S. Bureau of the Census 1970, Statistical Abstract of Latin America 1969 (U.N. data are for
latest available year, mainly 1965–1970).

pattern of this distribution is similar to that
of the distribution of per capita income. This
suggests that it is more than coincidence that
the developed countries of the world are the
urbanized ones.

**Figure 3-16 Percent of urban
population, by nation, 1970**

Definitions of urban areas vary from
country to country and over time. The
map shows the latest available U.N.
statistics for countries and employs
slightly different definitions of urban
area as reported by each country. The
countries are grouped into world
regions, with their average percent of
urban population shown. Variation of
tones within regions shows something
of the range in values which exists.
Especially in the large countries,
subregions would also show great
variation in percent of urban
population. (Data: *U.N. Demographic
Yearbook 1970*)

Table 3–4   World Urban Population, 1970

Region	Total Population (millions)	Urban Population (millions)	% Urban
Northern Africa	82.2	27.6	39
Western Africa	90.8	12.5	15
Eastern Africa	92.0	8.7	9
Middle Africa	28.2	5.1	18
Southern Africa	26.4	7.7	42
Northern America	199.3	140.0	70
Middle America	65.5	35.7	54
Caribbean	20.7	8.2	40
Tropical South America	121.4	60.1	49
Temperate South America	34.6	24.8	72
Southwest Asia	51.9	21.8	42
Middle South Asia	713.8	138.1	19
Southeast Asia	186.5	31.4	17
Mainland East Asia	658.0	99.4	15
Island East Asia	116.4	78.3	67
Northern Europe	80.1	56.6	71
Western Europe	145.5	80.8	56
Eastern Europe	102.4	53.1	52
Southern Europe	119.2	49.1	41
U.S.S.R.	241.7	136.0	56
Oceania	14.9	11.5	77

Source: *U.N. Demographic Yearbook 1970.*

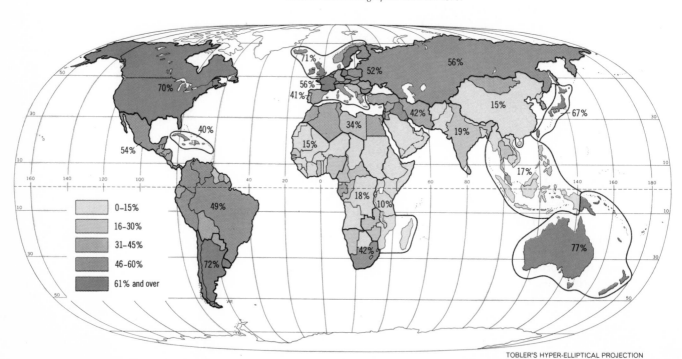

0–15%
16–30%
31–45%
46–60%
61% and over

TOBLER'S HYPER-ELLIPTICAL PROJECTION

Plaza of Los Angeles, about 1890. This is how the center of Los Angeles looked in 1890. Compare this photograph with the more recent photographs shown below. (Wide World Photos)

The Center of Los Angeles in 1957 and 1973. In 1957, the skyline of Los Angeles was rather flat and was dominated by the twenty-seven-story City Hall (white tower, top center). Building height restrictions, inspired by fear of earthquake damage, had resulted in no building over thirteen stories high except for the City Hall. The height restrictions were later lifted, and the downtown financial district now has several buildings over fifty stories high. Los Angeles is an example of a growing and changing city landscape which reflects complex interaction between environmental conditions, technological capacity, instutional control, and aspirations of its citizens. (Wide World Photos)

Cities are places to live. Whether it is Park Avenue in New York, a crowded street in Naples, or your own neighborhood, more and more of the world's people call the city and its suburbs home. In fact, it is safe to say that a majority of the students who read these lines already live in a metropolitan area or will move to one sometime during their lives.

Cities are places to sell and buy goods and to provide and utilize services. Employees in the Paris Bourse and the New York City Stock Exchange, seamstresses in the garment district and salesmen on Saville Row, bowling alley operators, insurance salesmen, grocery store cashiers, and air traffic controllers perform a few of the many activities that characterize urban life. Cities also provide people with enjoyment and education. Museums and zoos, theaters and restaurants are among the goals of tourists and weekend vacationers. No metropolis is without its colleges and at least one university.

Dominant Trade Areas

While the residents of cities fill some of the jobs and utilize part of the services offered by the urban places in which they live, the use of cities is not limited to urbanites. Neither are the manufactured goods produced in cities reserved only for local citizens. Every

city reaches out to serve and influence the area surrounding it. In return, what goes on in the city reflects the resources and character of the surrounding region. Midwesterners are familiar with the popular term "Chicagoland," which refers to the vast area dependent upon Chicago for supplies and services. New York City has a similar dependent area stretching far beyond its legal borders. In fact, every settlement has some geographical area larger than itself with which it interacts.

The ability of cities to reach beyond their legal limits can be illustrated by considering the distribution patterns of their daily newspapers. If a person traveling by car from New York to Chicago were to check the newsstands in all the towns along his route, he would find New York papers predominating on the "out-of-town" rack in New Jersey and Pennsylvania. As he moved westward, Chicago papers would begin to appear until finally their presence would predominate in Ohio and northern Indiana. The same relationship exists between Chicago and St. Louis or between San Francisco and Los Angeles, or between any two major cities. The dynamic activity and excitement of major metropolitan centers are of concern to the people living in the areas around and between them as well as to their own inhabitants.

Just as rural people depend upon cities,

cities must reach out for the supplies which support them. While a small town will usually use dairy products from some nearby source, large cities must depend upon distant farms. Figure 4-1 shows the sources of milk for the New York City area.

Figure 4-2 shows the area served and influenced by Mobile, Alabama. The complex nature of such urban influence is partially revealed by the seven boundary lines drawn about the city itself. Nearest to the city is a line showing the extent of the area in which

Figure 4-1 Sources of fluid milk for the New York area The fluid milk marketing area is a receiving zone for fluid milk in which wholesale milk prices are agreed upon under federal marketing orders. New York City is by far the largest market in this receiving area. Most of the milk destined for this area (89 percent) comes from the source areas shown under the federal marketing orders. Eleven (11) percent of the milk received comes from producers *not* under federal milk-marketing orders. Their sources are unknown, although very likely they are located in the same general territory. (Data from "Sources of Milk for Federal Order Markets by State and County," U.S. Dept. of Agriculture Consumer and Marketing Service, Dairy Division, C & MS-50, 1969)

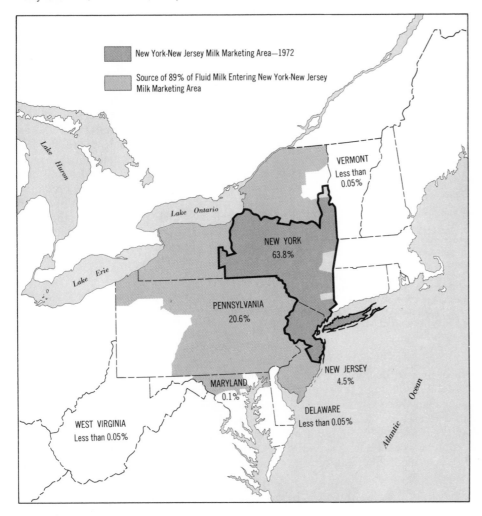

The City and Its Hinterland— the Effects of Distance

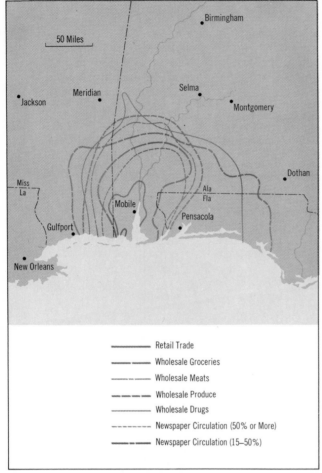

Figure 4-2 The areas served and influenced by Mobile, Alabama The first six lines are boundaries of territories around Mobile, Alabama, within which Mobile has 50 percent or more of the business in the particular trade or activity listed in the legend. (Edward L. Ullman, *Mobile: Industrial Seaport and Trade Center*, bound dissertation, University of Chicago, 1943, p. 58)

by the city's wholesale drug firms reaches farthest; in other places the farthest reach is shown by those places where more than 20 percent of all out-of-town newspapers originate in Mobile. At varying intermediate distances a variety of other indicators show the extent of the city's hinterland.

Each settlement, however large or small, influences and relates to the area surrounding it. Where wholesale and retail services are concerned, the area which a city serves is called its *dominant trade area*. Small settlements reach out only a few miles, while a city the size of Mobile, 70,000 at the time of the study, has an area of influence that extends more than 100 miles to the north and east. City size alone, however, cannot explain in every case the extent of the trade area or hinterland of a particular settlement. Distance measured in terms of the ease or difficulty of travel is also important. So too the influence or competition of neighboring settlements is significant in determining how far a city will reach beyond its borders. The effect of size, ease of travel, and location relative to dominant centers is shown by the newspaper distribution areas in the vicinity of Frankfort, Germany (Figure 4–3). Every aspect of cities and city-oriented life is influenced by population, travel conditions, and intercity competition. The sections which follow clarify the interrelationship of these and other variables and show how in combination they define the areas cities serve.

City-Hinterland Connections: The Journey to Work

Let us consider a trip with which nearly everyone is familiar. *The journey to work* may be nothing more than a housewife's walking from the bedroom to the kitchen in the morning. It may be as unusual as the travel pattern of one professor who teaches both in New York and at the Sorbonne in Paris and makes two round trips by air each week across the Atlantic. Between these extremes are found millions of American commuters who move

the people spent 50 percent or more of their retail dollar in Mobile. Although the area it encloses is smaller than those for other types of urban-based activities, it is still many times larger than the city itself. The outermost lines mark the boundary of Mobile's immediate influence. In some places the area served

daily by car from their homes in the suburbs to their jobs in the cities. This is, in fact, such a common occurrence that one way of functionally defining a *metropolitan area* is in terms of the commuting range of its inhabitants. This range is measured not so much by straight linear distance—since traffic conditions vary from place to place—as by the actual time required to drive to work. The average commuter will willingly drive about one-half hour both to and from work. Very few will consider extending the time for a one-way trip to an hour or more. This is also true for commuters who travel by train.

Figure 4–4 shows the frequency of commuter travel by train to New York City. The number of commuters declines rapidly with distance. Notice, too, how individual commuter stations appear like loosely spaced beads along some parts of the rail network. Figure 4–5 shows the commuting areas around various cities in the southern Great Plains and Rocky Mountains. In this figure cities with large commuter areas are most likely located in level areas and have good highways leading into them. Those cities with asymmetric commuting zones are often located adjacent to mountainous areas where driving is slower, or they may be connected to their hinterlands by poorer road systems in certain directions. Just as the unequal distribution of population within a city can be aggregated and shown by a smooth curve, the density of commuter travel as a function of distance (i.e., the number of commuters traveling between a city center and a particular distance ring) can be expressed by a similar curve (Figure 4–6).

Distance, travel effort, and distance decay functions

When we speak of the frequency of commuter travel and the spatial extent of city hinterlands, we are actually referring to varying degrees of participation in the processes which define urban life. A number of curves similar to that in Figure 4–6 describe the degree of partici-

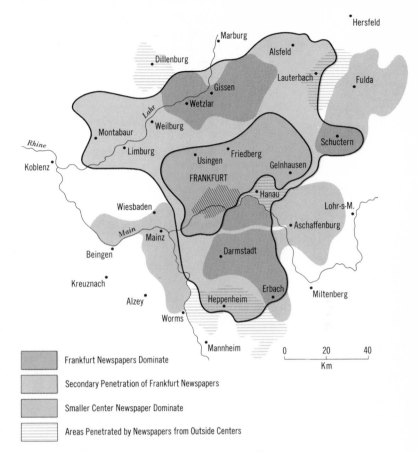

Frackfurt Newspapers Dominate

Secondary Penetration of Frankfurt Newspapers

Smaller Center Newspaper Dominate

Areas Penetrated by Newspapers from Outside Centers

Figure 4-3 Major distribution area for Frankfort newspapers (After J. Beaujeu-Garnier and G. Chabot, *Urban Geography*, Wiley, New York, 1967, fig. 38, p. 403; and W. Hartke, *Die Zeitung als Funktion sozial geographischer Verhaltnisse im Rhein-Main Gebiet*, Rhein-Mainsche Forschungen, 32, 1952, p. 21)

pation of people in an activity at a given site in terms of the distances they must travel to reach that point. A simple exercise will illustrate this on a regional and national scale. Plot the home addresses of a random selection of students attending your school. The largest proportion of students will come from nearby counties in the state in which your college is located, fewer will call states at intermediate distances "home," and people from the opposite side of the country and foreign students will appear least frequently. If you perform this exercise, however, you will notice exceptions to the regular diminishing of student numbers with distance. This can be accounted for in several ways. Obviously a nearby state with a very large population will be over-represented in absolute numbers because of its size. If the number of students from a given political unit is expressed as a proportion of the total population of that state or country, the participation curve which you plot will be much smoother. Other factors which might further influence the regularity of such a curve will be the per capita income of each state and perhaps the number and quality of its schools.

Figure 4-4 Frequency of commuter travel by train to New York City
Frequency zones have a maximum radius of 2½ miles from each station. Only trains entering within 5 miles of the city center (the area marked by the inner circle) are considered. (Adapted from David Neft, "Some Aspects of Rail Commuting: New York, London and Paris," *The Geographical Review*, vol. 49, no. 2, April, 1959, part A of plate II, figs. 3 and 4, copyrighted by American Geographical Society of New York)

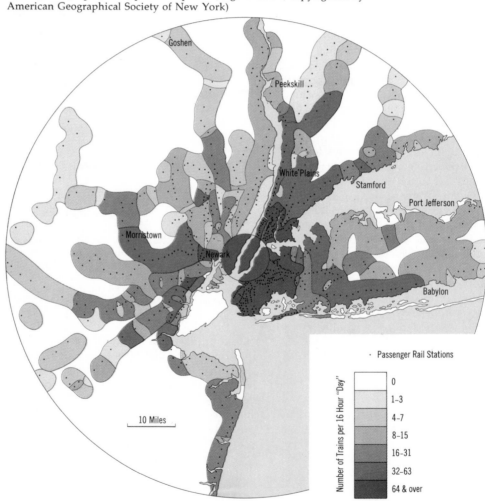

· Passenger Rail Stations

Number of Trains per 16 Hour "Day"

	0
	1–3
	4–7
	8–15
	16–31
	32–63
	64 & over

10 Miles

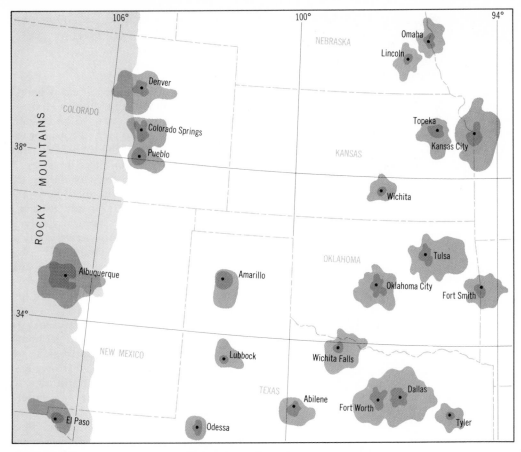

Figure 4-5 Commuting areas of some metropolitan centers in the Southern Great Plains and the Rocky Mountains (After Brian J. L. Berry, U.S. map in "Commuting Fields of Central Cities," University of Chicago, Social Science Research Council Committee on Areas for Social and Economic Statistics, in cooperation with the Bureau of the Census, Dept. of Commerce, Wash., D.C., April, 1967)

The same comments hold true for commuters to a city. The closer and/or larger the commuter suburb, the greater will be the absolute number of people traveling from it to the city each day. The number of job opportunities at home compared with those in the city will also be important. So too will be the nature of avail-

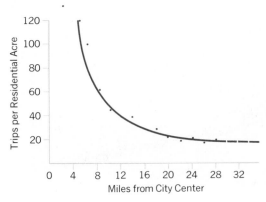

Figure 4-6 Frequency of commuter travel as a function of distance (Adapted from *Chicago Area Transportation Study,* vol. 1, parts of fig. 32, p. 61, published by the State of Illinois, 1959)

Washington, D.C., commuter traffic on Highway I-95 in northern Virginia.

So long as people insist on commuting by automobile the diurnal ebb and flow of commuter traffic from suburb to city and back again makes automobile congestion inevitable. Notice the difference in traffic density in the two directions. This picture, however, is of a rather special situation. An attempt is being made to induce people to use commuter buses by giving buses exclusive use of two lanes which can be changed to correspond with the directions of heaviest flow. A commuter bus is shown moving freely on these lanes reserved for it, while the inbound Washington auto and truck traffic is bumper to bumper. (Wide World Photos)

Returning from market along a mountain trail in Colombia, South America. The mode of travel and the quality of the route available greatly affect how far and how often one goes to market.

able transportation facilities and route conditions.

Variations in travel effort

We live in a non-Euclidean world where a straight line is seldom the shortest distance between two points. In order to understand this statement it is necessary to consider the *travel effort* instead of the linear distance involved in moving from place to place. If you have ever driven to the city during the morning rush hour, you will know how long it took you to fight the traffic and to find a parking place. On the other hand, if you have been fortunate enough to be leaving a city at that time and have moved swiftly along the nearly empty outbound lanes, it will be clear that the distance from city A to suburb B measured in time or effort may be much less at eight o'clock in the morning than it is from suburb B to city A. Just the opposite may be true during the five o'clock rush to get home. Thus, crowding and traffic help to skew the even geometry of the world in which we live.

Road conditions as well as traffic density also alter the symmetry of the commuter's world. Poor surfaces and narrow lanes will make certain routes slower than others. Steep road gradients, numerous sharp curves, and busy intersections can also delay the traveler and add extra costs of time and fuel to his trip. Figure 4–7 shows the total time required to go the same distance under varying road conditions.

Directional Differences: Geographic Circles

Variations in travel effort find expression in a variety of ways. City hinterlands as determined by commuter trips would be symmetrical about the center of a city on a theoretical isotropic plane. That is, if linear distance were the only consideration, all city hinterlands would be round.

Directional differences in travel effort act to create asymmetrical areas of influence. Thus, a geographic circle measured in terms of equal travel effort about some central point will rarely, if ever, resemble the perfect circles of Euclidean geometry. Figure 4-8 shows a set of geographic circles centered upon a business in a metropolitan area. Each line represents one minute of driving time away from the business under normal conditions. Such lines showing equal *time-distance* are referred to as *isochrones*. Travel along main boulevards and highways is easier and faster than on side streets. Generally speaking, this map shows that it is easier and faster to drive in an east-west direction than in a north-south direction. A major exception to this is travel along the northwest-southwest trending streets which cut across the area. The distribution of customers patronizing the business upon which this map is centered would conform closely to the asymmetric travel pattern shown by the isochrones. Such isochronic analysis can be a useful tool in understanding patterns of retail trade. By simple analogy, if we equate all the services offered by a city with those provided by a single store, it becomes easier to see why cities develop irregularly shaped hinterlands.

The geometry of city hinterlands

Not all variations in the shape of city hinterlands need be explained by variations in travel effort. A few simple geometric relationships also help to explain asymmetries such as the lopsided north-eastward extention of Mobile's influence (Figure 4-2). In order to examine this idea, let us return to our theoretical world with its cities situated upon an isotropic plane.

Figure 4-9 shows a generalized population density surface for a metropolitan area. A major city can be seen dominating the area along with three smaller suburban towns. This surface could also depict the total influence of each settlement and its inhabitants. If there were a single isolated settlement, a symmetric and circular cone of influence would extend outward from the CBD. In the example shown in Figure 4-9 cones of influence intersect one another much as the cones of adjacent volcanoes might build up around each other. This is further illustrated

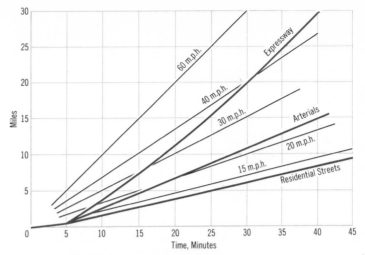

Figure 4-7 Time required to travel the same distance under varying road conditions On gravel and/or winding mountain roads, one can average between 15 and 30 miles per hour, depending upon conditions and number of stops. (Source: *The Dynamics of Urban Transportation*, Symposium of Automobile Manufacturers Association, Inc., October, 1962)

in Figure 4-10. Notice how the larger city at point A generates an area of influence which nearly engulfs that of the smaller settlement at B. Only the crest of city B's cone of influence rises above the slopes of A. The allocation of influence between two cities, or in this case between a major city and its satellite, can be visualized by drawing the line of intersection between the two cones. Thus points *x* and *y* in Figure 4-10 correspond to *x'* and *y'* in Figure 4-11, which is a map representation of the preceding three-dimensional view. Since the influence of the central city is greater on the side of the satellite settlement nearer to the larger city, the extent of the area of influence of the smaller place is less on that side. Conversely, the area of influence of the smaller, suburban town extends farther on the side away from the larger city. The resulting map pattern shows an asymmetrical hinterland belonging to the smaller town.

Figure 4-12A to D shows the relationships

Figure 4-8 A set of geographic circles centered on a business The lines represent one-minute driving time intervals away from the business location at the origin, under nonpeak-hour traffic conditions. The values were determined empirically by actually driving over the roads and measuring the number of seconds between checkpoints. The time lines were then determined by totaling the number of seconds from the business location along the shortest time route. Connecting the set of equal time points into a continuous line is obviously an abstraction because the vehicle cannot travel off the road network. This technique adds to the readability of the map, although adding an unreal character to it. Some interesting time-distance inversions occur as a consequence of a network of roads in which travel along some segments is much faster than along others. This is, however, the nature of the urban space in which we live.

between a large isolated city and its hinterland, the hinterlands of two cities of equal size, the hinterlands or areas of influence of a large- and medium-sized city, and a large city and a smaller satellite suburb. Compare these figures with the map of Mobile. The presence of New Orleans to the west of Mobile suggests that the asymmetry of its area

of influence results from the proximity of the larger metropolitan center.

Breaking points between city hinterlands

If two urban places have essentially the same number of shops and the same type and range of goods and offer the same services, how

*Human
Geography:
Spatial
Design
in World
Society*

68

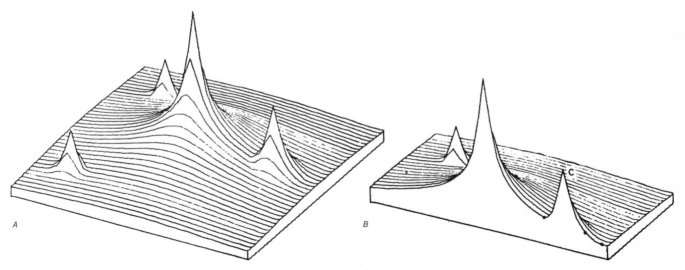

A

B

Figure 4-9 (*A*) Generalized population density surface of a metropolitan area. (*B*) Cross section of metropolitan density surface This model is a computer-calculated and computer-drawn density surface of a hypothetical metropolitan area. The model does not take into account nonresidential land use at the center of the cities and therefore does not contain the depressed central density pattern described in Figure 3-4*B*. The shape shown could be thought of as the rent surface or density of interaction in a metropolitan area with a central city and three satellite towns. (Robert S. Yuill, *A General Model for Urban Growth: A Spatial Simulation*, Michigan Geography Publication No. 2, Depart. of Geography, University of Michigan, Ann Arbor, Mich., 1970)

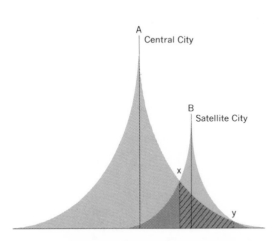

A Central City

B Satellite City

x

y

Figure 4-10 Allocation of influence between a central city and a satellite town Profile view of the zones of influence of a central city and its satellite town. The satellite's area of dominance is asymmetrical, being offset in the direction away from the central city.

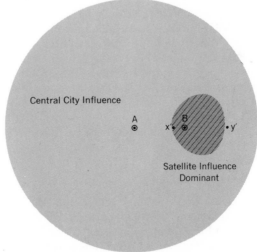

Central City Influence

A

x' B y'

Satellite Influence Dominant

Figure 4-11 Areas dominated by central city and satellite town Plan view of the zones of influence of a central city and its satellite town. At a distance beyond the satellite town, the central city reestablishes its dominance.

will customers located between them decide which center to patronize? In the real world, personal preferences as well as a host of other conditions play an important part in these decisions. Employment opportunities as well as consumer shopping habits vary considerably, and workers may commute from long-established homes in one town to new jobs in another city rather than change their residences. This process of city selection for work and shopping is extremely complicated. Although it is possible to draw a sharp dividing line between two such cities, a more realistic model would show zones of overlapping influence. In both cases the extent of influence will be a function of their characteristics. Population alone may give an indication of their relative attractiveness, or variations in job opportunities or the number of commercial establishments may also be used. Let us also assume that the number of opportunities for work and trade is directly proportional to city size. In this case, if transportation facilities are everywhere the same, the boundary between the market areas of the two cities will be a line marking equal travel effort in either direction. If the distance between two such places is 50 miles, then each will dominate an area 25 miles in depth. On the other hand, if one settlement is larger than the other and offers a larger number of more varied employment and customer opportunities, the market area or hinterland of the larger place will reach out farther from its CBD than that of the smaller. These relationships can be recognized in Figure 4-12.

Retail Gravity Models

The areal extent of city hinterlands can be estimated with the help of what are called *retail* and *social gravity models*. This approach for measuring the interaction between cities was first suggested by Henry C. Carey in 1858. Carey reasoned that an analogy might be drawn between the attractive force between two physical masses as stated in the physics equation

$$F = G\,\frac{M_1 M_2}{d^2}$$

and the interaction of two urban places. In this equation—which is familiar to all students who have had introductory physics—F is equal to the attractive force, M_1 is equal to the mass of the first body, M_2 is equal to the mass of the second body, and d^2 is the square of the distance between them. The constant G is an additional factor, the force of gravity, which must be included to make the computation correct.

William J. Reilly rewrote this equation in 1929 using populations instead of mass in order to describe the retail interaction between two cities. In his equation

$$I = \frac{P_i P_j}{d^2{}_{ij}}$$

P_i is the population of the first, or ith, city and P_j is the population of the second, or jth, city. The square of the distance between the two cities is shown by the notation $d^2{}_{ij}$. This says: The retail interaction between two cities i and j is equal to the product of their populations divided by the square of the distance between them. The interaction I may be a measure of the number of customers, sales, or some other exchange between the two places. Thus two towns of moderate size which are located a short distance apart may have the same amount of goods passing between them as two larger places separated by a greater distance.

In another of his *laws of retail gravitation* Reilly provided a similar equation which may be used to estimate the linear extent of the hinterlands of the two cities—that is, the location of the breaking point marking the mutual edge of their two areas of retail influence. When the breaking point separating two large populations is considered, it is important to remember that the model discussed here is deterministic rather than probabilistic. In reality the preferences of shoppers obey rules more complex than those imposed by simple linear distance or travel effort. If two

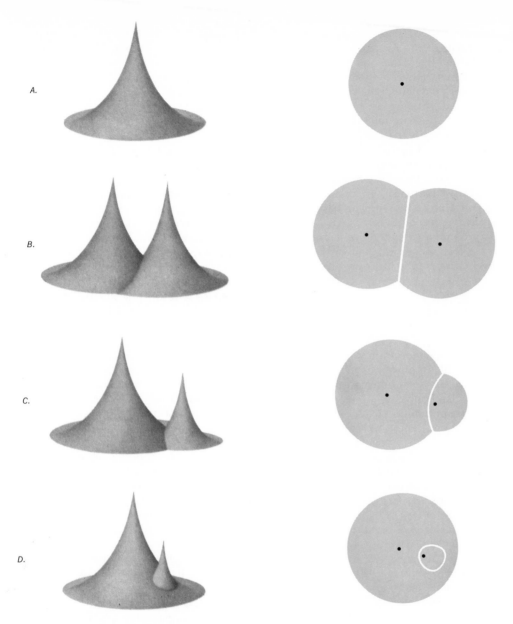

Figure 4-12 Cones of Influence around cities of varying size (*A*) single city, (*B*) cities of equal size, (*C*) city and independent small town, (*D*) city and satellite town.

large cities are relatively close to each other, people from either of the two may patronize establishments in the other. Suburbanites and rural residents between them will also base their choice of destinations on a number of factors and not just on travel effort. As a result of this, when we talk of the breaking point or dividing line between the hinterlands of competing cities, we refer to areas where the influence of one city predominates. In other words, more than 50 percent of the shoppers within a particular hinterland will utilize its central city on a regular basis although smaller percentages of people will make the trip to other competing settlements.

To estimate this theoretical halfway point between two cities Reilly used the formula:

$$D_j = \frac{d_{ij}}{1 + \sqrt{\dfrac{P_i}{P_j}}}$$

where D_j = the distance from city j to the breaking point
d_{ij} = the distance between the two cities i and j
P_i = the population of the ith city
P_j = the population of the jth city

This may be read: The distance from city j to the edge of its hinterland with city i is equal to the distance between the two cities divided by 1 plus the square root of the size of city i divided by the size of city j.

If we return to the case of Mobile (Figure 4–2), we find that the two cities, Mobile and New Orleans, are roughly 125 miles apart. The population of Mobile in 1940—when the map was made—was 70,000 and that of New Orleans 495,500. Substituting these values in the above formula we find that in theory the breaking point should occur approximately 35 miles west of Mobile. This point falls near the line denoting 50 percent or more of out-of-town newspaper circulation originating in Mobile. While this is only one of several measures shown by the various boundaries on the map, if we consider the sixth and seventh boundaries to refer to the same thing,

newspapers, then the edge of the hinterland defined by Reilly's method falls almost in the middle of the wide "border zone" indicated by all the commercial boundaries found through actual field study.

Problems associated with the gravity model

If only trips for one type of item are considered, and that item is readily available at all places with little or no variation in price and quality, then distance alone will usually determine the consumer's choice of market or market town. On the other hand, people will try to combine several errands on a single shopping trip, and larger towns with more choices and a greater variety of goods and services will attract customers from greater distances. As a result, the gravity model can only work where many trips and many travelers are concerned. A farmer may one day go to the nearest town to buy only groceries. Another time he may travel to a larger and more distant place not only to buy groceries but also to purchase a replacement part for his tractor and a pair of shoes for his child. More complicated models devised to take this type of human behavior into account are described in advanced texts.

A few moments' thought about the basic gravity model described above will reveal other complications. For example, is straight linear distance a good measure of true geographic distance? Ease of transportation may be very important. A superhighway leading to a farther city may offset the proximity of nearer places reached only on narrow, crowded county roads. If we consider city merchants who make deliveries to stay-at-home consumers, directional variations in freight rates or shipping charges may also make a significant difference in the customers' choice of stores. Several researchers have suggested that distance should be given greater or less importance depending upon the true effort required to overcome space. In order to do this the value d^2 might better be replaced by d^b where b would be some other value than the square of the distance. This might be the distance cubed in some cases where road conditions were poor, or the value might be something less than the distance squared where travel conditions were especially good.

Another thought to make us pause before using the simple gravity model would be the character of the populations involved. If three cities of equal size are equal distances apart but the average income in one city is considerably lower than those in the other two, the interaction between the two wealthier places might be much greater than between the poorer place and its richer neighbors. If we consider interaction on a world scale, cities of the same cultural background or ethnic composition might well interact with each other much more than with other urban populations speaking different languages or having different political beliefs. For greater accuracy an attempt must be made to weight each population according to some estimate of its potential for interaction. In one study of this kind cities in the South in the United States were considered to be less in the mainstream of national activity and were discounted by giving them a value only eight-tenths their true population size, thus reducing their interaction potential. In this manner some effort was made to adjust the gravity equation to assumed variations within the United States.

The subtle role of perception also must be taken into account. Many people say, "New York is a great place to visit but I wouldn't want to live there." This indicates a value judgment about the character of New York by nonresidents. In much the same way, our grandfathers longed to visit "Gay Paree" and made Paris the goal of European travel. Similarly, the public's image of certain national parks as desirable places to visit accounts for inequalities of recreational land use. On days when Yosemite National Park is so crowded that hikers and campers are being turned away, other beautiful campgrounds in the same area remain unfilled. The role of perception and attitude in spatial decision making is, thus, very important in accounting for real world patterns which otherwise might seem to contradict what we have said about the effect of distance on human affairs.

Social gravity models

Variations from culture to culture and between cities with different levels of income further complicate the basic equations of retail gravitation. John Q. Stewart and other social scientists more than 30 years ago recognized the need to take such factors into consideration. They suggested that the analogy with the equation for gravitation force can be used to measure many kinds of influence and interaction between population groups in addition to the retail function of cities. Several variations on Reilly's original equation have been put forward. One of the simplest, but more comprehensive, of these social gravity models takes the form:

$$I_{ij} = K \frac{P_i P_j}{d^b_{ij}}$$

In this equation the interaction I may be a measure of the number of telephone calls, intercity migration, commercial exchanges, or any of the multitude of ways in which society interacts. The constant K describes the intensity of interaction in a particular society. Its value must be carefully derived from field observation, for people interact with their neighbors in ways which vary significantly from culture to culture and from activity to activity. P_i and P_j are measures of size, and d^b_{ij} is the distance between the two places weighted by some exponential value b which again depends upon variations in travel effort.

Market Areas and Transportation Costs

The retail and social gravity models discussed above work only when aggregate conditions are considered. That is, the preferences and choices of individuals are so varied that for the purpose of understanding the spatial character of cities we must view society only in large groups. In this way personal and random variation in behavior is averaged, and we may look at the total behavior of a city's population as matching some type of normal distribution. While a few people may act in extreme and seemingly illogical ways, the average citizen's actions can be anticipated, although we cannot identify him as an individual.

Gravity models do not help us understand the *processes* underlying retail and social behavior as much as they provide *descriptions of the behavior* of large populations. Another way in which it is possible to view the delimitation of city hinterlands or market areas is to understand the role played in their formation by transportation costs. If we consider each urban place as a collection of stores or sales outlets for services and manufactured goods, we can simplify our discussion by considering the case of a single factory producing one particular manufactured item. Once we understand the processes by which one establishment defines the area in which its output is distributed, it becomes possible to view each city as the sum of all the stores and factories it contains. The total commercial activity within the city and the area served by such commerce in essence defines the hinterland or trade area of the city.

The threshold of a good

Every factory and every store must begin with certain basic necessities. Land on which to locate, a building or buildings to house the firm, equipment of all kinds, and a labor force and sales personnel must all be provided before the success of the establishment can be assured. All these things cost money, and all the money originally invested must eventually be returned to the investors through sales. If production costs are not met and exceeded by the returns from sales, failure results.

The minimum number of sales or the smallest total volume of sales which will allow a commercial establishment to prosper and give an adequate return to its owners is called the *threshold of the establishment*. This idea may also be expressed in terms of a single sale or a single item if the total costs of production are divided by the number of units

produced. This establishes the lowest price which may be charged for an item at the threshold volume of production which will meet production costs and also provide a reasonable return on the initial investment. This may be thought of as the threshold price of the good. From the customer's point of view every good and service has some maximum price more than which he is unable or unwilling to pay. When the price is unreasonable, the customer will go without or substitute something more reasonably priced. Obviously, to allow the firm to stay in business the threshold price must be less than the maximum a customer is willing to pay.

The range of a good

The above discussion omits one important cost in every transaction. Transportation must be paid by either the customer or the producer of every good and service. Shoppers must travel to the store, or the merchant must ship the purchase to the customer. Less tangible services are affected in the same way. You must visit your insurance salesman, or he must come to you. Medical doctors charge more for house calls than for office visits. The difference in price is their evaluation of the cost of their travel effort.

The cost of transportation varies considerably from item to item. If we consider only material goods for the moment, we can understand such variations in terms of the relationship between the volume or weight of an item and its total sales price. Generally speaking, small, lightweight goods with high value may travel long distances, while bulky or heavy items having a low value per pound or per cubic foot will travel less far. This simple relationship is shown in Figure 4–13. A fine camera with an expensive lens weighs at most 2 or 3 pounds. Even with adequate packing, equipment like this can be mailed long distances for only a few dollars. If we imagine a camera shipped from Japan to the United States by air, its total cost might be 300 dollars, of which 5 dollars might cover the necessary postage. Heavy bulk items such as bricks sell for only a few cents apiece. If a brick were shipped more than a few miles from the kiln in which it was baked, the price of transportation would soon exceed the cost of production and the combined production and transportation costs would be more than anyone would be willing to pay. Many items fall within this category. Soft drinks are essentially water with flavoring added. The bottle in which the beverage is shipped to the consumer also constitutes a significant part of the total weight. Glass and water are low-priced items and cannot be shipped long distances without unnecessary expense. Thus bottling works and brick kilns must be located close to their customers, while camera factories, in terms of transportation costs, can afford to locate in a few select places.

The unit cost for shipping various items 1 mile can be shown on a graph by vertical lines of different lengths. For each unit of distance involved an additional vertical transportation cost increment is added. Figure 4–14 shows this for two unlike types of goods. Notice how the resulting lines resemble two steps of stairs, one very steep and the other much more gentle. Since it is awkward to use stepped lines such as these on graphs, sloping lines representing the average increase in transportation cost with increasing distance are substituted in their place. In Figure 4–14 t equals the ratio of the cost of transportation Δc per unit distance Δd and is shown by the slope of the line.

When the transportation costs are added to production costs, it becomes apparent that goods can be shipped only finite distances before the costs of shipment make the products so expensive that customers will no longer buy them. This absolute limit on the demand for an item is called the *maximum range of a good*. Figure 4–15 shows the relationship between production costs, profits, and transportation costs for two hypothetical products, both of which cost the same amount to produce, both of which sell for the same price, but one of which is easily transportable and the other expensive to ship.

Value of Good

		High	Low
Volume or Weight of Good	**High**	Good Shipped Intermediate Distance Ornamental Building Stone Appliances	Good Shipped Short Distance Bricks Bottles
	Low	Good Shipped Long Distance Cameras Watches Radios	Good Shipped Intermediate Distance Table Salt Fertilizer

Figure 4-13 The relationship between volume of weight and value on the distance a good is shipped

Let us now translate these ideas into an areal context. Imagine a factory located on an isotropic plain across which potential customers are evenly distributed. Let us assume that 100 sales per year are necessary to offset the initial investment in the factory and all subsequent production costs: that is, the

Figure 4-14 Transport cost increment in relation to shipping distance The transport rate is the dollar charge per unit distance or the slope of the line. For linear transport rates of the type shown here, the total transport cost for shipping a given distance is found by multiplying the rate by the distance shipped.

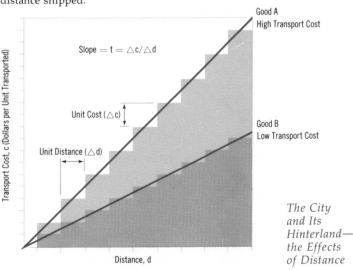

Slope = t = $\triangle$c/$\triangle$d

Unit Cost ($\triangle$c)

Unit Distance ($\triangle$d)

Transport Cost, c (Dollars per Unit Transported)

Distance, d

Good A
High Transport Cost

Good B
Low Transport Cost

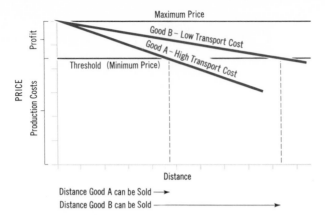

Figure 4-15 Relationship between production costs, profits, and transportation costs for two hypothetical products If two goods are sold at an equal price and profit but with a different transport cost for delivery, the good with the lower transport cost can travel farther.

threshold of the establishment is 100. In order to meet these initial costs the factory must be able to ship its products a distance *r* which represents the radius of a circular area surrounding the factory which will include 100 customers. This distance is called the *minimum range of the good*. At another distance *r'*, transportation costs will reduce consumer demand to zero. This second distance *r'* is called the *maximum range of the good* (Figure 4–16). All else being equal, in a densely settled area the minimum range of a good will be considerably less than in a region with sparse population. By the same reasoning, establishments with identical maximum ranges which operate in sparsely and densely settled areas would serve small and large numbers of customers, respectively.

A Regular Shape for City Hinterlands

Some commercial establishments in a city will have limited ranges, while others may serve the entire globe. This is shown in part by the varying ranges of the activities plotted on the map of Mobile (Figure 4–2). If we return now to our idea of the city as a collection of stores and factories, it is possible to think of the market area of an urban place as a combination

of the maximum ranges of many different goods and services. A settlement of a particular size might be characterized as having a typical average range for all its activities. Small settlements with few establishments would reach out a much shorter distance than larger ones with many specialized activities. How, then, do urban places share with their neighbors the territories which surround them?

The first consideration is the most efficient shape for the hinterland of a single settlement. Real world populations are seldom distributed with the regularity shown in Figure 4–17. People cluster together in settlements or along

Figure 4-16 The relationship between the threshold number of customers and the minimum and maximum range of a good The proportion of potential sales realized will fall with rising prices. This decline will occur as the base price is raised or as the delivery price is increased by the addition of the transport cost. The diagram shows both conditions. The base price cannot be so high that the firm is unable to achieve a market penetration of at least 100 customers—that is, its threshold of business. The customers are assumed to be spread evenly over the surface. Taking into account transportation costs, this threshold is met at the minimum range *r*. If the base price is lowered, greater market penetration is achieved locally and more distant customers will find it worthwhile to buy the good. At some distance *r'*, the transport cost precludes effective market penetration regardless of the base price (presuming it stays positive). This is the maximum range of the good.

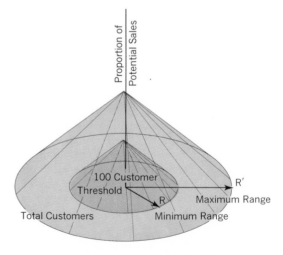

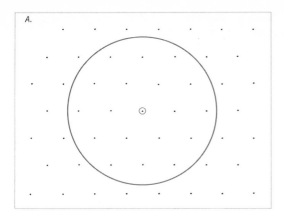

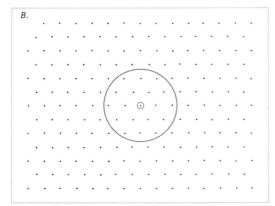

Figure 4-17 Minimum range of a good as a function of density Assume that an activity requires contact with eighteen locations other than its own to reach its threshold of business. The diagram illustrates that the range of the good, the radius of a circle centered at the firm, is inversely related to the density of customers. (*A*) Low density, large minimum range. (*B*) High density, small minimum range.

transportation routes, and near natural resources such as ore deposits or recreation sites. If every irregular distribution required a city hinterland with a new, perhaps unique shape, it would be extremely difficult for us to seek regularities in the spatial character of cities. What we need to find is a universal shape which will fit all hinterlands and yet contain the necessary number of customers to reach a given threshold requirement. On a plain having an evenly distributed population (Fig-

ure 4-18*A*) a circle meets these requirements. The only exception to this would be where two or more points might be exactly the same maximum distance from the center. If the threshold requirements were to change, the

Figure 4-18 Minimum market areas remain circular in a region of uneven population density An even population distribution is not a necessary condition for the existence of a circular market area. Parts *A* and *B* of the diagram show minimum market areas for firms with a threshold need for eighteen neighbors. Region *A* has an even distribution of population, and region *B* has an uneven distribution of population. It is always possible to draw a circle around the *n* nearest neighbors (ignoring ties for last place). The larger circles encompass eighteen additional neighbors for firms with double the threshold of the first case. Different radii are necessary, but the shape remains circular.

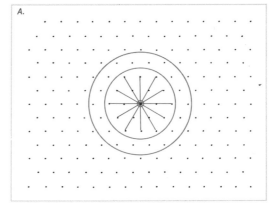

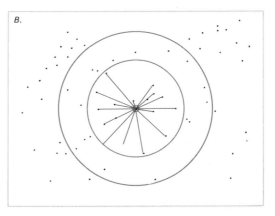

circle might grow larger or smaller, but we would not have to find a new shape.

It may come as a surprise to learn that regardless of the irregularity of population distribution, a circle is still the simplest universal shape that can be drawn to contain any specified number of points or customers. Naturally, odd shapes with all sorts of indentations and bumps might be drawn that could still contain a set number of points, but this could be done only by introducing confusing variety into our analysis. Figure 4–18B shows a highly irregular distribution of points within two circles, the smaller containing exactly eighteen and the larger exactly thirty-six. The circle drawn through the eighteenth most distant point from the center includes the other necessary seventeen but excludes the nine-teenth, twentieth, and so on. The same is true of the larger circle for the thirty-sixth point. Experimentation with an irregular point pattern of your own will quickly show that this holds true in every case. This means that in our search for universal conditions or constants we may take the circle as a possible regular shape that the hinterlands of settlements might take.

The next problem we must consider is how a collection of settlements with circular hinterlands might occupy a large area and share its resources, including space itself, or provide services and goods for the population distributed across it. We have dealt with single firms and single settlements in this chapter; therefore, a consideration of multiple settlements comes next.

*Human
Geography:
Spatial
Design
in World
Society*

78

5 | HOW CITIES SHARE SPACE: CLASSICAL CENTRAL PLACE THEORY

Cities and their uses of space are so complex that it is wise to begin our discussion of how urban places divide up the territories they occupy by looking at the simplest type of settlement. In most parts of the world subsistence-level farm villages provide shelter and basic needs but no real retail services for the peasants who inhabit them. Nevertheless, a hinterland, however small, is just as important for a village as a city. After all, the villagers depend upon the fields surrounding them for their very lives. At the same time, villagers "commute" to their fields rather than living near or in the center of their property. The village hinterland of fields and the farmers' daily trips to them are thus in many ways analogous to our preceding discussion of cities and commuters. Once we have established some basic rules about the spacing of villages, we can more easily move on to a consideration of larger settlements.

The Basic Pattern

What would be the optimum arrangement of farm villages across an isotropic plain of uniform fertility? Let us make the four following assumptions. (1) The land supports a uniform number of people per square mile. Let us assume in this case that the number is 25. Such an exact figure is solely a matter of con-

venience for the argument that follows. Poorer land would have lower population densities and greater distances between villages. (2) The typical farmer can afford to walk no more than 2 miles to work in the morning, nor can he trudge more than 2 weary miles homeward at the end of a long day behind plow or harrow. This distance represents the *maximum range* of the village as a self-sustaining farm community.

It follows from these two conditions that the total land available to a village must fall within a circle having the village at its center and a radius of 2 miles. The total area of such a circle is 12.56 square miles, which at 25 persons per square mile would provide for a population of about 314 people.

Our next assumption (3) is a simple one, that life is reasonably good and that there is slow but steady population growth. Eventually our 300-plus people will become 450 and even more—30 new families of 5; 150 new mouths to feed; an additional 6 square miles of land needed! Since the original population of 314 utilized all the land within 2 miles of the village center, young husbands and wives and their children who are old enough to work must walk more than 2 miles each way every day to find available land. When this trip to work becomes too great, the excess population will be forced to move. Let us assume that a *hiving-off* process will take place and a new village will be formed. But where?

The answer to this question in part depends upon our next and last assumption. (4) Villagers who hive off will try to stay as close as possible to older settlements in order to maintain important social bonds and linkages. The minimum distance between any two villages must be 4 miles, that is, at least twice the village radius. This distance allows adequate land for food production. At the same time, villagers will not move farther apart since they wish to minimize the travel distance required to maintain social contacts. Now let us see how the "offspring" of one parent village might fill up an empty and inviting area.

If we start with an empty plain and randomly place one "seed" village upon its surface, in succeeding generations that settlement will grow, hive off, and grow again. In turn, it will be joined by younger neighbors who grow and hive off in ever-increasing numbers. As each settlement grows beyond an optimum size defined by the trip to work and the carrying capacity of the land, it will become a mother for new colonies. This is shown in Figures 5-1A to D. In illustration 5-1A the primary settlement—designated A—reaches the hiving-off point and sends forth a nucleus which establishes itself two radii away at B. This distance will allow B when full-grown to extend toward A without competing for land needed by the mother community. In the next generation A again surpasses optimum size and hives off settlement C, while at the same time its first colony reaches optimum size, although it does not yet need to hive off excess population. In the third generation, A again sends out a colony which locates at D. In this and all subsequent cases new colonies are located so as to maximize contact with the most senior of the already existing settlements. B, having reached the point where hiving is necessary, sends out its own colony D', while C reaches but does not exceed the population which can be supported on land within 2 miles of its center. Subsequently, colonies are estab-

lished at all the points E, F, E', and F'. The pattern formed after eleven generations by villages following the above rules of growth is shown in Figure 5-1B. Notice too that by the time settlements E, E', F, and F' have been formed (Figure 5-1A), villages B and C are completely surrounded and will have to leapfrog their neighbors in order to send out colonies. Such a predicament would represent a resource shortage—in this case farmland. When this happens, the parent settlement has a limited number of possible actions. Its people may move beyond their neighbors to more remote resources, or new population increments may stay at home. In the latter case population densities will increase, and if no new sources of income are found, the general level of living will inevitably drop. Sometimes this crisis is met by an intensification of farming. Sometimes services and activities may develop with increasing settlement size, and a basic shift may take place in the pattern of living within these larger places. Figure 5-1C shows the accumulation of population in the original model assuming that everyone stays at home once empty neighboring land is used up.

Space packing: Circles into hexagons

Before leaving this example, let us consider the villages both as focal *points* and farm *areas*. Viewed as points, the pattern generated is a latticework consisting of equilateral triangles, each apex of which represents a settlement. When each point is thought of as the focus of a system of farming which utilizes the space around it, then the entire plain must be divided up among the settlements. This is shown by the neatly packed circular farm village areas in Figure 5-1A. One problem remains. Since circles do not fit tightly together, small open spaces, or interstices, exist everywhere. If these open spaces are divided equally among their neighbors (Figure 5-1D), the field of packed circles is transformed into a neat arrangement of hexagonal areas with no unaccounted space (Figure 5-1C). Locations within the small subdivided areas will be more than

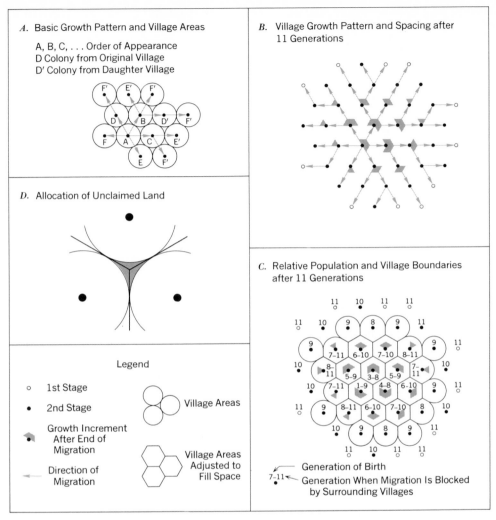

Figure 5-1 A growth model of village spacing Classical central place theory assumes as an initial condition that the underlying settlement pattern is an array of farm villages distributed at the nodes of a hexagonal lattice. A simple model of a settlement growth process that would result in such a pattern can be postulated. The key spatial assumptions necessary are that (*A*) each settlement requires a compact, finite, and local unit area for its functioning; (*B*) daughter colonies locate as near as possible to the parent colony when splitting off; and (*C*) an optimum size exists for the basic settlements. The process is described more fully in the text.

2 miles from any village center in our original model, but such excess distance will be very slight indeed; and in a more complex model we might start with slightly smaller circles which when changed to hexagons would not exceed a maximum distance of 2 miles. In any event, a triangular network of points and a field filled by hexagonal areas provide the best geometric solution to our original problem of farmers, farms, and farm villages.

How Cities Share Space: Classical Central Place Theory

Only three regular geometric shapes can be used to fill space without overlaps or leftovers: equilateral triangles, squares, and regular hexagons. Hexagons, being most nearly circular in form, are the best of the three shapes for minimizing the distance between a central point and the surrounding area which it controls. Thus, our model, generated with a simple set of geographic, social, and demographic rules, results in a pattern fulfilling the requirements of pure Euclidean geometry.

A Classical Theory of Central Place Hierarchies

The village pattern with which we have filled our isotropic plain relates man spatially to the land he occupies. But such settlements would be simple places where a traveler could find no cafe or teashop, no cobbler to mend his boots, nor any store to sell him provisions. The most humble peasant is linked to some sort of market economy which provides him with necessities, be they only flint and steel to light his fire, or, in more prosperous and modern times, a transistor radio with which to learn the latest news. In like manner, money for goods and services, and to pay the tax collector, marriage broker, and doctor, comes from his sale of crops. Such produce goes to middlemen who buy from many farmers and pass what they have collected to larger-scale wholesalers in their turn.

If we are to pull this simple model of spatial organization nearer to reality, we must provide our villagers with what they need; and we must also furnish goods and services necessary and suitable for a more urban life-style to the townsmen who supply the farmers. To do this let us introduce into our model a complete set of firms which will supply the entire population with whatever they need and can afford. In other words, the problem is *to find the best locations for a variety of establishments which have different thresholds and ranges for the goods and services which they provide.* While this complicates our model, we can continue to impose a certain simplicity

upon it by assuming that the population served by the necessary firms is evenly distributed in geographic space. Our network of villages will serve this purpose.

An interesting answer to the problem of regularly arranging points (firms) across an area (in this case represented by an evenly distributed population) was offered by Walter Christaller in 1933. Christaller, a German geographer, had noticed regularities in the settlement pattern of Barvaria in southern Germany. He attempted to explain these regularities deductively by creating a settlement model with certain fixed qualities and assumptions. At the same time, Christaller was interested in the distribution of different-sized settlements, villages, cities, and towns, which sometimes cluster together and sometimes are found far apart.

Another German, an economist named August Lösch, in 1945 independently derived an answer similar to Christaller's. Both concluded that *the best way to spatially provide a population with all types of services is to place such activities in a nested hierarchy of increasingly larger central settlements located at the nodes of a hexagonal network.* Both Christaller's and Lösch's schemes are essentially static. That is, their models are presented full-blown in all their complexity with no reference to how they might change through time. Christaller himself observed, "The state of rest is only fiction, whereas motion is reality." But both scholars stopped short of more dynamic models, and it may be said that their contributions have been as much to stimulate further geographic thought as to give us any absolute explanations of the real world.

Their answer, as given above, is phrased in a kind of geographical shorthand which needs clarification. To do this we will first give Christaller's rules and assumptions. We will also use this opportunity to follow through a sequence of theoretical reasoning in considerable detail. By doing this we hope to make the thought processes behind such exercises more explicit and understandable in order to demonstrate the value of this type of thinking. Next we will describe the system of central places which he proposed, and finally we will leave the static models of Christaller and Lösch and attempt to create a more dynamic description of a similar system as it might have developed in an imaginary kingdom, a useful place where everything goes according to plan. The remainder of this chapter will present examples of central place systems as they have been perceived and described in the real world.

The conditions underlying Christaller's model

Christaller began his deductions by limiting his model to the following conditions:

1. There exists an unevenly spread market on an isotropic plain.

The character of an *isotropic surface* should already be clear to us, and *an evenly spread market* simply means that everyone within the population has the same purchasing power and the same set of needs and desires.

2. There exists an equally spaced, discontinuous population.

All the conditions implied by this are met by the model of village distribution which has already been presented.

3. There exists a set of central place activities with different thresholds; these activities are point occupying and are ordered according to the size of their thresholds.

A central place activity or good is something needed by members of a population which they cannot provide for themselves. Such things can be material goods such as groceries, clothing, or equipment. They can be less tangible services like dentistry, haircuts, or insurance. They can also be socially defined, as are church services, Saturday night dances, or social clubs like the Elks, De Molay, and the Knights of Columbus. Such activities are considered to be *point occupying*. That is,

the spaces needed for their realization are so small when considered at the scale necessary for viewing the area in which their customers or participants live that they are reduced to dimensionless locations or points. In reality, such points are settlements of different sizes whose strategic central locations allow a maximum number of people to participate in the activities which take place there as well as to consume the goods and services they produce. Such settlements are referred to as *central places*. Thus, theory relating to them is known as *central place theory*. The notion of *different thresholds* relates on one hand to the number of participants necessary to make a social function succeed. For example, too small a crowd can turn a dance floor into an empty and echoing barn, while a congregation consisting of only a few people cannot support the regular services of a priest or minister. On the other hand, where goods and services are concerned, the number of people necessary to provide a living for a dentist will be different from the number needed to keep a barber in business. A small grocery store can survive on sales made within the local neighborhood of which it is a part, but a furniture store or farm tractor salesroom must draw customers from a far larger population in order to survive. If we take a set of activities which we assume includes all those necessary for leading a complete social and physical life, some will be able to get by with a low sales volume or with a few participants; others will need a great many. If in considering this set we rank its members in order of sales volume or number of participants from largest to smallest, we will have fulfilled Christaller's final condition.

We should also note in passing that with an unchanging and evenly distributed population *the threshold of a good determines the minimum range of a good*. For example, if a small grocery store needs 1,000 customers to survive (i.e., its threshold is 1,000) and every member of the population is a customer, then the minimum range of the grocery will be the radius of a circle the area of which includes exactly 1,000 people. Assuming a fixed and evenly distributed population, this area and therefore its radius will always be the same. Another establishment, needing a larger sales volume, would for the same reasons need to include more people within its sales area and therefore would need to be at the center of a circle with a larger radius.

Assumed relationships within Christaller's model

When Christaller specified the characteristics of his model as we have just described them, he created the environment in which his settlements, their activities, and their populations might interact. Such interaction depended in turn upon a set of *assumed relationships* which describe the manner in which all action would take place. These relationships can be summarized by the following four points.

1. The population of each central place is a function of the number of goods and services it offers.

By this is meant that a settlement offering few goods will be smaller than one offering many goods. The difference is in the number of storekeepers, service workers, and their families needed to offer a larger number of goods and services. In order to live continuously at a given place people need jobs. The population size thus depends upon the number of goods and services offered.

2. The central place hierarchy operates as a closed system.

Christaller, in simplifying the world in which his model operates, chose not to take into account the full activity of towns and cities. In this scheme his settlements serve only their own immediate hinterlands. They neither produce goods or services for national or international distribution nor import anything from beyond the limits of their own interlocking network of settlements. A second major simplification made by Christaller is that his cities exist as dimensionless points serving the areas surrounding them but not serving themselves. This notion creates a contradictory situation within Christaller's logic which needs further discussion. The existence of cities with large populations within the model would contradict a basic characteristic of its environment, that is, an evenly distributed population. In order to avoid this paradox, settlements must be treated as points with populations which have no needs of their own. This shows something important about deductive and theoretical reasoning. The abstract world of the theoretician also can have its pitfalls as well as its advantages. In the final analysis the real world is the absolute standard against which all our ideas must be judged.

3. A minimum number of central places operates within the system. (That is, each central place offers all goods offered by lower-order places plus an additional set with a larger threshold.)

This condition recognizes what economists sometimes call *economies of scale*. Every new firm will have overhead costs. These will be both in the construction and maintenance of the establishment itself and also in the provision of roads, new energy and water supplies, and other urban services for which the general population must pay. Therefore, the social and economic objectives of the population will be to cut down overhead wherever possible by clustering and sharing facilities. In terms of the settlement hierarchy, this means that each central place will offer as many goods and services as it can within the limits of the system. It also means that larger settlements offering very special services which have higher thresholds will also offer all the goods and services available in smaller settlements. To illustrate this in the briefest possible way: A small town might have a grocery store but little else; a larger town might have a barber but would also have a grocer; a city would have a dentist, and a barber, and a grocer. It also follows that dentists would not set up practice in isolated locations since that would necessitate new roads and other facilities already available in existing settlements.

4. The system operates under perfect competition and complete information.

Every firm and every customer will have complete and accurate information about all other customers and firms. This rather unrealistic but useful assumption means there will be no "shopping around" by customers. They will know beforehand that the goods and services they want will be exactly the same everywhere. Moreover, they will know which establishment is the nearest source for what they desire and go directly there. In other words all movement will be to the nearest place where the good or service is offered. No one will ever unnecessarily cross boundaries into another firm's hinterland. In the same way, *perfect competition* means that each establishment is so small when compared with the entire system that prices cannot be influenced by a single firm's dumping goods on the market to lower the price or hoarding goods in order to drive prices up. Likewise, firms cannot form monopolies for the same purpose. They all will be completely independent of each other, and all will have profit as their only motive. Finally, no establishment can have a price advantage because of differences in the quality of its product or through arbitrary price changes. In this model the only advantage which firms can experience is that of better or worse relative locations. Another way to say this is that all firms operate exactly at their thresholds, making just enough profit to survive. Since the *threshold of a good* determines the *minimum range of a good* where population is evenly distributed, the market areas determined by the minimum range will remain as small as possible and the maximum number of firms will be packed into the area served by the system.

Christaller's spatial model

Once Christaller had so carefully set the scene, there remained the task of constructing a spatial model matching the assumptions he had set forth. Given a set of activities ranked according to the size of their market areas, Christaller chose to begin with the largest settlements, while August Lösch began his considerations with the smallest. In this account, we will briefly describe the formal or geometric construction of a central place hierarchy from Christaller's point of view, while Lösch's choice—from small to large—forms the basis for the spatial history of our imaginary kingdom.

According to Christaller, each central place provides a complete set of activities associated with settlements smaller than itself. In addition, it has certain activities which can only flourish in places its size or larger. High-order central places (that is, very large towns and cities) are located across an isotropic plain, as were the villages in our earlier example. This results in a series of widely spaced settlements, each surrounded by a hexagonal market area representing the service with the highest threshold and the largest minimum range. In addition to their specializations, these large central places offer a *complete* selection of services to the population immediately adjacent to themselves. But because the market areas of these secondary services are smaller than those of the highest order, much of the population is not provided with these lesser activities. This is because the high-order centers are too far apart (Figure 5-2A).

In order to fill the needs of this unserved portion of the population, firms offering goods and services with smaller market areas are located in the unserved spaces between the largest market centers. The problem is to identify the most spatially rational locations for these smaller centers. Points farthest from the highest-order centers are logical places for the next tier or level of establishments. Such points of least accessibility are found at the exact center of each equilateral triangle formed by three adjacent higher-order places in the network. Figure 5-2B shows the total market area covered by high- and intermediate-order places. Finally, small towns and perhaps large villages (that is, low-order central places)

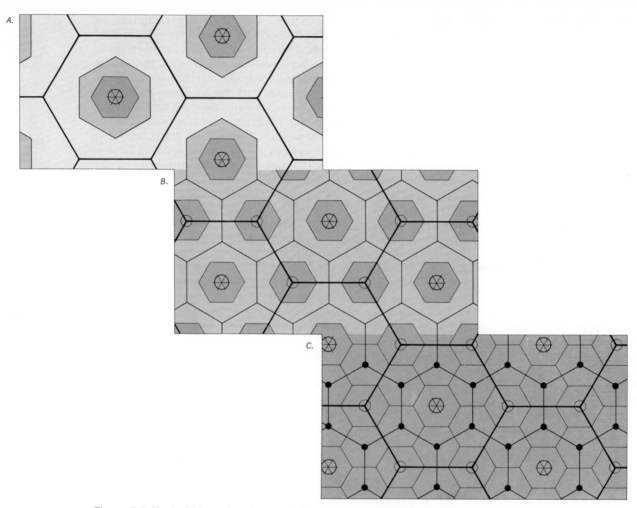

Figure 5-2 Nested hierarchy of central places and their market areas
(*A*) Partial hierarchy showing the network of largest market places and their market areas. This includes high-order goods (lightest shading), which require wide spacing of centers in order to reach their market threshold, intermediate-order goods (intermediate shading), and lower-order goods (darkest shading), with their shorter ranges. (*B*) Partial hierarchy showing the network of large and intermediate centers forming a nested hierarchy, which provides high-order and intermediate-order goods for the entire market area and low-order goods in their immediate locale. (*C*) Complete nested hierarchy in which the entire region is serviced with high-, intermediate- and low-order goods from a three-level hierarchy of central places. Close spacing of low-order centers allows goods with short ranges to reach the entire area.

are located in the unserved areas between large- and medium-sized settlements. Again, the best locations are the center points of the equilateral triangles formed by every three adjacent settlements in the existing network. This results in a landscape (Figure 5–2C) in which every place receives all the goods offered by the system. In this hierarchy a few large settlements furnish all customers with specialized services and also provide populations immediately adjacent to themselves with middle-range services and basic necessities. Medium-sized settlements in turn supply similar middle-range services to all customers not served by the largest centers; they also provide basic goods and services to their own neighboring populations. Finally, a network of small central places fills in the remaining gaps, thus bringing basic services to the rest of the population. The sum of all these settlements, the market areas of the small nested inside those belonging to higher-order central places, creates a *nested hierarchy of central places.*

Imaginary History of A Central Place System

There once was a Prince who lived in a kingdom which in the beginning had nothing but farm villages. He was industrious and imaginative, and liked a good time as well as the next fellow. Thus, it came about that the Prince began making mead in order to celebrate the good harvests, the coming of spring, summer, fall, and winter, and sometimes just to celebrate, so cheerful was his mood. Now mead is a drink made from honey; and honey, with an assist from the bees, comes from flowers. But flowers, belonging to that happy class of plants known as heliophytes, or sun lovers, cannot cluster at points but must grow widespread in order to soak up the sun which floods down everywhere. At the same time, bees, being busy but exceedingly small, do not fly long distances from flower to hive; and so it happened that honey was found everywhere in small quantities but never in large amounts at any one spot.

Thus many people in the kingdom could have made mead; but, strangely enough, few did. Our Prince's was the best. In fact his mead was so good he was soon not only providing drink for himself but also selling it to other people in his village. Now, this suited him very well, and he was soon referred to as the Merchant Prince by all the villagers, a title which was quickly shortened to Merp. Unfortunately, there were not enough customers in Merp's village alone to justify his becoming a full-time and profitable mead maker. In other words the threshold of his mead establishment was higher than the population of mead drinkers in his immediate village. Now it so happened that Merp's mead was very good and justifiably famous. Soon people from the neighboring villages closest to his own were walking across the fields to patronize his shop. In fact, some people from each of the six villages surrounding his own became regular customers. The fame of Merp's mead spread, and people from villages even farther away would send word that they wished that they too could buy some of his mead. But distances were too great, and so Merp's customers were limited to those in the nearest villages.

Now Merp fell to thinking about the meadless, thirsty people beyond the range of the good he had to sell. "Why not," he said, "set up branch mead shops in other villages in order to help the people celebrate their weddings and festivals and at the same time turn a pretty penny for myself?" (For the kingdom's coinage was particularly beautiful and the pennies were loveliest of all.) Merp quickly visited other villages beyond his nearest neighbors and found in them potential mead makers eager to give up farming for another way of life. Merp gave these people, one in each of the villages he chose, a franchise to become a mead maker using his famous recipe. In no time at all the landscape was filled with a network of mead shops serving the mead needs of the populace.

Now, in placing his branch mead shops Merp had had to take into account the short distance that customers were willing to walk. This meant that his network of mead shops was a closely spaced one and that shops in villages just one tier beyond his nearest neighbors became his competitors for the trade of the villages which lay between them. It fell out that people in a neighboring village who wished to purchase mead could choose one of three equally near mead-selling villages from which to make their purchases (Figure 5–3A). The result of this was that one-third of the customers in each such village journeyed to a different neighboring mead center. And so it came about that there developed a spatial hierarchy with mead-drinking villages representing first-order places and mead-selling villages becoming second-order centers.

This meant that Merp soon shared his customers with the six mead shops nearest his own. In other words, his shop could depend upon all the customers from his own village and one-third of the customers from each of the six surrounding villages. All in all, he could look forward to having the equivalent of customers from three villages patronizing his own establishment. This was also true for mead shop operators in all the other mead-selling villages throughout the land.

Time passed, and with the increase in mead

Figure 5-3 The three basic central place hierarchies The diagrams show the meaning of the K = 3, K = 4, and K = 7 central place hierarchies. These are the three smallest regular hierarchies that can be defined on a hexagonal lattice. A regular hierarchy is one in which the number of immediate subordinates is the same for each level.

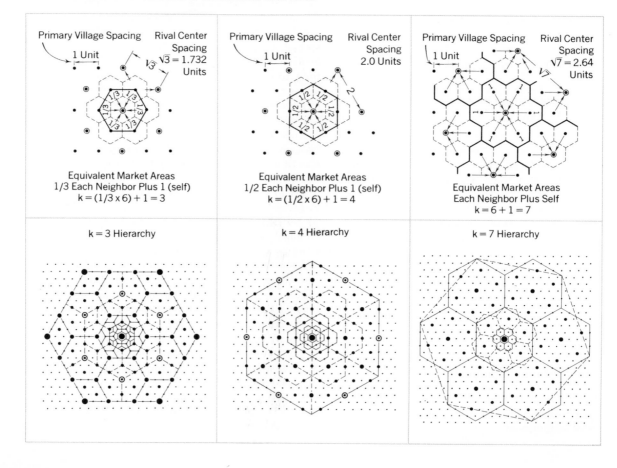

sales in every corner of the province there soon developed a shortage of copper kettles suitable for brewing mead. Merp had for a long time dabbled in copper kettle making for his own needs, and being farsighted, he anticipated that soon mead shops all over the land would feel the need for mead pots just as their customers had long before experienced an unsatisfied mead need. This was fortunate, for in order to justify the expensive equipment necessary for copper kettle making Merp had to provide copperware not only for his own village market area but also to the market areas equivalent to at least eight additional copper kettle-using villages. At the same time, his copper pots were heavy and hard to carry, and the farthest he could profitably transport them was just two times as far as people were willing to travel to obtain mead. In other words, he could sell his pots in his own village, in the six mead-selling villages closest to him, and in the six mead-selling villages beyond them. But this left the rest of the country without copper kettles. Thus Merp found himself once more doing for copperware what he had done for mead shops. He traveled throughout the land and set up a network of subsidiary copper pot emporiums in mead-selling villages beyond the maximum range of his own goods. Soon copper shops were flourishing in another, larger, more widely spaced network similar to the one he had set up for selling mead.

Again Merp felt the competition of the businesses established just beyond the maximum range of his own copper kettles, and again he found himself sharing customers from the outermost ring of villages with the subsidiary copper kettle makers nearest him. When things had sorted themselves out, he found that he was selling copper to his own village and the six mead-selling villages nearest him and winning one-third of the customers from the second tier of six mead-selling villages beyond them. Thus, his copper shop depended upon a number of customers equivalent to those found in nine village market areas.

Merp's Amalgamated Mead Makers were becoming famous, and their slogan, *Never a Greater Mead*, was on everyone's lips, just like their product. As Merp's enterprises became more and more prosperous, he realized that much of his success was due to the hard work of his helpers. Wishing to recognize their efforts, he designed a golden mead mug which he awarded for long and meritorious service. Since these mead mugs were solid gold, they were very valuable and could be shipped long distances for a small proportion of their total worth. Not every employee received a mug, however, and this last of Merp's products had the highest threshold of all. At the same time, its maximum range reached as far as the farthest person to whom one might be awarded. At last Merp had found something which he could supply without his having to set up subsidiary firms in other parts of the country. In fact, he supplied all the the twenty-seven village market areas which had developed within his province.

The K = 3 hierarchy

Let us end our story of Merp, the Merchant Prince and President of Amalgamated Mead Makers, with the above episode. Our point has been made. Starting with the smallest mead-drinking settlements (that is, villages or first-order central places), we have seen the progressive buildup of larger places offering mead to drink. These could be considered second-order central places. Thereafter, the addition of copper kettle manufacturing to another, less numerous set of settlements established a third order of central places, each containing mead drinkers, mead makers, and pot manufacturers. This process was repeated again for Merp's own settlement, a fourth-order central place, which produced in order from smallest to largest market areas mead, kettles, and golden mead mugs. This progression of central places offering more and more specialized services and goods depended upon a regularly increasing progression of customers. If these populations are thought of in terms of the number of village-sized market areas served in each case, the sequence is 1, 3, 9, 27, 81, . . . This progression by the square of 3 indicates the total effective market area which each order of central place serves

(Figure 5–3*A*). Lösch recognized this and gave systems incorporating this type of expansion a kind of shorthand designation. They are called *K=3 networks* and follow a *marketing principle* which had been recognized earlier by Christaller.

K=4 and K=7 hierarchies

Two similar progressions are described in Lösch's shorthand as K=4 and K=7 systems. The progression of market areas in the K=4 system is 1, 4, 16, 64, . . . , while that of the K=7 is 1, 7, 49, . . . Christaller also recognized these and suggested that the K=4 would also be useful for transportation networks and the K=7 for administrative purposes, although his comments predated Lösch's labeling.

In the K=4 network all settlements are located on roads leading directly away from the highest-order centers. This means that straight-line routes can reach all places, a situation unlike that in the K=3 network, where a zigzag route must be followed to reach all sizes of settlements. Central places in the K=4 network also provide a ranked order of goods and services. Starting at the bottom and moving upward, the minimum range of the lowest-order good is one-half the range of the next highest, which is in turn one-half the range of the third-order good, and so on for as many orders as are found within the system. Lower-order settlements are located exactly halfway between places of the next highest order and lie on the boundaries separating the market areas of those higher-order places (Figure 5–3*B*). It follows that a central place of a particular size has within its own market area the equivalent of four market areas of the next smallest size. It is this progression by fours which leads us to call this a K=4 system.

The K=7 network changes by a rule of seven. That is, each central place of a given size contains within its boundaries the equivalent of the areas associated with seven central places of the next smallest order (Figure 5–3*C*). This system is unlike the K=3 and K=4 networks, for each central place is located at the center of the area with which it is associated and is never divided by boundary lines of higher-order places. The advantage of this for administrative purposes can be seen at once. If a village or town lies equidistant from two or three larger places, its inhabitants, when shopping, can utilize some freedom of choice and go to whichever place they choose as long as their travel costs remain the same. Where administration is concerned and questions of legal jurisdiction are important, higher-order centers cannot share the allegiance of some smaller place's population, nor should questions of which code of laws, which police force, which tax collector be allowed to arise if the society is to function at all well. This is because law and administration in theory do not experience exponential decay with distance but remain fully enforced up to the boundaries of the administrative units in which they are applied. Thus, it is most efficient if each higher-order place clearly controls the territories of those places beneath it in the system. An examination of Figure 5–3*C* will indicate that the K=7 network satisfies this condition.

Other geometric progressions using still larger numbers are possible but not practical to present here. On the other hand, while our tale of the Merchant Prince may have seemed fanciful at times, there are many examples where knowledge of the geometry of central place systems can help clarify seemingly unsolvable complexities. The next section of this chapter discusses possible applications of central place theory to different societies.

Examples of Central Place Hierarchies
Relaxing the basic assumptions

The world is a chaotic place, and models of it which are useful because of their rigorous assumptions are remote from reality because of that rigor. We have seen the crystalline harmony of K=3, K=4, and K=7 networks. What happens when the assumptions which protect them are stripped away and we seek their counterparts on the face of the earth?

Christaller viewed his cities as dimensionless points serving the areas which surround them but not serving themselves. This is clearly unrealistic, but was allowed in order to maintain everywhere an even distribution of population. This also permitted the basic hexagonal market area of the smallest size to be everywhere the same. But we know that population clusters in cities. If we maintain a fixed unit of population, the hexagonal areas necessary to contain that basic population unit will be smaller where populations are large. That is, the minimum range of any good will become less as population density increases even though the threshold of the establishment remains the same. For example, if our basic threshold unit were 1,000 people, those thousand customers might live on one square mile in eastern Pennsylvania or the bottomlands of the Po Valley in northern Italy, or they might live on one city block in Chicago or Paris. It is more realistic to recognize that the basic unit of the hexagonal pattern will contract around cities and expand when far from urban places. Figure 5–4 shows a modular hexagonal pattern of this type which can be repeated over and over in all directions. Variations in this snakeskin allow adjustments to be made to the hexagonal network wherever sparse or dense populations appear.

Population density varies from place to place throughout the world as the result of many things besides urbanization. Some causes of this are cultural, some economic, some natural. Most often it is a combination of these and other conditions. An examination of the distribution of world ecotypes and world population on maps will show many different examples of population's becoming more sparse in very cold, very dry, or very mountainous areas. This thinning out can be shown graphically by the gradual change in size of a hexagonal network, with smaller hexagons representing wetter or warmer or more productive areas with dense populations and larger hexagons indicating colder, drier, or rougher areas with sparse populations (Figure 5–5).

Changes in the size of the basic network

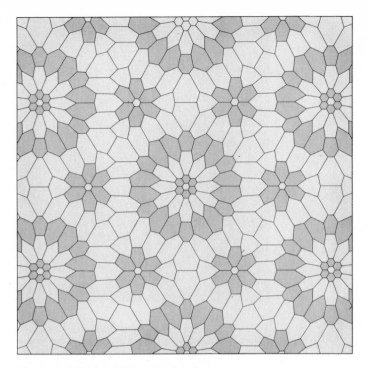

Figure 5-4 Modular hexagonal pattern An example of a hexagonal network constricted around certain cells and enlarged around others to adjust for differences in underlying density of central place customers.

help us to relax some of the assumptions in the central place model, but as long as central place hinterlands are defined by simple patterns, we must continue to assume that customers remain neatly at home in their own market areas. This is not the case in the real world. A distant store will offer credit while one nearby will not. The children like *that* dentist and can't stand *this* one. Vegetables are always fresher in the supermarket on the other side of town. At the same time, people will combine trips for the sake of convenience. Few customers would travel miles and miles just to buy a toothbrush. But if someone has made a long trip to a regional shopping center in order to buy a color television set, it is quite reasonable for him to step into the pharmacy adjoining the furniture store to make such a smaller purchase. When several

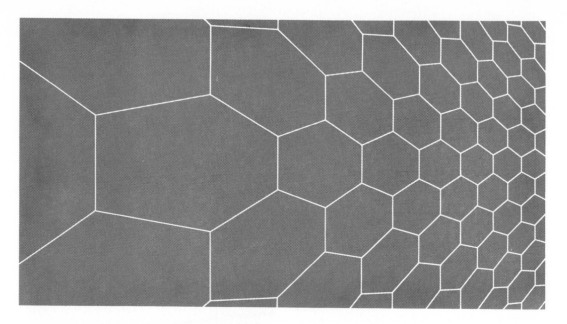

Figure 5-5 Logarithmic expansion of a hexagonal lattice A hexagonal network expanded by a logarithmic function in one direction. This network would be suitable for an underlying population that varied from dense to sparse along the east-west dimension.

similar errands are combined in one trip which thus has several purposes, boundary crossings can occur at any and all levels of the hierarchy.

Still other adjustments in the basic hexagonal network of settlements might deal with frontier situations. As settlement extends into less and less hospitable places, fewer and fewer amenities become available to the population. One might expect to find trading posts selling matches and ammunition, but sterling silver and vintage wines are only found for sale in large cities. In other words, lower orders of the central place hierarchy exist almost everywhere, but the complete system is limited to the most commercialized areas. The frontier development of a central place hierarchy is illustrated in Figure 5–6.

At the same time, random events or "shocks" may well skew or otherwise distort regular central place hierarchies into unrecognizable forms. In fact, it seems quite remarkable that there are locations where theory seems to be

reflected in reality. This is due in part to the relative regularity of the underlying environment in those places. Szechwan Province in China, Iowa and the northern Great Plains, and Ontario, Canada, provide us with a few such examples.

Permanent settlement hierarchies: China

A heap of flesh and a pile of bones, no matter how cleverly arranged, are not a living body. If the intended creature so described is to have life, blood must pump through veins and arteries and muscles flex in response to messages from the brain. So too with urban systems. In order for our ideas of settlement hierarchies to have validity and use we must be able to plot the paths taken through the system by people, goods, and messages. We turn now to mainland China, where over the centuries a hierarchy of central places has had an opportunity to develop an easily discernible pattern involving all sizes of urban places and levels of society. These elaborate systems of markets were described in locally prepared gazetteers, while additional information is available through newspaper accounts, some rural surveys, and personal information obtainable from Chinese emigrants now living outside the mainland. Among the scholars who have studied this subject is G. William Skinner, whose analysis includes much information on the spatial organization of traditional Chinese peasant society. The Chinese example is valuable for another reason besides its completeness. The age and stability of Imperial China allowed its system of settlements to attain a kind of spatial equilibrium of great interest.

Periodic markets Imagine a morning, dew-wet and bright, with the sun risen across the Chinese plain. We are standing at the edge of a small market town. It is one of the regularly scheduled market days, and since the harvest is nearly complete, the roads are busy with peasants bringing produce to sell and returning to their villages with their meager but necessary purchases. This is considered a "hot" day—not because temperatures are high but because business is flourishing within the market. On so-called "cold" days the market is nearly empty and local wholesalers may be on their way to nearby villages to bid for and buy the farmers' peanuts and grain. Barbers and blacksmiths also leave town on "cold" days to visit customers who ordered their services on a previous visit, usually during some "hot" market day.

The market undergoes regular or periodic changes. On certain days itinerant peddlers line the streets, making them noisy with their offers of manufactured items and goods not produced within the local region. The comings and goings of these footloose sellers follow complex and regular schedules. The low level of living and the frugal life of the village farmers generate only a small demand for imported wares at any given place at any particular time. The *threshold* or lower limit of sales needed to sustain such a peddler could not be met if he were to remain in one

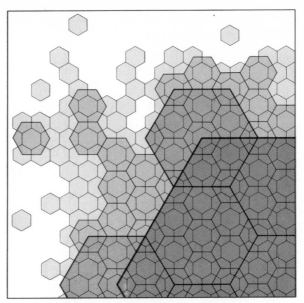

Figure 5-6 Frontier development of a central place hierarchy The assumption underlying this pattern of settlement is that usually only basic, low-order goods are offered on the frontier or edge of a settlement system, whereas larger thresholds are met in the central commercial areas and the full range of high-order goods is offered.

town waiting for his customers to come from villages within one day's walking distance. In theoretical terms the maximum range of the activity has fallen below the minimum range required to meet the threshold of the business. As a result, markets in the small towns of China as well as many other places in the world meet periodically rather than continuously. Towns with many nearby customers may have markets which meet every other day. Fewer potential customers result in markets' being scheduled less frequently, perhaps three times or six times each lunar month. On days when a market is not in progress in one town, the itinerant shops will travel to another "standard" market which is in session. In this way, by visiting a number of *periodic markets*, salesmen who might otherwise fail for want of sufficient trade manage to survive (Figure 5-7).

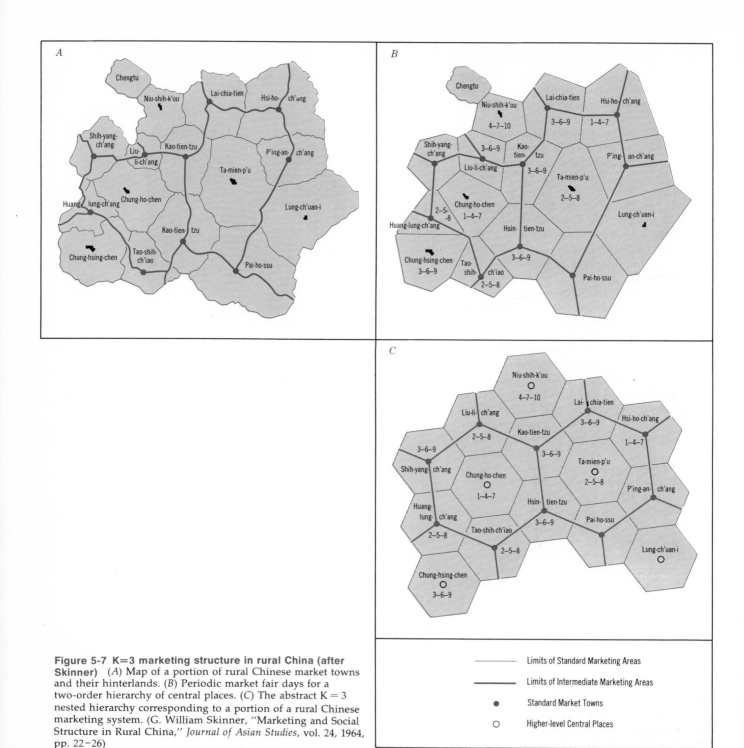

Figure 5-7 K=3 marketing structure in rural China (after Skinner) (*A*) Map of a portion of rural Chinese market towns and their hinterlands. (*B*) Periodic market fair days for a two-order hierarchy of central places. (*C*) The abstract K = 3 nested hierarchy corresponding to a portion of a rural Chinese marketing system. (G. William Skinner, "Marketing and Social Structure in Rural China," *Journal of Asian Studies*, vol. 24, 1964, pp. 22–26)

Limits of Standard Marketing Areas

Limits of Intermediate Marketing Areas

• Standard Market Towns

○ Higher-level Central Places

Standard markets If we were to walk through the market itself, we would see not only the temporary stalls of the peddlers but behind them a few permanent shops where tobacco and matches, candles and lamp oil, needles and thread, and brooms and soap can be purchased any day, "hot" or "cold." Teahouses and wineshops are often crowded with townsmen and villagers, while odors of cooking in food stalls and small restaurants season the morning air. Home workshops and small establishments also offer an ir-reducible minimum of needed goods and services. The carpenter's saw and the coffin maker's hammer sound in the street. In an-other shop, paper religious objects are made and sold. Other services, needed less fre-quently, are provided by the occasional visits of folk healers, tinkers, scribes, fortune-tellers, and musicians.

The business of the town is by no means limited to commercial activities. Eating and drinking establishments serve as headquarters for rotating credit societies where peasants can borrow money. Rich landlords may main-tain an office for collecting rents, and mer-chants and landowners may lend money or extend credit to their regular customers. Marriage brokers frequent the teahouses in market towns in order to learn of marriageable girls. Chinese secret societies which once controlled all aspects of life in the country-side also had headquarters or lodges in mar-ket towns. The control of commission agents who weighed the grain and dealt in livestock fell to these groups on market days. Religious festivals were often combined with annual fairs held in the standard market town. The local temple was the concern not only of townsmen but also of pious leaders from nearby farm communities. Thus a variety of social needs and obligations were met within the town, and the peasants in the surrounding countryside were dependent as much on their local market town as on their own small farm communities. At the same time, local officers of the imperial government collected taxes and administered the law, thus linking the peasantry and townsmen to the remote capital.

Itinerant merchants selling farm implements at a periodic market in Nepal. The merchants find it advantageous to line up with their competitors within the market, thereby facilitating comparison of the price and quality of their goods. This market is held only one day per week. The peddlers visit a market on its active day and move to another active market the next day, occasionally returning to a home base for resupply.

Higher-order markets Market towns like the one described above did not provide all the needs of every Chinese. Members of the educated and wealthier elite would have to seek still larger *intermediate* market towns if they wished to buy books and writing mate-rials. Better-quality cloth, unusual foodstuffs, and luxury items also seldom found their way to local markets and were supplied only in the larger towns and cities. The local elite and leisured class were accustomed to drink-ing their tea and wine in the establishments of larger towns where there was an oppor-tunity to meet others of their class. Beyond

How Cities Share Space: Classical Central Place Theory

95

such *intermediate markets* were those in larger cities which offered still rarer goods and more specialized services. A many-tiered system of markets, often paralleled by matching social and religious organizations as well as by progressively higher levels of government offices, spread its network across the Chinese landscape. *Minor markets* in villages where a peasant might trade a few eggs or vegetables with his neighbor were at the bottom. Next came *standard markets* and market towns which have occupied most of this discussion. Above them, *intermediate* and *central markets* were found in progressively larger towns. Beyond them, local and regional cities supported a complex variety of markets which supplied local, regional, and perhaps even national needs. Goods, money, and information moved both up and down through this system of settlements along paths, roads, and rivers.

China: K=3 and K=4 systems The mapped distribution of *standard* and *intermediate* market towns and their market areas located southeast of Chengtu in Szechwan Province in central China is shown in Figure 5–7*A*. Two simple analytical steps allow us to see the emergence of a K=3 network from the original map. In Figure 5–7*B* the boundary lines of the approximate standard and intermediate market areas have been straightened. (Numbers at settlements indicate the days within a 10-day cycle on which markets are held.) In Figure 5–7*C* the same boundaries have been standardized and reduced to diagrammatic form. These simple maneuvers quickly show the underlying order of the system. It should be noted that adjacent standard market towns may hold markets on the same days—for example, Kao-tien-tzu and Hsin-tien-tzu—but that the scheduling of such markets rarely coincides with market days in the intermediate market towns (i.e., those in the next highest order) with which they are associated. Conflicts are thus minimized vertically throughout the system, while horizontal conflicts are of little importance owing to the lack of lateral connections between settlements of the same order.

The same analytical steps have been repeated in Figure 5–8 for an area located northeast of Chengtu. In this case a two-step abstracting of the original map reveals a K=4 network with one market area unoccupied because of mountains. Notice that the only roads mapped connect higher-order and standard market towns, but that these direct routes join all the settlements with no detours except those imposed by topography. Again, market day scheduling conflicts for settlements within the same vertical systems are kept to a minimum.

Iowa: Crossing market boundaries

In matching our theoretical notions of settlement hierarchies to real world consumer patterns we need information about the actual shopping habits of the population. Recent investigations by Brian Berry and his associates near Council Bluffs, Iowa, tell us a great deal about Midwestern Americans and the hierarchy of settlements which they utilize. Figure 5–9*A* shows the area, while Figure 5–9*B* to *F* uses a series of star diagrams to indicate the origin of the rural customers and the settlements which they visited to obtain particular goods or services. This information was obtained by personally interviewing individual householders or by checking the addresses of customers or subscriber lists and charge account files at stores and offices. Once the origins and destinations of shoppers were learned, a straight line was drawn from each customer's residence to the urban place visited by him. The subsequent arrays of points and lines tell us many things about central place hierarchies.

The sequence of such goods and services in order from smallest to largest market areas is grocery shopping, office calls to physicians, women's coats and dresses, hospital services, and newspapers. This list, while incomplete, represents an entire hierarchy of central place functions from those with very short minimum ranges and low thresholds to others with high

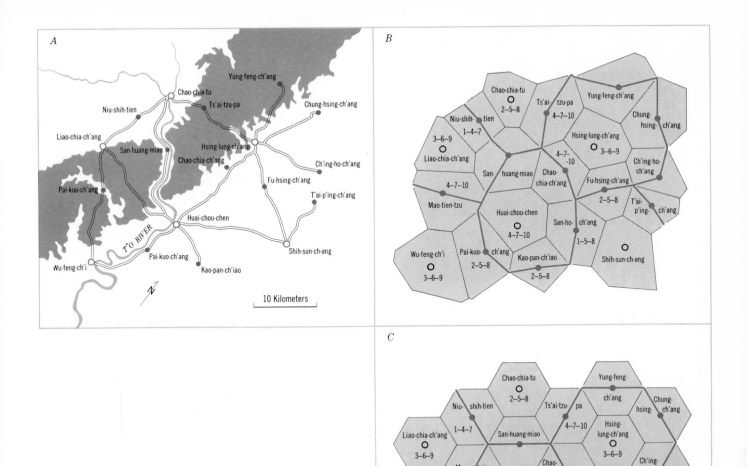

Limits of Standard Marketing Areas

Limits of Intermediate Marketing Areas

Roads Connecting Standard Markets to Intermediate Markets

● Standard Market Towns

○ Higher-level Central Places

Mountains Above 500 Meters

Figure 5-8 K=4 marketing structure in rural China (after Skinner) (*A*) Map of farm markets and their hinterlands, including a mountain zone. (*B*) Periodic market fair days for a two-order hierarchy of central places. (*C*) The abstract K = 4 nested hierarchy corresponding to a portion of a rural Chinese marketing system. Note the empty cell due to the presence of a sparsely settled mountain zone. (Op. cit. Figure 5-7)

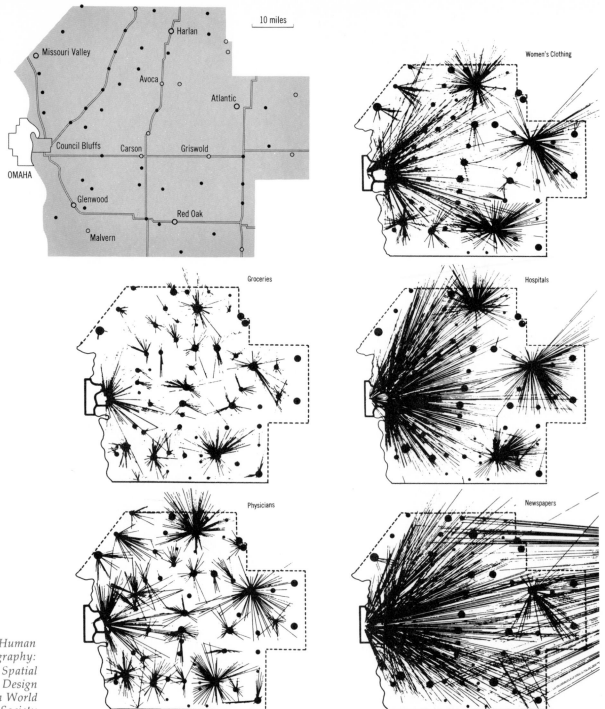

10 miles

Harlan

Missouri Valley

Avoca

Atlantic

Council Bluffs   Carson   Griswold

OMAHA

Glenwood

Red Oak

Malvern

Women's Clothing

Groceries

Hospitals

Physicians

Newspapers

*Human
Geography:
Spatial
Design
in World
Society*

98

thresholds and large minimum ranges. Notice, for example, that many people subscribe to newspapers originating in Des Moines, Iowa, far off the map to the east. This is interesting in itself, for Des Moines is smaller than Omaha, Nebraska, which is much nearer. However, in-state news originating at the state capital and presented by an excellent newspaper outdraws publications from the larger, closer city. Here is another place where simple theory and reality can differ. Affiliation with a political unit may influence consumer behavior to a degree which overcomes the friction of distance.

One of Christaller's original assumptions was that perfect competition existed and that consumers would not cross the boundary lines of their market areas. An examination of the Iowa maps shows that this is generally true but that there are enough exceptions to the rule that our theory needs some modification to match reality. Notice how in every diagram many of the rays emanating from urban places cross each other, clearly indicating that decisions were made on the basis of other criteria besides that of physical distance between customer and producer.

Given some knowledge of the expense of the item to be purchased and the number of times per year that such shopping might be done, we can understand differences in travel behavior. Grocery stores which are patronized on a regular daily or weekly basis have short minimum ranges, and settlements containing them are more or less evenly spaced throughout the study area. Clothing stores (Figure 5-9D) on the other hand are limited to far fewer places, attract more customers, have higher thresholds, and can expect customers to come greater distances but much less frequently. It is also important to note that while few customer triplines cross each other on the grocery map (Figure 5-9B),

many more do so on the map showing trips for women's clothing. This is generally true, for as specialization increases and considerations of travel time and short-run convenience decrease, the overlapping of market areas becomes greater and greater. This is also true where the investment required in the establishment providing the services becomes larger. Physicians' offices attract patients from medium-sized market areas, while larger, more expensive hospitals are fewer in number and reach out long distances for those who use their services.

The upper Midwest: Network distortion

The apparently endless, level miles of the northern Great Plains would seem a natural place to find an expression of Christaller's and Lösch's orderly landscapes. But subtle changes in the grassland's environment can create distortions in its settlement network just as certainly as do the high mountains which rise west of those buffalo-haunted plains. While the eastern half of this area is relatively flat, topographically speaking, rainfall along a line drawn between Minneapolis, Minnesota, and Great Falls, Montana, decreases steadily from 28 inches per year in the east to 12 inches in the west. At the same time, average annual temperatures decrease slightly from south to north. There are about 160 frost-free days at the southern limit of this area and approximately 110 such days along the United States–Canadian border. While most of the land is relatively fertile, northern Minnesota and Wisconsin are marked by the rocky outcrops of the Laurentian Upland or Canadian Shield. Aridity, cold, and poor soils all mean lower yields per unit of farmland. Lower yields mean reduced carrying capacities for the land, and if a high level of living is maintained by the population,

Figure 5-9 Consumer travel in southwestern Iowa   The lines represent a shopping trip from home to the central place offering the good or service listed. A variation in the range of the goods is clearly observable. Also, the market areas overlap to a considerable degree. (Brian J. L. Berry, *Geography of Market Centers and Retail Distribution* © 1967, pp. 11–12. Reprinted by permission of Prentice-Hall, Inc., Englewood Cliffs, N.J.)

farms must be correspondingly larger. As a result of this, it is reasonable to anticipate that farm populations will decrease from east to west and from south to north within this area. Figure 5–10, showing the distribution of farm units in thousands, confirms our expectations. At the same time, if the population is organized according to the spatial principles outlined so far, we would expect to find the basic Christaller network concentrated most densely in the southeast and most open or sparse in the northwest. This can be seen in Figure 5–11, where a regularly enlarging hexagonal network has been adjusted to match variations in the distribution of farm population. The resulting pattern is reminiscent of the expanding hexagonal lattice shown in Figure 5–5.

The upper Midwest: Hierarchies of functions

The distorted pattern in Figure 5–11 is admittedly a cartographic device meant to illustrate our argument. There is, however, a relatively simple way of testing the notion that a spatially organized hierarchy of central places exists in this area and that its network varies in size from southeast to northwest. This test necessitates understanding another aspect of central place hierarchies. When we spoke earlier of *nested hierarchies*, we indicated that in a particular culture and economy the

smallest settlements offer a few basic goods and services to the population adjacent to them. Larger central places offer the same things and, in addition, provide more and more specialized goods and services for bigger and bigger populations in increasingly larger areas. Since each good or service has a particular threshold which characterizes its place within the hierarchy, it is possible to compile a list of central place functions which allows us to predict what we should find in a settlement if we know its population.

In their investigation of Snohomish County, Washington, William Garrison and Brian Berry determined the threshold urban populations for fifty-two different urban-based activities. These are shown in Table 5–1, along with the average minimum populations associated with their first appearance in a central place hierarchy. For example, hamlets with populations of at least 275 people will contain some sort of restaurant or snack bar. Veterinarians' offices do not appear in settlements smaller than 575 people, and public accountants open offices in central places larger than 1,300 people. On the other hand, a town with a public accountant will very likely have both a veterinary and a restaurant. This list is based upon a somewhat complicated technique for determining average populations which need not concern us here. It should be noted,

Figure 5-10 Distribution of farms in the upper Midwest region The resources become more sparse to the north and west in the upper Midwest region, and the number and spacing of farms reflect the underlying resource base.

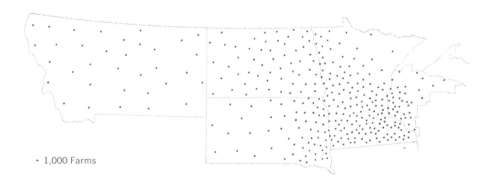

· 1,000 Farms

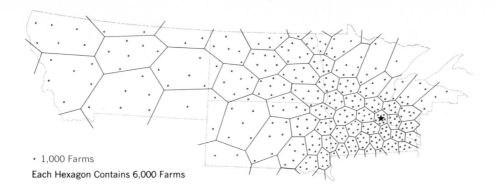

• 1,000 Farms

Each Hexagon Contains 6,000 Farms

Figure 5-11 A hexagonal net conforming to the underlying rural population pattern in the upper Midwest region

Table 5-1 Threshold Populations for Fifty-two Urban-based Activities

Class I_1		Furniture stores, etc.	546
Filling stations	196	Variety stores, "5 & 10"	549
Food stores	254	Freight lines and storage	567
Churches	265	Veterinaries	579
Restaurants and snack bars	276	Apparel stores	590
Taverns	282	Lumberyards	598
Elementary schools	322	Banks	610
Class I_2		Farm implement dealers	650
Physicians	380	Electric repair shops	693
Real estate agencies	384	Florists	729
Appliance stores	385	High schools	732
Barber shops	386	Dry cleaners	754
Auto dealers	398	Local taxi services	762
Insurance agencies	409	Billiard halls and bowling alleys	789
Fuel oil dealers	419	Jewelry stores	827
Dentists	426	Hotels	846
Motels	430	Shoe repair shops	896
Hardware stores	431	Sporting goods stores	928
Auto repair shops	435	Frozen food lockers	938
Fuel dealers (coal, etc.)	453	Class I_3	
Drug stores	458	Sheet metal works	1,076
Beauticians	480	Department stores	1,083
Auto parts dealers	488	Optometrists	1,140
Meeting halls	525	Hospitals and clinics	1,159
Feed stores	526	Undertakers	1,214
Lawyers	528	Photographers	1,243
		Public accountants	1,300
		Laundries and laundromats	1,307
		Health practitioners	1,424

Source: William Garrison and Brian J. L. Berry, "A Note on Central Place Theory and the Range of a Good," *Economic Geography*, vol. 34, no. 4, October 1958, pp. 304–311.

How Cities Share Space: Classical Central Place Theory

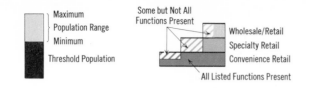

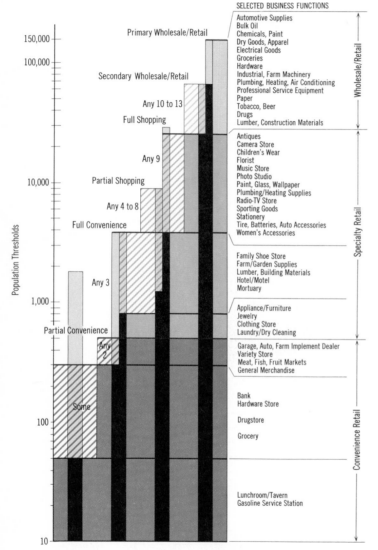

though, that these threshold numbers are not intended to be absolute or unchangeable. The important thing to realize is that the role of a settlement within a central place hierarchy can be roughly determined by learning the number of people living within its boundaries. If the type and number of functions available are known, the settlement's position within the hierarchy can be determined.

Figure 5–12 shows forty-six central place functions found in settlements across the northern Great Plains. They are grouped in the order of their appearance along with their approximate thresholds. Each general category of functions: convenience, specialty, and wholesale, indicates a higher level in the hierarchy. This list is not meant to be complete. It also varies somewhat from that of Garrison and Berry, but this might be expected as the result of regional differences in economic and social activities. The diagram also identifies four classes and six subclasses of settlements, from hamlets with nothing more than service stations and lunchrooms to wholesale-retail cities offering all forty-six types of functions as well as many more not listed. Again, our notion of a nested hierarchy of functions is confirmed.

The upper Midwest: Central place sequences The spatial distribution of settlements in the upper Midwest classified according to their place in a functional hierarchy is shown in Figure 5–13. The twin city metropolis of Minneapolis–St. Paul dominates the area and constitutes a special case not shown in the preceding diagram. Far to the west,

Figure 5-12 Trade center types (central place functions in the upper Midwest region)   This graph is a summary of the central place goods and services offered by the towns and cities of the upper Midwest region. There is considerable variation from town to town, but in general, the

expected low-order goods and services are available in nearly all small hamlets and villages, with increasingly more specialized, higher-order goods entering in towns and cities with greater populations. A population scale is shown on the left of the graph and the order of appearance of central place goods and services on the right. (John R. Borchert, "The Urbanization of the Upper Midwest, 1930–1960," *Upper Midwest Economic Study*, Urban Report No. 2, University of Minnesota, Minneapolis, Minn., 1963)

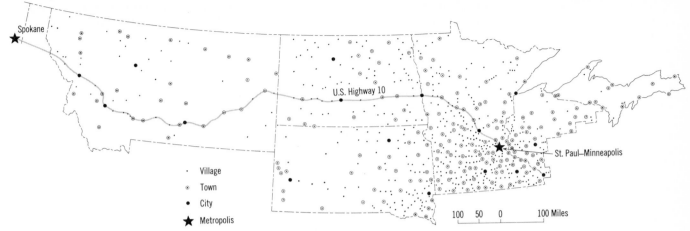

Figure 5-13 Upper Midwest settlement patterns The pattern of towns and villages in the upper Midwest conforms roughly to central place theory expectations. The wider spacing of towns to the west reflects the lesser resource base. The number and placement of villages, towns, cities, and metropolises also resemble a central place pattern. Obvious exceptions are the clusters of mining towns in southwestern South Dakota and western Montana. Mining is not a central place function. The sequence of villages, towns, and cities along U.S. Highway 10 may be taken as a sample central place sequence. (Op. cit., Figure 5-12)

Spokane, Washington, is a similar regional metropolis, although its population is considerably smaller than that of the Twin Cities. Beneath the Twin Cities are ranked four levels of commercial centers. Wholesale-retail centers, shopping centers, and convenience centers are subdivided for greater clarity, while hamlets constitute a single subdivision. The map shows that wholesale-retail centers are few in number and widely spaced. Shopping centers are more frequent; convenience centers more numerous still; and hamlets occur in the greatest numbers (Table 5–2). Two things instantly catch our eye: The distribution of settlements which, regardless of type, become more and more sparse to the north and west, and the bewildering mixture of settlement types scattered across the map.

The foregoing discussion of network distortions in large part explains the variation

Table 5–2 The Frequency of Trade Center Types in the upper Midwest

	Type of Center				
	Regional Metropolis	Wholesale-Retail	Shopping Centers	Convenience Centers	Hamlets
Number of Centers	2	17	169	482	1,647

Source: Op. cit., Figure 5-12, Report No. 3.

in settlement densities from place to place. What does central place theory tell us about the observed mixture? One of Christaller's basic observations which he sought to explain was the extreme variety in settlement size and function from one area to another. He answered his own query by pointing out that different-sized central places were required to meet the threshold and minimum-range requirements of various urban functions. This meant that straight-line routes across his hexagonal networks would pass through various-sized settlements in predictable sequences. Figure 5–14A shows such a series along a major line segment in a five-level K=4 hierarchy. Starting at a central place of the highest order and assigning the highest number to that place, the sequence from one highest-order center to the next is:

5-1-2-1-3-1-2-1-4-1-2-1-3-1-2-1-5

We are now ready to see if according to Christaller's reasoning there is any discernible underlying order in the settlement pattern of the upper Midwest. U.S. Highway 10 (U.S. Interstates 94 and 90) connects Minneapolis–St. Paul with Spokane, Washington. Its path—shown on Figure 5–13—goes from the edge of the humid Midwest, across the Great Plains, and through the Rocky Mountains. Ranged along U.S. 10 are all levels of central places

from regional metropolises to hamlets. If some type of K network exists within the area, we might expect to find settlements occurring along the highway in an orderly sequence corresponding to what theory tells us.

Figure 5–14B shows the sequence of central place types along U.S. 10. Hamlets have been omitted, as they have been from the following example of a K=4 theoretical sequence two units in length:

5-2-3-2-4-2-3-2-5-2-3-2-4-2-3-2-5

All central places have been evenly spaced in this diagram for convenience sake. To do this, we might imagine that a rubber band was drawn out along U.S. 10 and stretched proportionally more in sparsely settled areas than in densely settled ones. Knots tied in the rubber band would represent settlements spaced according to real world distances. If the rubber band were taken from the map and allowed to return to its normal length, every knot, each representing a settlement, would be regularly spaced with its neighbors. Such regular spacing within the diagram overcomes irregularities due to differences in resource endowments.

Upon first inspection, the U.S. 10 sequence still looks disorderly. However, if we examine only the sequence of settlement *size* changes, we find that it very nearly matches the theo-

Figure 5-14 Theoretical and empirical settlement sequence along a line through a 5-level k = 4 hierarchy (A) Theoretical K = 4 settlement sequence. (B) Actual U.S. Highway 10 settlement sequence from Minneapolis–St. Paul, Minnesota, to Spokane, Washington.

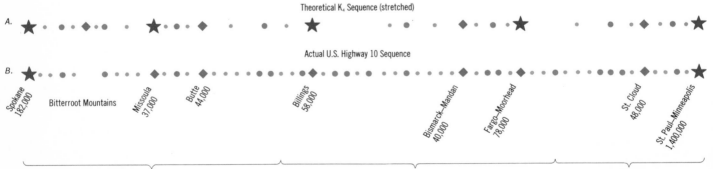

retical K=4 sequence of size changes given above. The variations that do occur are interesting. Three fifth-order places in the theoretical hierarchy coincide with fourth-order settlements on U.S. 10. High-speed motor transport may overcome the necessity for very large regional metropolises at these points. Furthermore, both Fargo-Moorehead and Billings, which in theory should be fifth-order places, have larger populations than St. Cloud, Bismarck, and Butte, which are also identified in the original study as the fourth-order places. The one area where settlements should be found in reality but are missing is the extremely rugged Bitterroot Mountains on the Montana-Idaho border, certainly the roughest terrain along all of U.S. 10. Finally, the model sequence seems to consistently underestimate the number of settlements found in the real world. This deserves special discussion in the next section. But before moving along, we can conclude that, although the correspondence between theory and reality is clouded by many variables, the existence of a hierarchy of settlement in the upper Midwest is strongly suggested by the sequence of observed settlement types.

The disappearance of Dakota: Adjustments in the central place hierarchy

The K=4 model apparently underestimates the number of settlements occurring on U.S. 10. If we divide the highway into three segments, one in the humid Midwest, one across the Great Plains, and one in the Rocky Mountains, and compare the number of settlements in each theoretical section with the number recorded in the equivalent portion of the real world, we find the relationships shown in Table 5-3.

Let us consider only the Great Plains, which differs most from our theoretical expectations. There are too many settlements. Is this a fair statement?

The Dakota Territory was slow to be settled by farmers. When statehood came to North and South Dakota in 1889, farm population was concentrated along the Red River Valley

Table 5-3   Number of Expected and Observed Trade Centers

Region	Expected	Recorded	% More Recorded Than Expected
Humid Midwest	8	13	162
Great Plains	9	23	255
Rocky Mountains	14	19	136

in the east. The Northern Pacific Railroad, completed in 1884, and the Great Northern Railroad, built by Jim Hill in 1895, crossed North Dakota to the Pacific Northwest. This opened up the marginal lands of the upper Midwest to dry wheat farming. Large numbers of Scandinavian immigrants along with smaller numbers of Russians and Germans moved out onto these windswept plains as dirt farmers homesteading quarter sections of farmland (160 acres) which they received free from the federal government. It was not an easy life. But the wheat market was good; the level of expectations of the people was low; and mechanization and communication improvements were just beginning to be felt throughout the land. Under these conditions many small farms were more or less evenly distributed across the area. Small, low-order central place settlements sprang up everywhere to serve the needs of these farm families. Years passed, and farm income relative to other employment fell. Larger and larger farms providing higher incomes but needing more and more capital became necessary in order to survive and meet the rising level of expectations of the American people as a whole. The depression and the droughts of the 1930s struck a blow at the farms. At the same time, growing metropolitan areas on the East and West Coasts lured many a young farm boy and farm girl away from home forever. Small farms were abandoned and were subsequently bought up and incorporated into the very large wheat ranches which survived. *Sidewalk* and *suitcase* farming became more and more common. In the former, the farmer lives in some nearby town and only visits his property to plow, plant, and harvest. In suitcase farming the farmer lives some-

How Cities Share Space: Classical Central Place Theory

105

☆ Secondary Wholesale-Retail

■ Shopping Center

□ Convenience Center

· Hamlets

0   50   100   200 Miles

**Figure 5-15 Distribution of declining trade centers in the upper midwest,
1930–1960** (Op. cit. Figure 5-12)

where away from the land most of the year, in Florida or New York, for example. He visits his wheat fields only when the seasonally determined workload demands. This means, in turn, that smaller hamlets, convenience centers, and shopping centers no longer have the rural population necessary to sustain them.

Figure 5–15 shows the distribution of declining trade centers throughout Minnesota, North and South Dakota, and Montana. Nor is this an isolated pattern. There is a large central belt of counties in the United States with declining populations. In the decade 1960–1970 the rural population of the eight Plains states was reduced by 420,000. Not even the South or Appalachia experienced so extensive a drop in population. In February 1971 a local high state official called for the consolidation of the two Dakotas into a single political unit to offset their declining populations. Perhaps most poignant of all is the front page feature story headline from the Sunday, February 14, 1971, New York *Times:*

THOUSANDS FLEE THE TOWNS OF
AMERICA'S LONELY PLAINS
(Dateline, McClusky, N.D.)

Abandoned towns, census tabulations, and

newspaper stories all help to confirm the notion, born of theory, that *in terms of recent economic developments and changes in transportation* the Great Plains may well be over-provided with low-order central places.

Cross-cultural Variations: Ontario

One important departure from theory may result from cross-cultural variations in the use of space. Much of our discussion of central place theory has emphasized cross-cultural similarities rather than differences in spatial behavior. This is particularly true for certain types of periodic markets and the development of higher-level market centers. An interesting and relatively unexplored subject is the point along a continuum of spatial behavior where cultural regularities give way to cross-cultural differences.

A comparison of Old Order Mennonite and "modern" Canadian consumer travel in Ontario Province will serve to illustrate the importance of cross-cultural spatial studies. Old Order Mennonites are known for their conservative religious beliefs, which are reflected in their homemade and somber clothing, their use of horse-drawn vehicles rather than automobiles, their very restricted use of electricity,

*Human
Geography:
Spatial
Design
in World
Society*

106

and their rejection of much of the modern world with its temptations such as moving pictures and television. Many Mennonite communities still provide their own teachers and education for their children. They are less conservative than other groups like the Old Order Amish in that they utilize modern farm machinery. All such groups are in sharp contrast with the other Canadians who surround them. These latter "modern" people have no religiously inspired restrictions of dress, nor do they shun contact with the outside world. In fact, differences between the two groups are great enough for us to talk of a *dominant culture* and a *subculture* where they are concerned.

The accompanying star diagrams (Figure 5–16*A* to *G*) of an area near Waterloo and Kitchener in Ontario are similar to those for Iowa and illustrate the shopping habits of the two diverse groups. A comparison of the origins and destinations of shopping trips made by the Mennonites and modern Canadians reveals cross-cultural differences. Distinctions in the two travel patterns are not in every case tied directly to settlement size or level in the hierarchy. Both modern and Mennonite Canadians travel intermediate distances for banking services and very little difference can be seen in their habits. In this case the service sought is relatively high in the spatial hierarchy and is impossible for individuals to do for themselves. In the case of travel for food, visible differences can be seen between the longer trips made by the modern Canadians as opposed to Mennonite journeys. This is a reflection of the Mennonites' simpler food preferences, greater self-sufficiency, and reliance on horse-and-buggy transportation. The use of horse-drawn conveyances for frequent shopping trips places time restrictions on Mennonite travel. It also means that whenever possible they will avoid going through busy Waterloo to reach Kitchener although it has a greater selection of goods and services. It is no fun trying to drive an easily frightened horse through downtown traffic. (In much the same way a study of the Old Order Amish in Indiana shows their preference for a super-market on the same side of a busy highway as most of the Amish colony's houses. A similar supermarket on the far side of the road had few Amish customers because of their reluctance to take horses into a dangerous situation.) Finally, Mennonite trips for yard goods are in sharp contrast with modern Canadians' trips for clothing bought off the rack. Most Mennonites dress conservatively and make their own clothes. They create little demand for store-bought attire, and there is little or no commercial response to their slight needs.

This part of Ontario has a well-developed spatial hierarchy of urban places just as our other examples have had. But differences can be found between Ontario and Iowa. Most important for our purposes are variations in consumer travel patterns between the two culture groups in Ontario. In many ways the spatial behavior of modern Canadians resembles that of people from Iowa more than it does the use of space by their Mennonite neighbors. Where modern goods and services are required, such as banking, both groups behave very much the same. But where traditional functions are carried out—and what could be more traditional than a culture group's habits of eating and dress?—modern Canadians travel much farther than do traditional Mennonites, who still live almost as their grandfathers did. We learn from this that even in a relatively small area with a single set of urban places, interesting and perhaps significant differences can exist on a cross-cultural basis. On the other hand, many spatial similarities seem to be shared by unlike cultures.

The way in which people communicate, the messages they send, and the way in which they organize space to do this are of great interest to geographers. Spatial hierarchies can be thought of as elaborate communication systems. Their design may help or hinder a group in its efforts to define and reach its goals. The next chapter examines the idea of human communications and the spatial systems which serve societies in their attempts to survive.

How Cities Share Space: Classical Central Place Theory

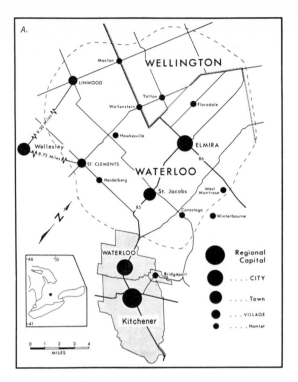

Figure 5-16 Shopping habits of Mennonites and "modern" Canadians near Waterloo, Ontario, Canada (A) The study area, (B) "modern" Canadian travel for banking service, (C) Old Order Mennonite travel for banking service, (D) "modern" Canadian travel for clothing and yard goods, (E) Old Order Mennonite travel for clothing and yard goods, (F) "modern" Canadian travel for food, and (G) Old Order Mennonite travel for food. (Robert A. Murdie, "Cultural Differences in Consumer Travel," *Economic Geography*, vol. 41, no. 3, July, 1965)

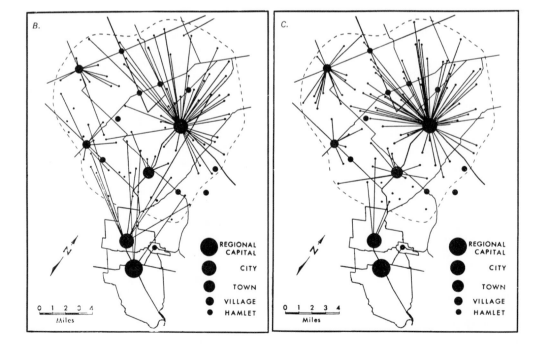

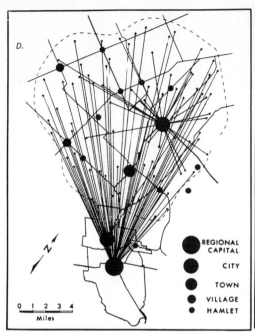

D.

REGIONAL
CAPITAL

CITY

TOWN

VILLAGE

HAMLET

0 1 2 3 4
Miles

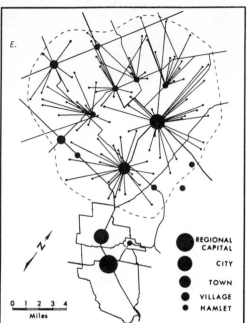

E.

REGIONAL
CAPITAL

CITY

TOWN

VILLAGE

HAMLET

0 1 2 3 4
Miles

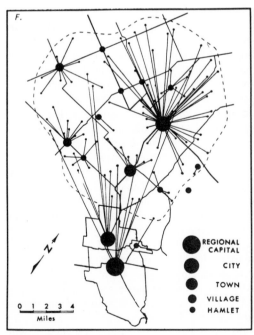

F.

REGIONAL
CAPITAL

CITY

TOWN

VILLAGE

HAMLET

0 1 2 3 4
Miles

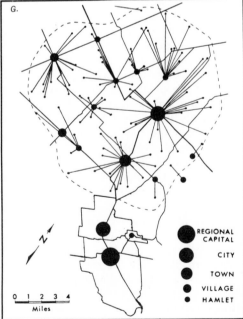

G.

REGIONAL
CAPITAL

CITY

TOWN

VILLAGE

HAMLET

0 1 2 3 4
Miles

6 | COMMUNICATION AND ORGANIZATION: CHARACTERISTICS OF INFORMATION SYSTEMS

The Importance of Connectivity

As I was going to St. Ives,
I met a man with seven wives.
Every wife had seven sacks,
Every sack had seven cats,
Every cat had seven rats.
Rats, cats, sacks, and wives,
How many were going to St. Ives?

St. Ives is everywhere. The man of St. Ives, trailing his retinue of wives, cats, and rats like a comet's tail, might be taken as symbolic of communication hierarchies. In pages past we have talked about the organization of space with strong emphasis upon *distance* and *direction*. Only when we maintain those two basic elements are we able to discern portions of the hexagonal networks by means of which space is most efficiently organized. But those qualities are no more important than a third: *connectivity*. In some static system, a picture in *Mother Goose*, with all the characters frozen at one moment in time, the man of St. Ives might have his wives and their minions ranged around him in some neat geometric pattern. But once we start the cadence of the verse and begin chanting it like a marching song, sending all those people and creatures jogging and skittering along imagination's winding roads, all spatial order

will be lost. The wives will gather and gossip, or hurry to harrass their man. The cats and rats will do all the things cats and rats have always done, and the scene will appear to be near chaos. And yet the connectivity is there that links them all into an old and familiar rhyme. The whole thing is much like an army on the parade ground and an army caught up in battle. On parade the relationship between staff and officers and men, divisional headquarters, regiments, companies, platoons, and squads is given some spatial expression. That regularity is soon lost when army meets army in battle, but the connectivity of the system, in this case expressed as a chain of command, keeps the whole organization operating through charge and countercharge, defeat and sometimes even victory.

Administrative hierarchies are what we are discussing here. They might be expressed in terms of locational analysis as $K=7$ systems. At the top is a central figure or a central place which administers its immediate surroundings as well as having authority or dominance over six adjacent places or positions of the next lowest order. Each of those six would in turn administer its own area and six still lower-order places. A message starting at the top and moving through the chain of command outward and downward would split and split again until every level, place, or person was reached. This pattern is shown in Figure 6–1. We have returned momentarily with this figure to a geometric ordering of space to make a by now familiar point. If this diagram is redrawn in a more abstract form, emphasizing the system's connectivity, the subsequent pattern resembles the orderly branching of a tree. Figure 6–2 shows such a diagram that matches a K=7 network, but many systems can be diagrammed in tree form.

It should not be thought that hierarchies shown as trees are necessarily one-way systems. The election of the President of the United States every four years is a good example of the reversal of such a system. Ideally, every person casts one vote, which is recorded at some local polling place. Counts from neighborhood polls are aggregated at city and county and state levels, until finally the nation as a whole learns what party and which man the populace has chosen. In this case many small messages start at widely dispersed points. By virtue of their aggregation at higher and higher levels they become a single directive by means of which the President receives his power. The people's decision is then given expression by means of Presidential decisions

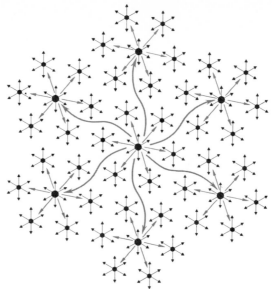

Figure 6-1 Flow pattern for a K=7 spatial hierarchy

or commands sent back down through the hierarchy until individual voters are again involved, this time by the need to comply with new laws or to pay new taxes.

Figure 6-2 K=7 tree hierarchy This hierarchy may be thought of as representing an organization chart of a regular K=7 hierarchy. The circles could be foremen or supervisors. Topologically it is identical to the spatial hierarchy shown in Figure 6-1.

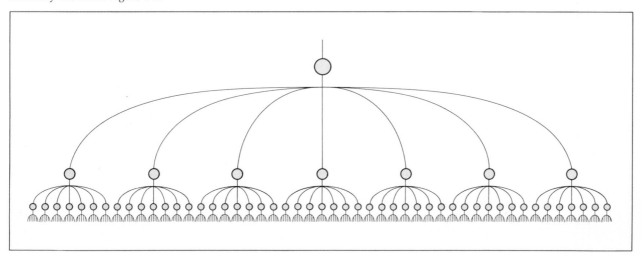

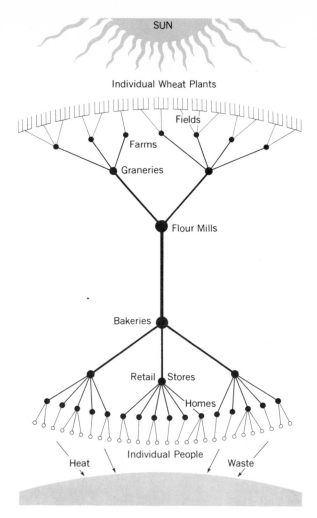

SUN

Individual Wheat Plants

Fields

Farms

Graneries

Flour Mills

Bakeries

Retail Stores

Homes

Individual People

Heat

Waste

Figure 6-3 Energy pathways in the wheat-to-bread food chain Many systems display a dumbell, or "complete tree," spatial network. Energy and material are assembled, change of state occurs, long transport hauls are completed, and products are distributed for use and, finally, returned to the environment after use.

plants – fields – farms – graineries – mills – bakeries – stores – homes – individuals – heat and waste—can be shown as a complete tree (Figure 6-3). Tiny increments of solar energy and soil nutrients are concentrated by each wheat plant into kernels of grain. Grain is harvested and concentrated in grain elevators for shipment to flour mills. Flour in turn moves to bakeries from which bread is shipped to numerous retail outlets and finally to individual homes. Once eaten, the energy is released; everything else that remains is waste. The energy is used to perform work which creates heat as its final by-product. The waste, either garbage or sewage, eventually breaks down into its component parts, releasing a final increment of heat energy back into the earth environment. Thus the whole system represents a coming together and a dissipating of energy through space and time.

This forms a basic dumbbell-shaped system of concentration and dispersion similar in form to a real tree with both roots and branches. Consider how leaves concentrate the sun's energy for long trips to the tips of root tendrils, and roots in turn absorb moisture from the soil to help maintain the tree's metabolism. On the next warm day lie down on the grass near some tree, and in your prone and sideways view see both ends of the tree, one in air and the other in soil. Imagine the system in its entirety and enjoy seeing birds and worms as similar, each species living in and around the energy system that is the tree, and each an energy system organized in its own way along hierarchial lines (Figure 6-4).

In brief, hierarchies are an efficient way to fill space with different-sized settlements. Settlements are typified by different types of activities or by different stages in the same system of activities. Thus our wheat – bread – energy system in Figure 6-3 could be shown in part as a farm – village – town – city – neighborhood – house settlement system. Neat and formal arrangements of space are often lost or undecipherable, but in any system, either natural or social, the connectivity which binds its many parts together can be shown

Another way in which hierarchies as systems become important to us is the gathering, processing, distribution, and use of resources of all kinds. This is such an important point that we will return to it again and again, but a single example will suffice for now. The following simplified food system—sun and

as treelike series of paths or links connecting together hierarchically arranged focal points. At such foci, energy, materials, or ideas are concentrated, perhaps changed into another form, and sent along to higher or lower centers for further concentration or distribution. *Trees* of this kind are found everywhere and ultimately can be thought of as communication and transportation systems which organize and hold together all human and natural phenomena.

Transportation and Communication

Society operates in geographic space by means of communication and transportation systems. As time passes, society reaches greater and greater levels of complexity through the use of hierarchies and through special handling of materials and messages. It follows that the properties of these systems are important in the conduct of all our activities. Any limitations on the movement of things and thoughts through these hierarchies become, in turn, constraints on the functioning of society. Limitations may be physical, institutional and cultural, or psychological. Each type of constraint has spatial characteristics. As technology and human aspirations change, making possible new connections and sometimes closing off old routes, the constraints within the systems also change.

We begin our discussion of these things with an exploration of some physical, institutional, and cultural limitations of movement systems. Our first subject is the nature of messages as the binding elements of social interaction. We then consider the characteristics of transportation and communication systems over which things and ideas travel. Communication and transportation systems share or have analogous properties as a consequence of their parallel operation. To understand one we must be aware of the operation of the other. While we are at present essentially concerned with information systems as *control mechanisms*, we will continue to draw examples from systems transporting more tangible objects. Furthermore, in order for

Figure 6-4 A complete tree system The tree is a system which transfers energy and material between two volumetric domains via a hierarchical network.

material systems to operate, information sent as messages must precede the movement of goods and people. Consider these examples.

People usually must know that an airplane is scheduled to leave before they will come to the airport. The airline, in return, must have some estimate of the potential number of travelers. Goods are seldom shipped blindly to retail outlets. Consumer demand must first be gauged and reported to the wholesale suppliers. Newspapers and magazines base their weekly production on feedback from previous newsstand sales plus subscriber lists. Universities have registration and pre-registration in order to match students to classes. As a result, sometimes new sections are added in popular courses; sometimes unfilled classes are canceled. In every case, the movement of vehicles, goods, the printed word, and students is triggered and in large part controlled by advance information sent through a communication system paralleling the system of transport. As the transportation system continues to function, additional messages about new developments will be sent. Even when the initial transportation job is done, information either halting the system or indicating it should continue will be necessary.

One of the things emphasized in this chapter is the role of *standardization* and *routinization* in maintaining efficiency at high volumes of interchange. These characteristics, however, must be balanced against the need for *flexibility* and *freedom of choice* which allow the *innovation* and *adjustment* necessary for survival in changing world. But before discussing these points in detail we must consider the ways in which members of a society communicate with each other. What kinds of thoughts and words are essential to our well-being and in what ways do we exchange them?

Types and Techniques of Communication

If someone you love reaches out and touches your hand as you pass by, you have received one of the best kinds of messages. When a relative telephones and says, "Come home, we need your help," you have received another communication. The world is full of communications and messages, many of which we scarcely recognize and some of which we fail to realize at all. Each one of us at least once in our lives has given a message, perhaps not in words, to someone we hoped

to know much better. And too often from the sender's point of view the message is never read, the invitation to friendship passed over. On the other hand, stop and consider the next time you get a parking ticket that you have received a message. Not just to "pay the two dollars," but a more complex communication, a comment by society about the values it places on transportation and terminal facilities, and another one in which a whole system of courts and agencies combines to enforce a tiny part of our culture's code of conduct.

Table 6–1 gives examples of the means of communication employed and the numbers of people between whom messages are sent. The columns are divided between *personal means*, in which nothing gets between the sender and the receiver, and *mechanical means,* in which mechanical and electronic devices are used to move messages. The *Mechanical* column is further subdivided into *Instant* and *Stored* categories to accommodate obvious differences in types of communications.

Going from left to right in every row of the table leads us from immediate face-to-face experiences with strong emotional overtones to more and more remote events. Since electronic communication is for all practical purposes as quick as or quicker than direct human speech, the difference between the first two columns in any row is one of increasing distance. The third column, *Mechanical-Stored,* indicates that senders and receivers can be far apart in time as well as space. It is very hard for us to predict where we, the authors of this book, will be when you, the reader, see these pages. Many miles and many years may separate us. It is the same with old letters and diaries. Some of the most evocative reading materials available are your own old messages to others and to yourself.

Similarly, the quality and nature of messages change from the top to the bottom of the table. The ideas and emotions exchanged between two and only two people have elements lacking in mass communication. The reverse is also true; mass media can do things personal chats never could. President Franklin D. Roosevelt, in the early days of

*Human
Geography:
Spatial
Design
in World
Society*

114

Table 6-1 Means of Communication by Numbers and Types

Number Involved in the Exchange	Type of Contact		
	Personal	Mechanical	
	Instant	*Instant*	*Stored*
One to one	Talk, touch	Telephone	Letters
One to many	Lectures	Television	Textbook
Many to one	Town hall meeting	Group lobbying by telephone and telegram	Contracts
Many to many	Symphony and applause	Conventions	The law

radio, recognized these differences and bridged the gap between face-to-face and mass communication by holding "fireside chats" on national networks.

To summarize the characteristics of communication as arranged in the table, in the upper left we find face-to-face spontaneous, repetitious, fluctuating, give-and-take between couples. The lower right is reserved for the massed voices of society speaking across the years. Information flow between sender and receiver changes from the upper left to the lower right of the table. Going from conversations to constitutions, such flow becomes increasingly more routinized, more inflexible, and more one-directional in character. This accounts for the frustration felt by individuals when they attempt to deal with communication elements further and further along this continuum. Student protestors are less successful than they wish since they almost always use face-to-face–personal–instant communication techniques in their attempts to change many-to-many–mechanical-stored messages embodied in laws and constitutional articles. The best political strategists will choose a variety of types and techniques of communication in order to achieve their goals and are realists about the social inertia of the things they want to influence and change. Each one of us operates

across this spectrum of communication, and our happiness and sense of personal effectiveness are tied largely to our ability to send appropriate messages along the right channels.

Overload in Information Systems

All systems must have a constant flow of messages, materials, or energy moving through them in order to function. Flows move from focal point to focal point along routes or paths. The carrying capacity of these routes is finite, and there are limits above which they cannot operate. Some examples where breakdown results when these upper limits on the carrying capacities of systems are exceeded include blowing a fuse just as you plug in the iron after turning on the air conditioner, a traffic jam, and a flooding river. People as part of communication systems are also affected. A worker pushed beyond endurance by the increasing tempo of his task refuses to continue working or behaves irrationally and botches the job. The latter situation is one of the high points of Charlie Chaplin's film *Modern Times*, in which he is overwhelmed by his work on the assembly line and goes temporarily insane. In every case, when the upper limit is exceeded, the system suffers from *overload* and breaks down.

While every system which includes paths

with finite carrying capacities is subject to overload, whether it is a highway network or the human body, for the moment we will consider *information overload* rather than the physical overwhelming of some system. Information overload can be defined as *receiving too many bits of information per unit of time for adequate appraisal, processing, and response.*

To understand this, let us consider automobile driver reaction time. A good driver must be constantly aware of the events surrounding him and be able to respond to them quickly and rationally. The more events or objects per mile, the slower a person must drive in order to see and safely respond to his environment. There is a definite upper limit on the number of things a driver can take into account. If he speeds up, the flow of information bits past his eyes becomes too great, and then he may well have an accident.

The main difference between an expressway with limited access and a city street is reduced information per unit distance. On a freeway, the number of information bits and subsequently the number of necessary choices per mile which face the driver are reduced and the speed with which the system operates can be increased. But this also means that the choices open to a driver on an expressway are decreased. Efficiency, measured in terms of the time necessary to cover a fixed distance, is improved, but at the expense of decreased flexibility and an accompanying hazard, boredom. Seemingly endless miles of uninterrupted superhighways can induce drowsiness which spells disaster or at the very least the utterly frustrating experience of missing your exit and having to drive on another 12 miles to the next turnoff.

There is a trade-off between freedom of choice with less efficiency and greater efficiency but increased inflexibility. Ultimately, however, nearly every system can be subjected to intolerable loads. Cities as communication systems are no exception, nor are their inhabitants safe from similar stress. In an urban world it is a matter of survival for us to understand the nature of information overloads in urban terms. To do this, we must identify the physical elements important in communication systems and their transportation counterparts.

Communication and Transportation Components

Whenever things, people, ideas, and energy are moved, three elements are always present. These are *carriers, routes,* and *terminals.*

Carriers

Carriers come in all manner of forms and sizes. Automobiles, buses, airplanes, trains, and ships are carriers for people and goods. Mosquitoes, fleas, and rats are often the carriers of disease. Sound waves carry speech, and speech in turn is a highly symbolic carrier of ideas. Radio waves and electric impulses also carry information, as do books, newspapers, and letters. Migrants, salesmen, and gossips also serve to spread culture, information, and hearsay. In still another form, coal, oil, wood, and radium are all carriers of energy and are in turn transported from place to place. In other words, *a carrier in any communication-transportation system can be thought of as a container for whatever is moved.* Sometimes the container is self-propelled; sometimes it is not. Often it is as simple as a box on wheels; just as often it is a complex, living organism.

Routes or domains

Routes are the media through which carriers move. Veins and arteries are the routes along which blood travels in the body; viruses, such as serum hepatitis, are carried by the blood. Carriers and routes are matched to each other and have special characteristics. Railroads move huge quantities of materials from one place to another but sacrifice flexibility of destination in return for volume. Individual trucks and cars have a much greater choice of where to begin and end their trips but carry smaller loads than trains. The differences as routes between railroad tracks and highways is obvious. Rivers and canals are very much like highways in their linear roles as routes for carriers, but lakes and oceans offer almost unlimited choices for the middle part of trips, becoming restricted only as shore is approached. The atmosphere allows voices to spread ideas for short distances near the earth's surface, while the ether affords interstellar opportunities for broadcasting as long as the transmitter's energy is sufficient. Thus routes are not necessarily linear, and we sometimes refer to the medium in which carriers move as the *domain* of travel.

In all cases the efficiency of the system is a function of how well the carrier is matched to the physical characteristics of the route. The choice of destinations is in turn limited by the dimensions of the system. A linear system such as a ski lift may connect two points with no other choices. Skiers have only one path up the mountain. By *path* we mean the trace of an individual trip along a route. A snail's route is the sidewalk; the silvery line he leaves behind marks his path. A two-dimensional system—say, an ocean with numerous ports along its shores—offers a different magnitude of possible pathways. A moment's thought will show how this line of reasoning is a direct consequence of our earlier discussion of point, line, and area relationships.

Terminals

Terminals act as exchange mechanisms between different types of domains. As a result, terminals always mark the contact, or *interface*, between two or more environments whether natural (a seaport), social (a hotel front desk), or economic (a customs shed). Terminals also serve as scale transformers which may either combine or divide anything transported or communicated into different-sized bundles depending upon overall need and the characteristics of the systems involved.

An airport terminal, for example, operates at the interface between the two-dimensional land surface served by one-dimensional linear routes and the volumetric sky with an almost unlimited number of paths. Of course, no system is ever as simple as it at first appears. Airplanes cannot land wherever their pilots wish but are limited to special types of landing surfaces and the presence of navigational aids. Even in the air, pilots are not free as birds and must stick to carefully monitored traffic patterns near airports as well as following specific flight plans when flying in busy areas.

Airports also serve as scale changers. Passengers arrive by ones, or twos, or threes in private cars at low speeds. Most commercial airliners have capacities in excess of 100 passengers, and craft like the Boeing 747 can accommodate more than 350 people. The speed of commercial airplanes is roughly a magnitude greater than the speed of automobiles (60 versus 600 miles per hour). Airports, therefore, must be designed to change the scale of operations between automobile- and aircraft-utilizing systems, keeping the two types of carriers out of each others' way, and at the same time minimizing the distance which passengers must travel on foot between the two carriers. Note that pedestrian traffic within the terminal constitutes another system serving as a bridge between the first two.

Numerous other examples come to mind. Seaports act as transformers at the interface between two types of domains. Bulk shipments brought long distances by sea must be broken into smaller parcels for distribution over land. A recent innovation to smooth this transition is *containerization*, in which goods are shipped in standardized containers designed to be easily transported by ships, trucks, and rail without repackaging. At the same time, large ships can approach the shore in only very special places with particular loading and unloading facilities. As another example, radio and television systems are made possible by special terminal facilities. As you read this sentence, you are surrounded and penetrated by radio impulses from all sides. But unless you have truly exceptional fillings in your teeth, you are unaware of the information carried by the radio energy around you. Terminal facilities such as receivers and transmitters are necessary for the systems to work.

If we wish to transmit ideas in printed form from person to person, books and newspapers require special terminal procedures and mechanisms for their successful use. Here again, scale changes are important, for what one man writes, a million may read. Wide-scale literacy depends in large part upon high-speed presses in order that sufficient copies can be distributed. On the other end of the same system we each spend years learning to read and comprehend what we see in print. The carrier is the printed page; the routes are the streets used by the newsboy; the terminal facilities include presses and literate people. One advantage of the written word is its ability to endure through time and carry people's thoughts from one age to another.

Over-the-Road Versus Terminal Effort

These several examples all suggest a further aspect of communication-transportation systems. The effort and energy required at either end of a trip or transmission is almost always much greater than that required by the portions of it en route. The cost of radio receivers and transmitters as opposed to the free ether is self-evident. In computer systems, remote control computer terminals can be connected to the central computer by means of regular telephone lines. The terminal keyboard, computer, and print-out mechanisms are far more expensive than the route along which data, instructions, and results travel.

A human example familiar to all students is the variation in effort we all experience on our way to lectures. The crowded stairs and elevators in the dormitories require much more time and effort to traverse than do the open walkways across campus. The same thing is true at the far end of the trip to lecture. Entering a crowded lecture hall, particularly when the preceding class is streaming out, again takes considerably more effort then the walk en route. Commuters undergo similar experiences every day as they enter the city. The nearer their destination is to the

CBD, the more congested will be the streets which they must use and the more difficulty they will have in finding a parking place. The trip home is perhaps even worse, for the custom of letting all businesses out at the same time in the late afternoon creates costly pedestrian and automobile traffic jams.

A particularly interesting problem in over-the-road versus terminal effort in transportation relates to air travel. Innovations in jet aircarft pose terminal difficulties which make increased advantages en route less persuasive arguments for more and more speed. Pound for pound and passenger for passenger the 747 is more efficient than smaller airplanes such as the 707. However, the traveler may lose more than he gains if on returning from Europe he disembarks from his 747 along with the more than 150,000 scheduled passengers arriving at J.F. Kennedy International Airport on similar aircraft any late afternoon in July or August.[1]

In much the same way, all high-speed flight presents special terminal problems. As airplanes need longer and longer runways and takeoff and approach paths, new airports must be located at greater distances from the centers of metropolitan areas. This means the ground portion of the trip from city to terminal will increase with added costs in time and effort. Similarly, while the flight time across continents and oceans grows steadily less, additional hours in the air may be added at the traveler's destination due to congestion aloft. Strict rules must be followed by all aircraft. This necessitates queuing for both takeoffs and landings. The latter action is often referred to as "stacking" the aircraft in a holding pattern. As traffic increases, it is becoming common for New York City flights originating in San Francisco to be stacked near Denver, Colorado, before being allowed to advance into the New York metropolitan airspace.

As the number of aircraft increases, the quantity and quality of information processed by air terminals must increase even more

[1]*The New York Times*, Apr. 9, 1972, sec. 2, p. 1.

rapidly. The upper limit or capacity of airports will ultimately be determined by the upper limits of their communication systems as much as by physical crowding. Just as world population growth has necessitated increased spatial organization, so must our ability to communicate keep pace with growing congestion. It follows that cities, like airports, present special problems. But before we look more closely at the special role of communication in cities, let us consider some ways in which the capacities of information systems can be changed.

Increasing System Capacity

The efficiency of any communication system is proportional to the number of messages exchanged between its participants. Of course, this means messages which are understood and acted upon. Too many messages, too much information, as we have already said, will simply break down the system. As organizations grow larger and more complex, new ways to increase capacity must be found. This becomes evident, for example, if we contrast ancient and modern forms of government.

A Greek city-state (*polis*) could operate democratically by calling an *assembly* of all its citizens in the marketplace or amphitheater in order to carry out the business of legislation. To be sure, not every inhabitant of a *polis* was a citizen. Citizenship belonged only to adult males whose fathers were citizens before them. Given this Greek definition of the electorate, the number of decision makers remained manageable. In all of what is now Greece only Athens had 30,000 or more citizens so defined. And in all the Greek world just two other city-states, Syracuse and Agrigento (Acragas) in Sicily, were as large. At the time of the Peloponnesian War, Athens's total population numbered perhaps 175,000 men, women, and children, who were slaves, alien residents, and free Athenians. This meant that one in every five or six inhabitants had the right to vote. Since not every citizen could regularly find time to help run the govern-

Terminal congestion. Automobiles are taking up more and more space in central city areas. Notice the expressway in the background. Rather than relieving congestion, such installations shift the crowding to terminal areas. Storing commuter automobiles is a very inefficient use of space, especially if many commuters drive into the central city alone, and many do. This scene is near the center of Atlanta, Georgia.

ment, daily business was conducted by an appointed *Council of 500*, 50 from each of 10 tribes. Turnover in the council was rapid, and every citizen had to serve his turn. The arrangement, therefore, was relatively fluid, and each participant knew and could actually see and hear all other persons who debated and cast ballots.

The city of Socrates and Plato was a far cry from modern nation-states such as our own. In the election of 1972 more than 73 million voters cast their ballots for President, and even then, less than 70 percent of those eligible to vote did so. Such populations are far too large to gather at one place, let alone give every citizen a chance to be heard. Instead, we must use telephones, radios, and teletype machines to gather and tabulate votes beyond the precinct level, while voting machines are used almost everywhere. Sheer size forces us to use new methods of decision making and vote taking. If governments are to represent the will of the electorate, the channel capacities of their political systems must

Communication and Organization: Characteristics of Information Systems

be increased to accommodate more and more people.

How then can we alter the systems we use to meet new demands? An obvious answer is to enlarge the channels through which information flows. This could mean larger auditoriums for public meetings. Another way would be to add additional, parallel channels the same as those that already exist. In this case we might try to hold duplicate city council meetings to handle overflow crowds of citizens. However, simply increasing the size of a system will not necessarily increase its efficiency. There are other ways in which the capacities of systems can be increased without making them larger.

Standardization and *routinization* are two such means. The degree to which these qualities exist within systems imparts particular characteristics to them. Therefore, it is important to recognize such features, their attributes, and the advantages and disadvantages which accompany them.

Standardization

A standardized system is so designed that it has only a limited number of types of inputs and outputs, whether this refers to information or material objects. By doing this, fewer choices need to be made within the system and a smaller number of steps can be taken in order to process information and materials flowing through it.

We constantly encounter standardization in our daily lives. We may complain of the dreary sameness of major motel chains offering bland anonymity in every corner of the land. This is not a conspiracy of mediocrity. This is a prime example of standardization and its advantages and disadvantages. If travelers want and demand a certain level of comfort within a fixed price range, and if they want reliable food every meal and not a gourmet's delight one night and a ptomaine parlor the next, they seek out standardized hotels and restaurants.

Companies that deal in nationwide accommodations must be able to provide reliable food and lodging in every location. They tend to avoid local or regional variations, no matter how picturesque or appetizing they may be. Thus a chain restaurant may be nothing to write home about—since there is probably one back home anyway—but it is almost always dependable and reasonably priced, and offers those same French fries that always keep Junior quiet at meal times. Travelers who want variety and higher quality must pay for it with time, by seeking out good restaurants in unfamiliar places; with money, since unusual and good-quality items almost always come in smaller quantities at higher prices; and with patience, for if we experiment we inevitably make some mistakes.

Other systems using standardization include buses which require exact change when you board them and colleges with rigid entrance requirements. In each case—and you can add dozens of examples with a few minutes' thought—the system more efficiently processes customers, passengers, or students by limiting the type of inputs it will accept. In every case freedom of choice is sacrificed for increased carrying capacity.

Routinization

Routinization limits the number of paths through a system. We have already noted than an expressway will take you quickly from one side of a city to the other but offers only one path with few entries and exits. Freedom and flexibility are sacrificed for efficiency. The same is true at another scale for assembly lines. Factories produce enormous quantities of standardized products by limiting the number of paths materials can take through their systems, and workers must perform the same task over and over at an appointed spot along the line. Engineering and medical schools which train students to meet certain specific and rigid standards of performance set by the state offer fewer electives than do departments in the humanities which follow different standards of excellence and attempt to graduate no two students exactly alike. By reducing the number of paths through a system, the number of decisions open to the participant are limited and the efficiency of the whole operation increases. Improvements are gained by adopting *standard operating procedures*, whether these are routines operating within the system or actual physical pathways along which things move.

One further way in which efficiency is gained is by making the boundaries of the routes or paths more and more impenetrable. This can best be explained with the help of a simple example. Consider three kinds of garden hose: The usual kind is an impervious tube, another has holes regularly spaced along its length, and a third is made out of heavy canvas through which water can seep at any and every point. The force of the water reaching the end of the hose farthest from the faucet is greatest in the first kind and least in the third. Conversely, water reaches the ground along the entire hose when it is made of permeable canvas; only the ground at the far end of the impervious hose receives liquid. There is a trade-off here between efficiency, measured as the force of the water at the far end, and linear coverage, which is greatest where the walls of the hose are easily penetrated. End points, remote from each other, are best served by paths with impenetrable boundaries or walls. An example comparable to the garden hoses is the role of different types of boundaries in transportation networks. City streets have low curbs, few protective devices, and many open driveways. On the other hand, the borders and median dividers on superhighways are very often reinforced concrete posts with corrugated steel panels in between. The latter boundaries are literally impenetrable in most cases. City streets provide access to local areas; expressways connect widely separated points. Their boundaries match their functions.

Changing capacities of carriers and terminal facilities

We must be careful not to assume that specialization applies only to routes and not to carriers and terminal facilities. In fact, whole systems can become so adapted to a single use that their specialization makes them unsuitable for any other purpose. Iron ore shipment on the Great Lakes is a good example of this. This system, by means of huge ore boats, supplies iron ore from the Mesabi Range near the western end of Lake Superior to steel mills along the shores of Lake Michigan and Lake Erie. Similar cargoes of coal are carried from railroad terminals on Lake Erie in Ohio and Pennsylvania to other points farther removed from the coal fields of the central and eastern United States. At first, ore and coal boats were more or less motorized barges of relatively small size. With the passing of time, the ships became larger and larger. At first they became wider, deeper, and longer, but the physical geography of the Great Lakes imposed certain design limits on these lake craft. The ship locks at Sault Sainte Marie and the channel in the Detroit River between Lake Huron and Lake Erie are relatively narrow and shallow. Furthermore, it would be exceedingly expensive to enlarge these bottlenecks in the natural system. After the ore boats had reached the maximum width and depth permitted by the narrows described above, their capacity was further increased by making them longer and longer without changing their draft or beam. By mid-century these ships had become so long that they were unseaworthy in the open waters of the Atlantic, where the crests of large ocean swells can be far apart and the ships could literally be broken in two. Along with this set of interacting constraints special docking and loading and unloading facilities were developed at both ends of their voyages. The mass movement of bulk ore and coal has been highly perfected, but the ports specializing in these cargoes cannot be used for any other type of vessel or activity. Thus, the bulk movement of raw materials on the Great Lakes has become highly specialized, but the system is inflexible to the point of being unable to accommodate other cargoes or to use its carriers elsewhere. If the sources of coal or iron were to drastically change, or if new technology ruled out ore or coal in their present form or

Communication and Organization: Characteristics of Information Systems

quantities, the system would automatically become obsolete. Here again the choice has had to be made: specialization with greater capacity and accompanying inflexibility or more general, less efficient, but more flexible and lasting carriers.

Institutions as Communication Systems

Institutions of all kinds, public and private, may be thought of as communication systems. Routes, terminals, and carriers can be identified within them, and in every case information flow is an important part of their functioning. Institutions are organized for special purposes and are always standardized to some degree. Prisons, factories, armies, and universities are all institutions. Different as are the purposes they serve, they still resemble one another, for all of them are hierarchically organized and structure the space they occupy according to their functions.

Prisons

Prisons represent one extreme along a continuum of institutional systems. When society decides that one of its members is dangerous or should be punished, he is put in prison—that is, he is denied the unlimited use of space. At the same time, if too many prisoners are kept together in one area, they may become unmanageable. Prisons are spatially organized into separate buildings or wings, cell blocks, and cells. The warden is aided by assistant wardens, who in turn direct guards and trustees in the prison routine. Thus the spatial organization and administrative hierarchy parallel one another. Traditionally, prisons have had almost no methods for their inmates to communicate upward through the hierarchy. Since prison conditions often give much for prisoners to complain about, prison riots should not come as surprises. Such disturbances serve as mechanisms for penetrating the nearly impervious boundaries imposed on information flow by stone walls and an inflexible chain of command.

Factories and armies

Factories and armies are very similar. In each case their members are given greater freedom of movement than prisoners. But specialization and routine are built into each system. Participants must be in proper places at appointed times in order for both these systems to work.

In either case, highly organized hierarchies must send information from the top to the bottom of the system. There must also be some feedback. Quality control tells factory management when production processes are going astray. Shop stewards and union representatives keep the owners aware of the workers' feelings. One of the reasons for strikes is the breakdown of normal information flow between management and labor.

Army terminology—front, flank, rear, advance, retreat, strong point—is particularly spatial in character. Generals must know the progress of battles, which are in turn made up of thousands of individual encounters. Movement through space is a key factor. Reinforcements must be sent to bolster weak points or to take advantage of the enemy's mistakes. Supplies and ammunition must go forward, and intelligence and the wounded need to be sent to the rear. Here again, information flow directs the movement of men and materials just as management needs information to run a factory. *Regimentation* is important in both examples. In fact, the words *regime* and *regiment* share a common root with *regimentation* and provide clues to the way in which these and similar institutions are organized.

Universities

Universities are also hierarchically ordered institutions which occupy space. They, however, are found near the opposite end of the continuum along which we have ranked communication systems. Their goals are to maximize independent and imaginative thought. To do this, freedom of choice and independence of decision are most important. Here, as in our other examples, we are talking about an ideal situation. Freshmen, particularly, may find it hard to believe the above statement, but even an underclassman will appreciate the freedom of university life if he has just come from the army or an assembly-line job.

The main purpose of a university is to generate new ideas and change in the minds of students and faculty. This is done in order to create new knowledge which may eventually find practical application, or to bring forth works of art with which to satisfy our innermost needs. The university, then, is ideally a place where the minds of men are allowed complete freedom to generate new ways of looking at the world. Once imagination has produced ideas, they must stand the test of debate and challenge in the academic cockpit. Professors and students should challenge each other. Out of such interchange will come new and better ideas. The best and most efficient way to do this is by prolonged face-to-face communication with as many different people as possible.

The spatial and functional organization of the university matches these needs. A large number of classes meet every hour. At regular intervals participants change classes and rooms, and new combinations of students and professors are formed. A single student may hear three or more teachers in a single day and may come in contact with completely different students in each class. The frequency of contact with bearers of new ideas is enhanced by this continuous shifting about. Certain other focal points exist on campus for the exchange of information. The library, a storehouse for knowledge, is one of these. Students and professors come and go during their lifetimes, but the materials in libraries generally remain in one place longer and are more available than humans. Thus, books and documents have a kind of inertia which places them on the lower right side of the table of communication types (Table 6–1). Access to information of this sort gives stability and continuity to academic life, although even printed knowledge ages, becomes less pertinent, and, as it were, dies.

On the other hand, cafeterias and coffee shops are also important parts of universities. At these points intense, fleeting, face-to-face encounters take place between students and faculty. The university in this way has a full range of information exchange mechanisms from very large, highly structured introductory courses through smaller classes, seminars, and libraries all the way to personal conversations and arguments. All such exchanges take place in an ever-changing variety of locations. The effect is kaleidoscopic and may seem confusing to new students until they realize that the strength of the university as an information and communications system is in its flexibility and freedom.

The Balance between Routine and Change

Even universities need some routine and specialization. In this way the capacity of the system is increased in order to provide more and more people with the educations they want. This imposes problems of increasing systems capacity while maintaining an opportunity for innovation. Sometimes whole schools are organized to meet the needs and purposes of students and faculties. Dentistry, engineering, and medicine are examples of more highly structured, tightly organized parts of the university. In such cases, the students must prepare for examinations imposed by external licensing agencies like state governments. We would scarcely want to drive across an imaginative but untested bridge, or have our tonsils removed by someone long on imagination and short on skill.

This brings a basic problem in universities to our attention. Universities, like any other institutions, need to be organized. Their students need to learn basic skills, be they surgery or sonnets. But all such organization stifles the opportunity for radical new departures, that is, the imaginative breakthroughs by which mankind always advances. To the ex-

Communication and Organization: Characteristics of Information Systems

tent that students are not allowed to make their own choices, the university becomes a think factory turning out identical products who may serve society but not advance it. On the other hand, to the extent that students have absolute freedom, there is less and less chance of any finished product. In other words, institutions of all kinds in order to survive and improve must find a balance between routine and change.

Every one of us constantly works within or alongside not one but many institutions. If we think of them as spatial systems with routes and walls, terminals, and carriers, as well as feedback and storage mechanisms, our ability to understand and cope with them will improve. In every case, institutions, like any systems, can suffer from overload and breakdown. Since cities are in large part collections of institutions, all that we have said so far about information flow and communication systems applies to urban places. The concept of settlements' being organized into spatial hierarchies is particularly useful at this point. In the pages that follow we will consider cities as communication systems which are in turn nodes in the overall system which makes up the modern world.

7 | URBAN COMMUNICATION: INFORMATION FLOW AND THE MEAN INFORMATION FIELD

Switching Points

Cities are like the refreshment table at a party. When you want to meet that fascinating person across the crowded room or escape a boring conversation in which you're mired, you excuse yourself and go get something to eat or drink. Somehow you don't return to your original partner but begin talking to someone else. If that new conversation doesn't work out, there's always the need for another sandwich, another trip to the switching station. Even at room scale, space is not homogeneous. Certain places offer more opportunities for contact and exchange than do others.

Cities are the same. Their huge daytime populations, the pedestrians crowded together on the streets, thousands of stores, hundreds of institutions, and scores of theaters and museums all provide the opportunity for face-to-face contact between people. Karl Deutsch likens the metropolis to a telephone switchboard with hundreds of lines leading into it and an efficient means of making connections between any two wires. The potential for communication in such a system is enormous.

Transactions and Commitments

In every society communication fills a variety of needs. At the simplest verbal level a baby gets pleasure from hearing his parents exclaim and coo over him and from goo-goo-gooing in return. Adults participate in what are sometimes called *idiot greetings* when they say "Hi" and "Hello" to the same classmate or co-worker whenever they see him, even if it's twenty times a day. All these constitute verbal assurances that we are part of a social group and that we are approved of and loved.

Almost every communication is intended as a *transaction*; it is part of the way in which the business of living is conducted. We communicate our needs and desires; we ask, plead threaten, fuss, and persuade. We listen, in turn, to countless messages directed at us. Such exchanges of messages are transactions and often result in one or both parties committing themselves to do something or provide something for the other person. Transactions and commitments can be between individuals or between people acting for firms, corporations, institutions, and all manner of social groupings. The marriage vow formalizes a commitment between two people arrived at after lengthy transactions. Contracts and mortgages are similar formal statements of agreements between people and institutions. Business deals, life insurance sales, and theater tickets and the performances that follow all can be thought of as transactions and commitments. The opportunity for these interactions is greatest in large cities, and is one of the major reasons for their existence.

Quaternary Urban Activities

The words *quarternary activities* are a convenient way to say *information handling and management*. Our use of *quaternary* implies that *primary*, *secondary*, and *tertiary* activities also exist. Let us place these terms and the activities for which they stand in a proper context. If we consider all the pursuits in which man engages, all the different jobs he does, we can order such activities along a continuum of resource manipulation. For example, a man can be a miner, a metal worker, a steel salesman, or an economist for a firm which buys and uses structural steel. Each type of activity relates to the same resource, but as we move along the above list, we find that each subsequent person's contact with the actual physical resource has grown less. At the same time, influence and decision-making ability increase steadily from miner to salesman to management economist.

Activities involving the actual procurement of raw materials—for example, mining, farming, and lumbering—are designated *primary activities*. Those during which raw materials are physically manipulated and changed into more refined and manufactured products— iron and steel, furniture, bread, gasoline—are called *secondary activities*. All the jobs which relate to the buying, selling, transporting, and stockpiling of manufactured items can be called *tertiary activities*. We also include under this designation all services such as repair and maintenence, clerking, and entertainment. Many of these jobs are not directly concerned with the manipulation of physical resources. The term *quaternary activities* refers to the handling and management of information and knowledge. Thus, most managerial positions would be included under this phrase. Accounting, banking, stockbroking, publishing, librarianship, basic research, and teaching are also included. The term *quaternary* was suggested by the geographer Jean Gottman in his attempt to describe the characteristics of Megalopolis.

Generally speaking, the larger the settlement, the greater the importance of information handling to its survival. Nevertheless, it is difficult to show the role of quaternary activities, for to do so we would have to follow various important messages and orders for goods and services step by step from desk to desk, from office to office, from town to city. If we plotted enough of these routes on maps, we would see lines converging on major metropolitan areas. Unfortunately, information suitable for making such maps is often confidential and, usually, almost impossible to track through the administrative labyrinths of big business and government. We must try instead to find *surrogate measures* of the central role played by cities in quaternary activities. Such *surrogates* would stand in place of more direct measures; that is, they would be *reliable substitutes for the real thing*.

Certain things suggest themselves as reliable substitute measures for information flow and handling. The quantity of mail sent and received, the number of library books available to the public, the number of books, magazines, and newspapers published or the number of publishers, the number of computers in use at a given location, the number of telephones and/or telephone calls, and the points of origin of television programs and radio broadcasts all serve to show where the action is in today's world.

It would belabor the obvious to display elaborate statistics proving that New York City is the source for an overwhelming majority of direct news broadcasts and "live" radio and television shows. Prerecorded programs such as "specials" and weekly series may be made in Hollywood or elsewhere but almost always are sent to New York City for rebroadcasting down through the hierarchy of television and radio stations. Figure 7–1 shows two major broadcasting networks, both originating in New York City, the home of all major broadcasting companies in the United States. Just as New York City dominates

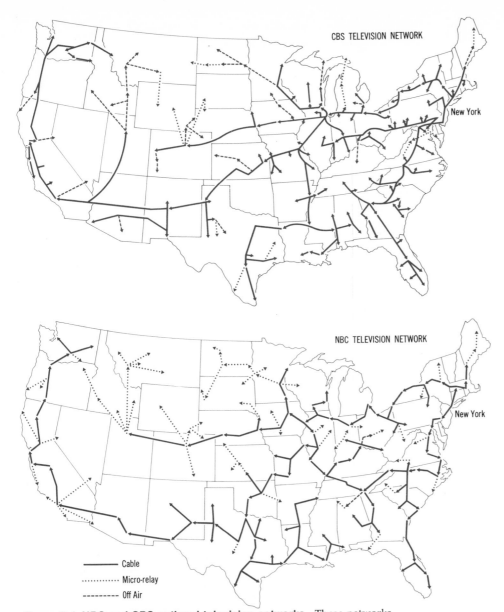

Figure 7-1 NBC and CBS national television networks   These networks consist of line-of-sight microwave connections or physically connected cables. Both networks originate in New York City. They employ quite different route patterns to reach the same areally spread TV market. Neither network is very redundant; that is, there is usually only one route from New York City to a given station. This implies either that their equipment is very expensive and alternative routes are not financially feasible, or that the equipment is very reliable, or both. (*International Television Almanac 1967*)

Table 7-1   Dominance of New York in Communication Industries and Services

City	Population of Surrounding SMSA (nearest 1/10 million)	No. of Textbook Publishers	No. of Daily Newspapers	No. Employed in Printing and Publishing	No. of Companies in Data Processing Products and Services, 1968	No. of Airlines
New York	12.0	131	11	125,100	236	63
Los Angeles	7.6	1	3	42,400	49	31
Chicago	7.0	18	7	96,900	115	26
Philadelphia	5.0	12	3	38,600	36	26
Detroit	4.3	1	2	19,800	17	17
Boston	2.8	11	4	24,100	18	16
Washington, D.C.	2.9	7	3		29	17

Source Data: *Editors and Publishers Market Guide 1970*; textbook publishers: list of members of the American Textbook Publishers Institute; data processing–computer companies: *Computer Yearbook & Directory 1968.*

communication media in America, every nation has a major city which is its communication hub. London, Paris, Rome, Tokyo, Moscow, and Buenos Aires, for example, dominate the electronic flow of information in their own countries.

Table 7-1 shows the dominance of New York in book publishing and data processing companies. The major urban areas of the country account for a very high proportion of all communication industries and services.

Another measure of the information-handling potential of a population is its accessibility to private means of communication. The telephone is most important. Figure 7-2 plots the number of telephones of all kinds (private, commercial, government) for a selection of cities in the United States and Turkey as a function of their size. The first thing that we see is that the data form two discrete groups. Turkey, an emerging nation, has fewer telephones per capita in every case. Generally speaking, in both the United States and Turkey there is a direct relationship between city size and the number of telephones. However, New York City, Washington, D.C., Istanbul, and Ankara all have proportionately more telephones per capita than the other settle-

ments. This is a clear indication of their central role in the communication complexes of their respective countries.

It is interesting to note that cities in both nations show a nearly straight line or *linear* relationship on the graph. Turkish settlements, however, are scattered farther on either side of the trend line describing the relationship between telephones and population. In other words, their *variance* is greater. This indicates that there is a greater degree of variation in the communication capacity of Turkish settlements than for those in the United States. Large cities in both cultures play inordinately important roles in their countries' quaternary systems.

The emphasis placed upon large cities can be shown by another, more comprehensive measure. Large companies maintain their headquarters offices in major cities. This is confirmed by the data shown in Table 7-2 and Figures 7-3 to 7-5. The data given in Table 7-2 clearly indicate the predominant role played by New York City and Chicago in business management. Other American cities also serve as headquarters for far-flung business empires, but to a lesser degree. The maps that follow illustrate the connectivity which exists between New York City, Chicago, Pittsburgh, Los Angeles, Detroit, and the rest of the coterminus United States and Canada.

This clustering of management results in a geographic focusing of information flow upon a few large cities. When the absolute numbers of people and messages in the world were small, the urban experience within such central places was comprehensible and manageable. Now that we are undergoing runaway growth of both population and information, cities are becoming more difficult places in which to live.

The communication revolution

The communication revolution which has taken place in the last few decades has changed all our lives. The invention of new ways to record, store, and transmit information, as well as the development of additional approaches to logic and thought, has accelerated the world's flow of information. Every century has seen an increase greater than the one before. Every decade, particularly in the last hundred years, has experienced a geometric growth of information handling. For example, in the nineteenth century type was set by hand at a top speed of about 1 character per

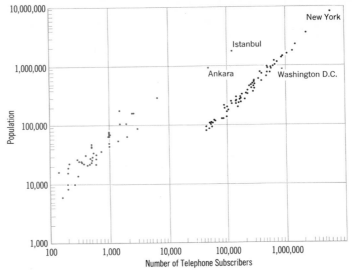

Figure 7-2 The number of telephones by size of city in Turkey and the United States, 1970 The number of telephones as a function of the size of a city in Turkey and the United States yields linear but separate trend lines when plotted on double logarithmic graph paper. The difference in the location of the trend lines reflects the much greater use of communication in the advanced nation compared with the emerging one. The closeness of the points to each regional trend line indicates a unity or system of communication in each region, with the two largest cities far and away the most important communication centers. In Turkey, Istanbul is the largest city and Ankara is the capital. The same relationship exists in the United States between New York City and Washington, D.C. As one would expect, Wahington, D.C. has more telephones per capita than normal. This can be seen by its location off the trend line to the right, even though there are other cities which both are larger and have more telephones than the capital city. (Compiled from data in *Statistics of Communications Common Carriers,* Dec. 31, 1968; Turkish telephone directories; *Census of Population by Administrative Division,* Republic of Turkey Prime Ministry, State Institute of Statistics, 1965)

Table 7-2   Location of Headquarters of the 500 Largest U.S. Industrial Corporations, 1971

City	No. of Corporations
New York	115
Chicago	38
Pittsburgh	15
Cleveland	14
Los Angeles	11
Philadelphia	11
St. Louis	9
Detroit	8
Minneapolis	8
Milwaukee	8
Other cities	263

Source: *Fortune,* May 1971.

second. Mechanical typesetting machines built during the last 75 years have raised this to about 5 characters per second. At the present time photographic typesetting machines with mechanical character selection achieve rates of 500 per second, and electronic composing machines have reached speeds of 10,000 char-

Urban Communication: Information Flow and the Mean Information Field

129

Figure 7-3 Location of plants, by state, for the 500 largest U.S. corporations with headquarters in New York City (After William Goodwin, "The Management Center in the United States," *The Geographical Review*, vol. 40, no. 1, January, 1965, pp. 8–10; data from *Moody's Industrials*, 1962; and *Thomas' Register of American Manufacturers*, 1961, copyrighted by American Geographical Society of New York)

Figure 7-4 Location of plants, by state, for the 500 largest U.S. corporations with headquarters in Chicago (Op. cit., Figure 7-3)

Figure 7-5 Location of plants, by state, for the 500 largest U.S. corporations with headquarters in San Francisco and Pittsburgh
(Op. cit., Figure 7-3)

A view of midtown Manhattan. Manhattan Island contains a concentration of corporation headquarters, financial institutions, advertising firms, and radio/television companies. All these and many more business, governmental, and cultural institutions rely very heavily for their operation on information exchange among themselves and with the rest of the world. New York City is well equipped to facilitate such exchanges by the complexity and high density of human affairs conducted here.

*Human
Geography:
Spatial
Design
in World
Society*

132

acters per second. This increase in the ease and speed of typesetting is paralleled by improvements in high-speed presses, publishers' accounting procedures, and the shipment of books and newspapers to readers throughout the world. The resulting flood of reading materials of all kinds is illustrated by two sets of data shown in Tables 7–3 and 7–4. The United States' mails are a major means by which publications reach the American reading public. In the 20 years between 1948 and 1968 the volume of materials shipped at the library postal rate increased 20 times by weight! In the 6 years from 1963 to 1968 the value of all types of books sold in the United States rose by more than 50 percent.

This incredible increase in communication by the printed word has been matched by similar increases in radio and television. Here, as in any communication system, terminal facilities are important. Commercial broadcast stations in the United States and its territories increased by nearly 1,000 from 1965 to 1968. Receiving sets of all kinds increased by more than 250 million in the period from 1950 to 1967. Tables 7–5, 7–6, and 7–7 show similar increases for other countries throughout the world. The number of phonographs in use in the United States in the same 18 years rocketed from 16.8 to 51.0 million. In banking, another area of communication and information handling, similar expansion has taken place. Examine the next check that comes your way. You will notice a set of numbers printed in the lower-left-hand corner. Those numbers are printed with a special shape so that optical scanners can read and sort them. All such checks are routed to their home banks by automatic devices which sort and channel thousands per hour. An indication of the explosion in information handling that has taken place is that if all such checks were sorted by hand, this job alone would require the labor of every man in the United States between the ages of eighteen and forty!

And so we arrive at another paradox in our lives. We cannot handle, unaided, the immense communication burdens within a mass society. But as we solve problems of volume by greater and greater standardization and by substituting more and more machines to do our work for us, we inevitably change our life-styles. There is no way to go back to the simple agricultural world of our grandfathers and still keep the conveniences which serve us. Who among us is ready and willing to sacrifice postal service and printing presses, radio and television, credit cards and checking accounts for the quiet life? And yet part of our modern world is a nearly unmanageable flood of data and information which all these things pour in upon us. What happens to human beings in the path of such an onslaught and what alternatives do they have?

Information Overload in City Systems

If the average person lives 75 years and sleeps one-third of each 24 hours, his waking life will be 50 years long. Within this period of consciousness it has been estimated that 10^{16} (ten thousand trillion) bits of information will be processed by him. The rate at which this huge store of information can be handled depends upon the means by which the information is transferred, the individual's health, and his skills. Experiments indicate that reading is perhaps the fastest and most effective way for humans to process information. If we take this as the optimum case, then a well-trained speed reader might average 3,000 bits of information per minute. Not everyone can read so rapidly, and the prospects of bringing every reader up to his fastest reading rate through special training are slight. It is reasonable, therefore, to take the average reading rate for the general population as closer to 1,500 bits per minute. Richard L. Meier suggests that at this rate a person who reads 350 days per year for 12 hours each day could accommodate an information flow of 400 million bits of information per year. Even at double the assumed rate the total figure still would be less than 1 billion per year. We must also keep in mind the rather unrealistic assumptions that our

Table 7–3 Pounds Shipped by Mail at the Libraries Materials Rate in the United States

1948	5,746,751
1953	7,133,881
1958	45,586,019
1963	69,327,734
1968	101,240,000

Source: *The Bowker Annual of Library and Booktrade Information* Bowker, New York and London, 1970, pp. 59.

Table 7–4 General Books Sales of All Types in the United States, in Dollars

1963	1,673,000,000
1968	2,568,000,000

Source: Table 7–3, op. cit., p. 28.

subject would read without stopping, that he would not have to react to what he read beyond passively assimilating the information, and that all forms of communication could be made as efficient as reading.

The discrepancy between Meier's estimate (50 Billion bits in 50 years) and the first estimate of 10^{16} bits in the same period occurs because the larger number includes all the nonverbal messages contained in our environment as well as those on the printed page. For example, a picture is a two-dimensional or areal array of information, while printed matter is one-dimensional (linear) in form. In other words, one picture really is worth 10,000 words. Consider, in turn, the even greater amount of information contained in the volumetric environment that surrounds us.

Meier further estimates that the current growth rate of per capita information transmission is between 3 and 6 percent per year. Furthermore, there is no indication that this rate will diminish. Table 7–8 shows his estimate that the per capita flow of information in a modern city is about 100 million bits of information per year. At a conservative growth rate of 3 percent the information available per person would reach 200 mil-

Table 7-5 Increase in Communication Media for Selected Countries

Country	1972 Population (millions)	Per Capita Gross Natl. Income (U.S. $)	Radio Receivers Thousands 1960	Radio Receivers Thousands 1970	% Increase	Per 1,000 Inhabitants	Television Receivers Thousands 1960	Television Receivers Thousands 1970	% Increase	Per 1,000 Inhabitants
United States	209.2	4,240	170,000	290,000	71	1,412	55,600	84,600	52	412
Sweden	8.2	2,920	2,744	333*		41	1167	2513	115	312
France	51.9	2,460	10,981	15,796	47	314†	1902	10,121†	432	201†
Japan	106.0	1,430	12,410	25,742	107	255†	6860	22,658	230	215
U.S.S.R.	248.0	1,200	58,600	94,600	61	390	4788	34,800	627	143
Argentina	25.0	1,060	3,500	9,000	157	370	450	3,500	678	144
Mexico	54.3	580	3,300	14,005	324	276	650	2,978	358	59
Turkey	37.6	350	1,352	3,072	127	87	1	25†		0.7†
Colombia	22.9	290	1.971	2,217	12	105	150	800	433	38
Algeria	15.0	260	596	700†	17	52	60	100†	67	7†
Egypt	35.9	160	1,500	4,400	193	132	50	475	850	14
Kenya	11.6	130	57	500†	777	48†		16		1.5
India	584.8	110	2,148	13,387	451	22	0.4	25		0.05
China	786.1	Est. under 100	7,000†	115,000		16	10	300†		0.4†
Nigeria	58.0	Est. under 100	143	1,275	791	23	1	75		1.4
Afghanistan	17.9	Est. under 100	24	248†	933	16†				

*Decrease due to combined radio-TV licenses.
†1969 data.
‡Estimate.
§1965 estimate.
Source: *U.N. Statistical Yearbook 1971* and Population Reference Bureau, Inc., 1972.

Table 7-6 World Distribution of Telephones

Region	Thousands 1966	Thousands 1970	% Increase 1966 to 1970	Telephones per 100 inhabitants 1966	Telephones per 100 inhabitants 1970
Africa	2,618	3342	28	0.8	1.0
North and Cen. America	108,151	132,294	22	36.1	41.2
South America	4,469	6,137	37	2.6	3.2
Asia	20,603	33,229	61	1.2	1.6
Europe	59.720	80,776	35	13.3	17.4
Oceania	4,540	5,879	29	25.4	29.1
U.S.S.R.	7,872	11,000	40	3.4	5.0
World	208,500	272,700	31	6.2	7.4

Source: *U.N. Statistical Yearbook 1971.*

Table 7-5 (cont.)

Country	Newsprint Consumption Kilograms per capita		Telephones Thousands		Per 100 inhabitants	
	1955–1959	1970	1966	1970	1966	1970
United States	35.7	43.5	98,789	120,218	50.3	58.7
Sweden	23.8	42.7	3,573	4,307	46.0	53.7
France	10.4	11.9	6,554	8,774	13.3	17.2
Japan	6.0	19.1	16,012	26,233	16.1	25.1
U.S.S.R.	1.6	4.0	7,872	11,000	3.4	5.0
Argentina	6.7	10.8	1,527	1,748	6.7	7.5
Mexico	2.4	3.1	928	1,506	2.1	3.1
Turkey	0.7	2.0	386	577	1.2	1.6
Colombia	1.7	2.4	500	809	2.8	3.8
Algeria	0.7	0.3	143	184	1.2	1.3
Egypt	1.0	1.0	335		1.1	
Kenya	0.3	0.4	57	77	0.6	0.7
India	0.2	0.4	927	1,175	0.2	0.2
China		0.7				
Nigeria	0.1	0.1	73	80	0.1	0.1
Afghanistan		0.04	9‡		0.1	

Table 7-7 Estimated world book production, 1955–1969

Region	Book Production by Number of Titles		Number of Titles per Million Inhabitants		Percentage Distribution of Book Production		Percentage Distribution of Population	
	1955	1969	1955	1969	1955	1969	1955	1969
Africa	3,000	8,000	13	23	1.0	1.6	8.3	9.7
America, North	16,000	71,000	66	226	5.6	14.3	9.0	8.8
America, South	9,000	12,000	72	64	3.2	2.4	4.6	5.2
Asia	70,000	100,000	47	50	24.6	20.2	55.0	56.0
Europe	131,000	225,000	320	489	46.0	45.4	15.2	13.0
Oceania	1,000	5,000	68	265	0.3	1.0	0.5	0.5
U.S.S.R.	55,000	75,000	279	313	19.3	15.1	7.4	6.8
World total	285,000	496,000	106	140	100.0	100.0	100.0	100.0

Source: Unesco Statistical Yearbook 1970.

Urban Communication: Information Flow and the Mean Information Field

135

Table 7–8 Information Transmission in a Metropolitan Area of 5 Million Population

Mode of Reception of Social Communications	Time Allocated (in millions of person-hours per year)	Estimated Receiving Rate (in bits per minute)	Estimated Flow (in millions of millions of bits per year)
Reading	4,000	1,500	360
Television	6,000	400	144
Lecture and discussion	4,000	200	50
Observation of environment	3,000	100	20
Radio	1,500	300	30
Films	160	800	8
Miscellaneous	5,000	100	30
Total			642
Per capita average—100,000,000 bits per year.			

Reprinted from Richard L. Meier, *A Communications Theory of Urban Growth,* published for The Joint Center for Urban Studies of the Massachusetts Institute of Technology and Harvard University, by permission of M.I.T. Press, Cambridge, Mass. © 1962, p. 130.

lion bits in 36 years and the practical limit of human processing in 72 years. If the faster rate is selected for our calculations, the 400 million limit would be reached in 24 years—just about the year 2000. Obviously, something will happen before urban man is faced with such an overwhelming and unrealistic flow of information! Automation and computers may relieve us of some of the burden but cannot spare us completely. Other psychological defense mechanisms exist within us to protect us from too much stress. The unconscious use of such defense mechanisms accounts in large part for what we take for granted as typical urban behavior.

Responses to urban overload

The moose challenges Captain Kangaroo to a game of catch and tosses him a table tennis ball. The captain catches it and returns it quickly. Moose then tosses two at once; again returned. Four, five, a dozen, the captain frantically grabs at the cascade of balls and flings back a few. Finally a flood of table tennis balls pours down on a silent, unresisting figure. The captain, overwhelmed, has *turned off*. His response to too many table tennis balls

may be a standard joke on children's television, but the effectiveness of the scene comes from how well it matches realities we all have experienced. When too much of anything comes our way, something has to give.

Stanley Milgram has suggested a number of ways in which city dwellers adjust to conditions of urban overload. A person walking near Times Square in New York City will have the opportunity of face-to-face contact with 220,000 people within 10 minutes of his hotel room or office. Across the Hudson River in Newark, New Jersey, he would be able to meet only 20,000 people in the same 10-minute walking radius. Still farther out in the suburbs this figure would decrease to 11,000 or less. The hordes of pedestrians encountered near Times Square are overwhelming. In order to accommodate themselves to such numbers New Yorkers have adopted patterns of behavior for which they are famous. First of all, they always seem to be in a hurry. Another way of stating this is that city dwellers apparently *allocate less time for each transaction or casual contact.* Money is thrown down on the counter and a newspaper snatched up; subway tokens are purchased hurriedly and without comment. When the number of contacts or information inputs increases drastically, less time can be allocated to each encounter.

City dwellers are often accused of being callous and unconcerned with the plight of their fellow man. At face value, this may well be true. But in terms of the community or social group of which they feel themselves a part, they will be no better or worse than rural folk. When a New Yorker steps over a drunk collapsed in the entryway of his apartment building, he is again responding to urban overload by *disregarding low-priority inputs.* Energy and time, money and emotion must be carefully parcelled out when there are so many drains upon each person's limited supplies.

City living forces people to constantly *redraw the boundaries that define their lives in order to spare themselves and shift the burden to the other party.* Stores selling faulty merchandise will disclaim responsibility and send the frustrated buyer to the factory representative. The City Department of Streets will tell an apartment dweller that the broken sidewalk in front of his building is the responsibility of the landlord. The landlord will reply that it is the job of the city to repair such things.

Urbanites reduce or block off reception of all kinds before it's allowed to happen. Everyone seems to wear sunglasses in the city. All the pretty girls have blank eyes like plexiglass curtains drawn between themselves and the passing crowd. No businessman, lawyer, or doctor will see anyone without an appointment; and the usual comment of the famous to the press is "No comment."

Associations within the city are often fleeting and superficial. *The intensity of inputs is diminished by filtering devices.* Many people seek the anonymity of city life. Both fugitives from justice and celebrities weary of recognition welcome city crowds into which they can merge unnoticed. Friendships are formed among a person's co-workers and not geographically. People can live for years in the same apartment building, pass each other in the halls, stand together in the elevators, and never become acquainted.

Finally, *special institutions are formed to absorb inputs that might otherwise overwhelm the city dweller.* Peddlers and parades must be licensed, and police enforce noise abatement laws. Welfare departments care for the poor, who might otherwise ring every doorbell and stop every pedestrian in search of alms. Everyone "lets his fingers do the walking" in the classified pages rather than personally traveling from store to store in search of what he needs.

On another level of interaction, ethnic neighborhoods can be considered informal institutions which have grown up over long periods of time. These neighborhoods become habitats which are familiar and therefore less stressful for specific social groups. Greenwich Village with its counterculture and the Bowery with its bars and bums tend to segregate and institutionalize life-styles in New York City just as do the Left Bank in Paris and Soho in London. In this way, ghettoes may represent in part the self-imposed, protective clustering of minority groups. This is not to deny that powerful forces beyond the control of minorities constantly work to keep them contained in undesirable areas. But just as the dependents of American military personnel form "little Americas" in foreign cities, so may people speaking the same language or practicing the same religion voluntarily seek each other out for protection and relaxation. Zoning laws provide a more formal way of institutionalizing certain kinds of land use. This creates special city environments by excluding industry, determining street widths and property setbacks, and providing open space in the form of parks. All these measures tend to lessen the density or rate of information flow, thus protecting the individual.

The relationship between cities, information flow, and people can be outlined quite simply. One of the chief reasons for the existence of cities is the opportunity for face-to-face contacts which are important for service (tertiary) and information-handling (quaternary) activities. So many people and so many communication outlets may accumulate within the city that its inhabitants become overloaded with information. The alternatives resulting from conditions of information overload are the breakdown of the system or the creation of mechanisms and attitudes which protect or buffer individuals. Flight to the suburbs and special institutions are two of many such mechanisms. An entire set of attitudes which distinguish city dwellers from their country cousins may also develop. These distinctions are described below.

Urban and rural attitudes

It is possible to characterize the sharp contrast between urban and rural society by the phrases *city slicker* and *country bumpkin*. Other contrasting pairs of words like *cosmopolitan* and *bucolic* also suggest themselves. The city is thought of as a place of innovation and change, while the small town stands for tradition and stagnation. The city dweller is sophisticated; his behavior is *cool*. That is, little or nothing surprises him or makes him flustered. The tourist from the small town, on the other hand, is overwhelmed by the tall buildings, the crowds, the thousands of sights. He is what comedian Fred Allen called a *yuck*, the provincial who gapes at skyscrapers. These contrasting behavior patterns are easily explained in terms of adjustments to information overload. The city dweller, accustomed to the flood of contacts at the urban core, has developed attitudes which protect him, His noncommittal sophistication is simply one way of making a virtue out of omitting what he can't handle. The unsophisticated visitor has not yet had time to overload and responds to the same situations in a naïve manner.

Personal appearance becomes very important in the city. Since most contacts are fleeting in urban situations, the clothes one wears become symbols of status and attitude. Hair styles, particularly men's hair length, also assume the function of costumes telling the role a person plays. In the small town, conformity to some accepted norm is more im-

portant. Everyone knows who everyone else is, so why hide it? Along with all of this is the utilitarianism of city life. It's not a man's background that counts, but rather his skills, accomplishments, and bank balance. In small towns, conversely, family ties and length of residence are more important. There are still some places in New England where people, residents for 50 years or more but born elsewhere, are considered newcomers or strangers.

The city dweller views the world as changeable, and he values material progress. This comes in part from his emphasis on the material appearance of the people with whom he has brief contacts. Anything goes as long as it leads to success. Geographically speaking, high land values near the city center increase competition for land use. Buildings are continually being torn down and new ones built in their places. The actual environment in which the city person lives is more likely to change than are the ageless country hills. On the other hand, truly rural people, subjected to the unpredictable whims of weather which make or break farmers' fortunes each year, may be more fatalistic. That is, they accept whatever fate has in store for them, for their chances of changing the course of events is slight. This notion is again reinforced from a geographical point of view if we consider the high population density of cities combined with the immense concentration of wealth in these central places. A natural disaster which might wipe out a few rural families and go unnoticed except by the unfortunates will evoke massive efforts of aid and reconstruction if it strikes a city. Not only is the city able to marshall people and wealth, it is also located at a focal point of communication lines and news media which report its condition to the world. Some cities dominate the world news. For example, while New York City's problems are of spectacular proportions, New York City is not alone in its troubles. And yet for every newspaper article or news item telling about the woes of Pittsburgh, Calcutta, or Buenos Airies, there are several relating Manhattan's problems. This is in large part a reflection of the concentration of news media, writers, and broadcasters in the area.

Contrasts between rural and urban life-styles and attitudes result many times from differences in the geographical scales at which people view their environments. Inhabitants of both very large and very small settlements identify with events occurring in their home areas more than they do with those in other places. A man may think of himself as a New Yorker, or he may identify himself, for example, as a Shadypointer if he happens to live in Shadypoint, Oklahoma. New York City has a population of nearly 8 million; Shadypoint has only 300. And yet if a New Yorker reads of crime or violence anywhere within the far-flung limits of his city, he will feel his security threatened just as much as would the citizen of Shadypoint if trouble happened there. It matters very little that New York is 25,000 times larger than Shadypoint, for the *vulnerable space* of each person matches the approximate dimensions of the settlement in which he lives.

The boundaries of the world perceived by people in large and small settlements vary in much the same way. The big-city dweller will be accustomed to seeing strange behavior and dress; his perceptual horizon will extend to include other city modes in the world system of which he is a part. Rural people, at the other extreme, draw the perceived boundaries of their world along nearby landmarks. Even if the daily mobility of two people from large and small settlements is much the same—let us say each travels 5 miles to work and 5 miles home—the richness of the urban scene will expand the worldly experience of the city dweller more than any village environment will.

The Mean Information Field

Frequency of contact between people, their mobility or use of space, and the richness of information within their environment all play a part in shaping a population's life-style. The geographical concept of the *mean information field* (MIF) of the individual can be used to operationally define the relationship between human contacts, mobility, and information availability.

Nonspatial variables

Every environment contains information of many kinds in very large quantities. Only a portion of the total amount of information which surrounds a person will be available to him. Just as we receive information from all sides, so do we communicate messages to the people and environment which surround us. Not everything we transmit outward is received or understood. Sometimes we refuse messages; sometimes our own messages are rejected by others. The ability and willingness of people to receive and send information depend upon their education, training, and culture. This ability to communicate is also a function of a person's chronological age. Very small children find little to enjoy at motion pictures. An illiterate wandering in a library will be as isolated from information as he would be on a desert island. An observant, well-trained farmer reads much more from the landscape than does a city dweller.

Daily contact space

Our ability to communicate with other people also depends upon our ability to overcome the *friction of distance*. Distance as a geographic variable has been discussed at length in Chapters 3 and 4. We can translate those ideas into the individual's ability to communicate with others by observing that the people we contact most frequently are those closest to us in space. The farther from us a person is located, the less likely are our chances of communicating with him. Our ability to communicate across space depends upon our access to means of transportation and communication. If you do not own or drive a car, if you cannot write letters or read, or if you do not have the price of postage or of a telephone call and can't afford a bus ticket, the range of your communication is very limited.

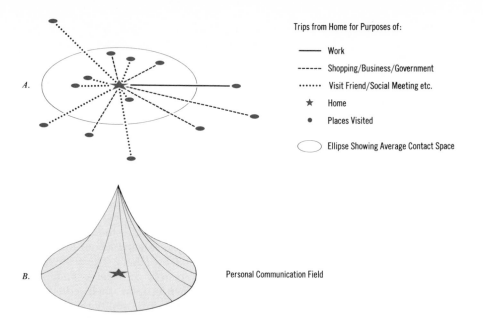

Figure 7-6 Daily contact space and personal communication fields A
person is usually counted for census purposes at his place of residence. But
people are not always at home. Part *A* of the diagram represents a typical
collection of other places visited at varying frequencies and distances from
home. The ellipse shows the average distance to these other locations
appropriately weighted by frequency of contact. It is only with in this
space that a person has contact with other people and with communication
devices. Part *B* shows an idealized personal communication field which
indicates the range and intensity of potential contact. This idealized cone
would vary by culture and by individual.

The *mobility* or *space-using capability* of each
person is important in determining his ability
to send and receive information. Shut-ins
and stay-at-homes lead impoverished lives.
Housewives detained by small children in
suburban kitchens sometimes show signs of
having been kept in solitary confinement. On
the other hand, people commuting to the city
share two worlds, suburban and urban.

The average or usual area across which a
person moves each day enhances to a greater
or lesser degree his ability to communicate,
for the size and character of this area will
help to determine the number and type of
people with whom he comes in contact. This
daily contact space of the individual deals
with regularly occurring events rather than
those which are out of the ordinary. In other
words, the daily contact space of a person
would be defined by his trip to work, shopping
trips, and normal journeys for social purposes. Once-in-a-lifetime migrations and
unusual trips such as journeys while in the
armed services are excluded. To create or
draw the daily contact space of an individual,
his usual trips are plotted on a map. This may
be shown as an actual pattern of moves or
generalized as a simple form such as an ellipse
(Figure 7–6).

The daily contact space of people varies with
age, occupation, and culture. A baby's contact
space is limited at first to his crib and his
mother's arms, then to one or two rooms,
next to a house and yard, and finally to a
neighborhood as the child grows older. Young
adults are probably the most mobile in Ameri-

*Human
Geography:
Spatial
Design
in World
Society*

140

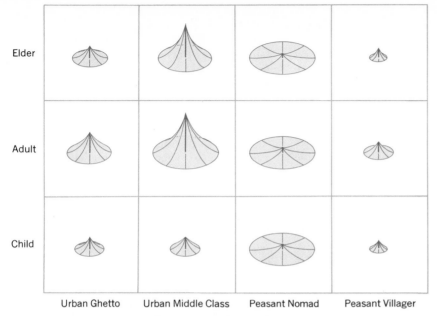

	Urban Ghetto	Urban Middle Class	Peasant Nomad	Peasant Villager
Elder				
Adult				
Child				

Figure 7-7 Hypothetical communication field, by age and culture
Personal communication fields can be expected to vary by age, occupation,
and culture. In most societies, working adults håve the greatest spatial
range and are engaged in more transactions than the young and old. Nomads
travel widely but with fewer transactions per day.

can culture, while increasing old age restricts the geographical area which people utilize in their daily lives. Businessmen commuting to the city cover more space than do their wives, while traveling salesmen see more of the world than do typists and desk-bound administrators. Women in some cultures are confined for most of their lives to harems visited only by husbands, sons, and brothers. Nomads may wander over miles of pasture, while peasant farmers tend only a few restricted acres of land. The *daily contact space* of people is shown in Figure 7–7 as part of their *personal communication fields.*

The mean information field

We may think of each person as standing at the center of a cone-shaped tent, the inner volume of which represents all the contacts he makes with others. This tent (Figure 7–6)

can be referred to as his *personal communication field.* Its shape describes the *allocation* of his contacts over space. The height of the center pole is proportional to the general probability of his communicating with someone nearby in contrast with his communicating with someone farther away. The slope at which the walls of the tent fall away is the rate at which his contacts diminish with distance. The diameter of the tent is a measure of his ability to overcome distance through his own mobility and his use of communication devices. However, the actual number of people contacted by an individual varies as a function of his age, occupation, and culture. Therefore, we must multiply this personal communication field by the total number of contacts made by the individual in a given time.

Obviously, a baby will interact intensely with an extremely limited number of people nearby. His *actual contact field* will be very

*Urban
Communication:
Information
Flow and
the Mean
Information
Field*

141

peaked, steeply sloping, and small in volume. An urban middle-class adult will occupy a communications tent with more gently sloping walls, a larger diameter, and a significantly larger volume of contacts. Conversely, as the elderly communicate with fewer and fewer people, their fields become smaller. The size of actual communication fields also varies from one socioeconomic group to another and from culture to culture. Figure 7–7 also shows the actual communication fields of people from different cultures at different ages. Because personal and actual communication fields vary greatly from individual to individual within any culture, it is useful to aggregate or summarize such fields in order to show the behavior of particular populations. Each of these aggregates is referred to as a *mean information field* (or by its abbreviation, MIF).

Operationalizing the MIF

If we wish to apply these ideas to the real world, we must find ways of assigning values to the terms we have introduced. In other words, we must make them operational rather than theoretical. The question is, how much and over what distances will the average member of a society exchange information with other people? That is, what will be the shape of the communication tent he occupies, regardless of its absolute volume?

The Swedish geographer Torsten Hägerstrand pioneered attempts to make the concept of the MIF operational. Recognizing that it is impractical if not impossible to learn every movement and every exchange of information in an entire population, Hägerstrand searched for surrogate indicators of total communication. He chose local migration patterns as one measure of the general communication potential of a group living in Asby Parish in central Sweden. This choice was based upon the premise: "The intensity of migration must consistently be in close proportion to the frequency of communicative impulses."

Hägerstrand reasoned that few people will permanently change their homes without considerable information about the place to which they are moving, and that the more known about an area, the more people will move there. Such information must result from previous contacts and messages flowing back and forth between the place of origin and the migrants' destinations. Migration data for Asby Parish showed that most outward moves were to nearby places and that the number of migrants rapidly diminished over distance. When the frequency of migration was plotted against the distance migrated, a curve showing the effect of the friction of distance on communication could be drawn (Figure 7–8A). Similar data were gathered by William Garrison and others for Cedar Rapids, Iowa. In this case all members of 250 households kept records for 30 days of every trip they made for any purpose. It was assumed that travel frequency would serve as a surrogate indicator of the intensity of total communication within the Cedar Rapids community (Figure 7–8B). Tables 7–9 and 7–10 give the number of moves and their distances for Asby Parish and Cedar Rapids.

Both of the curves plotted on the basis of the data in Figure 7–8A and B have shapes which show a distance decay function. The formula for these curves is expressed as $Y = aD^{-b}$, where Y will be the expected number of resettled migrants per square kilometer (in the Swedish case) or the expected number of trip contacts (in the American case), D will be the distance from the point of origin, and a and $-b$ will be constants determined by the empirical data shown in the tables.

In order to determine their spatial distribution the data could be plotted as bulls-eye patterns centered on the point of origin of the migrants and householders. But it is more convenient if we transform the data into rectangular matrices which can be easily multiplied and otherwise manipulated. Using the above equation, we can fill in a 5 by 5 grid containing 25 cells, each 5 kilometers on a side, with the number of migrants and contacts we might expect to find in cells at given distances from the central point of origin. Tables 7–11a and 7–12a show the expected distri-

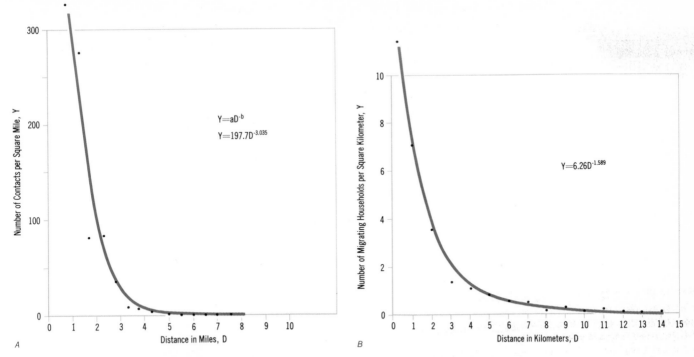

Figure 7-8 *(A)* **Number of migrating households per square kilometer from the Asby district, Sweden** These data were compiled from birth and migration records for the Asby area.
(B) **Number of contacts per square mile from residences in Cedar Rapids, Iowa** These data were compiled from travel diaries kept by a sample of households in Cedar Rapids, Iowa. The location of all places visited for a one-month period were used to establish the personal contact field.

bution of migrants in Sweden and household contacts in Cedar Rapids.

If we try to compare the two grids, we are immediately faced with a near impossibility of matching the data recorded in corresponding cells. How can we equate hundreds of migrants with thousands of household trip contacts? A further manipulation of the data is necessary in order to attain comparability. If we assume that the contacts in all 25 cells represent 100 percent of the contacts for the community in question, then we can change the raw data in each cell into the percentage equivalent of the total by dividing the value in each cell by the sum of all the cells. After

doing this we end up with grids showing the cell-by-cell percent distribution of the total communication within each community (Tables 7–11*b* and 7–12*b*). Note that the values in the latter grids total 1.0000. Since the total value in each case equals unity, we may think of it as 100 percent. We may also describe such grids as the distribution of probabilities of a contact being made somewhere within the total area represented. For example, in the Swedish case, out of every 10,000 migrations we could expect, 4,432 to terminate within 5 kilometers of their point of origin, that is, inside the center cell of the grid. Out of the same 10,000 migrations only 96 would termi-

Urban Communication: Information Flow and the Mean Information Field

143

Table 7-9 Observed Local Migration in the Asby Area, Sweden

Distance in Kilometers	Number of Migrating Households	Ring Area in Sq. Kilometers	Number of Migrating Households Per Km.²
0.0- 0.5	9	0.79	11.39
0.5- 1.5	45	6.28	7.17
1.5- 2.5	45	12.57	3.58
2.5- 3.5	26	18.85	1.38
3.5- 4.5	28	25.14	1.11
4.5- 5.5	25	31.42	0.80
5.5- 6.5	20	37.70	0.53
6.5- 7.5	23	43.99	0.52
7.5- 8.5	18	50.27	0.36
8.5- 9.5	10	56.56	0.18
9.5-10.5	17	62.82	0.27
10.5-11.5	7	69.12	0.10
11.5-12.5	11	75.41	0.15
12.5-13.5	6	81.69	0.07
13.5-14.5	2	87.98	0.02
14.5-15.5	5	94.26	0.05

Source: Duane F. Marble and John D. Nystuen, "An Approach to the Direct Measurement of Community Mean Information Fields," *Papers and Proceedings of the Regional Science Association,* vol. 11, 1963; adapted from Torsten Hägerstrand, *Innovations förloppet ur Koroloquisk Synpunkt,* Meddelanden fran Lunds Universitets Geografiska Institution, Avhandlingar XXV, Gleerupska Univ.-Bokhandeln, Lund, Sweden, 1953.

nate in the northwest corner cell. Chances of householders in Cedar Rapids, Iowa, contacting people over 5 kilometers away are even less. Out of every 10,000 trips 8,992 were to destinations within 5 kilometers of the starting point. Only 6 out of 10,000 would end up in each of the corner cells.

Let us return now to the assumption that the data on which the above values are based serve as accurate measures of the general ability and willingness of individuals to communicate. This distribution of probabilities can be described as the *mean information field* for an average individual located at the source of the data. In one case, Asby Parish would occupy the center of the grid; in the other, Cedar Rapids. In this way, we have been able to give values based upon empirical evidence to the general ideas started at the beginning of the discussion.

Weighting the MIF

The MIF described above assumes an average and centrally located person whose mobility has been included as part of the surrogate measure chosen to represent him. That is, he is considered to be stationary in the center of his daily contact space. The probability of his contacting another person extends outward from him in a regularly diminishing and symmetrical field. The problem is that regardless of his potential ability to interact with people, he can only do so if there are people with whom to interact. But population is not homogeneously spread across the land in real life. People cluster in cities and disperse in rural areas. In order to better match reality the matrix of the MIF should have squares with different values or weights according to underlying population distributions.

If the friction of distance in connection with other variables results in his having half his communication potential distributed within the central grid cell which he occupies but no other recipient actually shares the cell with him, then half his potential is lost for lack of co-communicators. *The potential number of contacts is shown more realistically as the product of the potential probability (shown by*

Table 7-10 Observed Personal Contacts in Cedar Rapids, Iowa

Ring	Number of Contacts	Contacts per Sq. Mile
0.00–0.50	1661	2115.92
0.50–1.00	770	326.69
1.00–1.50	1082	275.53
1.50–2.00	442	80.41
2.00–2.50	584	82.72
2.50–3.00	301	34.88
3.00–3.50	73	7.15
3.50–4.00	80	6.79
4.00–4.50	47	3.52
4.50–5.00	4	0.268
5.00–5.50	4	0.242
5.50–6.00	18	0.996
6.00–6.50	9	0.458
6.50–7.00	8	0.377
7.00–7.50	4	0.176
7.50–8.00	0	0.000
8.00–8.50	35	1.350
8.50–9.00	2	0.069
9.00–9.50	0	0.000

Note: The mean distance of the sample households from the Cedar Rapids CBD was 1.35 miles.
Source: Duane F. Marble and John D. Nystuen, "An Approach to the Direct Measurement of Community Mean Information Fields," *Papers and Proceedings of the Regional Science Association*, vol. 11, 1963.

the MIF) and the actual distribution of population. Figure 7–9 illustrates this for the MIF of the Asby area (Table 7–11b). It should be noted that the probabilities weighted by population add up to more than 1.0000. Again, it would be difficult to compare this grid with any other, so we must *normalize* it by dividing the value in each cell by the total value, thus assigning a percentage of the whole to each cell. The normalized probabilities again total 1.0000, although the distribution of values is no longer symmetrically arranged around the center cell.

Communication and Spatial Diffusion

When gold was discovered at Sutter's Mill in California, relatively few people knew of it for the first week or two. This was because, regardless of the discoverer's desire for fame or secrecy, there were not many persons nearby to receive and pass on the message. As word reached San Francisco and finally found its way to the Eastern states, more and more carriers and recipients became available. The news *diffused* to every corner of the land, and the gold rush was on. The rate at which that information spread was a function of the MIF and the population distribution of the people involved. Once the idea reached densely populated areas, it spread rapidly. We can imagine how this process works if we consider that each person who receives the message immediately becomes a new sender. As more and more senders are created, the news descends from all sides upon those still ignorant of it. At the same time, the advance of the news into untouched territory proceeds in a stepwise fashion from one communication field

Table 7-11a Expected Migration Grid for the Asby Area

2.38	3.48	4.17	3.48	2.38
3.48	7.48	13.57	7.48	3.48
4.17	13.57	110.00	13.57	4.17
3.48	7.48	13.57	7.48	3.48
2.38	3.48	4.17	3.48	2.38

Source: Duane F. Marble and John D. Nystuen, "An Approach to the Direct Measurement of Community Mean Information Fields," *Papers and Proceedings of the Regional Science Association*, vol. 11, 1963.

Table 7-11b Percent Distribution of Total Communication in the Asby Area

.0096	.0140	.0168	.0140	.0096
.0140	.0301	.0547	.0301	.0140
.0168	.0547	.4432	.0547	.0168
.0140	.0301	.0547	.0301	.0140
.0096	.0140	.0168	.0140	.0096

Note: The entries in each cell denote the probability of a receiver in that cell coming in contact with a carrier of information who is assumed to originate in the center cell. Cells are 5 × 5 km.
Source: Duane F. Marble and John D. Nystuen, "An Approach to the Direct Measurement of Community Mean Information Fields," *Papers and Proceedings of the Regional Science Association*, vol. 11, 1963.

Urban Communication: Information Flow and the Mean Information Field

Table 7-12a Expected Personal Contact Grid for Cedar Rapids

2.62	5.30	7.48	5.30	2.62
5.30	21.42	60.98	21.42	5.30
7.48	60.98	3677	60.98	7.48
5.30	21.42	60.98	21.42	5.30
2.62	5.30	7.48	5.30	2.62

Note: Cells are 5 × 5 km.
Source: Duane F. Marble and John D. Nystuen, "An Approach to the Direct Measurement of Community Mean Information Fields," *Papers and Proceedings of the Regional Science Association,* vol. 11, 1963.

Table 7-12b Percent Distribution of Total Communication in Cedar Rapids

.0006	.0013	.0018	.0013	.0006
.0013	.0053	.0149	.0053	.0013
.0018	.0149	.8992	.0149	.0018
.0013	.0053	.0149	.0053	.0013
.0006	.0013	.0018	.0013	.0006

Note: Cells are 5 × 5 km.
Source: Duane F. Marble and John D. Nystuen, "An Approach to the Direct Measurement of Community Mean Information Fields," *Papers and Proceedings of the Regional Science Association,* vol. 11, 1963.

to the next. The greater the overlap of communication fields, the faster it will spread.

Geographers are concerned primarily with the spatial aspects of diffusion processes. They share this interest in particular with anthropologists who have studied the idea of *culture hearths* and *culture areas*. A culture hearth can be thought of as some location on the earth's surface inhabited by a group of people whose inventiveness creates ideas, traits, customs, and inventions which move or diffuse outward until people in possibly remote areas also utilize them. Similarly, a culture area is a geographically defined portion of the earth's surface the population of which shares a set of ideas, traits, customs, and inventions which distinguish that group from all others. The distinction between the two is the *originality* of things moving outward from the hearth; the inhabitants of a culture area in most cases share a collection of

things which have come from all over, though a few may have originated at home.

Distance-dependent diffusion processes

In the above respect, culture hearths are thought of as generating *diffusion waves* which, moving outward from their source, carry "messages" like ripples expanding outward from a rock thrown into a lake. While these ideas were originally discussed in qualitative terms by anthropologists Clark Wissler and A. L. Kroeber, it was Hägerstrand, using his work with the MIF, who first simulated quantitative measures of diffusion. Hägerstrand's treatment of diffusion looks at the process over a number of time intervals. At every succeeding time the "wave" moves farther through space from its source. Models such as this are *distance-dependent* and *spatial* in character.

Hägerstrand's work with diffusion models warrants closer inspection, although what we present here, of necessity, must be only the bare outline of his ideas. Hägerstrand's initial interest was in developing a theoretical explanation of the spread of innovations. In order to test his ideas, he needed data giving both the times and places at which an innovation was accepted as it spread from its point of origin. In searching for such sets of data, he became interested in the spread of Swedish government subsidy programs for farmers throughout rural Sweden. These included the acceptance of government pasture subsidies by farmers who were willing to fence in their land in order to protect forests from grazing animals, and the use of tests to detect bovine tuberculosis. His efforts to understand the processes by which use of pasture subsidies spread from farm to farm provide us with an introduction to his work in general. Figure 7-10A to D shows the farms in a portion of western Sweden which accepted government subsidies in the period from 1928 to 1933. By accepting such subsidies, farmers received money to fence in and improve their pasture lands. One might think that such aid would

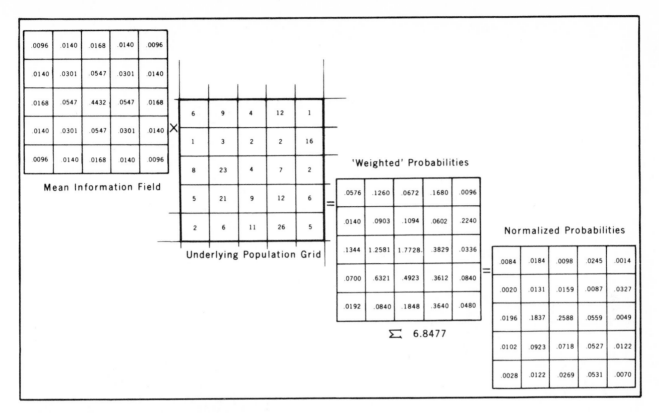

Figure 7-9 Mean information field weighted by underlying population distribution See text for explanation. (Peter Gould, *Spatial Diffusion*, Association of American Geographers Commission on College Geography, Resource Paper No. 4, Washington, D.C., 1969, p. 32)

be immediately accepted by all the eligible farmers in the area, but an inspection of the maps shows that acceptance was at first slow and spatially irregular. The western part of the area developed ahead of the eastern section, which lagged behind. The diffusion process, as revealed by the maps, appears to have been complex and to have had a strong spatial character. Many more acceptances occurred among farmers adjacent to neighbors who already had the subsidy, and far fewer occurred in more remote spots. Hägerstrand reasoned that if he could simulate such a pattern of spatial diffusion, using as few and as simple rules as possible, he would gain valuable insight into how development and change take place in a spatial context.

His first attempts to simulate patterns resembling those shown in Figure 7–10 used a single source, or "knower," located on a homogeneous and isotropic plain with an evenly distributed population of potential "acceptors." He assumed that such a knower, or innovator, would tell one neighbor after another, and that once told, a neighbor would accept the subsidy without further persuasion. Thereafter, each new acceptor would subsequently tell his neighbors. Hägerstrand further assumed that information was spread only when two people exchanged messages. Such paired meetings would take place at constant intervals. One person would tell another in the first generation, or time period; two would tell two more in the next generation; and so

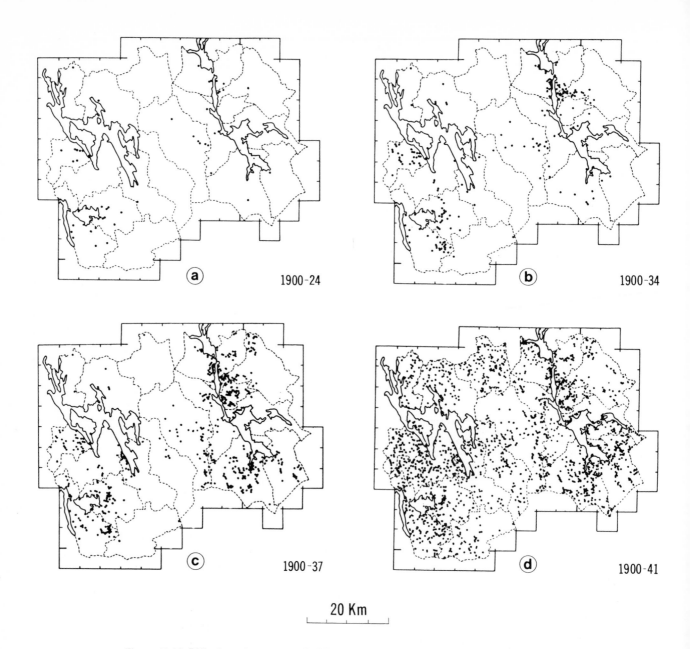

20 Km

**Figure 7-10 Diffusion of pasture subsidies in the Kinda-Ydre district,
Sweden, 1928–1933** The dots represent farms accepting the subsidy
program. (From T. Hägerstrand, *Innovation Diffusion as a Spatial
Process*, trans. by Allan Pred. Chicago: University of Chicago Press,
1967. The original book was published in Swedish by C. W. K. Gleerup,
Lund, Sweden, 1953)

forth. The probability of one person's telling another would depend upon the linear distance between those who had already adopted the subsidy and potential acceptors. In other words, those nearby would have a greater chance of learning than those far away. Also, such probabilities for contact would depend upon some empirically derived measure of the MIF in Sweden. In this case, the MIF for Asby was used (Table 7–11*b*). While some of these conditions might seem unrealistic, the simplicity which they imposed upon the model had greater advantages.

To activate the model, Hägerstrand at each time period "floated" the MIF of Asby over every acceptor from the previous generation one at a time, and one new paired contact was randomly chosen for each acceptor. The farmer contacted thereupon became a knower or message sender in the next and all subsequent generations. As more and more farmers accepted the innovation, the contribution of the central cells to the spreading pattern became less important. At the same time, if an acceptor was hit for a second time in some subsequent generation, that effort was considered redundant and was therefore not counted.

The results of Hägerstrand's initial efforts showed similarities to the actual distribution, but nevertheless they were somewhat disappointing. Too much variation occurred between the model and reality and also between one run of the simulation and another. In order to correct for such variation, Hägerstrand introduced further modifications into his model.

In his next effort, he weighted the MIF by the underlying uneven distribution of population and also introduced barriers which either prevented or slowed communication. These barriers in large part represented the lakes which broke up the area in western Sweden. Hägerstrand also began his diffusion with twenty-two original knowers rather than a single subsidized farm. Figure 7–11*A* to *D* shows the actual diffusion of pasture subsidies for four time periods. Impenetrable barriers are shown by solid lines and semipermeable

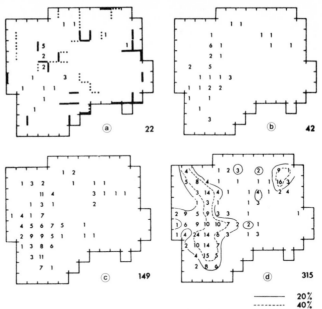

Figure 7-11 **Actual diffusion of pasture subsidies in matrix form** The data have been prepared in this form for easy manipulation. (from T. Hägerstrand, "On Monte Carlo Simulation of Diffusion," *Quantitative Geography*, ed. by W.L. Garrison and D.F. Marble, Northwestern University Studies in Geography, no: 13, 1967, p. 17)

barriers by dotted ones. Any cell lying on the leeward side of such a barrier—that is, the barrier falls between the teller and the potential acceptor—is either prevented from receiving the message in the impenetrable case or, for example, can receive the message only 50 percent of the time if the barrier is 50 percent permeable.

Runs with the improved model were conducted much as were those with the original one. In the improved case, the MIF was floated over each of the twenty-two original knowers in turn. The MIF was then weighted according to the underlying population distribution, as shown in Figure 7–9. (It should be noted that since the distribution of population varied relative to the location of each innovator, the weighted MIF was different in each case.) After that, one paired contact was randomly chosen for each innovator. In the next time period, or generation, the original inno-

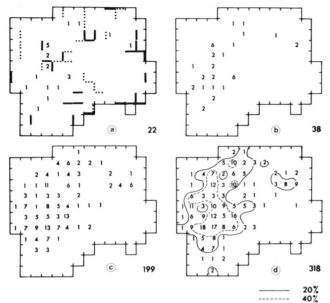

Figure 7-12 Simulated diffusion of pasture subsidies in matrix form The model includes barriers and is adjusted for underlying population of farms. Map A depicts the arrangement used at the start of the simulation. Compare the actual pattern with the simulated one. (Op. cit. Figure 7-11)

vators again were allowed paired meetings, but so were those with whom they had come in contact the previous time. The simulation was stopped when the number of acceptors approximately matched the actual number shown in 7–11D.

This method of choosing locations randomly but according to an underlying set of probabilities (in this case, shown by the weighted MIF) is called the *Monte Carlo method* and can be used for many purposes. Hägerstrand can be said to have created a *Monte Carlo model of spatial diffusion*. The results of his second attempts were very good. The simulation at four different time periods is shown in Figure 7–12A to D. A visual comparison shows remarkable similarity between the actual and the simulated final patterns (Figures 7–10D and 7–12D). In fact, if we consider the simple set of premises underlying the model, we should be impressed by its power of predic-

tion. Among other things, this model did not take into account the influence that mass media, such as newspapers, radio, and government agencies, might have. Word of mouth communication through paired meetings has been the principal medium of diffusion assumed by the model. The success of the simulation indicates that such contacts are extremely important in spreading ideas and innovations.

The Monte Carlo method of simulating spatial diffusion has subsequently been tested with other examples. Hägerstrand went on to show that it could clearly describe the spread of tests for bovine tuberculosis on Swedish farms. Leonard Bowden used similar techniques to study the decision to drill wells and use irrigation water from underground sources as that technology spread across the plains of eastern Colorado. Starting with the location of forty-one wells in 1948, his simulation of the location of 410 wells in use in 1962 was so close that he went on to predict the location of 1,644 wells that may be in use in 1990. One of the rules Bowden incorporated in his 1990 model was that no more than 16 wells could be drilled in any one township. His study was so persuasive that the local authorities adopted the 16-well-maximum rule. It will be interesting to watch that area and learn in the years ahead how close Bowden's prediction comes to reality, particularly since the acceptance of the 16-well rule makes the process something of a self-fulfilling prophecy.

Richard Morrill, using similar techniques, simulated the spread of the black ghetto in Seattle, Washington, from 1940 to 1964. His work was particularly concerned with the mechanics of "block busting" whereby real estate speculators take advantage of the unfounded fears of white home owners that black neighbors will drive down property values. In this case, more than one contact had to be made before a white resident would sell out or a black family move in. In the words of Peter Gould, "A certain threshold value had to be reached before the barrier crumbled."

Ideas such as the threshold concept can be incorporated into spatial diffusion models, making them even more accurate and, incidentally, more complicated. Students continuing in geography will want to examine the work of Hägerstrand and others more closely. We, however, would like to point out that the above studies using the Monte Carlo method were carried out at both regional and neighborhood scales and that these techniques meet the geographers' criterion of being useful at many different spatial levels.

Figure 7–13 shows the distance-dependent diffusion of the Brazilian honeybee *Apis mellifera adansonii.* Technically speaking, these bees are not "knowers" but, rather, an expanding life-form. However, the diffusion they follow in hiving off and swarming to new locations is analogous to the spread of disease or rumors or even the spread of knowledge of domesticated plants among early man. This bee was originally imported into Brazil from Africa in 1956. In 1957, twenty-six swarms were accidentally released in São Paulo, Brazil. The rapid spread of these insects is of particular importance because of their aggressive and unpredictable behavior, their danger to man and animals with whom they come in contact, and their ability to replace other bees. These bees have spread rapidly through the mechanism of hiving off and swarming to new homes over relatively short distances.

If this bee were to reach North America, it might mean the end of the beekeeping industry in the United States, since their viciousness would necessitate their destruction. The resulting loss to American agriculture through inadequate plant pollination has been estimated at as much as 5 billion dollars annually. A committee of the National Research Council has monitored the advance of these bees across South America. The committee points out that control of the bees in the vastness of the Amazon basin is beyond anyone's means. They recommend that every effort be made to stop them at the Isthmus of

Figure 7-13 Spatial diffusion of the Brazilian honeybee This honeybee, which is unusually vicious, poses a threat to the people in the areas it invades. There is a proposal to try to halt its advance at the Isthmus of Panama, thus preventing its spread to Central and North America. (Gerald S. Schatz, "Countering the Brazilian Honey Bee: Aftermath of a Biological Mishap," *News Report, National Academy of Sciences*, vol. 22, no. 8, October, 1972)

Panama by placing new types of breeding bees with more desirable genetic characteristics in their path. Some colonies will also have to be killed or given new, less dangerous queens in order to control the menace in the heavily populated areas of South America. In any event, knowledge of diffusion processes provides scientists with better means of becoming ecological watchdogs.

Hierarchical diffusion processes

Another type of diffusion study derives more from the work of sociologists who view

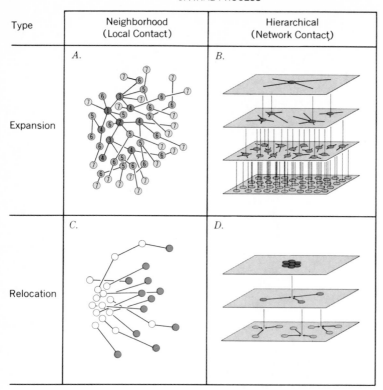

Type	Neighborhood (Local Contact)	Hierarchical (Network Contact)
Expansion	*A.*	*B.*
Relocation	*C.*	*D.*

Figure 7-14 Types of diffusion Examples of each type of diffusion include: (*A*) neighborhood spread of a rumor or disease, (*B*) hierarchical spread of a national fad, (*C*) shift of frontier homesteads, (*D*) migration to a metropolis.

Human Geography: Spatial Design In World Society

diffusion as an interaction process between individuals which can take place between peers without reference to their geographic locations or by moving up and down social or administrative hierarchies. Such models are *hierarchial and nonspatial* except in the sense that movement from one level of a hierarchy to another represents changes in scale. Another aspect of diffusion studies concerns whether the number of people sharing the thing diffused increases with each move or time period or whether the number of such "knowers" remains constant.

Various combinations of these traits are possible. For example, the movement of styles from one metropolitan center to another and then outward from those points to surrounding cities and thereafter to towns is both hierarchical and spatial. Figure 7-14 presents four basic combinations: in two the "knowers" remain constant in number but move either spatially or hierarchically; in the other two the numbers increase with each time period although the process can be either distance-dependent or hierarchically structured. The diffusion processes where numbers increase have particular significance in terms of human and other ecosystems. The spread of irrigation wells and that of honeybees are examples of neighborhood diffusion.

One example of spatial hierarchical diffusion is the growth of the Sierra Club, an organization dedicated to helping people explore and protect wilderness areas (Figure 7-15). The club was founded by John Muir and a group of friends in San Francisco in the year 1892. For many years it remained only in that vicinity. However, individual membership became increasingly widespread. In 1906 the members living in the Los Angeles area wished to form their own local chapter. Thereafter, there was a short-range diffusion of chapters in California. By 1930 a chapter was opened in New York City. Several years later the Great Lakes chapter located in Chicago was organized. In 1960 the club members decided that they could become an effective national organization, and further hierarchical growth took place from New York, Chicago, and other early centers. At the present time the Sierra Club is among the major environmental lobby groups in the United States.

Communication as a Catalyst for all Urban Activities

Geographic theory suggests that the manipulation of information and knowledge has been a major reason for the existence of cities. Certainly, the transactions which take place in urban places trigger and control most of the world's activities. This viewpoint, however, does not describe or explain most of what

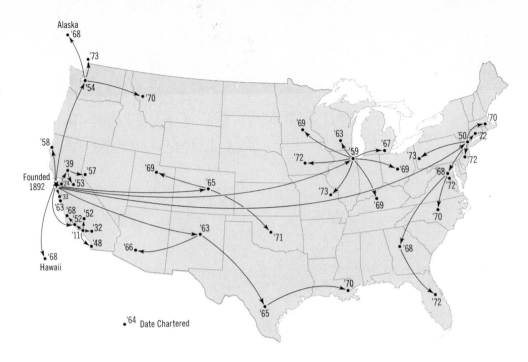

Figure 7-15 Growth of the Sierra Club—an example of hierarchical diffusion The hierarchical diffusion linkages are defined wherever a descendent chapter is formed from territory previously assigned to antecedent chapter. An example is the Mackinac Chapter territory in the state of Michigan, which was formerly a portion of the Great Lakes Chapter, including eleven states with chapter headquarters in Chicago.

actually takes place in settlements of all sizes. In fact, quaternary and tertiary activities provide the economic foundation only for what we call *service centers* or *central places.* Many towns and cities depend instead upon manufacturing or the production of raw and semi-finished materials for their survival. The flow of information through the hierarchy of urban places may direct all such activities but in most cases furnishes them with very little direct economic support. Information, rather, serves as a catalyst producing much greater reactions. While centrality and connectivity are significant in hierarchies of central places, other factors are important in the location of primary and secondary industries. The next chapter looks at additional elements which help to create patterns of production. But no matter what other geographic elements fall within the limelight, no matter how slight the role played by information flow seems, we must remember that without a steady flow of messages nothing would take place.

Come to the highest peak in the land and view the sweep of the continent. Let imagination extend our vision in order to see not only the plains, mountains, and coastlands with their routes and cities, but also the origin and movement of messages, goods, and materials everywhere across the land. If we exercise our wits a bit more, we can liken the scene in its entirety to some complex form of life with nervous and circulatory systems, in fact, to one endowed with all the parts necessary for maintaining its dynamic, moving form.

If quaternary activities and the cities which support them can be compared to the brain and nervous system of this gigantic organism, then the tertiary services are analogous to the functions performed by veins and arteries distributing oxygen, nutrients, and fluids throughout its body. In this fanciful comparison, the raw materials produced by fields and mines become similar to the food and water consumed by every living thing. There remains the role played by the digestive tract and glands, for which we need seek a comparison. And such a comparison comes immediately to mind: The manufacturing complexes of the world and their activities can be easily equated with those organs which change raw food into substances the body can use. Finally, of course, both the body and the land must be able to dispose of waste products quickly, easily, and safely.

It is not our intention to carry this comparison any further. We use it only to point out the interrelatedness of urban activities with those in rural areas and of the important systems, both man-made and natural, which bind them together. If the world is to remain healthy and suitable as the home of man, its many parts must function well together. If each of us is to contribute to this state of global health as well as help to maintain and restore it, we must understand earth's physiology and metabolism. Nor is it worthwhile or practical to separate man and his works from those of "nature." Ultimately, we live in and with nature and are part of it. If it falters or perishes, so too, inevitably, will we all.

The centers of secondary production where manufacturing takes place are just as important as quaternary and tertiary activities within the man-land global system. The ideal function of manufacturing complexes is to provide for all material human needs in a manner and at a rate which will bring no cumulative harm to the total life-support system on earth. This aim may be further divided into two interdependent ones, the first being to maximize production while minimizing economic cost, the second to assure continuing production at a minimum of costs or damages to society and nature. This second aim has received scant attention until recently. Now we are concerned with maintaining a clean environment while at the same time finding sources of energy capable of allowing humans a sufficient and acceptable level of living. Since only a few short centuries ago North America and the other parts of what is now the modern industrial world contained only the simplest of Neolithic or preindustrial manufacturing activities, it is worthwhile to consider the patterns of urban and industrial growth in space and time that have led to the present world condition.

Urban History: A Geographic Point of View

Economic development, urbanization, and population growth interact in many ways. The thumbnail urban history which follows is a simplified description of an extremely complex situation. As such, it depends for its organization upon the dimensional concepts which we have already reviewed. We hope it demonstrates how the geographical point of view can be used to clarify a complex subject.

For this discussion we may think of settlement history as consisting of three stages, each representing a set of demographic and urban conditions, each lending itself to certain geographical concepts. The first, or earliest, period begins about 8,000 to 10,000 years ago with the beginnings of urban settlement. It continues until the first part of the Industrial Revolution in the eighteenth century, and could be called *the period of settlement foundation*. The second starts with the Industrial Revolution and promises to extend for some time into the immediate future. This might be called *the period of settlement consolidation*. The third period is less clear; but beginning sometime in the years ahead, it should extend for a very long if unpredictable span of time and might be called *the age of world urbanization*. The lines between these periods are indistinct. History is seldom divided into neat compartments. Nevertheless, unless some immense disaster overtakes the human race, this discussion about future conditions is probably reliable in view of present and past circumstances.

In the first period of urbanization, populations were small and scattered. Growth was sporadic. Sometimes a series of good years would allow a rapid increase in some favored area. Later, disease, famine, or other catastrophes might reduce or reverse population trends in the same area. Meanwhile, another spot might experience slight population growth. At first, no true cities existed. Settlements were little more than collections of farmhouses which might appear on regional maps as point locations. The archaeological evidence from Jarmo, an early Near Eastern example of this period, shows a cluster of farmhouses first appearing about 8,750 years ago. In the centuries that followed, food supplies became more secure and some social differentiation and technical specialization took place. By 4250 B.C. small cities appeared in the lowlands of Mesopotamia. Those early cities contained homes of artisans. City populations were nevertheless very limited, and those settlements were either built in easily defended locations or surrounded by walls and moats. Each city controlled the territory around it much as the Greek and Italian city-states did in later periods of history.

As farming technology improved, bringing increased supplies of food, populations slowly enlarged. Better weaponry, the growth of administrative skills, and an accompanying increase in transportation technology gradually brought neighboring towns and cities together under the control of larger, more powerful governing bodies. Heads of state usually lived in urban settlements, and these capitals very often grew more rapidly than their neighbors. Trade developed and exchanges of goods and raw materials increased, especially where water transportation was possible.

Perhaps the most important phase of city growth in ancient times was the development of the Greek *polis*. The independent Greek city-states produced some of mankind's finest political, literary, architectural, and artistic achievements in the few centuries in which they flourished. At the same time, the Greeks characterized their world as being divided

Patterns of Development: Process of Regional Growth

into two parts, the core, or *oecumene*, and the lands beyond. The *oecumene*, from the Greek point of view, was the hearth of civilized behavior and all important activity. Beyond the *oecumene* were the lands of the Barbaroi, the uncouth, uncivilized barbarians. This concept of a core area as a separate and important world has been revived in modern times and given a special meaning which will be described below.

By the end of this long and complex period of settlement foundation, nations and empires had appeared and disappeared many times over. But throughout most of this time, the world's cities were surprisingly tiny. Estimates of city size for ancient, and even medieval, times are "educated guesses" at best, but the measures of the magnitude are still small. Rome, the dominant urban example of the classical world, according to one estimate had perhaps 350,000 people in the first century A.D. London in Roman times was little more than a modest town, nor did it grow rapidly afterwards. By 1377, its population was a scant 35,000. Meanwhile, Rome's population in 1526 had been reduced to 55,000. In this sense, our initial view of cities as points when compared with the areas of the regions they controlled is not unreasonable. The importance of cities in this first period was in their development of a way of life distinct from that followed by the more numerous country folk surrounding them.

The second period of urbanization, which began in the eighteenth century, was ushered in by the Industrial Revolution. Actually this revolution was characterized by dramatic changes in many fields, not just in methods of manufacturing. Scientific farming with mechanization, improved seed and stock breeding, better fertilizing techniques and field crop rotations meant more food with less investment in labor. Medicine developed preventive as well as curative skills. The steam engine radically changed land and sea transportation. The telegraph was invented, and communication of all kinds improved. The possibility of disaster areas going unaided through lack of news became less

and less likely. As a result populations increased. Subsequent rural crowding and dislocations, combined with opportunities in the industrial cities, led new generations to seek lives centered on urban patterns and places. London in 1800 had grown to 850,000 people. Amsterdam increased 2.25 times to 224,000 in the years between 1650 and 1850. By 1950, Greater London had grown to nearly 11,000,000 while Amsterdam in 1963 had 868,000 inhabitants. Rome in 1965 had just less than 2,500,000 people.

While the whole world in 1800 contained perhaps only one or two urban areas which exceeded 1 million people—and those were in East Asia—the United Nation's 1970 *Demographic Yearbook* listed fifty-five cities and urban concentrations with over 2 million. At the same time, the physical size of cities dramatically increased. The invention of the internal combustion engine and hydrocarbon fuels resulted in the rapid outward expansion of built-up areas from their original sites. Electricity and new building techniques also altered and expanded the urban landscape. New terms used to describe urban places have found their way into the language. Census books now list "standard metropolitan statistical areas" larger than incorporated cities. The built-up urban area of southeast England which centers upon the City of London is officially known as the "Greater London Conurbation." The word *megalopolis*, coined by Jean Gottman to describe the continuous strip of urban development incorporating several independent cities between Washington, D.C., and Boston (Figure 3–7), is now being used to describe similar areas in the Midwest and Europe.[1]

Cities now extend over large areas, and thinking of them as point phenomena becomes less and less practical. Los Angeles covers more than 454 square miles; Detroit, within its city limits, exceeds 139 square

[1]It is interesting to note that Gottman's term which was originally intended as a proper noun describing a specific geographical location has now become a generic term indicating a type of place and has thus become nominal rather than locational in its meaning.

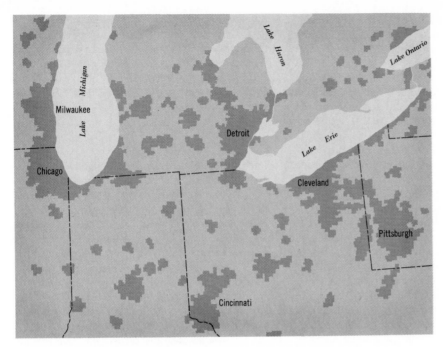

Figure 8-1 Upper Midwest megalopolis, United States, 1970 Areas of high-density urban development which are made up of coalescing metropolitan areas appear in several places around the world. The Upper Midwest of the United States has such a development. (Adapted from *Atlas of the United States of America,* U.S. Dept. of the Interior, Geological Survey, Washington, D.C., 1970)

miles. In 1961, the 3.2 million people living in the Central District of the Greater London Conurbation occupied 117 square miles; the total conurbation was much larger, containing 616 square miles and 8 million people. While no one knows the exact amount of the earth's surface covered by urban or "built-up" features, one estimate of the area occupied by the 668.1 million people living in cities and urban places of more than 100,000 exceeds 8,100 square miles. This is equivalent to a city almost the size of Massachusetts, or one-half the size of Denmark.

The second stage of urbanization, which has been called a period of city consolidation, is continuing at the present time. Numerous urban areas already exist, and more are appearing on all the world's continents except Antarctica. Note that the emphasis here is on the term *area*. Each urban area is not only expanding, but is already joined to all the others by increasingly complex transportation links. The competition for space to expand is growing, and cities as distant from each other as San Francisco and Los Angeles may vie for the same resources such as drinking water supplies. Typical of these coalescing urban areas is the incipient Midwestern megalopolis growing up around and between Detroit, Toledo, Cleveland, Buffalo, and Toronto (Figure 8–1). Similar conurbations in the German Ruhr, the Randstadt in the Netherlands, and the Tokyo-Yokohama area of Japan also exist, nor do these few examples exhaust the list.

The third probable stage of urban growth will take place in a world inhabited by more than 6 billion people. This period can ap-

Patterns of Development: Process of Regional Growth

propriately be called the age of world urbanization. Some time after the year 2000, when world population numbers between 6 and 20 billion, favorable sites for city expansion will be almost completely occupied. At that time area–area urban relationships will be at their fullest. The major cities of each continent will have expanded until no space remains unfilled in the more habitable areas along the main lines of communication connecting them. Instead of many very large cities there will be a smaller number of megalopolislike urban regions (Figure 3–12).

Perhaps these regions will merge into a single world-city which has been given the name *Ecumenopolis* by Constantinos Doxiadis the Greek planner and architect. It is fitting that the ultimate city should be named by a Greek whose ancestors coined the word *oecumene* to describe the civilized limits of their world. However, if it comes to pass, Ecumenopolis promises to be something very different from what we have already experienced. The problems inherent in managing, servicing, cleansing, and policing a city of such gigantic proportions would be nearly overwhelming. Whether this vision of a future urbanized world may seem apocalyptic to some readers or exciting to others, the statistical projections of current urban and demographic trends substantiate the above description of the development of settlement as a spatial process. That is, steady demographic increase from small to vast populations inevitably will lead from settlements as sets of points to one great network of interconnected areas taken up with urban structures and activities of all kinds and surrounded by almost unpopulated agricultural and waste lands. Let us now look at the economic and technical growth of regions, particularly in the United States, in order to more fully appreciate the implications of such processes.

The Economic and Technical Growth of Regions: The United States

The United States is among the great manufacturing countries of the world. However, within its boundaries there is great variation in production from region to region. What characteristics describe those parts of the United States that grew into powerful commercial and industrial centers? Why did some places never grow industrially and why have some declined?

Some historical conditions

The United States is rather a special case, for it is one of the few countries which was "born free." That is, the growth of the nation and the nation's industries coincided with the general rapid increase in technological and productive skills which we have come to know as the Industrial Revolution. The American population from the very beginning had no significant traditional society of peasants and nobility within it. At the same time, like it or not, the native American Indian population had been in large part removed from its original lands and partially destroyed. The formative years of industrial development needed an enormous labor force which was supplied by the importation, family by family, of the uprooted masses of Europe. We often refer to the America of the nineteenth and early twentieth centuries as *the melting pot*, wherein people of many backgrounds and persuasions were merged. But it might be more accurate to call it the *grinding mill* between the stones of which immigrants, largely stripped of their native cultures, had of necessity to conform to new modes of life. The changes in society necessary for industrial development were harder to bring about in complex traditional societies such as those which existed in Europe and Asia.

The economic growth of America can be viewed in terms of three factors or inputs designated by classic economics: capital, labor, and raw materials or resources. A fourth element worthy of consideration is the role of the entrepreneur, who provides managerial and organizational skills. As geographers we will consider the importance of relative situation or locational advantage in the growth of industry. It is also important to consider the way in which political processes influence development. These factors are intertwined in every system, whether "Western" or communist or feudal.

In the early United States private profit was the major motive underlying the growth of industry. The rapid influx of unskilled workers provided a labor surplus available at low wages. Before union organization forced a more equitable distribution of profits (an issue still considered unresolved by many), wealth went to the organizers of industry and commerce. This was the era of *robber barons* and *captains of industry*. The former raped the land of its natural resources; the latter ground the faces of the workers in the quest for profits.

Stage one: Initial exploitation

At first, direct exploitation of natural resources was the means of gaining wealth. The gold fortunes of California are a prime example, but there are many others, including those made from:

Fish and lumber in New England

Coal in West Virginia

Lumber, iron, and copper in Michigan

Silver and gold in Colorado

Lumber in the Pacific Northwest

Grasslands and petroleum in the Great Plains

The soil itself throughout the South and Midwest

Development of these resources took capital which came from (1) foreign investment, (2) Eastern financiers in well-developed areas far behind the advancing frontier, and (3) local money, especially from *nouveau riche* entrepreneurs first on the scene. It was not the miners, or lumbermen, or fishermen who got rich. It was the saloon keepers, merchants, and early manufacturers.

Stage two: The takeoff point

In every case the accumulation of capital led to a *takeoff stage* marked by a period of rapid expansion and enormously wasteful exploitation of resources. Only the cream of the land was skimmed off. The buffalo were slaughtered; Michigan white pine and California redwoods devastated; the seas emptied of herring and the whale herds reduced to isolated individuals. It was a time of *once-and-for-all, git-and-git-out* exploitation of nonrenewable resources. High-grade gold, silver, and copper were taken, shallow petroleum fields emptied, hardwood forests cut; and even now the fossil water from beneath the high plains of eastern Colorado is irrigating fields from subterranean reservoirs never to be refilled.

But we must not be completely harsh in judging the pioneers and early businessmen. Hindsight is easy, and current standards may not have always applied. The rapid exploitation of a resource to exhaustion sometimes yields another cycle of growth *providing the profits earned are reinvested in productive local industries.* For example, the hardwood forests of Michigan and Indiana provided profits which helped to create the furniture industry for which Grand Rapids is famous. In much the same way, white pine and copper fortunes were subsequently invested in the Detroit automobile industry. Early investments in machine industries, buggy manufacturing, and marine engines were an intermediate step between the mines and lumber camps and the assembly lines at Willow Run and River Rouge.

Stage three: The drive to maturity

A drive to maturity characterizes manufacturing's third stage of growth. Industry begins to import raw materials and to export finished products beyond the limits of the region. With standardization and routinization, low labor skills are required of a large labor force. This pool of workers is usually encouraged to immigrate by increased job opportunities. European migrants working in the late nineteenth century textile mills and garment factories of New York and Boston are a good example of this. Black people and Southern whites flocking to the mills and factories of Detroit and Chicago also fit this roll. At this

Aerial view of the Ford Motor Company complex, steel mill, and auto assembly plants at River Rouge, Michigan. The Ford Motor Company's River Rouge industrial complex near Detroit, Michigan, is a vertically integrated system in which basic raw materials, including iron ore, limestone, and coal, are used to produce steel which, within a few days, is incorporated into the engines, frames, bodies, and parts of completed automobiles. (Photo courtesy of the Ford Motor Company)

stage organizational capacity becomes the key to development.

At the international level, raw materials often move between countries. In this case, most of the profits will accumulate at the point of manufacturing rather than at the source. This might be described as *economic imperialism*, and in the past was accompanied by the military occupation of the resource-producing regions and the development of classic political imperialism. Nearly every large manufacturing country which has passed into the third level of industrial growth has trod the boards of this stage. The role is not always a comfortable one, as the British learned with their Empire, the French with their colonies, the Russians with East Europe and parts of inner Asia, and the United States with its many international woes and responsibilities.

At the regional level, to again cite the example of Michigan's industrial development, automobile manufacturing arose as the second great source of wealth in the state's history. Thousands of migrants were drawn there. As long as the expectations of the newcomers remained low, or as long as the environments from which they came offered an even less attractive mode of living, Michigan's urban areas and industries seemed to prosper. However, the auto industry soon became too large for the region, and remote investment opportunities had to be found for the new profits. Funds were dispersed to far-flung stockholders, were invested in national and international enterprises, and also went to create nonprofit organizations such as the Ford Foundation. From a global or national point of view these activities were quite rational, but seen regionally perhaps too little was reinvested in creating the social infrastructure necessary for further growth potential in the immediate area. As the third stage of regional development reached its peak, education became more and more important at all levels. It may be argued that not enough was invested in local schools and training programs to ensure the ultimate health of the region. More of this in a moment.

Stage four: Specialized industrial development

As the fourth phase, *specialized industrial development,* is approached, less and less depends upon the presence of unskilled labor. Automation begins to take over, and machines become more and more complex in their operation. The resulting vision of the future is a technological one. A skilled and affluent labor force becomes more and more a necessity. It must be skilled to increase productivity per worker as well as the valued added through manufacturing, and it must be affluent in order to purchase the products which result. Automobiles are again a prime example of this. Approximately 20 percent of the United States' gross national product is derived from automobiles, roads, and associated activities. (An interesting comparison can be made with the federal budget, which also represents about 20 percent of the gross national product. Since about half of the federal budget is allocated to the Department of Defense and aerospace industries, this means that the automobile industry and all its accompanying activities are twice the size of our defense effort.) The working middle class buys most of the cars produced in America and must, in turn, earn wages which allow it to support the industries which employ it.

Thus, the ideal preparation for the fourth stage of industrial development should include investment in the education and aspirations of the general population. Let us phrase this for a final time in terms of Michigan and its industry. This single industrial state is only one of several such in the United States, and yet it is more powerful, more populous, and more affluent than most nations of the world. In fact, it consumes more electrical power than all but twelve nations. In other words, more than 90 percent of all the nations use less. Detroit, its largest city, is the largest automobile manufacturing region in the world. The rest of Michigan is the world's second largest automobile manufacturing region. We say this not out of some chauvanistic or hucksterish pride but rather to emphasize that this industry and its region are sustained by an innovative, skilled, organized, and wealthly population. *Yet each generation is born without skills.* Training a stream of young people in the intricate ways of a complex industrial society is one of the most important tasks within this sort of region. Without a continuous flow of new talent as well as materials and investment funds, such a region may eventually decline. Another cause for concern is too heavy an emphasis on a single activity. As the energy shortage continues, and as gasoline becomes more and more scarce, car sales may diminish and workers may be laid off. Diversification is thus an essential yet too frequently overlooked necessity for the health of industrial regions.

Meanwhile, another element in the equation of success is the social and natural environment which results from industrial activities. The migrant poor, filling the lowest ranks of employment, are least likely to receive the education so necessary for future success. The pattern of movement of the wealthy owners and managers to the suburbs is followed in succeeding generations by the flight of affluent workers from the inner city. We need not recount the resulting urban woes discussed in earlier pages. We simply want to point out again the interconnectedness among the elements introduced in this book as it progresses.

Spiral and Cumulative Patterns of Growth

The preceding account of growth in an industrial region is largely literary in content. It will help to order some of our thoughts about the subject before moving on in the next chapter to specific and more technical details concerning the location and growth of manufacturing firms and complexes.

Following the model suggested by W. W. Rostow, we have described the four stages of growth as *initial exploitation, the takeoff stage, the stage of maturity or sustained growth,* and *the stage of specialized development.* It is tempting to add a final stage, decline and death, but such a fanciful addition would carry our analogy with the history of some living organism much too far. Since the time of the Industrial Revolution, and perhaps since the foundation of modern West European society in the Middle Ages, there has been no major geographical shift from the centers of industry which were first established. New ones have been added in America, South Africa, Australia, and Japan, but there seems no immediate or predictable demise in store for any of the world's major industrial regions. However, industrialized nations with few local sources of energy will operate under increasingly difficult circumstances.

We can picture the region of our choice and its stages of growth as a stack of horizontal slices in time. This is shown in Figure 8–2. In the lowest of our time slices the region is a small one, based largely on the exportation of raw materials. This outward flow is indicated by the broad arrow leaving the designated surface. At the same time, other elements are moving into the picture. Foreign investment, imported manufactured goods and machines, and migrants are represented by the three flow arrows focused upon the regional center. All these inward flows serve to build up the region. Local entrepreneurs accumulate savings and seek outlets for venture capital. It is not unusual for these frontier types to like to keep close track of their money and to seek nearby investment opportunities. At the same time, capital in the form of ma-chines, buildings, and stocks of goods may gradually accumulate. Population may grow through continued in-migration and natural increase, and with luck, the people's skills and education, aspirations and ability to consume more products will also grow. Increases in the size of the market will allow businesses with higher thresholds to appear. That is, the first firms to appear will supply the basic needs of the original population. Grocery stores, hardware shops (or historically, blacksmiths' forges), and food and drink establishments, all with very limited ranges and all needing relatively few customers to survive, will come first. Thereafter, firms needing larger and perhaps wealthier populations from which to draw their support will be established. Now dressmakers will appear as more women enter the population. Select foods instead of pork and beans will be stocked for the more affluent, and doctors, dentists, and printers will get their start. As the service population and the population served increase, the need for other kinds of goods will grow, and at some point local raw materials will be used for the internal production of goods once shipped in from outside the region.

While the above description has been given a slightly "boomtown" flavor for effect, the story is a true one. In pre-Revolutionary America raw materials were sent to England for manufacture into clothes and equipment which were then returned to the colonies. In a short time Yankee merchants and manufacturers had taken over the production of most imported goods, and even fine glass and silver, such as the metal work of Paul Revere, were being produced in New England. In more recent times, California exported fruit and gold and lumber in exchange for almost all manufactured goods from the East. Then, as population increased, automobile and other *assembly plants* were established. Machine and automobile parts were shipped to the West and put together there, a practice which resulted in considerable savings on freight. Finally, independent branch plants of large Eastern firms were established to

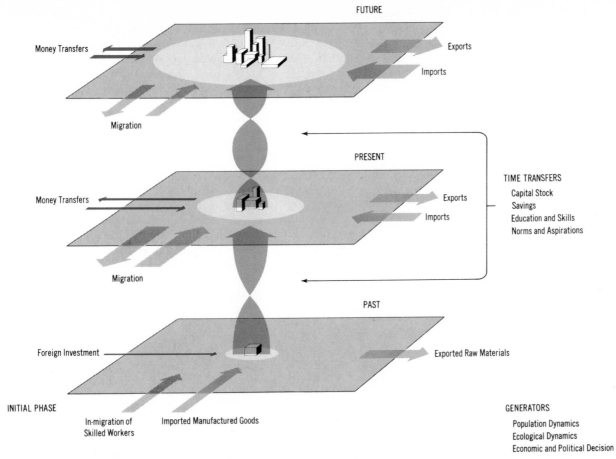

FUTURE

Money Transfers

Exports

Imports

Migration

PRESENT

Money Transfers

Exports

Imports

TIME TRANSFERS

Capital Stock
Savings
Education and Skills
Norms and Aspirations

Migration

PAST

Foreign Investment

Exported Raw Materials

INITIAL PHASE

In-migration of
Skilled Workers

Imported Manufactured Goods

GENERATORS

Population Dynamics
Ecological Dynamics
Economic and Political Decision

Figure 8-2 Regional development—circular and accelerative growth
Population dynamics include demographic change, levels of education and skill, social norms, and aspirations. Economic and political dynamics include inertia of venture capital and labor, piecemeal innovation, uneven writeoff, social overhead investment, neighborhood copying effect, changes in business thresholds, and supportive and social legislation. Ecological dynamics include depletion, overload, pollution and concentration, and secondary effects.

fabricate the parts themselves from local raw materials or those shipped in bulk from great distances. Last of all, special industries such as electronic equipment and aircraft were located particularly in the Los Angeles area. The same story could be told of countless developing countries which before their independence provided raw materials for Europe but which following the establishment of their autonomy developed industries of their own, often out of national pride and an urge for self-sufficiency.

In this sense the pattern of growth which develops is both spiral and cumulative. It is spiral in the sense that each stage leads to the next and provides the seeds for further growth; it is cumulative in that growth allows new activities and attracts additional businesses and factories which could not exist under previous conditions.

Patterns of Development: Process of Regional Growth

The middle time slice shown in Figure 8–2 illustrates this stage of sustained growth. Now imports and exports of materials and goods more nearly balance each other. The region may continue to provide raw materials for other places, but it also exports finished products in large quantities. Two additional transfers keep these flows in balance. On the one hand, money transfers move capital in and out of the region as it accumulates or is needed. At the same time, migration now moves in both directions as demands for more labor develop locally or as surpluses of particular types of workers develop. All in all, the region continues to grow in wealth, complexity, and areal extent.

Next the possibility for specialized development becomes apparent. Local capital still will be available for investment, but even more money from outside the region will become available if things look good to national and international investors. A labor pool with specialized skills may also form and provide incentive for other firms to open nearby. Less-skilled workers will move away to regions where earlier stages of growth still exist. Typical of this would be the continuing emphasis in Connecticut and Massachusetts on skilled artisans. At first gunsmiths, brass workers, and clocksmiths developed a tradition of precision work in that area. Subsequently the emphasis on precision, control, and feedback mechanisms required in the work led to present-day electronic firms and the production of modern precision instruments. At a still later date, the growth of research firms and universities further increases the emphasis on data handling and decision making and provided new paths for development. Knowledge becomes a commodity, and a shift to quaternary activities may result.

Inertia and change

Various forms of inertia work for the smooth flow of events described and illustrated above. Labor and venture capital have strong tendencies to stay at home. People become com-

mitted to a region for reasons other than their jobs, and few want to move, once having invested in homes and schools. Similarly, the amortization of industrial investments, that is, the time necessary to "write off" the initial costs of equipment and structures, is slow and uneven. Nothing ever wears out all at once, and it is usually cheaper to keep making replacements and repairs rather than to abandon a site and begin over again somewhere else. Meanwhile, people nearby learn by watching the earlier firms, and a *neighborhood copying effect* further increases the size of the region as observers become participants. Finally, the investment in social overhead may be immense. As we have already mentioned, schools and homes all cost money. So do highways, shopping centers, museums, and cinemas. The inertia exerted by all these things serves to keep industrial regions intact.

Perhaps the major negative forces which may cause the modern industrial world to rethink its priorities and to seek new spatial locations are the ecological dynamics which inevitably accompany partially planned industrial growth. By "partially planned" we mean development without due regard for the total balance of man and nature. Sometimes the depletion of a raw material will cause the decline of an industrial center, but this is rarely the case. American and European steel mills as well as those in Japan depend now upon ore and scrap from sources halfway around the globe. It is more likely that the overloading of the environment with pollutants from factory smokestacks and workers' automobiles as well as with wastes of other kinds will eventually create environments which neither management nor the workers can tolerate. Moreover, if the concentration of firms demanding commonplace yet essential resources such as pure water and fresh air becomes too great, the firms themselves through overcrowding will ruin the environment that originally made the site so desirable. The developing energy crisis may also play an important role in these matters. If fuel costs continue to increase, less efficient firms, or perhaps even regions, may find it impossible to compete with better-organized or better-endowed industrial areas. This sequence of urban growth and decay in its entirety can force or induce firms to shift their sites to more favorable areas. In the final analysis, it is these factors which may well tell the story of success or failure for the developed world in the decades ahead—or perhaps for the entire world.

The reader may ask at this point, "Yes, but what about development in socialistic and other economies different from our own?" We recognize that such cases have unique problems, but the important thing in every economy is to get the profits from resource use into the hands of people who are able and willing to reinvest the money in further development. In nineteenth century America those were the captains of industry whom we have already mentioned. In other places and at other times the entrepreneurs may have the guise of bureaucrats or national planners. We are not saying that all the profits in socialist economies are spent wisely or for the good of the people; we simply imply that the flow of resources, both natural and financial, needs to generate new cycles of growth rather than being hoarded, squandered in the pursuit of pleasure, or transferred out of the region. At the same time, we are not defending this spiraling cycle of growth; we are simply describing it.

Transportation and Regional Development

One might think that the character of a region depends solely upon its own resources, but its external relations are just as important. A significant element in Figure 8–2, "Regional Development, Circular and Accelerative Growth," is the movement into and out of the developing area at any given time. Such movements are often taken for granted, but the role of transportation is too vital to leave unnoted.

We have already shown how interaction and connectivity are essential elements of city growth. In much the same way, in order for a nation or the regions within a nation to grow there must be a progressive extension of the transportation network binding their respective parts together. This can be thought of as the spatial consolidation of the areas involved. With time, more and more point locations will be served by more and more carriers. Similarly, carrying efficiency and capacity will increase as the travel time and cost between places diminish. We are again tempted to use an analogy with living organisms, the more advanced the creature, the more complete and specialized will be its nervous, digestive, and cardiovascular systems. In order to understand this in terms of regional growth it is useful to sketch the historical development of transportation in the United States.

Historical development of transportation in the United States

Water carriers   When the European invasion of North America began, the newcomers faced a continent with more than 9 million square miles of roadless wilderness. The area that is now the contiguous forty-eight states represented somewhat more than 3 million of the total. Spanish settlement came first in Florida and the Southwest, but the main thrust of expansion came in the seventeenth, eighteenth, and nineteenth centuries from the newly established ports along the East Coast. It is not surprising that water played the most important transportation role in early times. Little investment was needed in rivers and lakes as routeways, and wood for the original small craft was everywhere available. The first input which we might think of as being modern in nature was John Fitch's steamship service which by 1790 plied regularly on the Delaware River between Philadelphia and Trenton. By 1807 Robert Fulton's steamship line had joined New York City with Albany, a 150-mile journey taking $32\frac{1}{2}$ hours. The crossing of the Appalachians and the opening of the Midwest and Great Lakes region spurred the construction of the Erie Canal, which opened in 1825. Canal after canal extended

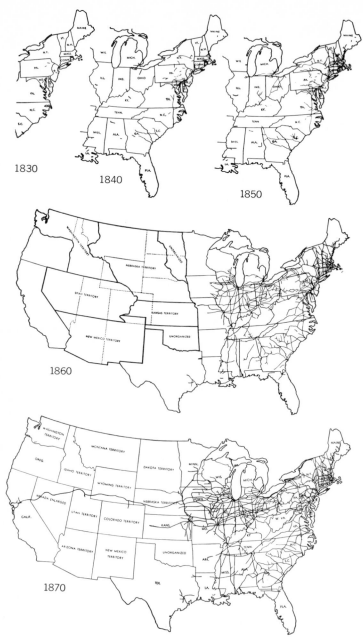

1830

1840

1850

1860

1870

the network, and by 1850 much of the north-eastern United States was served by some 4,460 miles of canals in addition to natural waterways.

The heyday of the railroads in the late nineteenth and early twentieth centuries saw a period of relative quiet for water carriers in the United States. The Mississippi–Ohio river system declined as a passenger route to almost nonexistence, while barges maintained some freight traffic along the waterway. Throughout the last hundred years, however, the Great Lakes have remained enormously important in the development of the iron and steel industry along the shores of southern Lake Michigan and Lake Erie. This was accomplished by the completion of the Sault Sainte Marie Locks in 1855 which allowed larger ore boats to ply between Lake Superior and the other Great Lakes. Finally in 1959, the St. Lawrence Seaway connected the Great Lakes and the Atlantic, thus allowing large oceangoing vessels to reach the Midwest. Surprisingly, though, the Seaway has lagged behind the expectations for its use. Containerized shipments in which pre-packaged goods can be shipped on railroad flatcars or flatbed trucks have made it possible for shippers to send their goods directly to East Coast ports which do not face being closed by ice for the winter as do those on the Great Lakes. Similarly, the canals and rivers of the Seaway still impose limits on the size of ships which can use them. The cost of deepening or widening bottlenecks like the Detroit River are prohibitive. Nevertheless, by 1968 about 287 billion ton-miles (approximately 15 percent of the total freight hauled that year in the United States) was carried on 25,260 miles of usable inland waterways.

Human Geography: Spatial Design in World Society

Figure 8-3 Growth of the United States railroad network, 1830–1870 A. The early stages of railway development in America are shown on these maps. During the decade 1830–1840 the total length of completed railroad increased from 23 to 2,818 miles. In the next ten years more than 6,200 miles of rail-

road were opened, bringing the total network to 9,021 miles in 1850. During this period the population of the United States nearly doubled. By 1860 the nation's rail network had increased to 30,626 miles of track. B. The Civil War halted many railroad projects, but work was rapidly resumed after the conflict, and by 1870 there were 52,922 miles of railroad in the country, including the first railroad connection to the Pacific Ocean. (*Railroads of America,* Association of American Railroads 1966.)

Railroads Water carriers have obvious limitations, and other means of transport soon developed in the United States. The Baltimore and Ohio Railroad, chartered in 1827, was in regular service by 1830. The pattern of rail development in America followed the same general pattern found in developing countries today. At first scattered ports were the source of short feeder lines. Longer lines penetrating the interior from a smaller number of more favorably located ports followed next. Feeder routes were built outward from rail towns located back from the coast, and eventually all major settlements were interconnected by additional lines. Figure 8–3 shows the growth of the rail network.

The length of track within the United States grew steadily from 1830, with a pause during the Civil War, until maximum mileage was reached in 1916. In 1869 the West and East Coasts were linked by rail when the Union Pacific transcontinental rail line between Omaha and San Francisco was completed with the driving of a golden spike at Promontory Point, Utah. The difference caused by such developments is easily demonstrated. In 1866 a horse-drawn stage carried 6 passengers daily from Topeka, Kansas, to Denver, Colorado. By 1870 up to 500 passengers per day were traveling on railroads between the same two points. By 1890, the pattern of railroads in the United States was complete, and today's routes have maintained essentially the same configuration (Figure 8–4).

The half century since 1916 has shown a steady decline in railroad service (Figure 8–5). Although freight in ton-miles in 1966 was twice the 1916 figure, it dropped from 77 percent to less than 43 percent of total intercity freight. And while the nation's population doubled, the 1916 figure of 35 billion passenger miles dropped to 12 billion by 1969, and passenger trains run on only about a third of the track in operation. This amounted to only about 1 percent of total intercity passenger travel, with the bulk accounted for by automobile traffic (86 percent) and air travel (10 percent). Intercity passenger trains, which numbered close to 20,000 in 1929, declined to less than a

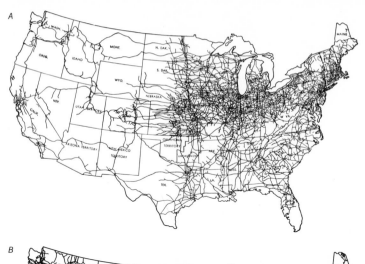

A

B

Figure 8-4 American railroad network, 1890 and 1966 A. The twenty years prior to 1890 saw rapid expansion of the railroad network. The total completed mileage stood at 163,597 miles. The major railroad network had been established by this time. B. The maximum railroad mileage, 254,037 miles of track, was reached in 1916. Since that time, there has been a slow decline in the amount of track in use. In 1966 there were 209,292 miles of track in service. (Op. cit. Figure 8-3; current map courtesy Association of American Railroads)

thousand by the end of 1967. However, trains continue to predominate wherever bulk shipments are made and in this sense are still the most critical transportation element for American industry. In like manner, gasoline shortages and rationing will inevitably reestablish the importance of railroad passenger traffic.

Patterns of Development: Process of Regional Growth

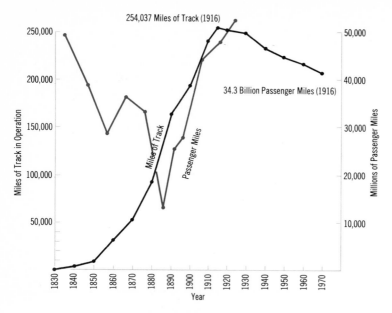

254,037 Miles of Track (1916)

34.3 Billion Passenger Miles (1916)

Miles of Track

Passenger Miles

Figure 8-5 Growth and decline of American rail-road mileage and passenger travel The rise and fall of railroad passenger travel has been dramatic. In modern times the railroad passenger service has been unable or the railroad companies unwilling to compete effectively with the automobile on relatively short trips and airline service on long trips. On the other hand, the railroads are still the major freight carrier. The drop in total miles of track in service probably reflects efficient consolidation, of the network and technological improvements. Total tonnage of freight moved continues to grow. (Data from *Historical Statistics of the United States, Colonial Times to 1957, Continuation to 1962 and Revisions; Statistical Abstract 1972*, U.S. Dept. of Commerce)

Highways Road transportation and construction did not come into its own until the invention and improvement of the automobile. The federal government was slow to take over the responsibility for highway construction and maintainence. Philadelphia and Lancaster, Pennsylvania, were linked by the first of the *privately* owned *turnpikes* in 1794. State and local governments east of the Mississippi helped private entrepreneurs to extend the system of toll roads in the decades that followed. In fact, the development of railroads stimulated the construction of local feeder highways in order to supply stations along

their lines. Farmers also wanted better roads on which to bring their produce to market. And, curiously enough, the growing fad of bicycling created an active lobby which demanded better roads for the new pastime. (It is interesting to note that history repeats itself, and now nearly a hundred years later bicyclists are once more lobbying for safe, usable cycle paths.)

However, it was not until the turn of the twentieth century that the automobile age really began. State highway departments, state road systems, and state-sponsored highway aid laws became common by 1915. By 1920 the Ford Motor Company had an annual production of more than 1 million cars. The Federal Aid Road Act of 1916 offered limited support to states which had established highway departments. Government involvement increased slowly until in 1956 the Federal Highway Act authorized the payment of 90 percent of construction costs of the interstate highway system. Thirteen years later 29,640 miles of interstate highway were in use, while another 11,000 were under construction or contemplated (Figure 8-6.) The impact of the energy crisis on the use of private automobiles is, at this writing, somewhat obscure. But in the long run, the era of the private automobile seems to be past its peak.

Air transportation Air transportation has added its part to the spatial consolidation of the continent. Aviation entered the scene after its infancy in World War I. A series of acts were passed by Congress which authorized the federal government to conduct business with and to subsidize both airlines and the airports which serve them. The Kelly Act of 1925 made it possible for the United States Post Office to ship mail by air. In 1926 the Air Commerce Act directed the Secretary of Commerce to establish airways and navigation facilities. The Civil Aeronautics Act of 1938 and the Federal Airport Act of 1946 helped to improve the facilities of the largest airports throughout the country. All these aids to aviation reflect its more recent arrival on the scene and the special terminal facility problems which this type

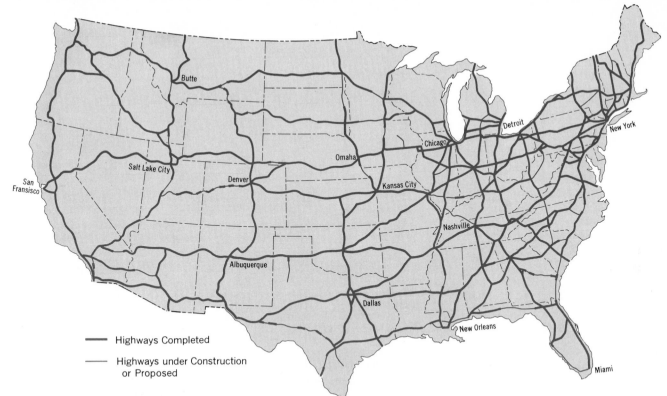

Figure 8-6 The status of the national system of interstate and defense highways, September 1972 (U.S. Department of Transportation, Federal Administration)

of carrier encounters. Passenger growth has been most spectacular (Figure 8–7), while air freight is limited to high-value, low-volume, or low-bulk goods. Few raw materials find their way to factories by airplane.

Pipelines One of the first pipelines in the United States was constructed in 1879 and brought oil from Titusville, Pennsylvania, to the Reading Railroad 110 miles distant. From such modest beginnings pipeline transportation has grown to become the third most important freight carrier in the United States, sometimes accounting for 20 percent or more of the total volume of freight per year. The "Big Inch" and "Little Inch" pipelines built during World War II from the Texas oil fields to the industrial Northeast ushered in a rapid

expansion of the carrier throughout the nation. At the present time, no part of the forty-eight coterminus states is farther than 200 miles from a pipeline route. While this means of transportation has been limited to liquids until recently, experiments show that solid materials can be converted to a powder mixed with water and pumped as a slurry through pipes. Limestone, sulphur, and coal have all been moved this way, and this technique may someday allow pipelines to compete with railroads as the nations major bulk carrier.

Interpretations of Transportation and Regional Growth

The pictures sketched above of regional growth and the increasing importance of transporta-

Patterns of Development: Process of Regional Growth

169

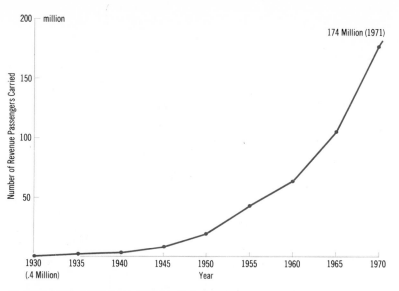

Figure 8-7 Growth of Air Passenger Travel Air passenger service continues to expand rapidly, despite increasing difficulty in air traffic control, terminal congestion, and inefficient ground transporation connections with the large metropolitan airports.

tion, particularly in a developed nation like the United States, need further interpretation. To understand the underlying geographic principles we must seek theories which can account for the actual processes we have described. To do this we first will use as an example the role of railroads as an element in regional growth. We then consider the general conditions necessary for resource development. In the next chapter, we describe development as a set of abstract processes occurring on an isotropic plain. This latter approach will introduce us to some of the geographical theories which account for the locations industries choose.

Railroads as an economic force

The development of the vast network of rails shown in Figure 8–4 has been a major force in shaping the nation and its industrial complexes. Leland H. Jenks has characterized three stages in the growth of railroads, in each of which they play a different role. These should be considered as points along a continuum of development. First, the prospect of railroads stimulated growth long before their actual presence on the land. Next, railroads required an enormous investment of capital and material in order to create the actual physical network. Finally, after being constructed, their presence changed land uses and land values and helped to create new markets through changes in transport costs and general accessibility.

In the first stage, the *idea* of the railroad does not refer to the design of roadbeds and locomotives but rather to the stimulation of developmental thought that follows from the promise of improved transportation. Early railroad promoters in the United States were not simply engineers or financiers working in the narrow realms of design or profit. They were often visionaries who saw the "Civilizing Rails" as the means to transform wild nature into a landscape of grain fields, orchards, and cities.

In the second stage, the construction of railroads helped to create and sustain large portions of the early industrial establishment. They required new combinations of land, labor, and capital. The actual land upon which the rails were laid represented very little investment. However, as soon as a route was completed, the land adjacent to it on either side increased enormously in value. Labor also was in great demand, and by the 1880s probably as many as 200,000 men were at work building railroads in the United States. Many of them were married and supported families, and everyone, single or married, demanded food and goods. This in itself was an important stimulus to the economy. But even more important, perhaps, was the demand for sleeper ties, iron rails, locomotives, cars, and even shovels and picks. During the height of railroad construction in the second half of the nineteenth century, American iron and steel production could not keep pace with the many demands placed upon it. Much was imported from England and Wales, and in the 1890s more than 20 percent of all pig iron made in the States was turned into railroad bars. These demands provided the impetus needed by young American industrial towns such as Pittsburgh and Youngstown to "take off" into the era of sustained growth.

The money to pay for all of this came from local, national, and international sources. The story of railroad finance is long, complicated, and none to clear, for the records of various holding companies which managed the investments have in most cases never been made public. Nevertheless, the desire for profit led many a large foreign investor into the American market. British, Dutch, and German capitalists invested an estimated 2 billion dollars in the United States during the first nine years after the Civil War, of which half a billion went directly into railroads. On the other hand, the purchase of government bonds by foreigners allowed banks to use released funds for investment in railroads and industry. The American government also subsidized the railroads by giving them substantial land grants along right-of-ways.

American companies learned to innovate in the management of money, and as their profits began to roll in, they often reinvested in further development rather than paying stockholders with their initial receipts. This internal financing of corporate growth was an American invention and led to still further advances in the manipulation of money. (If we return momentarily to our notion that information handling and flow is an important aspect of city growth, we can see how money management kept pace with regional development and urbanization). Out of this came a new type of tycoon whose specialty was investment. These laissez faire capitalists of whom so much has been critically written nevertheless played an important role in the development of America's industrial complexes.

The third way in which transportation developments aided industrial growth is even more directly geographical. It is simplest to say that no resource, however rich, can have true value unless it can reach a suitable market without incurring crippling transportation costs. Table 8–1 clearly illustrates the advantages of railroads over earlier modes of land transport.

Railroads allow other advantages to industry as well. Goods and materials can be exchanged

Table 8–1 Advantages of Rail Over Earlier Types of Transport, 1873

Cost of Moving Army Troops	
Average rate per man per mile rail	$0.0675
Average rate per man per mile stage	$0.1375
Rates	
Rate per 100 pounds per 100 miles:	
Union Pacific Railroad rates	$0.4005
Wagon rates	$1.4600

The Quartermaster-General of the U.S. Army estimated that the cost of moving troops and supplies by stage and wagon was 66 percent higher than by rail.

Source: Robert S. Henry, "The Railroad Land Grant Legend in American History Texts," *The Mississippi Valley Historical Review,* vol. 32, no. 2, September 1945, Footnote of a letter from Quartermaster-General •Meigs, p. 192, relating to savings of the War Department as a result of the building of the Union Pacific Railroad.

rapidly between companies supplying portions of a finished product. Vertical integration of organizations thus becomes possible. Factories can also have the option under certain conditions (which we will discuss in the pages ahead) of locating near the market rather than at the source of energy or raw materials. Also, in the days before highways and airplanes, railways became an efficient means of moving large numbers of migrants to new homes and new roles as workers and customers in developing areas.

"The Role of Transportation and the Bases for Interaction"

Our second interpretation of regional development is drawn from the work of Edward L. Ullman whose definitive essay provides the title for this section. We have already seen that increased transportation allows people at greater and greater distances to share goods and ideas. The result is that the world is becoming more homogeneous. On the other hand, regions no longer need to be self-sufficient; their populations can specialize in doing the things they know best and import whatever else is needed. This tends to make the world more heterogeneous. Thus, we can think of two opposing processes at work, one resulting in regional similarities, the other in regional differences. Both are important in regional development, and both depend upon the intensity of spatial interaction. Edward L. Ullman, whose definitive essay provides the title for this section, describes three factors which relate to the growth of interaction between people and between industries.

Complementarity is the first factor which stimulates interaction and subsequent regional development. This means that if one place has a surplus of a material or product and a second place has a matching need, an exchange will take place. However, just being different is not enough. The surplus of milk in New Zealand does little to encourage the shipment of dairy products to China. Even if politics and economics permitted, the avoidance of milk and milk products in the Chinese culture would prevent such an exchange. There must be a *supply* in one place and a *demand* in the other for interaction to occur. Where modern transportation allows the shipment of low-value bulk materials for long distances, strange alliances occur. West African iron ore finds its way to American steel mills, as does ore from Venezuela and Labrador. On the other hand, where two places produce similar things, the likelihood of exchange becomes considerably less. While some wheat is shipped in both directions across the Canadian-American border, the amount is slight compared with the amounts that are sent to other destinations.

The second factor which may promote or inhibit interregional exchanges is a presence or absence of *intervening opportunity*. This is a question of relative location—if a demand exists at some place and two or more sources of supply are available, all else being equal, the source nearest the consumer will be used. We have already seen how the Mennonites of Ontario trade in Waterloo rather than go farther to Kitchener with its more numerous stores (Chapter 5, Figure 5-16). The world is full of other examples. The forests of the Pacific Northwest became a source of lumber for Eastern states only after the forests of the upper Midwest were depleted. The iron ores of Africa and South America were sought out only after the great deposits of high-grade ore in Minnesota were essentially exhausted. At a personal scale, analyze your own use of space. How often do you go across town to a more distant park to walk your dog or play ball if some nearby place will serve just as well? Recreation places can be considered as resources, and in order for their users to travel from afar the sites must have some unique quality, like the slopes of Aspen or the geysers of Yellowstone. Otherwise, remote areas will go unused while nearer spots will attract all the customers.

What about winter ski trips to the Alps instead of Aspen, or exotic cheeses available in the supermarket next to those produced in Wisconsin or New York? Reasonable transportation cost, or *transferability*, accounts for such movements. The Alps have become available to some people for Christmas skiing as the result of large, fast aircraft, charter flights, and comparatively low prices for food and lodging in foreign areas. In other words, modern air technology has made people more transferable than before. Cheeses from France and Germany compete with American products because of low sea transportation costs. Coal and iron ore are available from remote sources because the technology of transportation has made their bulk shipment possible at low cost. In these examples low-cost transport makes it possible to supply materials in sufficient quantities. Conversely, if a product is too bulky or heavy and its market price too low to sustain proportionately large transportation payments, it cannot be used and a less expensive substitute must be found to take its place. For example, poor populations in developing countries find it difficult or impossible to pay the proportionately high costs of shipping lumber and coal and oil from distant sources. Because of this, throughout much of the arid parts of the world where trees are scarce dung is burned for fuel and mud or adobe used for building walls and even roofs. It may seem incongruous that the beaches of the Pacific Northwest are piled with driftwood free for the taking while elsewhere poor families use animal droppings for fuel. But driftwood's low value and great bulk create a lack of transferability which makes all the difference. Similarly, the plastic bottles thrown out in such profusion from American homes would be considered valuable containers anywhere in the developing world, but the cost of moving cheap plastics farther than the nearest refuse heap places them impossibly out of reach for those unable to pay the costs of transportation. Free for the taking at one point does not mean free delivery at another.

Thus for development to take place with the aid of transportation: (1) *complementarity* must exist between the developing region and other areas; (2) there should be no *intervening opportunity;* in other words, there must be a need to develop the resources within the region rather than seeking similar materials at some place nearer the market; and (3) the cost of transporting materials, people, and information must be such that they have a high degree of *transferability.* Only after these conditions have been met can development become reality. In the next chapter we will return to our isotropic or homogeneous plain in order to see how such conditions, stated in theoretical terms, influence the location of industry and industrial complexes.

Parallel to the growth of cities is the increasing complexity of the regions which contain them. This is particularly true of the industrial concentrations around which so much of the modern world revolves. We have already mentioned that in wealthy economies labor becomes its own best market. When many industries cluster together, they not only share a common labor pool and market but also reinforce each other by supplying component parts for each other's products. Since the suppliers are close to the consumers, transportation costs of such parts are low and another advantage is gained. Industries in modern times have moved closer to centers of population. It is true that there has been a recent shift of some factories from the city to the suburbs, but on a regional scale such moves are relatively insignificant. The map of the industrial regions of the United States (Figure 10–16) could almost be used to show the concentrations of population in the nation.

Nevertheless, the location and procurement of raw materials and energy supplies cannot be overlooked. Every factory must in some way solve the problem of where to locate in terms of materials, labor, and customers. Some succeed; others do not. While a variety of reasons account for the location of industry, transportation plays a particularly important role. In order to fully appreciate this, we now examine several theoretical examples of industrial location.

The Spatial Equilibrium of Individual Firms

Let us start on a flat plain with a single factory utilizing an evenly distributed raw material such as some agricultural product. In this general case, the consumers and the labor force are also spread evenly over the plain. Factory operations involve three types of costs: the cost of procuring the raw material, production costs, and the cost of delivering the finished product to the consumer. For the firm to stay in business the market price must cover these costs plus a reasonable profit. Let us assume such a balance is achieved. This would result in a finite supply area around the plant from which the raw material would be provided at some average price. If this supply area were enlarged, the average price for the raw material would go up by the additional transportation cost involved. The factory would also be a definite size, that is, capable of a certain volume of output at a given cost. Everything else being equal, an equilibrium would be established which would result in a fixed wholesale price. If in order to expand the size of the market area production were suddenly increased many times without a parallel price increase, the firm would find itself in trouble. Difficulties would occur from an inevitable rise in the cost of raw materials as well as from problems in procuring additional labor and capital equipment. Management, as it sets about establishing a firm's scale of production, must therefore keep in mind the spatial constraints on procuring raw materials and labor.

The market area served by a factory is also finite. Management must take into account the number of customers who will purchase their product at the price offered. At a given factory price, additional customers are available only by enlarging the market area. This, however, would mean a price rise for all the customers in order to absorb added delivery costs. Thus, for the factory to operate successfully, all these factors must be in balance spatially as well as economically. Under such conditions it is not very practical for management to tell their salesmen to "go find new customers," for they could only find customers by going greater distances. The resulting rise in travel costs would require a price increase, which, in turn, would very likely reduce the number of customers per unit area in the original market zone. Another way to describe this is to say that most products are *price elastic*. This is an economist's term indicating the change in volume of sales that accompanies a change in price. As the price rises, more and more customers will switch to other products or do without the commodity. In our example, if the price becomes too high because of increased transportation costs, the market area will yield fewer and fewer customers and the firm's sales will drop below the break-even point.

The economics of business are embedded in a matrix of spatial constraints. The equilibrium of a firm can be upset by spatial changes such as innovations in transportation, changes in population density, and raw material yields per unit area, just as dislocations can result from changes in nonspatial attributes such as shifts in the elasticity of demand or improvements in internal economies. Similarly, nonspatial innovations may often improve a firm's productivity, but sometimes such changes have accompanying spatial consequences that can make the firm's location no longer tenable. Both parts of the picture must be clear for management to prosper.

Methods of Solving Locational Problems

The linear case

Imagine an electronic parts manufacturer serving a number of assembly plants located along a single-track rail line. The industry is a *footloose* one: that is, it can locate anywhere it chooses without changing its production costs. Parts must be delivered from the factory to each of the firms it serves, but deliveries are limited to only one firm on each trip. Where along the line should the factory be located in order to minimize the distance traveled in delivering parts to all its customers?

If it is not possible to concentrate the factory and all its customers in the same place, thereby doing away with transportation costs, travel efforts may be reduced by locating the factory at the point of *minimum aggregate travel, the point at which the sum of the travel efforts to all points in the system is at a minimum.*

Figure 9–1 shows the situation graphically. Firms F_a to F_g have fixed locations along the route. Our factory can be placed at any point along the line, including the same point as one of the assembly firms. There are at least two points which may suggest themselves to the reader. Most of us might think that the *mean,* or *average,* location along the line would be most efficient. Others might think the *median point,* with the same number of firms on each side, would represent the solution. Who is right?

We compute the *mean value,* that is, the *center of gravity,* by starting at either end, summing up the distances to each firm, and dividing by the number of firms. The mean location is at the sixth unit of distance from the left. The median location with three firms on either side would be at F_d. If we compute the aggregate distance to each milepost along the line from all of the

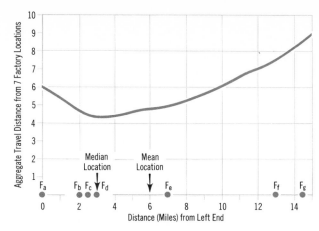

Figure 9-1 Locating the point of minimum aggregate travel for an odd number of factories along a line In a linear pattern with an odd number of elements, the point of minimum aggregate travel is the median point, that is, the point at which half the distribution is on one side and half on the other. For an asymmetrical distribution, the mean location will be some distance from the optimum aggregate travel location.

Figure 9-2 Locating the point of minimum aggregate travel for an even number of factories along a line The optimum location for the aggregate travel distance in a linear pattern of an even number of elements is indeterminate. It is located at any point along the line between the two most central elements in the distribution. The zone of optimum location could be quite large if these two points happen to be far apart.

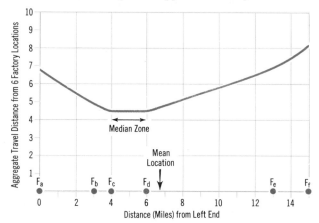

firms, we can plot the values as a curve shown on the upper part of the figure. *Notice that the minimum total distance coincides with point F_d.*

The situation is not so simple when an even number of points must be served. Let us consider the same case, but with six firms instead of seven (Figure 9–2). Now the median point of the distribution lies somewhere at or between the two most centrally located firms. In fact, there is no median point; rather, there exists a line segment with half the firms to the right of it and half to the left. The factory supplying parts may be located at either of the two centrally located firms or anywhere along the space between them. As long as the factory is located between the two central firms, the increased distance incurred in moving from one central firm's location is compensated by a decrease in distance from the other central firm. In other words, there is a stretch of spatially neutral territory along which any location will do. While this may seem somewhat contradictory, we will see a similar situation in the two-dimensional example that follows. The real world implications of this are important. Within industrial regions there are sometimes large areas which have such nearly equal transportation advantages that other factors, such as environmental conditions, become more significant in the final process of location.

The two-dimensional case

Let's face it, geographic reality is almost always areal rather than linear. How do we find the point of minimum aggregate travel when the points are in an area instead of along a line? Where in a park would we put a hotdog stand? Where is the best spot in a city to locate a bakery? Where in the nation should we build our assembly plant? Let us mention in passing that *the mean value, or center of gravity, of a two-dimensional distribution does not necessarily coincide with the point of minimum aggregate travel.* This is simply an extension of our same observation for the linear case.

It would be useful if there were some quick and simple way to extend the analysis of the median point from one dimension to two, but none is known. The problem is that as the observer moves around the periphery of an array or cluster of locations, the point which appears to be the median shifts according to his location. A simple example will explain this. Imagine that you are standing at the edge of a field upon which are growing a random scattering of trees. Looking straight at the field and viewing it from right to left or left to right you see a fixed sequence of trees. But since some of the trees will be nearby and others far away, as you stroll around the edge of the area the trees will appear to change their relative positions.

Because there is no simple method for finding the point of minimum aggregate travel for a set of locations on a two-dimensional plane, it is necessary to use some sort of *iterative solution*. By an iterative solution we mean a method which first approximates an answer, and thereafter, using the first results, attempts to find a better answer the second time, and so on, and so on. Each time an approximation is attempted, the results come closer to the correct answer, although it may never be reached exactly. The process of iteration is stopped when the approximate answer falls within some limits of acceptability determined by the needs of the person solving the problem.

One firm with several customers

Imagine that the electronic parts manufacturer in the linear example now wants to locate within a region across which are randomly scattered the same seven assembly firms mentioned in the linear case. This situation is shown in Figure 9–3A and B. Where should the manufacturer locate in order to minimize transportation costs, all else being equal? The answer to this question is the point of minimum aggregate travel. To find such a point we must use an iterative solution. One simple rule to start with is that the point of minimum aggregate travel must lie within the polygon formed by lines connecting the outermost of the scatter-

ing of customers (Figure 9–3A). Consider the sum of the distances from all of the firms to each of a set of regularly spaced points covering the entire polygon. One such set of distances is shown on the diagram. Each point has associated with it a total travel distance to all the customers. Some of these values will be relatively large and others small. The one with the smallest value is our first approximation of the point of minimum travel. If we think of the values at each of the points as tent poles of varying height sticking up above a flat plain, then we can imagine the cloth of the tent touching the tops of the vertical lines. This forms a continuous surface like the one in Figure 9–3B, which is really more like a sagging awning than a peaked tent. This surface shows the continuous change in aggregate transportation distance from any point on its surface to all the firms. If we made a physical model of the surface and released a steel ball upon it, the place where the ball would come to rest would be the point of minimum aggregate travel. This would not necessarily correspond with our shortest tent pole, but it would be nearby. This is because in the first step of the iteration the regularly spaced points are relatively far apart. To improve on this we may repeat the process by centering upon the first solution a smaller lattice with points closer together. Once more we measure and sum up the travel distances to the points in the finer lattice. A finer-grained estimate thus becomes available in the vicinity of the first minimum. We repeat this process until the change from one iteration to the next is so small that further improvement would not be worth the effort. The surface which we have constructed showing aggregate travel effort is a smooth one shaped like a shallow bowl. All the down gradients lead to the minimum point. There are no rolling hills; nor are there pits or wells on the surface. This is because there are no significant differences in the character of the transportation surface from one place to another.

A special difficulty can occur in finding the point of minimum aggregate travel if the bowl-

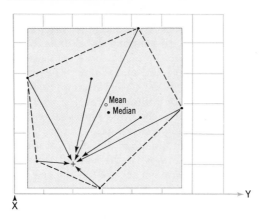

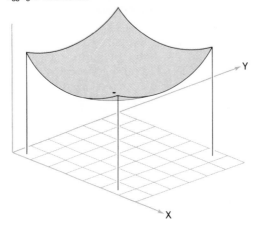

Figure 9-3 Finding the minimum aggregate travel location and the mean location of a two-dimensional point pattern (*A*) An iterative search solution is suggested for finding the point of minimum aggregate travel in a two-dimensional pattern. A lattice of points is constructed over the region in which the elements are located. Distance and travel effort are measured from each element to a lattice point, and the sum of these values is determined. The procedure is repeated for each lattice point. This set of values lies on the surface shown in part *B*, and the surface can be approximated from them. The procedure may be repeated in the vicinity of the lowest value for increased accuracy. The minimum point found in this manner is always only an approximation of the true optimum.

An analytical solution for finding the mean location is available. Project the location of the elements on two perpendicular axes. Find the ordinary arithmetic mean of the projected values on each axis. The two mean values will be the coordinates of the mean location in the two-dimensional array. This will not ordinarily be the point of minimum aggregate travel.

(*B*) An aggregate travel value may be calculated for any arbitrary point in the region in which a collection of elements is located. The collection of all such values would trace out the surface shown in the diagram. The problem then is to find the lowest point on the surface. The surface contains an infinite number of points, and therefore, the approximating method suggested above is used to approach the optimum as closely as desired. Other search methods could also be employed.

like surface is extremely shallow or perhaps even flat over part of its area. Think again of the steel ball analogy. If a ball were released at the lip of a nearly flat bowl, it would travel in a complex pattern rolling back and forth many times. Its path would depend upon where and in what direction it was started, and it would take a long time for it to settle down. If the surface were in part actually flat, there would be an area where the ball could settle just as well at one place as another. Contrast this situation with that of a funnel-shaped surface with steep sides. On such a surface

the ball would reach a single resting place almost immediately (Figure 9–4 *A, B* and *C*).

The lesson we learn here is that if there is very little difference in the values near the absolute minimum, a zone of indeterminate location will exist which depends upon the cutoff value chosen for the iteration. In a situation where there is no marked difference among several near-optimum locations, it may be a waste of time to search for the absolute value or optimum. A typical problem in the real world would be evaluating the location of a new regional hospital. It would make sense to locate such a facility at the point of minimum aggregate travel since the time used in an emergency trip to the hospital might be very critical. However, if the gradient of the aggregate travel surface were nearly flat in the vicinity of the optimum site, alternate locations nearby might be just as good for all practical purposes. If the exact optimum point were already occupied by another building or function which could not be easily displaced, then another one nearby would do nearly as well, and would be much less expensive.

A further step in this type of analysis might be to deal with several variables simultaneously. That is, we might first want to solve the problem in terms of the point of minimum aggregate travel and then consider land values as shown by a rent surface similar to those discussed in Chapters 3 and 4. The two surfaces could then be added together, or to look at it another way, they could be stacked on top of each other and their depressions and elevations combined. This is shown in a simple case in Figure 9–4C. A major problem in such a maneuver is to find some unit of measure com-

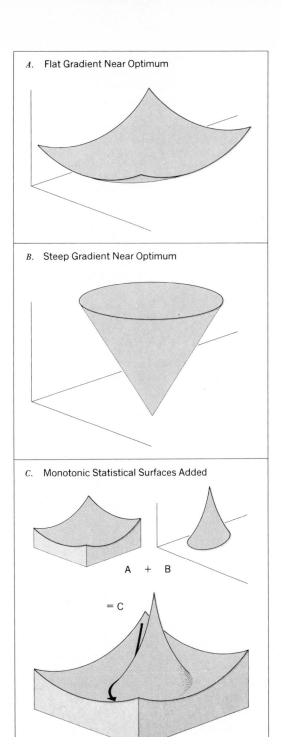

A. Flat Gradient Near Optimum

B. Steep Gradient Near Optimum

C. Monotonic Statistical Surfaces Added

A + B

= C

Figure 9-4 Monotonic statistical surfaces A surface is monotonic if there is always a downward path from any point to the minimum point on the surface. Clearly, search procedures are much simplified if the surface is monotonic. It may be monotonic but very flat in the vicinity of the optimum, as in part *A* of the diagram. A rather broad zone of indifference regarding the separation of the true and approximated optimum may be tolerated with such a surface. This would not be the case when a steep gradient to the surface exists near the optimum, as shown in part *B*. In some instances, but not all, the sum of monotonic surfaces is also monotonic. Simple search procedures may then be employed to find the minimum. The usual problem in adding statistical surfaces is finding a proper weighting of one relative to the others. If one rides higher or lower on the others, the minimum point will be shifted. If the choice of relative value involves some ethical or moral judgment, a scaling factor may be impossible to determine. The researcher must then seek a consensus of opinion. Objective procedures will not suffice.

Transportation and Location: The Search for Optimum Sites

mon to both surfaces. In the case of the hospital, one measure is in value or rent per acre; the other is in minutes or seconds of accessibility. How much is a minute less in an ambu-

Figure 9-5 Production and transportation costs associated with a single firm (*A*) Profile of production, terminal, and carrier costs. (*B*) The profile rotated through a full circle. Contour lines on the surface projected to the plane show costs rising with the distance from the production location.

A. Production, Terminal and Carrier Costs

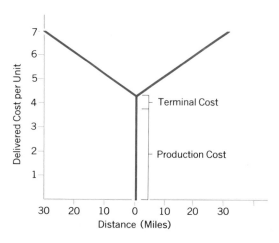

B. Total Delivery Cost in Two Dimensions

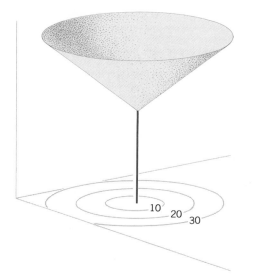

lance worth to an accident victim relative to the cost of buying more expensive land for the hospital? In cases like this, no analytic method will by itself give an answer. This is the kind of decision making that requires inputs other than those provided by science.

A panel of citizens would probably be needed to render such a decision. Medical personnel might give the panel some idea of the cost in lives attributed to the length of time between accident and hospital treatment. A cost analysis would indicate the land cost contribution to anticipated daily patient costs. Some relative weight would have to be assigned to the two types of surfaces in order to add them together. Once this was agreed upon, the analysis could be completed. The problem would not be avoided by simply adding the two surfaces without considerable soul searching. Lack of such an effort would imply that money and lives were exactly equal and the same. One value of the initial analysis is that it at least pinpoints the alternatives and forces the decision makers to consider ethical and human values. As in most things, there is no final, easy path to wisdom.

If the surfaces we add together are complex or numerous, the end result will be a rough terrain with many possible choices. At the same time, it would be nearly impossible to consider surfaces with fifty or a hundred points without the assistance of electronic computers, for thousands of calculations would be required for each iteration. In this case, we have been considering the location of a factory or business serving a number of scattered customers. Another, similar problem arises when we wish to locate a single firm having several sources of raw materials.

Best locations given multiple transport costs

Consider a mine or other source of raw materials. In order to extract the substance and prepare it by concentration, refining, or other means for shipment, certain terminal costs are inevitable. These might be shown by a vertical line such as that in Figure 9–5*A*. Once the material has been loaded on a carrier, transportation costs will make it increasingly expensive with each mile it travels away from its source. This is also shown in Figure 9–5A. Terminal and carrier costs combined make up the total cost of transportation. If we picture such costs three-dimensionally, they will take a shape much like an umbrella blown inside out (Figure 9–5B). Such costs can be mapped on a two-dimensional surface as a set of concentric rings (sometimes called *isotims*) increasing in value with increasing distance from the center. Now let us consider a factory which uses three such raw materials, each of which has different production and terminal costs and different shipping costs and originates at a separate point location. In all three cases, the shipment costs could be shown as a set of concentric rings increasing outward from the center (Figure 9–6). It is possible to determine the combined costs of bringing all three materials together at any point. In Figure 9–6 the combined cost of transporting materials to point A would be 10 dollars a ton for the first material, 10 dollars a ton for the second material, and 15 dollars for a ton of the third material. If we assume that all three materials are needed in equal quantities, the best location for a factory would be where the sum of these three transportation costs is least. The way to determine this point or area is to add up the three values at a large number of points on the map (Figure 9–7A). These summed costs can then be used to draw another map of the combined transportation cost surface (Figure 9–7A and B). Points having the same values may be joined by lines (sometimes called *isodapanes*) similar to those on a contour map. The lowest point on such a map is the ideal spot for a factory if transportation costs are the most important factor. This would be point X in Figure 9–7B.

We know that in reality such regular conditions as those just described rarely if ever occur. Special transportation rates may be assigned one material or another. Terminal costs may depend upon whether a port or mine has automated loading facilities or whether the work is all done by hand. Moreover, some shipments may travel by rail, while others come by barge or truck. In every case the sur-

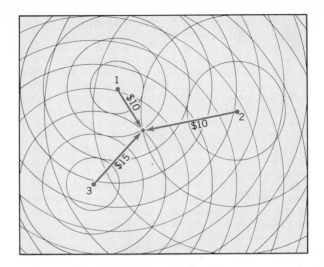

Figure 9-6 Transportation costs from three separate raw materials sources The total cost of moving raw materials from each point source to an arbitrary location, such as point A, can be estimated by use of the cost contour lines (isotims).

face representing the combined transportation costs shows high costs in some places and low costs in others.

The same thing is true for the distribution of finished goods. In this case we might consider three major cities, each representing a consumer market. Where should we locate our factory in order to minimize the costs of reaching the entire market? Isotims can be constructed around each city, and summing their values at any point, as described above, allows us to construct isodapanes similar to those describing least-cost locations for assembling raw materials (Figure 9–7B).

The principle of the *median location* can be important in the two-dimensional as well as the one-dimensional or linear case. If a particular city has more customers than the other market cities combined, it may be considered as the median location and the best spot for the factory. This can be easily illustrated. Suppose three cities, A, B, and C, have 200, 300 and 600 customers, respectively. If the factory is located in city C, there will be zero transport costs for 600 customers and some other com-

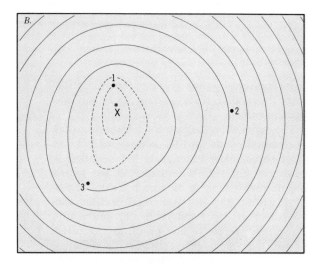

world this is one of the most persuasive arguments for large population concentrations attracting more and more industry, particularly if consumer goods are the item of production.

A final case might be where some of our centers represent markets and others are sources of raw materials. A contour surface showing increasing transportation costs could be constructed for each type of center. All such surfaces could be added together, and the resulting map of aggregated costs for both getting to the factory and getting from the factory to the market would indicate the places with lowest total transportation costs. All else being equal, the low spot on this map would be the best location for a factory.

Differential Transportation and Production Costs

Suppose we have two factories in direct competition with each other. How will they divide up their market areas? The simplest case would be where both have the same terminal costs of assembly and production and the same transportation costs for the finished product. Figure 9–8A illustrates this example. Factory F and factory F′ have equal production and terminal costs shown by the two stems; their transportation costs increase regularly with distance from their locations. The point X at which the transport lines intersect represents the limit of each factory's market in the area between them. The lower part of the figure

Figure 9-7 Least cost location for assembling raw materials from three separate sources (A) Estimating cost surface by calculating assembly costs for a lattice of points in the space. (B) Contouring the statistical surface estimated in part A. The contours are called *isodapanes*. The minimum point may be found by the methods described in Figure 9-3.

Figure 9–8 Competition for market area by two firms under varying conditions of production and transportation costs (A) Transportation and production costs are equal for the two firms. The market boundary is a straight line dividing the space between the two firms. (B) Transportation costs are equal; production costs are unequal. The market boundary is a hyperbola bending in the direction away from the firm with lower production costs. (C) Transportation costs are unequal; production costs are equal. The market boundary is a circle surrounding the firm with higher transportation costs. (D) Transportation and production costs are unequal. The market boundary encloses an egg-shaped region surrounding the firm with higher costs.

Human Geography: Spatial Design In World Society

bined cost based on a total of 500 customers located in cities A and B. If we were to move out of city C and approach cities A and B, no matter how much we saved reaching the customers in A and B we would have an additional loss of 100 units in departing from C. In the real

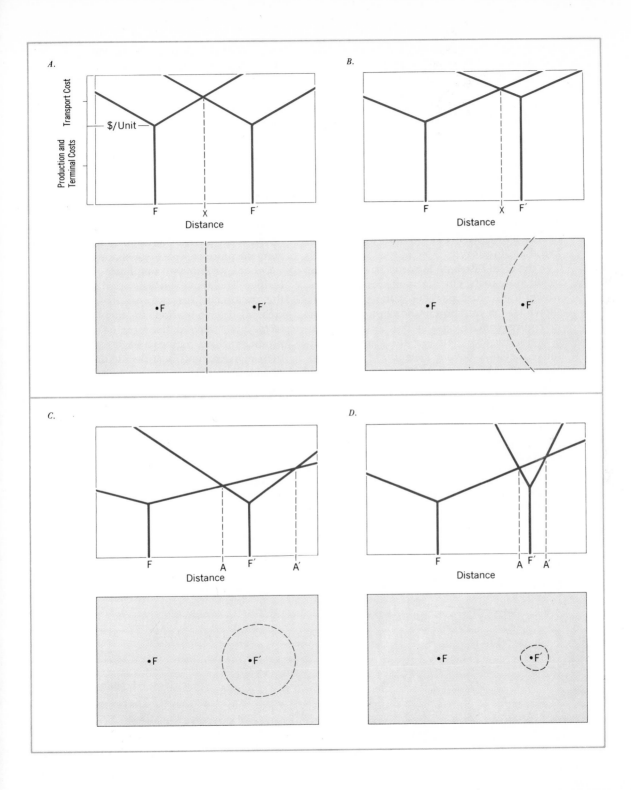

shows a map view of the same situation. Note that the intersection of the two sets of equal cost lines is a straight line. This is a reflection of the complete symmetry of the costs involved.

Now suppose that one factory has substantially greater production costs although transportation remains the same for both. In this case (Figure 9-8B), the factory with lower costs has a distinct advantage in the area between the two. The point X has now shifted at the expense of factory F'. Again the lower portion of the figure shows a two-dimensional view. But now factory F has an advantage which allows its market area to partially enfold that of factory F'.

In the third case both factories have the same production costs but the transportation rates which they must pay are different. This is shown by the variation in the slope of the lines in Figure 9-8C Factory F has an advantage both in the area between them and also at some distance beyond factory F'. The two points of intersection of the transportation lines (A — A') show the limit of the second fac-

tory's market area in the linear view. The map illustrates how an advantage in the transportation costs allows factory F to completely encircle the market area of factory F'.

The progression we have followed leads inevitably to the fourth, most complicated case. In this, the factories have unlike terminal costs and unlike transportation rates for their products. Obviously, given these conditions many variations are possible. A typical case might resemble that in Figure 9-8D, which is similar to the pattern formed in Figure 9-8C. In the third example the smaller hinterland is circular in form; in the fourth the hinterland assumes a more complex egg shape.

Other variations complicate things still further. The above analysis applies only when the customers directly bear the costs of increasing transportation. In many instances a factory will have a fixed or list price for its products within a given area. If that is the case, then management must decide just how far it is willing to ship goods, all the while absorbing increasing transportation costs. If two or

Figure 9-9 Comparisons of transport costs by different types of carriers
Truck transport generally has lower terminal costs but higher carrier, or over-the-road, costs than the other types of carriers. Railroad carriers are intermediate in terminal and overhead costs between truck and ship. Water transport has very low distance costs but high terminal and overhead costs. The result is that trucks compete most efficiently at short distances, rail carriers at intermediate distances, and water carriers at longest distances.

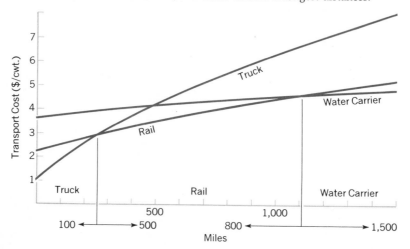

more firms are engaged in a price war, customers at considerable distances may benefit from not having to pay increased transportation. Such benefits are usually short-lived, however, and once a firm has driven its competitors out of a territory, prices may suddenly go up. In fact, subsequent prices charged by a victorious firm may actually include the costs incurred during the previous battle and pass them along to the customer! One indication of differentials in pricing based on transportation is the legend seen in certain advertisements: "Prices higher west of the Mississippi."

Variations in the Cost of Transportation

No interaction can take place without movement, and no movement has zero transportation costs. In the preceding sections we have been primarily concerned with the location of raw materials, industries, and markets. Let us now consider some basic differences in the transportability of materials and goods. Different types of carriers offer different advantages; at the same time certain commodities or materials are either more expensive or less expensive to ship than others. Finally, institutional arrangements such as special rates or other preferred treatment impose variations on the cost of transportation. Figure 9–9 illustrates differences in the cost of several types of carriers. Some commodities may serve the same end purpose but may have different forms, different content, and different degrees of transportability. Table 9–1 illustrates this for one of the most general of all commodities, energy, in some of the many forms in which it is moved. In this instance, terminal and over-the-road costs have been included in a single figure. We have omitted human porters from both figures, for their use results in astronomical costs. If a coolee or a porter on safari were to eat 1 pound of rice per day and could carry a 100-pound load, and if his trip out and back from his starting point were to last 50 days with no "refueling" stops along the way, half his load on the trip out would be "fuel" for the journey!

Table 9–1   Costs of Moving Energy*

Type	Cost, $
Coal by oxcart (labor only)†	190,056
Lignite by rail	4,456
Fuel wood by rail	3,866
Manufactured gas by pipeline	3,866
Electricity (at 60% load factor)	2,345
Oil by tank truck	2,005
Coal by rail	1,725
Natural gas by pipeline	1,720
Oil by rail	1,372
Oil by pipeline (high estimate)	600
Coal by freighter (normal)	483
Oil by tanker (high estimate)	170
Oil by pipeline (low estimate)	105
Oil by tanker (low estimate)	85

*Various fuels converted to electrical equivalents. Dollars per million killowatthour moved a distance of 500 kilometers. Assumed rate of energy return: 20 percent of the contained energy. Loading and carrying costs combined.

†Estimate by Kolars based on criteria similar to those cited in the source note below. Oxcart, labor only: per ton per kilometer, $0.62; with 1,220 pounds coal (yielding 1,000 killowatthours) gives $0.378 per kilometer for 1,000 killowatthours. Loading cost assumed to be the same as fuelwood: $1.056 per 1,000 killowatthours.

Source: *Energy Sources of the World*, U.S. Department of State Publication 3428, June 1949.

Weight-gaining and weight-losing industries

Certain products weigh more and more as they move from one stage to another of their production. These are called *weight-gaining* commodities. Other finished products weigh less than the original materials from which they are made. These are called *weight-losing* commodities.

Bottled soft drinks are a good example of a weight-gaining commodity. The initial ingredient is usually a concentrated syrup produced at a few regional locations. The syrup is shipped to local bottling plants where locally available water—by far the largest and heaviest ingredient—is added. Bottles, another heavy part of the end product, are also most often procured locally, even from the market

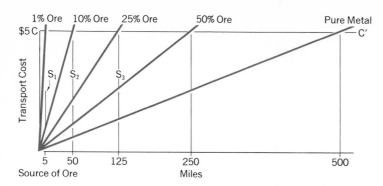

Figure 9-10 Adjusted transport rate, by grade of ore and distance range, for a constant transport charge The diagram shows the effect of ore grade on the distance an ore can be shipped. An ore is valued by the amount of pure metal it contains. It takes twice as much ore to get the same amount of metal from an ore with half the metal content of a higher-grade ore. Consequently, for a fixed transport cost on the usable part of the ore, a low-grade ore cannot travel as far as a high-grade ore or the pure metal. Very low-grade ore—e.g., 1 percent or less—can hardly be moved from the ore deposit. Therefore, smelters for low-grade ores are found at the ore deposit. Higher-grade ores may be moved toward the market.

itself in the case of returnable bottles. Most of the total transportation costs are incurred in the last few miles between the local plant and neighborhood retail outlets. Such industries will be consumer-oriented.

The iron and steel industry is a good example of a weight-losing activity. Ore, coal, limestone, scrap, water, and other materials are used in very large quantities to produce smaller amounts of the end product. In cases such as this, producers will try to minimize the distances that raw materials are hauled, while finished goods will travel farther. In other words, the factory will be located nearer the raw materials than the market.

This relationship is clearly shown in Figure 9-10. This diagram assumes the location of a mine or metal source at the intersection point of the two axes. The rays or lines extending outward from that point indicate the accumulation of transportation costs with increasing distance for five kinds of mate-

rials ranging from a completely pure one ready for further processing to an ore containing only 1 percent of the desired substance. This figure assumes that the cost of moving a ton of pure substance will be the same in all cases and that the cost of moving less than pure materials has been *adjusted* in direct proportion to the amount contained. That is, it will cost twice as much to move a ton of iron in the form of 50 percent ore as it will to move a ton of iron in the form of 100 percent pig iron. Typical metals in the form of ore would include high-grade hematite ore, which is 50 percent iron; bauxite, which is approximately 25 percent aluminum; and copper ore, which often contains 1 percent or less of the sought-after metal. The cost of moving a ton of pure material is shown by the horizontal line c—c'. If that cost represents the maximum amount allowable for transporting any raw or semi-finished material, then the intersection of each of the transportation cost lines with c—c' will mark the farthest that that particular substance could be shipped from its source. Thus, hematite could travel from the mine to a smelter at S_1; bauxite from the mine to S_2; and copper ore from its source to S_3. In all these cases, the more waste material accompanying each pound of metal, the more quickly the allowable transportation costs of the metal will accumulate and the closer to the mine will the smelter or refinery, of necessity, be located. Though in reality such shipments become much more complicated, the above conditions are still the essential reasons that the processing of weight-losing raw materials is located far from the market and nearer to the sources.

A special case of particular historical interest is manufacturing prior to the Industrial and Transportation Revolutions. Until the nineteenth century the materials used and the goods produced by a single craftsman weighed considerably less than the food consumed by him during the year. Thus, the total transportation costs involved could be minimized by locating the workshops of artisans in agricultural areas. The term *cottage industry* takes on a new meaning when viewed this way. It was cheaper and more efficient to bring the materials to the workers than to transport food long distances to workers living near sources of raw materials. It was also less costly to move the finished products to the cities than it was to support large numbers of workers in urban areas. Only with the improved transportation and manufacturing techniques developed during the nineteenth century could settlements grow through large cityward migrations of workers. Before then the cost of moving food and raw materials was greater than the cost of transporting the finished goods.

Rate structures

Another important variation in transportation costs results from different rate structures, that is, different methods of assessing aggregate transportation costs. In general three types of rate structures are used for determining the cost of transportation. The first is a *postage stamp* rate in which a single charge for transportation is made regardless of the distance the item is shipped. The second is a *blanket rate* in which the area served is divided into zones or regions, each with a uniform freight rate throughout but with farther zones having higher rates charged. Figure 9–11 shows a typical blanket freight rate structure for lumber originating in the Pacific Northwest. The third type of charge is a *mileage rate*. In this type there is some direct or proportional charge made for each unit of distance a commodity is shipped.

Rates often vary from straight linear relationships, for economies of scale are gained by shipping the same quantity of something longer and longer distances. Most carriers charge high per mile costs for local shipments, intermediate costs for shipments to

Figure 9-11 Blanket freight rate structure The map shows freight rates for lumber, in cents per 100 pounds, originating in the Pacific Northwest. Large sections of the country can be reached for the same cost. Values for the nearer Western states are not shown. Flat rate zones are much smaller for shorter hauls, if they exist at all. (R. J. Sampson, *Railroad Shipments and Rates from the Pacific Northwest,* Bureau of Business Research, University of Oregon, Eugene, Ore., 1961, p. 45, map 1)

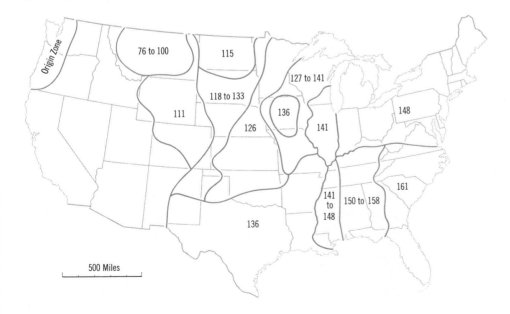

Transportation and Location: The Search for Optimum Sites

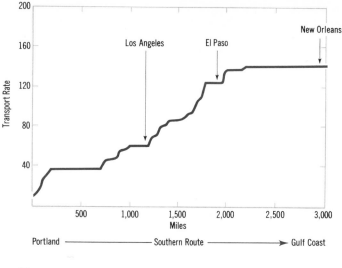

Portland ————— Southern Route ————→ Gulf Coast

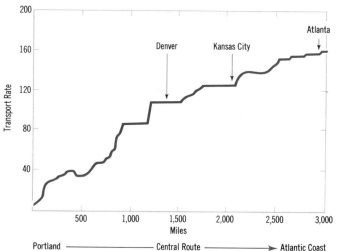

Portland ————— Central Route ————→ Atlantic Coast

Figure 9–12 Freight rate profiles Costs of transporting lumber and plywood from Portland, Oregon, across the United States via the central route to the South Atlantic Coast and via the southern route to the Gulf Coast. (Op. cit., Figure 9–11, pp. 40–41, charts 2 and 3)

distances when this type of shipping rate is utilized. This results in an irregular, gradually flattening profile for the transportation cost line leading away from the source of the materials shipped. Figure 9–12 shows this for lumber and plywood from Portland, Oregon, destined for the southern United States. Imagine the complications encountered if transportation lines as irregular as the one shown here were to be used in the figures illustrating the models in the preceding section. In the real world not only do the complications increase, but strange situations are often found. Notice in Figure 9–12B how it is actually cheaper to ship things 500 miles from Portland than to ship them 400 to 450 miles. A similar example exists for an area beyond Kansas City at a distance of about 2,300 miles. In these and many other cases the rates charged by shippers reflect the competition of local products or other means of transportation. Thus, railroads often lower their rates on routes parallel to navigable waterways so that they can compete with the water transportation. But rather than examine all the changes possible in these matters, we simply call them to your attention and push on to a case study of one commodity, shipped in the United States, which we hope will illustrate the foregoing comments on locational strategies.

The Case of the *Angelo Petri*

Recognizing that the above discussion may at times have been a bit dry, we consider it appropriate to conclude with a case of wine. In the Central Valley of California ship canals penetrate 60 to 70 miles inland from the port city of San Francisco. Among the ships you might see on those canals would be the *Angelo Petri* bound for Stockton on a regular voyage. The *Angelo Petri* is a converted oil tanker fitted out to carry wine in twenty-six huge stainless steel tanks. On each trip it is capable of carrying 2½ million gallons, which amounts to nearly 1½ percent of the total wine consumption of the nation. The wine is shipped in bulk from California to the East Coast where it is bottled and sold. Wine in such large

Human Geography: Spatial Design In World Society

somewhat farther places, and relatively low costs per unit distance to remote places. This has the advantage to the shipper of extending his market area beyond its normal limits. Nearby customers may actually underwrite the transportation costs of customers at greater

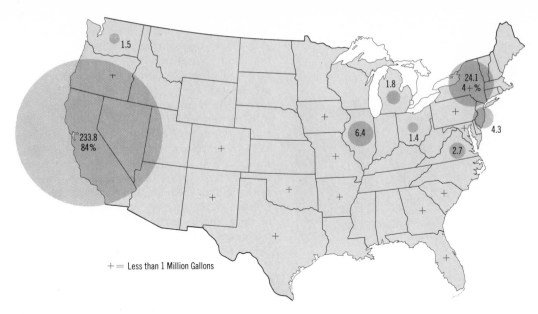

+ = Less than 1 Million Gallons

Figure 9-13 United States still wine production, 1971 Wine is a type of commodity whose production is concentrated in a few regions. Since the market is the general population, such industries are faced with major transportation problems, especially if their production is located outside the densely populated Northeastern region of the country. (Compiled from data in *Alcohol and Tobacco, Summary Statistics, Fiscal Year 1971,* Dept. of the Treasury, Publication 67 (3-72) NO-Cp:AT-82, Table 62, p. 55)

quantities must be handled efficiently, and its transportation is treated by the company as a problem in industrial logistics.

First of all, the wine storage tanks on the shore in Stockton must be full and waiting when the ship arrives. This prevents the ship's having to linger in port. Powerful pumps move the wine through pipelines from the shore tanks to the ship. Speed in loading is not only economical but necessary to minimize the exposure of the wine to air, which is bad for it. This is just a single judicious use of transportation technology skillfully applied at various well-chosen locations along the route from vineyard to consumer. Considerations such as these are important not only to the wine industry but also to any firm which ships large volumes of materials long distances. The story of how this wine ship was built and brought into use is for this reason

particularly interesting and incorporates many of the principles that we have presented earlier in this chapter.

Spatial distribution of production facilities and markets in the wine industry

Although wine grapes can be grown nearly everywhere in the United States, they grow best in California (Figure 9-13). That state produced 80 percent of the wine consumed in the national market. A logistics problem arises whenever a relatively small region produces large amounts of some good which is then marketed throughout the country. Wine consumption in the United States— that is, the wine market—matches the distribution of population although it varies somewhat because the popularity of wine drinking differs from region to region. The problem,

Transportation and Location: The Search for Optimum Sites

California vineyard. This vineyard is located a few miles north of San Francisco Bay in one of the regions best suited for growing quality wine grapes. The best grapes are typically grown on slopes without irrigation in regions where mild, moist winters and summer fog prevent extremes in temperature.

therefore, is to find the best way to move the wine from its optimum place of production, California, with its Mediterranean climate, to its major area of consumption, the industrial northeastern United States.

Most wine sales are handled by only a few companies. These are often cooperatives in which many farmers have banded together to market their products. United Vintners, which owns the *Angelo Petri*, is one of these large wine-producing and -marketing companies. Many years ago these companies began to ship their wine in bulk to Eastern markets in railroad tank cars. Such tanks are either made of stainless steel or lined with glass. They are sealed at the beginning of the journey to prevent "shrinkage" (usually from pilfering) along the way. Bulk shipments save the cost of moving bottles and make possible lower rates. Such savings are important for industries whose production facilities are far from major markets.

Processing and distribution systems

The geographical strategy of an industry can be understood by considering the industry's requirements at each stage of production. Wine is an agricultural product derived from the land. Vineyards take spread-out areal forms in order to gather solar energy. Fresh grapes are very perishable once they are picked. They must be harvested at just the right degree of ripeness and moved quickly to the winery for crushing to avoid spoilage and uncontrolled fermentation. As the time from harvest to crush is critical, space must be conserved at this stage. That is, the journey from field to factory must be short. In order to have short hauls of fresh grapes by tractor or truck, many small wineries that are spread out among the vineyards are needed rather than a few large ones. At the same time, there is little to be gained by economies of scale in the fermentation stage once vats or barrels holding several thousand gallons are used. Nobody finds it useful to ferment wine in vats holding millions of gallons.

These factors provide an explanation for the geography of the first stage of wine production. Vineyards are located in the sunny Central Valley of California as well as in several smaller valleys surrounding San Francisco Bay. The long axes of these latter Coast Valleys, as they are called, are parallel to the Pacific shore and are excellent wine grape country. Most of the fine California wines are produced here on hillslopes without irrigation. Sufficient moisture and summer fog produce a mild environment best suited for growing quality wine grapes. Production in tons per acre is small compared to the Central Valley where *vin ordinaire* is produced from grapes grown on flat, irrigated land in very hot sun. There, the result is a much higher tonnage per acre of grapes suitable for *vin ordinaire*. This explains why the wine ship moves along the canal to Stockton, for that city is in the center of the bulk wine country. Many wineries scattered throughout the entire wine-growing region help fill the shore tanks before the ship arrives, although most of the wine comes from nearby Central Valley locations. The wine is moved on this leg of the journey in glass-lined tank trucks similar to the large tank trucks which bring fresh milk to urban markets.

There are economies of scale in the bottling and storage stages of wine production, and unlike fresh grapes, wine stores well so that time is not a critical factor in the trip from the winery to the bottling plant. In fact, food storage is one of the reasons for converting grapes to wine. Controlled fermentation greatly extends the useful life of the perishable fresh fruit. The fact that an entirely different and delicious concoction results from fermentation is a happy, added benefit of the ancient art of fermentation for preservation.

One geographical consequence of all this is that subsequent stages such as bottling are not tied to the site where the wine is produced. For example, United Vintners has three bottling plants, one in California, one in the Chicago area, and one in New Jersey.[1]

After bottling, the wine is moved to wholesalers, sometimes through two or more tiers of a retail hierarchy. Transportation is by truck. The wine may be bought and sold several times and may be sold under many labels. In fact, wine companies buy from each other to make up shortages in the various types of wine they offer.

Figure 9–14 is a summary of the spatial pattern for this process. It is the familiar dumbbell or complete tree form of concentration, transportation, and dispersion. The product moves through an assembly stage, a long-haul stage, and a distribution stage. Only in California where the long-haul stage is absent does the region of the market overlap with the production region.[2]

The national distribution problem

Let us now consider the national distribution problem of the company which eventually purchased the *Angelo Petri*. Given three bottling plants, the firm was faced with a direct prob-

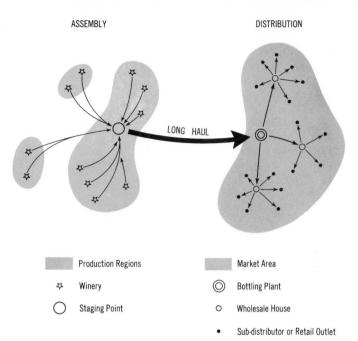

ASSEMBLY   DISTRIBUTION

LONG HAUL

Production Regions   Market Area
☆ Winery   ◎ Bottling Plant
○ Staging Point   ○ Wholesale House
                            • Sub-distributor or Retail Outlet

Figure 9–14 Typical stages of production and distribution in the wine industry There are sub-assembly and assembly stages of production followed by long hauls to market regions, where the product is distributed and subdistributed by wholesale and retail networks. Consider the spatial patterns in the production of bread from flour (see Figure 6–3), or automobiles, radios or other consumer products. The pattern is a general one.

lem in logistics: What should be the market area of each plant? It was rational to seek a least-cost delivery system for the entire firm since the bottling plants do not compete with one another. With this in mind, we can consider the analytical steps the company found necessary in order to answer the above question.

Let us simplify the analysis by assuming that the staging point for the start of the long-haul shipments is located at the storage tanks in Stockton. Some bottling can be done at this spot if needed. This location is represented by the point at the far left of the diagram in Figure 9–15A, C and E. The horizontal axis of this diagram represents distances across the United States. The Chicago and New Jersey bottling plants are shown at their respective distances from California. Total delivery costs

Transportation and Location: The Search for Optimum Sites

[1]Details of our story are somewhat hypothetical because the authors have no intimate knowledge of the company's operations.

[2]In addition to the wine sent by ship, another part is shipped directly by railroad tank car or is bottled in California for distribution on the West Coast. Prior to the introduction of the wine ship most of the wine shipped to the East went by railway either in bulk or sometimes in bottles.

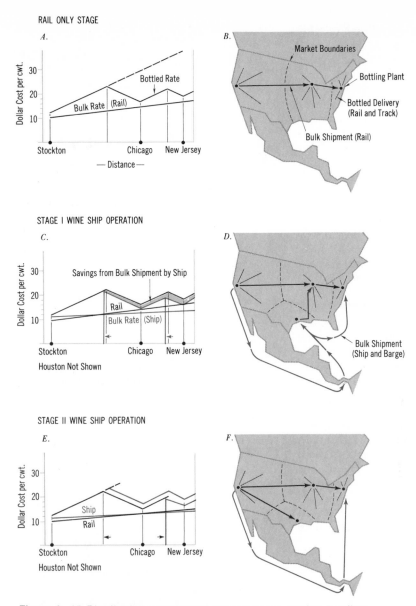

RAIL ONLY STAGE

A.

STAGE I WINE SHIP OPERATION

C.

Houston Not Shown

STAGE II WINE SHIP OPERATION

E.

Houston Not Shown

Figure 9–15 Distribution system and market areas of wine-bottling plants The wine industry takes advantage of flatter rates for shipping bulk wine compared to shipping bottled wine by establishing bottling plants closer to markets than to the production region. Parts *A* and *B* of the diagram show a situation in which bulk shipment by rail is used to move wine from the West Coast to the East Coast and Midwestern markets, where it is then bottled and shipped at the higher bottled rate. Parts *C* and *D* show the cost and market area adjustments, which resulted from the entry of a wine tanker into the long-haul phase of the distribution. Parts *E* and *F* show final distribution patterns after the railroads had responded to the presence of the ship by lowering rail rates on long hauls of bulk wine.

are shown on the vertical axis. A market location is reached either directly from California with bottled goods or indirectly through bulk shipments to the other bottling plants and then onward in bottled form to the market. The resulting market areas are shown in Figure 9–15B, D, and F.

As shown on the graph, the bottled wine transport rate is considerably more than the bulk wine rate. For example bulk wine is delivered to Chicago for $1.25/cwt (cwt = hundred weight), and the case goods (bottled) rate is $3.52/cwt. The difference would be even more for wine if we adjusted the case goods rate by first subtracting the weight of glass and packaging material in the containers. The costs of production, storage, and bottling are shown on the diagram as vertical columns at the locations where those activities take place. The diagonal lines indicate transportation rates for bulk and bottled movements. Linear (straight-line) transport rates are used for simplicity; actually such rates would increase at a decreasing rate in the stepwise fashion discussed earlier in this chapter. Nearly all the case goods shipped from the Eastern bottling plants move by truck, but we indicate the bottled rates from all plants to be the same. Truck rates in reality would be somewhat higher than rail rates for case goods from California.

Under these simplified assumptions it can be clearly seen that it would be foolish to ship only bottled products from California. The delivery price using this mode only is shown as the projected line in Figure 9–15A for bottled delivery. The delivery cost on the East Coast would be prohibitively high (although by using linear rates we exaggerate this effect in our example). Much lower costs can be achieved by shipping the wine in bulk to the Eastern bottling plants and then sending it on to the customer in bottles. This is shown in the diagram by the flatter bulk rate lines to the bottling plants in connection with the combined cones of rising delivery cost from each plant to its entire market. The points (or lines in the map examples) where these cones intersect divide the national market into segments which are assigned to each plant according to the lowest delivery cost.

In general, if the opportunity arises to choose the location of a production stage, it is advantageous to work back from the market locations as well as forward from the raw material sites in making the decision. The volume produced by each bottling plant should be adjusted to these market boundaries and not the other way around. That is, the boundaries which allow each plant to dispose of its products should be set first and plant capacity brought into line with the customers in each retail region. In fact, however, many manufacturing firms historically have been *production*-oriented rather than *market*-oriented. Convenient or traditional production sites were developed first, and then the management sent their salesmen out to "find new markets."

The size of the plants cannot be estimated from our diagram because we have not specified the variation in density of wine drinkers. We also take as given that the bottling plants are located near Chicago and New York. Given a choice of locating two bottling plants east of the Mississippi—a decision predicated on estimates of economies of scale—the minimum aggregate travel locations would very likely occur at those population peaks since they are the first and second largest metropolitan concentrations.

Figure 9–15C shows the situation shortly after the entry of the wine ship into the picture. The cost of moving wine by oceangoing vessel through the Panama Canal and up the East Coast is approximately three-quarters of the cost of the bulk railroad rate for the same origin and destination. The red lines indicate the advantages gained through use of the wine ship. There is a higher cost for storage and facilities at the staging point in Stockton, but the delivery costs to Chicago and New York are significantly less. At this time the company had the ship deliver wine to a newly opened bottling plant in Houston which was to serve the Southwest market. Wine was also transferred from the ship to two company-owned barges for shipment up the Mississippi and along the Illinois waterways to Chicago. This first stage of operations was later discontinued for the following reasons.

With delivery costs lower at the distant bottling plants the company adjusted the market area for each of its plants. The subsequent boundaries are shown in Figure 9–15E and F for the original three plants. Notice that the most distant New York plant gains relatively more territory because it receives a greater absolute benefit from the lower transportation rate. Of course, the California-based transportation rate for bottled shipments changed not at all, and therefore the Chicago plant gained some territory at the expense of the California plant. We have omitted Houston from the graphs in the figures, but the same principles hold.

Results of transportation innovations

The new conditions required several management decisions. The lines on the graph indicate delivery costs but say nothing of prices charged for the wine. The company made a savings which it could have passed on to its customers in the hope of enlarging total sales at the expense of competitors. Several factors acted against such a decision. First, in certain states, prices for alcoholic beverages are regulated by the state government. Sluggishness in price changes is characteristic of markets where prices are administered. If the company petitioned for a lower price and succeeded, it might experience difficulty in raising the price of its goods at a later date if that became necessary.

Secondly, there are not many wine shippers. The market in this industry may be described as an *oligopoly*. An oligopoly is a market economy dominated by a few large firms. In an oligopoly, lowering prices to gain customers at the expense of your competitors is likely to be met by a price reduction on their part. As a consequence a *quid pro quo* situation often develops in which prices are not changed very often. Under conditions in the United States market, collusion is illegal but letting

well enough alone is common. Savings not easily matched by competitors are simply taken in the form of larger profits.

An advantage of lower prices is that new customers may substitute wine for other beverages. Economists call the degree to which this will happen *the price elasticity of the good. The elasticity of a product is the ratio of the change in the volume purchased to a change in price.* However, it appears that a substantial price change would be required to lure beer drinkers over to wine in this country. The transportation savings described here were not large enough to warrant such expectations. For these three reasons the retail price of wine brought to the East by the *Angelo Petri* remained nearly the same.

However, other changes were triggered by the new ship. The nearly 2½ million gallons of wine per trip that the ship could carry was a significant part of the entire market. This meant a significant loss of trade for the railroads, especially since long hauls are relatively more profitable for the railroads.

As a result of the competition of the ship, which began in 1957, by 1964 the railroads had introduced lower rail rates for shipments of wine by single carriers with over 150,000-pound capacities.[3]

The 150,000-pound minimum was a consequence of an innovation in rail transport: the introduction of "jumbo" tank cars capable of holding 20,000 liquid gallons. The innovation was borrowed from other industries which required bulk shipments of various industrial liquids such as acids, caustic soda, and petroleum products.[4]

By lowering the rates, the railroads apparently won back the Chicago market, because in 1964 the wine ship discontinued the Houston stop and the barge shipments up the Mississippi. Since that time the ship has confined its trips to the New Jersey terminal with Houston and Chicago again being served by rail tank cars. This result, which is shown

[3]Rates on carriers with lower minimum loads of 50,000 pounds and 64,000 pounds were also adjusted downward.

[4]The smaller minimums were associated with the then standard 6,000-gallon and 8,000-gallon tank cars.

*Human
Geography:
Spatial
Design
in World
Society*

194

in Figure 9–15*E* and *F*, had implications for the other companies selling California wine to the Eastern markets.

Railroad rates are regulated by the Interstate Commerce Commission (ICC). Any commodity rate change naturally applies to all companies. If the railroads did indeed respond to the competition from the wine ship—a point that has never been made public—then the company that bought and operated the ship had provided a windfall gain for its competitors by getting all their transportation rates reduced as well.

Backhaul problems

Another interesting problem facing the company was the need to find a suitable backhaul for the wine ship. Carriers from raw material- and food-producing regions travel fully loaded to industrial and consumer regions, but on the return trip they often lack a bulk cargo and are forced to return empty. Since the carriers must be returned regardless of whether or not they have a cargo, railroads and other carriers offer "backhaul" rates that are lower than normal. Any revenue is better than none, and offering a lower rate may induce some traffic. In the case of ocean vessels an additional factor makes it necessary for something to be in their holds. Ships lack stability and cannot make way without cargo for ballast. For example, oil tankers on their return hauls ·take on seawater as ballast. (Incidently, the used water is then normally pumped out and spreads as a polluting oily bilge on the ocean.) Many backhauls result in curious anomolies in the economic geography of the world. Refrigerated ships which carry meat to Great Britain from Australia-New Zealand on the return leg bring ice cream to East African ports. Popular British brands of ice cream are sold in Mombasa at approximately the same price as in London as a consequence of very low freight rates. Similarly, in the nineteenth century immigrants traveling in steerage from Europe to the New World were able to go for very small fares because the ships were primarily engaged in carrying raw materials, especially lumber and grain, from America to the Old World. The immigrants were essentially a backhaul cargo.

Consider the long-term industrial location consequences of lower backhaul rate policies. An industrialist planning to open a new factory which would distribute to the entire nation would probably find it best to locate in the industrial region of the northeastern United States. Not only is the population and therefore the market concentrated there, but the cost of reaching the other regions of the country would be less. This would be true because manufactured goods might well receive advantageous backhaul rates on the carriers used to bring bulk raw materials the opposite direction. Backhauls thus tend to increase industrialization in the most industrialized region at the expense of outlying regions. Although this is not a major factor in industrial concentration, it is another small way in which advanced regions are favored for further cumulative and spiral growth.

In view of the above considerations what backhaul would be suitable from New Jersey to California? New Jersey is in the center of the industrial region. California has a rich market of 20 million persons and is a food-producing region. The population is engaged in many tertiary activities on the one hand and primary food production and extractive industries on the other. It lacks significant amounts of secondary manufacturing. The wine ship needed a liquid industrial product as the backhaul cargo. The solution was liquid detergents. Detergents are better than seawater as ballast because of the revenue such cargo yields, and besides, the tanks needed to be cleaned after each trip!

The role of competition between carriers in industrial locations

The wine industry has special characteristics, but it is not unique in the problems it faces. Most industries have stages of production in which logistics enter as an important variable. All such firms are concerned with seeking the best location for their facilities and with obtaining the best transportation rates bargaining can provide.

The American aluminum industry offers a parallel to that of wine. Aluminum is made from bauxite, a 25 percent ore, the bulk of which is now imported from Caribbean and South American deposits (Jamaica, Surinam). Bauxite is processed mechanically and by heat to yield aluminum oxide (alumina) which is 50 percent aluminum by weight. Facilities for this stage are found in the Gulf port cities such as Mobile, New Orleans, and Baton Rouge. The final stage of reduction to pure aluminum is accomplished by electrolysis and requires a large energy input. It takes 13,000 kilowatthours of electricity to make 1 ton of aluminum. The industry has great incentive to locate this stage of production in a region where energy is plentiful and cheap. For a time the Pacific Northwest was the best location for aluminum reduction mills because of the low-cost electricity made available by the well-developed hydroelectric power plants of that region. In the 1960s, however, advances in the generation of electricity by coal-fired steam plants made the Ohio Valley, with its cheap coal resources, attractive to aluminum companies. The Pacific North-west plants require a very long rail haul from the Gulf ports, and then much of the finished aluminum must travel back across the country to the industrial East with its aluminum fabricating plants which make up a large part of the wholesale market. A considerable transportation savings was achieved when most of the new aluminum plants ended up on the banks of the Ohio. Not only could the river water be used for cooling, but also it made possible barge delivery of the aluminum oxide processed on the Gulf. The railroads offered rail rates competitive with the barge rates, and as a result, none of the aluminum plants use the Mississippi-Ohio river system for barge traffic. One could still say, however, that they have benefited from the presence of the river, for if the threat of barge transportation did not exist, the refining mills' bargaining power with the railroads would be diminished.

One of the results of optimizing locations is that certain areas of the world become identified with particular activities. These areas can be thought of as land use *regions*. The next chapter describes methods of identifying types of regions whether they are formed by spatial optimizing activities or other unrelated processes.

10 | DIVIDING SPACE AROUND AND WITHIN CITIES: REGIONAL ANALYSIS

Regions as Mental Constructs

We succeed as living creatures largely through our ability to impose some sort of mental order on the infinite combinations of reality which surround us. We do this by continuously learning to classify and categorize all our impressions and perceptions of the world. A baby soon learns that the world it inhabits does not consist of an immense number of unique items and actions but rather is made up of sets of similar things. Thus, the first door a toddler sees may seem entirely different from the second one, but in a very short time he learns to lump all such contraptions into a single set called *doors* with certain attributes.

Space is one of the most important things about which babies and children learn, and as they grow up, they acquire more and more knowledge about the locational geography of their environments. All of us go through similar stages of development. These processes are usually intuitive and take two forms. We construct maplike images based on the geography we have encountered. Such *mental maps* help us to navigate from place to place. In all cases, we identify specific portions of the earth's surface, place limits of some sort around each one, and form emotion-filled value judgments about every area thus identified.

Areas to children may have the rich nuances of the playpen, living room floor, grassy yard, city street, or playground. For adults, areas may evoke all manner of responses from fear and anger to pleasure and longing. This is particularly true as we begin to think about and become concerned with areal locations such as *the Deep South*, *the industrial Northeast*, *Harlem and Westchester*, *North and South Vietnam*, and *the Near East*. Whenever we identify some geographical area, we are *regionalizing* earth-space. That is, we are categorizing and assigning qualities and values on a locational basis. We are delimiting *regions*, however intuitively, and as a result have become practicing geographers.

We regionalize our environments in order to simplify, understand, and manipulate them. That is, once we have identified a specific area and assigned certain attributes to it, we can act in terms of the good or bad qualities it represents to us. This is such a natural way to behave that we seldom stop to analyze the process by which we perceive and identify these regional constructs which bring order to our lives. If we do think closely about what we are doing, we soon realize that regions are strange things. We could not survive without our ability to categorize space, and yet as we attempt to be more and more precise in defining the places important to us, the less successful we become. Ask yourself a few questions about the regions which concern you most, such as the area in which your house is located, the political unit in which you pay local taxes, or any of the potential war zones throughout the world. Where are the exact boundaries of your neighborhood? If you are now part of a college community, is your town geographically split between "town and gown"? If so, can you draw the geographic border between the two sectors? If you want to move to the suburbs or you already live there, where is the line separating them from the city?

If we are going to organize our lives geographically by means of regions, we should know more about them. Let us look at some examples of how the regions important in our lives can be most evasive mental constructs and why we need to be more specific in their use. This entails several problems, among them problems of regional definitions, problems of scale, and problems of distributions and their intensities.

Problems of Defining Regions
The Near East

For years the newspapers have been filled with stories about the latest crisis in the Near East. Just to confuse matters, the same crises are occurring in the Middle East, which apparently is the same place; or is it? Let us simplify matters for the moment and call the region by either term. The United States and Russia have come close to war as the result of power struggles in that part of the world. If the area known as the Near East is so important, it should be easy to define.

What do you think constitutes the Near East? There is desert there, so we might be able to define it by drawing a line on a map marking the areas with 10 inches or less of rainfall per year. But such a line does not do the job. The areas of the world falling within the 10-inch rainfall line include deserts on every continent except Europe. That will not do!

The Near East is where the Arabs live. But Arabs also form a significant minority in part of East Africa. At the same time other places which we might have strong intuitive feelings for including in the region are populated almost entirely by Jews (Israel), Turks (Turkey, Northwest Iran, Soviet Central Asia), Persians (Iran), and Copts (Ethiopia). Try again.

Well, the geographical distribution of Islam, one of the great monotheistic religions of the world, should identify the Near East. But Islam is the major religion of both Bangladesh and West Pakistan, Indonesia, and much of East Africa. Besides, what about the beliefs of the Black Muslims in America?

It is clear that aridity, ethnic origin, language, and religion do not define the Near East. What about purely political definitions which give simple lists of countries within the region? Table 10–1 lists some of the various country-by-country definitions of the Near (Middle) East during the last 75 years.

We cannot exhaust all the possible definitions of the Near East at this point. For the moment we wish only to emphasize that the confusion outlined here is not unusual when it comes to defining particular regions. Let us just remember that when the fate of nations hangs in the balance, we need to keep our terms straight—and that includes regional definitions.

Nodal regions and uniform regions

Regions are one way of simplifying and describing phenomena which are distributed through space and which, therefore, have the potential for being locationally defined. If we turn to the earlier chapters of this book, we quickly see that two classes of map patterns have been used to illustrate the many different comments regarding man's use of space. The first shows the extent and linkages of hierarchially organized systems. Typical of these would be the maps in Figure 5–14 illustrating the shopping preferences of two culture groups in Ontario, Canada. The second type of map includes all those showing the spatial distribution of sets of like objects, activities, and conditions. These distributions appear on the maps as intensities such as those in Figure 1–3,

Table 10-1 Political Definitions of the Near (Middle) East

Source	Countries
D. G. Hogarth, *The Nearer East,* 1902	Albania, Montenegro, Southern Serbia, Bulgaria, Greece, the Ottoman lands of Asia, the entire Arabian peninsula, the southern two-thirds of Persia
Middle East Air Command (Great Britain, on the eve of World War II)	Egypt, Sudan, Kenya
Commander in Chief, Middle East Operations, World War II	Egypt, Sudan, Cyprus, Iraq, Aden, British Somaliland, the Persian Gulf area (a region within a region!), Eritrea, Lybia, Greece, Crete, Iran
Middle East Institute, Washington, D.C. (post-World War II)	Morocco to East Pakistan and Russian Turkestan
American Friends of the Middle East—Executive Vice President, 1953–1954	"The Middle East can be defined as comprising those countries between the Pillars of Hercules and the Straits of Macassar in which, if an injustice is perpetrated in one, a protest will be raised in the others— plus Israel"

Source: After Roderic H. Davison, "Where is the Middle East?" in *The Modern Middle East,* Richard N. Nolte (ed.) Atherton, New York, 1963, pp. 13–29.

where per capita income is divided into subclasses ranging from poor to rich. Another kind of intensity shown by maps is a binary or dichotomous one. That is, every observation has simply a *yes/no* or *exists/does not exist* value. Political units are good examples of this. Point Barrow, Alaska, is just as much in the United States as is Topeka, Kansas. But cross 1 inch beyond the border into Canada and you are absolutely in another country with different rules based on a different government.

In the first type of map, movement, linkages, and organization are important. The regions depicted by these maps are organized around foci or nodes and are called *nodal regions,* or sometimes *functional regions.* The second type of map shows regions which are uniform or homogeneous throughout and which are not thought of in terms of their organization. Regions of this latter type are called *uniform regions;* they are also sometimes referred to as *formal* or *homogeneous regions.*

Dividing Space Around and Within Cities: Regional Analysis

A scale view of nodal and uniform regions

In a few minutes you will probably lay down this book and casually glance at the tabletop upon which it rests. Your immediate impression of the table's surface will be one of a uniform or homogeneous surface. But look closer; stains and scratches, differences in the finish, perhaps variation in the material from which it is made, create a kind of heterogeneity. Now stand back from the table. Its surface will again assume a uniform appearance. In turn, the table will become part of a mixture of furniture and furnishings which make up your room. Similarly, every part of the building in which you live will seem unique and designed for a particular purpose. But if you leave your residence and travel some distance from it, you may very well think of it and the property upon which it stands as a single unit called *home*. Thus at each successive change in scale we alternate between heterogeneous and homogeneous interpretations of the world.

When we view the human organization of space, we see areas composed of many similar units, such as farms, having little horizontal connectivity but with major linkages leading to distant focal points. The repetition of like objects in general creates an impression of areal uniformity. If we look at a larger, more encompassing area, the focal point of the system becomes apparent and appears as a nodally organized portion of a hierarchy. The alternation of our view is between uniform regions and nodal regions.

Multiple property regions

The hinterland of Mobile, Alabama, discussed in Chapter 4 is an example of a nodal region. In this case, a complex city forms the central hub from which all manner of things, including newspapers and services, flow outward and into which supplies and customers find their way. One set of preference lines or linkages cannot show all the activities which define the city and its hinterland. Neither does a single boundary serve to delimit the farthest

reach of Mobile. Here is a case where multiple criteria define the urban region which interests us. The problem is to choose an average boundary for the city's hinterland representing several factors instead of a single boundary for a single activity.

There can be as many boundaries drawn around a city as there are types of retail, wholesale, service, administrative, and all other functions available within it. Because of this, Ullman's study of Mobile shows a kind of transition zone marking the outer limits of the city's influence. This zone is actually defined by several boundaries, not just one. Regional boundaries are often delimited in this manner. An analysis of the boundary between the hinterland regions of New York City and Boston further illustrates this point. Figure 10–1 shows the division of southern New England between the two metropolises based on seven indicators. Three areas are clearly defined: a region belonging exclusively to Boston, another to New York City, and a wide transition zone between the two. There is considerable areal overlap between many types of nodally organized hierarchies centered in Boston and New York. The solution to the problem of assigning areas to either of these two central nodes is found by determining the direction of dominant movement for whatever indicator is used. For example, the suburbs of Boston are classed within the hinterland of that city because an overwhelming number of telephone calls are directed from them to Boston's downtown area. A very large number of calls are also made from Boston's suburbs to New York City, but the dominant direction of movement is to Boston. This same idea of dominance determining association can apply to many kinds of indicators and to many problems of regional delimitation.

Continuous and discrete observations

Consider two uniform regions: a field of wheat and the climatic zone within which it is found. If we walk through the field, we will see that it is composed of individual plants largely independent of their neighbors. Now let us consider temperature, one aspect of the climate of the area. Since the sun shines everywhere upon the air above the field, there is no part of it which is not affected by radiant energy. In fact, by definition, even the absence of radiant energy constitutes a measure of temperature. No matter how small an area we choose to observe, no matter how finely we subdivide our climatic area, we can always assign a temperature to the area under observation. This is not to say that the temperature will be everywhere the same. Differences in the slope of the ground, the reflectivity of the surface, and numerous other conditions introduce variations from place to place. But temperature will exist everywhere; only our observations of it are discontinuous. In other words, phenomena such as temperature are continuous variables over space. This is true of human as well as of natural phenomena. We have previously referred to the dichotomous and therefore continuous character of political jurisdictions. You cannot for purposes of observation subdivide a nation into areas so small that they will fall through the sieve of political jurisdiction and land in some apolitical space. On the other hand, almost all economic observations, whether per capita income, productivity, or capitalization, are based on discrete units of observation. We may describe Appalachia as a poverty region, but in the last analysis our figures are based on the incomes of individual human beings. Furthermore, the uniformities we plot on per capita income maps are aver-

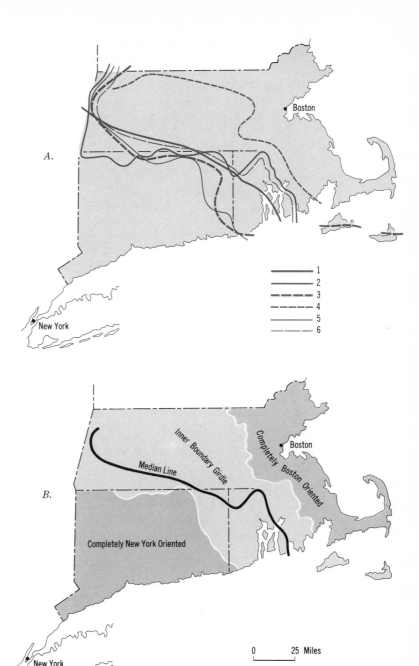

Figure 10-1 Delimitation of hinterland boundaries between Boston and New York City (*A*) The median boundaries for a selection of activities were established in New England between Boston and New York City. The activities were (1) railroad and coach passenger flows, (2) newspaper circulation, (3) telephone calls, (4) business addresses of directors of manufacturing firms, and (5) correspondent banks. Two other indicators not shown on the map were metropolitan origin of vacationers and an estimate of truck freight movement. (*B*) The median, or middle line, of the seven functional indicators was then used to define the boundary between hinterlands of the two metropolises. The boundary zone on either side of the median line shows the zone of partial dominance, (Maurice H. Yeates and

Barry J. Garner, *The North American City*, Harper & Row, New York, 1971, p. 102; after H. L. Green, "Hinterland Boundaries of New York City and Boston in Southern New England," *Economic Geography*, vol. 31, no. 4, October, 1955)

ages or means and incorporate paupers below the level shown as well as rich people hidden in the crowd. In every case where we deal with uniform regions it is wise to keep in mind whether the phenomena dealt with are discrete or continuous.

The space-time framework for regionalization

The frequency and timing of our observations will also affect our interpretation of whatever we analyze. Both of these conditions can be thought of as scale differences, but one operates in time while the other operates in space. The two together constitute a space-time frame of reference of immense importance.

If we study the expansion of the United States across North America and choose to view the process only at 100-year intervals beginning in 1776, we will learn few details about the order in which statehood occurred (Figure 10-2). The time interval chosen is inappropriate for our purposes. We would do better to look at the country every decade, as in Figure 10-3. On the other hand, if we wish

to study commuter patterns in metropolitan areas, we must sample the area at least every six hours. Measures made by the decade are of scant use for planning better traffic patterns and controls.

Returning to our spatial point of view, we must study the territorial expansion of the United States using all North America as our spatial frame and using states, whatever their size, as the statistical subdivisions. To make sense out of commuter patterns we need to look at entire metropolitan areas with reasonably small subdivisions, since most commuters leave the central cities when their work is done but at the same time do not travel far from them. As in all research the upper and lower limits of the scale of investigation should be carefully considered. We must always avoid using too many units or too few. This applies to time as well as space. Too many units— that is, too fine a filter—will hide significant relationships by isolating each observation in its own location and moment in history. Too few units—a sieve with too large a mesh —will allow clots and clusters of data to pass unobserved by hiding significant rela-

Figure 10-2 Statehood at 100-year intervals.

1776

1777-1876

1877 to present

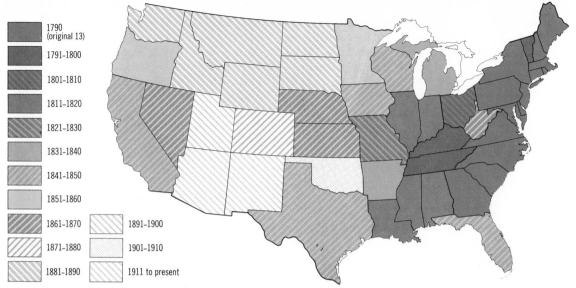

Figure 10-3 Statehood at 10-year intervals.

Legend:
- 1790 (original 13)
- 1791-1800
- 1801-1810
- 1811-1820
- 1821-1830
- 1831-1840
- 1841-1850
- 1851-1860
- 1861-1870
- 1871-1880
- 1881-1890
- 1891-1900
- 1901-1910
- 1911 to present

tionships within statistical averages compiled for meaningless aggregations.

Methods of Identifying Regions

When we attempt to identify a region, we are most often concerned with several characteristics rather than a single feature of the area. Single-feature regions like the retail outlets and customer distributions to which we have already referred are less of a challenge to define than more complicated regional types. In order to illustrate methods of regional identification we now present some problems necessitating more complicated regional analysis.

Areal overlays

One of the simplest and best ways of locating multiple uniform regions consisting of overlapping criteria is to plot each of several characteristics either on the same map or on transparent overlays which may then be superposed upon each other. The area having the greatest number of overlapping portions may be defined as the region or at least as the core of the region in question. This technique has paral-

lels in the mathematical use of Venn diagrams and in set theory, which will be commented on after the following example.

The overlay technique can be illustrated by a very practical problem recently solved by one of the authors. A large bank wished to establish a branch office in the suburbs of its home city. According to the law of its state, branch banks may be located in unincorporated suburban territories but only in *established community centers*. In other words, outside the city limits of any settlement, new banks can only be opened in recognizable settlements although such places have not yet incorporated or formed legal identities for themselves. In the case in question, the parent bank hoped to prove that a certain small unincorporated collection of homes, businesses, and service establishments constituted a viable community despite its lack of legal identity. If this could be proved, the bank could then build its branch office there and conduct business. The problem of establishing the functional validity of the settlement in question was a very geographic one.

As in any regional problem there were three steps necessary in its solution: (1) The term *established community center* had to be defined in a way which would allow the area in question to be systematically compared with the theoretical definition; (2) a suitable scale of research had to be determined; (3) actual research techniques and analysis had to be decided upon and carried out.

The problem of definition was met by use of the same kind of geographic reasoning which we have already presented in earlier chapters. The following is an excerpt from the formal argument presented to the Federal Comptroller of Currency, who decided the case.

Economic, political and social organization of metropolitan areas takes the form of nested hierarchies. Some functions are regional in scope, others metropolitan and still others local. An economic example of such a hierarchy is retail shopping centers. Some are regional in character, serving large regions in the metropolitan area. Others are community retail centers and still others serve as local convenience shopping centers. Political organization follows the same pattern. Some administrative services have regional jurisdiction and a similar tax base, others are county-wide and others local. Similar social organizations exist. Club memberships, church groups, and school districts organize the community at the local scale for social purposes. Unincorporated villages are a type of community organization at the lower level of this hierarchy. We may claim that a concentration of such local activities, when not an incorporated place, is still the organizing focus of the surrounding territory out to at least half the distance to the next concentration of services of comparable size. Natural and man-made barriers may modify the extent of this influence. A branch bank, which is a local economic activity operating at the convenience level, may be expected to seek out such a cluster of community activities as the most effective location in which to reach the people of the local community.

By this definition, proof of the viability of the settlement in question depended upon being able to demonstrate its centrality or focality from an economic, administrative, and social point of view.

The scale of investigation was more or less pragmatically determined. An area including and larger than the settlement had to be shown. At the same time, a very large area including numerous such settlements was unnecessary since similar settlements would subdivide the area into roughly equal-sized low-order hinterlands. Therefore, an area roughly 6 by 6 miles with the settlement near its center was selected (Figures 10–4 to 10–6).

Three research techniques were used in the analysis. To begin, five overlapping service areas were plotted on the map: (1) fire districts, (2) police districts, (3) voting precincts, (4) elementary school districts, and (5) postal districts. The subsequent overlap of these services is shown in Figure 10–4. Next, the addresses of a random sample of local library patrons were plotted on the map along with similar samples of a cleaning establishment's customers, members of the local Veterans of Foreign Wars post, and members of the Rotary and Kiwanis Clubs (Figure 10–5). These distributions represent a more nodally organized set of activities but again helped to confirm the evidence of centrality presented by the first analysis. Finally, the number of urban land parcels per quarter square mile were counted for the entire 64-square-mile area. It was reasoned that urban-sized land parcels rather than farm-sized properties are a de facto proof of urbanization. The density of small-sized land parcels shown in Figure 10–6 coincides rather neatly with the overlap of service areas on the first map and the cluster of customers and members on the second. To make a long story short, the central area in question was judged to be an *established community center*, and the case was decided in favor of the bank. From the point of view of this discussion, the analysis had established the functional validity of a small, low-order urban region.

A note on Venn diagrams and set theory

Readers with some background in logic or mathematics will recognize certain similarities between the technique of overlaying one regional characteristic on another and the use of

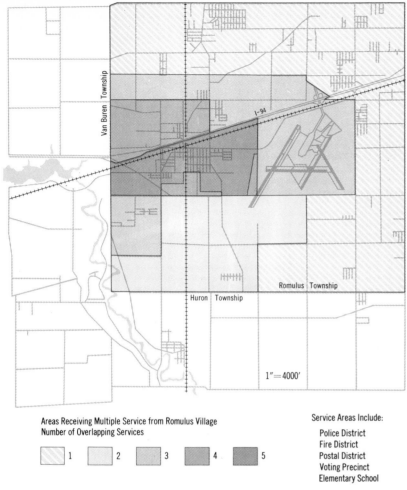

Van Buren Township

I-94

Huron Township

Romulus Township

1″=4000′

Areas Receiving Multiple Service from Romulus Village
Number of Overlapping Services

1	2	3	4	5	

Service Areas Include:

Police District
Fire District
Postal District
Voting Precinct
Elementary School

Figure 10-4 Public service jurisdictions of the unincorporated village of Romulus, Michigan   An unincorporated village, by definition, has no boundaries. The central office or facility of each of the services listed was in the built-up section of the unincorporated village of Romulus. Each public service jurisdiction was plotted separately on the map. A functional definition of the village territory was defined as the zone with maximum overlap of the service jurisdictions.

Venn diagrams to sort out overlapping phenomena. Any collection of related or like things or activities can be thought of as a *set*. For example, all types of land use found in cities might be a single set. An individual and particular land use, such as a park or rail yard, is considered an *element* of the set. Closely related land uses—parks, playgrounds, bicycle paths, ball fields—can be thought as *subsets* within the set of urban land uses. Sets of one kind of element may overlap other sets and become subsets of more than one set. For example, the set of land uses known as *recreational* can be found as subsets of *urban land use* and *rural land use*. The largest grouping which includes all elements under consideration is called the *universal set*.

As Peter Haggett points out, maps may be

Dividing Space Around and Within Cities: Regional Analysis

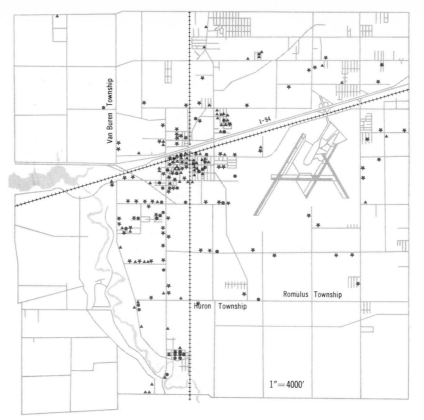

Van Buren Township

I-94

Romulus Township

Huron Township

1" = 4000'

* Members Kiwanis, VFW Post, Rotary Club
• Cleaning Establishment Customers
▲ Library Users

Figure 10-5 Home place sample of members and customers of Romulus-centered activities The range of certain central place functions of the unincorporated village was established by plotting the home address of a sample of members and customers of Romulus-based activities.

considered a special type of Venn diagram. Thus you may think of all the countries in the Western Hemisphere as a universal set, the countries of South America as a subset, and a single South American country as an element within both the set and subset. In this case, spatial contiguity plays an important role. In the more general case, nonspatial characteristics define at least some of the characteristics of the elements. For example, the universal set might again be all the countries of North and South America, but the subset could be major producers of wheat and beef. Elements within the latter subset would then include Argentina and the United States, which, obviously, are noncontiguous. This emphasizes the necessity of keeping the operational definitions of the problem clearly defined. It is also necessary to keep in mind that most Venn diagrams are maps not of geographical space but of abstract spaces often specified by nonmetric definitions.

Venn diagrams deal often with a finite and rather neat geographic world containing well-defined units with clear characteristics. Reality is messier than that.

The most widely used method by means of which complex associations of variables can be simplified is factor analysis or principle component analysis. The next section shows

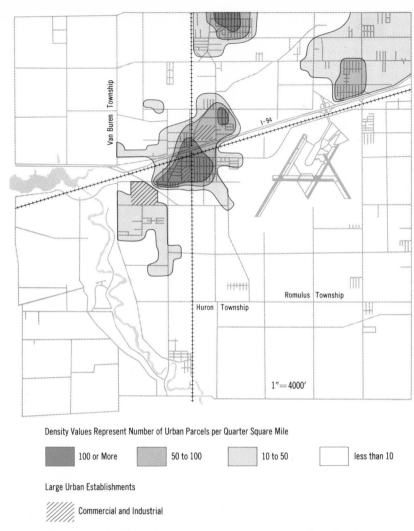

Density Values Represent Number of Urban Parcels per Quarter Square Mile

| | 100 or More | | 50 to 100 | | 10 to 50 | | less than 10 |

Large Urban Establishments

Commercial and Industrial

Figure 10-6 Urban land parcel density in the vicinity of Romulus, Michigan A land parcel map was employed to determine the density of land parcels in the vicinity of the unincorporated village of Romulus. A lattice of points was laid over the map, and the number of parcels of land within a square centered on the point and half a mile on each side were counted. A density surface was so defined, and contours on that surface revealed the contiguously built territory of the village. This method of establishing boundaries is morphological rather than functional. The two methods described in Figures 10-5 and 10-6 were functional. Counting housing density or street intersections would be two other morphological techniques for defining urban areas.

how this technique has been used to look at the distribution of economic development throughout the world.

Factor and principle component analysis

Regions, like people, are complicated and unique but at the same time share similarities. Just as everyone has a head and two arms and two legs, so may regions share commonalities such as similar population densities, climates, and vegetation. If we look closely at people, however, we observe different skin pigmentation, as well as straight hair and curly hair; blonde, brunette, and black hair; big noses and small ears; big ears and small noses. But the important thing is that despite a confusion of physical detail, we can perceive apparent if sometimes elusive patterns by means of which we can tell one group from another. For example, if we encounter a collection of people with high cheek bones, a fold of skin at the inner corner of the eye, and straight black hair, we might classify them as Mongoloid rather than Caucasoid or Negroid peoples. With additional effort and analysis we might be able to identify or categorize them as Japanese or Chinese. If we went further and took their cultural attributes into consideration, our identification would become almost positive. There would be exceptions to our general description of all people claiming Japanese ancestry, but the probability of such variations would be low, since the Japanese share a common cultural heritage as well as genetic background. To put it another way, we can describe a range of physical and/or cultural attributes belonging to a particular people by using a single comprehensive term, in this case *Mongoloid* or, more specifically, *Japanese*. The problem is to sort out the details into sets of related characteristics and to arrive at systems of classification which can account for all the details in terms of a few basic types.

One analytical technique by means of which numerous characteristics associated with any phenomenon can be compared, sorted, and accepted or rejected on the basis of the similarities they share with each other is called *factor analysis*. We might start out by observing ten different characteristics in a human population and find that of the total six features are always closely associated. We might also find that three of the remaining four features are also found in mutual association but independent of the first six. A third set of one feature also exists. That is, changes or variation in the group of 6 will not be accompanied by changes in the group of 3 or the group of one. However, all three groups are needed to describe the population. We might further be able to use a single measure to describe how much of the variation in the total population could be explained by the six characteristics in combination. Such a grouping and measure is called a *factor*. Once several such factors have been identified which characterize differences within a particular population, it is possible to determine the percent of overall variation that can be attributed to each factor.

Thus, if we take our example of ten traits and reduce them to three basic factors or patterns, we would "collapse" the ten to three and still be able to adequately describe the population. We might also be able to separate each individual from the population and describe him in terms of the three factors (let us call these *A*, *B*, and *C*) that we have already identified. We could thus assign him an *A* value, a *B* value, and a *C* value which taken in combination would describe him in terms of the three factors, which in turn would represent ten different physical traits.

Two similar techniques exist by means of which this can be accomplished. If *all* the variation within a population is assigned in part to each of the identified sets of characteristics, the technique is called *principle component analysis*. If some small percentage of the variation within a population is left unassigned and attributed to error, the technique is called *factor analysis*. The difference between these two techniques is a technical one, and for our purposes we will speak of the two interchangeably. Moreover, we will

Table 10-2 Indices of World Economic Development

1. Kms. railroads p.u.a.*	13. Imports p.c.	28. Crude birth rates
2. Kms. railroads p.c.†	14. % Exports to N. Atlantic	29. Crude death rates
3. R.r. freight ton-km. p.y.p.c.‡	15. % Exports raw materials	30. Pop. growth rates
4. Ton-km. freight p. km. r.r.	16. Kw-h. electricity p.c.	31. Infant mort. rates
5. Km. roads p.u.a.	17. Energy cons. in kw-h.	32. % Pop. in cities >20,000
6. Km. roads p.c.	18. Energy, cons. p.c.	33. Physicians p.c.
7. Motor vehicles p.c.	19. Comml. energy p.c.	34. % Land area cultiv.
8. Motor vehicles p.u. road	20. % Energy cons. comml.	35. Wheat yields
9. Motor vehicles p.u.a.	21. Energy res. in kw-h.	36. Rice yields
10. Value for. Trade	22. Energy res. in kw-h.p.c.	37. Pop. p.u. cultiv. land
11. For. trade p.c.	23. % Hydro pot. dev.	38. Newspaper circ. p.c.
12. Exports p.c.	24. Hydro pot. dev. p.c.	39. Telephones p.c.
	25. Fiber cons. p.c.	40. Mail flows p.c. domestic
*p.u.a. = per unit area.	26. Petrol. ref. capc. p.c.	41. Mail flows p.c. internat.
†p.c. = per capita.	27. Pop. density	42. National product
‡p.y. = per year.		43. National product p.c.

avoid a detailed, "cookbook" discussion of how analysis based on these mathematical techniques is carried out and concentrate instead on the results and their regional implications.

Some nations are rich and some are poor, but are these national units clustered together geographically into regions or are they randomly distributed? In other words, are there regions of the world which might accurately be described as developing as well as those which are developed? Also, do groups of nations share nearly similar characteristics of development and closely resemble one another, or do they "string out along various continua which measure relative development"? Brian J. L. Berry in a global study of the regionalization of economic development has used factor analysis to examine these and similar questions.

The first step in this exercise in regionalization was to decide upon a broad definition of "economic development." This condition is generally thought of as a high level of production and consumption of energy and material goods matched by a high level of literacy, good health, and similar demographic con-

ditions. Next, data were collected for forty-three various measures of development for each of ninety-five world political units. A selection of these indices is shown in Table 10-2. The countries are listed in Table 10-3 and shown on the maps in Figures 10-7 and 10-8. Other indices of development and additional countries might have been added to these lists, but nearly impossible difficulties arose in getting comparable data for more political units or measures of development. It was also felt that the large number of countries would sufficiently describe the entire world, while the forty-three indices were more than adequate to indicate the relative position of a given nation.

The countries were ranked according to their position for each indicator, and a 43 × 43 correlation matrix comparing each of the indices with all the others was computed. Factor analysis was then used to find which combinations of the many indices best described the countries. The forty-three indices fell into four basic patterns by means of which the ninety-five countries could be described. The first factor or pattern accounted for 84.2 percent of the observed variation, while the second factor

Dividing Space Around and Within Cities: Regional Analysis

Table 10-3 Political Units Considered in Developmental Study

1. Canada	33. Ireland	65. Rhodesia & Nyasaland
2. United States	34. Italy	66. Fr. Equatorial Africa
3. Colombia	35. Netherlands	67. Fr. W. Africa
4. Costa Rica	36. Norway	68. Madagascar
5. Cuba	37. Portugal	69. Angola
6. Dominican Republic	38. Spain	70. Mozambique
7. El Salvador	39. Sweden	71. Afghanistan
8. Guatemala	40. Switzerland	72. Ceylon
9. Haiti	41. United Kingdom	73. India
10. Honduras	42. Algeria	74. Pakistan
11. Mexico	43. Egypt	75. China
12. Nicaragua	44. Libya	76. Taiwan
13. Panama	45. Morocco	77. Hong Kong
14. Venezuela	46. Tunisia	78. Japan
15. Argentina	47. Cyprus	79. S. Korea
16. Bolivia	48. Iran	80. Br. Borneo
17. Brazil	49. Iraq	81. Burma
18. Chile	50. Israel	82. Indonesia
19. Ecuador	51. Jordan	83. Malaya (& Singapore)
20. Br. Guiana	52. Lebanon	84. Philippines
21. Surinam	53. Syria	85. Thailand
22. Peru	54. Turkey	86. S. Vietnam
23. Paraguay	55. Ethiopia	87. Australia
24. Uruguay	56. Ghana	88. New Zealand
25. Austria	57. Liberia	89. U.S.S.R.
26. Belgium	58. Sudan	90. Czechoslovakia
27. Denmark	59. Union of S. Africa	91. E. Germany
28. Finland	60. Belgian Congo	92. Hungary
29. France	61. Br. E. Africa	93. Poland
30. W. Germany	62. Gambia	94. Rumania
31. Greece	63. Sierra Leone	95. Yugoslavia
32. Iceland	64. Nigeria	

Source: Brian J. L. Berry, "A Statistical Analysis," part VIII, in Norton Ginsburg (ed.), *Atlas of Economic Development*, University of Chicago Press, Chicago, 1961, p. 110.

accounted for another 4.2 percent. Such a high percentage of explanation allows us to skip factors 3 and 4. Factor 1 indicates that among the forty-three original indicators, accessibility, transportation, trade, external relations, technology, industrialization, urbanization, national product, and the organization of the population are all closely associated along a single new measure or dimension which is referred to by Berry as the *technological scale*. Factor 2 emphasizes those indices least repre-

sented by factor 1: birth and death rates, infant mortality rates, population growth rates, population densities, and population per unit of cultivated land. This second factor is referred to as the *demographic scale*.

Once the major patterns had been identified, the countries were reranked according to their positions on these two new scales. At this point the new list of ninety-five countries was divided into five equal groups of nineteen countries each. This arbitrary

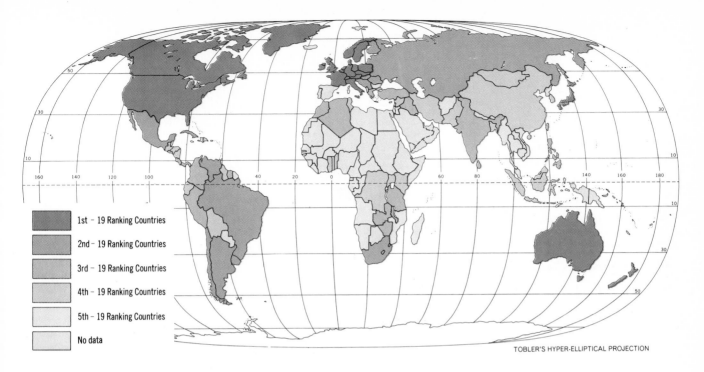

1st – 19 Ranking Countries

2nd – 19 Ranking Countries

3rd – 19 Ranking Countries

4th – 19 Ranking Countries

5th – 19 Ranking Countries

No data

TOBLER'S HYPER-ELLIPTICAL PROJECTION

Figure 10-7 The technological pattern Countries ranked according to a composite score on a "technological scale" as determined by a factor analysis of ninety-five world political units and forty-three measures of development. (Brian J. L. Berry, "A Statistical Analysis," Part VIII, in Norton Ginsburg (ed.) *Atlas of Economic Development*, © 1961 by the University of Chicago. Published 1961. Composed and printed by the University of Chicago Press, Chicago, Ill., p. 111)

division allowed a middle group and two other groups on the higher and lower sides. Maps were made using the two sets of five groups of nineteen countries each. The result is shown in Figures 10–7 and 10–8. These two maps show us that high productivity, energy use, consumption of goods, and access to transportation are accompanied by good health, literacy, and low infant mortality rates, to name a few of the indicators represented by the two factorial scales. Conversely, measures typical of low energy consumption and minimal production and consumption of goods and services are paralleled by poor health, high death rates, and high population densities per unit of cultivated land. The resulting map patterns indicate that a con-

siderable degree of spatial contiguity or regionalization does occur in terms of nations sharing similar characteristics. While Berry went on to test and analyze the relationship between the demographic and technological scales, our purpose is served at this point. Given refined analytical techniques it is possible to "boil down" vast quantities of data into manageable map patterns representing regions. However, in the study just described human judgment was still important, as it is in all regional analysis. The forty-three basic indices on which the analysis was made were first identified through familiarity with the phenomenon of economic development. Later in the study the division of ninety-five countries into five groups of nineteen each

Dividing Space Around and Within Cities: Regional Analysis

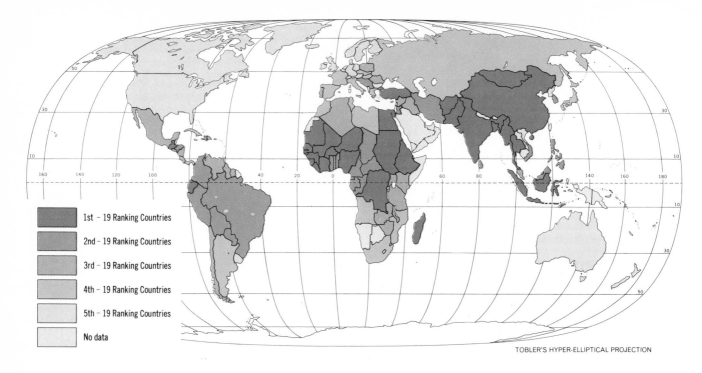

1st – 19 Ranking Countries

2nd – 19 Ranking Countries

3rd – 19 Ranking Countries

4th – 19 Ranking Countries

5th – 19 Ranking Countries

No data

TOBLER'S HYPER-ELLIPTICAL PROJECTION

Figure 10-8 The demographic pattern Countries ranked according to a composite score on a "demographic scale" as determined by a factor analysis of ninety-five world political units and forty-three measures of development. (Op. cit., Figure 10–7, p. 112)

was again a matter of cartographic convenience. Nevertheless, the resulting maps confirm our notions of the distribution of development throughout the world. In Chapter 12 we will examine a theory which accounts for the particular distribution we have just described. In the meantime, let us continue our discussion of regionalization.

The Topology of Geography

Regionalization is a basic technique by means of which we organize our impressions of the world in which we live. Our interest in regions could be justified by this aspect alone, but a second reason exists. We might call this reason the topology of geography: a consideration of the shapes areas take and of the real world conditions resulting from those forms.

Gerrymandering

The most famous or infamous manipulation of geographic shapes has been given the name *gerrymandering*. This practice is essentially the drawing of political boundaries in such a way as to give unfair numerical advantage to a particular party when voting takes place. The name itself is derived from that of Elbridge Gerry, Governor of Massachusetts, who in 1812 led his party in a redistricting of state counties in order to gain unfair political advantage in forthcoming elections. The strange shape given Essex County in the northeastern part of the state (Figure 10–9) led critics to call it a *gerrymander:* Gerry + (sala)mander. The practice which remains common today in local politics, is similar to the manipulation of the segregation indices discussed in Chapter 2.

Spatial efficiency

Not all boundaries are redrawn for the purpose of gerrymandering. The "one man, one vote" ruling of recent years has led many states, counties, and cities into spatially redefining their political subunits to ensure the voting rights of citizens. In other words, the voting districts have been made more *spatially efficient*. Another subject demanding greater spatial efficiency is the matter of drawing the boundaries of school districts to minimize racial inequities and also to minimize the distances that students must travel to reach their schools. If we consider a school as a central place to which students travel, then its district will constitute a hinterland from which it draws its student population. If the hinterland is shaped in a strange or inefficient way, some students will have to travel excessive distances. In this case a measure of spatial efficiency would be the sum of the distances all students attending a school would have to travel in order to reach the school. The smaller this figure, the more efficient will be the region served by each school.

A knowledge of geography and of regionalizing techniques need not be an abstract exercise. Good regions can mean savings to taxpayers, the more equitable distribution of voters within voting districts, and the rational matching of consumers and resources. In this way geography can create its own social topology. But regions in themselves tell only part of the story. The world is most interesting where one region or realm contacts another. In fact, the edges of regions are where the real problems of regional delimitation are found. Therefore, we next consider boundaries, their problems, and their role in the world around us.

Boundary Problems and the Edges of Regions

One example of this deals with the edges of homogeneous regions or the contact zone between them. Take, for example, the problem of defining the edge of a typical urban area

Figure 10-9 The original gerrymander The original gerrymander was depicted in the *Boston Gazette* of March 26, 1812. The name refers to a senatorial district designed to concentrate Federalist votes. It was at first likened to a salamander but later became known as a gerrymander, after Governor Elbridge Gerry, who signed the districting law.

as shown in Figure 10–10. Long fingers of built-up area extend into the countryside with urban outliers beyond the contiguous edge. Empty spaces form deep embayments with pockets of unoccupied land here and there within the city. Where does the city begin and end? One approach to this question might be to define the urban CBD and to work outward from the center to the edge. The techniques we have already covered in this chapter, in large part, have adopted this strategy. Another way of considering regions is to worry about their edges. That is, if we can define their edges, the centers will take care of themselves. But to define the edges of one or more regions we must consider the processes at work within them. Let us consider a con-

Dividing Space Around and Within Cities: Regional Analysis

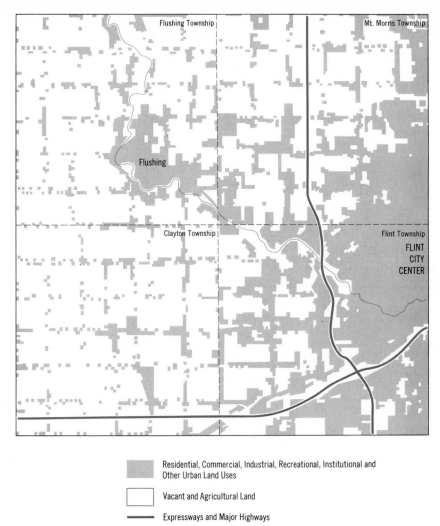

Flushing Township

Mt. Morris Township

Flushing

Clayton Township

Flint Township

**FLINT
CITY
CENTER**

Residential, Commercial, Industrial, Recreational, Institutional and
Other Urban Land Uses

Vacant and Agricultural Land

Expressways and Major Highways

**Figure 10-10 Urban areas of the western half of Flint, Michigan, and
adjoining townships** Where is the boundary of the urban area of Flint?
(Based on Genessee County Metropolitan Planning Commission map, "Existing Land Use, Genessee County, 1968")

figuration found in nature and how generalization can be drawn from complexity.

Epsilon measures and local operators

Suppose we wish to locate the boundary between the North American continent and the
Atlantic Ocean southward from New York
City. Nothing could be simpler, you might at
first think. However, questions of scale would

immediately raise their heads like monsters
from the ocean depths. Does our map need to
show all the embayments and peninsulas
illustrated in Figure 10–11A? Or would a much
smoother outline as in Figure 10–11B do? You
may reply that the closer we come to reality,
the better off we are, and that the first map is
the best. But if we were to look at a large-scale
Coast and Geodetic Survey navigational chart

*Human
Geography:
Spatial
Design
in World
Society*

214

of a portion of the same area, we would see how lacking in detail even the first map is. And yet, armed with the best maps available at the largest scales, if we were to walk along those same shores, we would become aware of many additional things the map makers had missed. If we were planning to sail southward along the coast from New York City in a small boat, and if that boat could turn easily in twice its own length but could never safely venture more than a few hundred yards from shore, we would be interested in all the crinkles and crenulations of the coast. On the other hand, if we were skippering a giant oil tanker whose keel rode many feet beneath the surface and which needed several miles in which to turn if it were using its own engines, we would avoid the coastal shallows at all cost. Our route would take us well out to sea, and the inlets and shoals nearer in would not interest us at all.

In order to depict the coast at the level of smoothness or detail suitable to our purposes we can use a simple, mechanical technique. Let us say that the diameter of an area in which a supertanker can effectively navigate is 25 miles. Next, let us cut out a circle of cardboard the radius of which is proportionate to 12½ miles on the map shown in Figure 10–11A. Now let us roll that disk along the coast, marking all the while the line of contact it makes with the intricate land-water boundary shown on the map. Notice that the edge of our disk cannot penetrate many bays and inlets. Note too that almost all the detailed features of coast fall on the landward side of the line of tangency between the effective operating radius of our ship and the heavily indented shoreline. The resulting line which we have drawn along the coast shows a much smoother contact between the continent and the sea than the one with which we started (Figure 10–11B). What we have ended with is a new map showing the edge of the domain of very large ships on the Atlantic. In using this method of defining a boundary we assume that the ship's captain will keep his vessel as near to the center of his circle of maneuvering ability as possible. The actual boundary falls at the perimeter of the circle, but if the ship were to be found there, it would be in dangerous waters and in trouble.

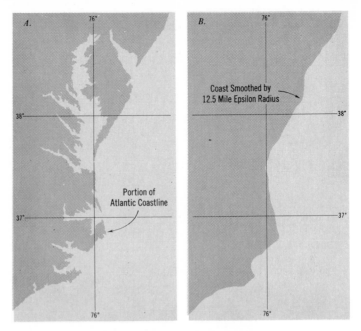

Figure 10–11 Portion of Atlantic coastline of the United States at different levels of boundary generalization (*A*) A detail map of the Atlantic coastline showing Delaware and Chesapeake Bays. (*B*) The same coastline as in part *A* generalized to a curve, with curvature not greater than that of a circle with a twenty-five-mile diameter.

The radius of the circle used to delimit the effective boundary between two types of regions or domains is called an *epsilon radius*, sometimes simply shown as the *E* radius. This radius may differ from one circumstance to another, and the size of its circle, which effectively delimits the intricacy or smoothness of a border, depends upon the processes at work within the region or regions defined. In the case of the oil tanker it was large; in the case of a sailing dinghy it would be small. In every case, the process or agent of action by which the epsilon size is determined is referred to as a *local operator*.

Boundary dwellers and boundary dwelling processes

The zones of contact between two or more regions are places of particular interest. Let us

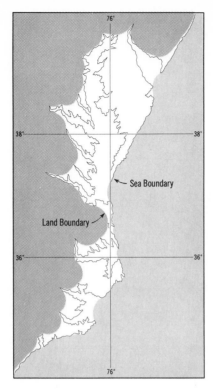

Figure 10–12 The coastline of the Chesapeake and Delaware Bay region smoothed on both land and sea sides by an epsilon radius of 12.5 miles

consider perhaps the single most important boundary zone on earth. The seashore or littoral marks the contact between land, water, and air. As the tide rises and falls, sometimes more, sometimes less land is exposed to the atmosphere. The shallow waters lapping the shore of the continents conserve or store the sun's energy and often become hospitably warm. At the same time rivers and runoff of all kinds bring nutrients from the land into the neighboring seas. Such foods are particularly available at the mouths of large rivers. There estuaries and deltas often present interfingerings of land and water. If we were to choose an epsilon measure of large radius, representing the daily life space of the larger fish and sea mammals, we could define the outer limits of the coastal zone by moving such a disk along

the map edge of such a shore. In the same way, if we chose another epsilon representing a continental- or land-based process, such as the outer coastal boundary for a railroad which would not require too many tight turns, causeways, or bridges, and moved this second epsilon disk along the landward side of the coastal zone, we would define two boundaries for the land and sea. These boundaries would approximately parallel each other, but in many places a kind of no-man's-land of tidal marsh and windswept headland, consisting of both land and sea and yet belonging completely to neither, would be defined (Figure 10–12).

Boundary zones such as these offer opportunities for processes which could not endure in the homogeneous environments on either side. In like manner, they are often noted for a unique set of inhabitants adjusted to peculiarities resulting from the interfingering and interaction of adjoining domains. Consider the map of Chesapeake Bay in Figure 10–13. Oysters are sea creatures which need rich sources of food as well as energy in the form of sunwarmed water. They are bottom dwellers and therefore live most often in shallow water. If the coastline is straight and steeply sloping, the zone available to them where the necessary conditions of shallow, nutrient-rich water are met is too narrow to sustain more than a modest population. At the same time, a straight coastline is more readily exposed to the pounding of surf which might easily destroy shellfish and crustaceans. The deep inlets of the estuary give protection from the sea's excess energy. This relationship of the boundary zone to its inhabitants is evident on the accompanying map. In much the same way, a major theory regarding the origins of life on the earth suggests that it may have first appeared in the shallow coastal waters of primordial continents.

For our immediate purpose of understanding urbanization we should transfer these ideas into the realm of human activities and consider the boundary effect in settled areas. Certainly the zone of deterioration surrounding the CBD in Burgess's concentric ring theory of city growth represents the contact between the business district and viable residential

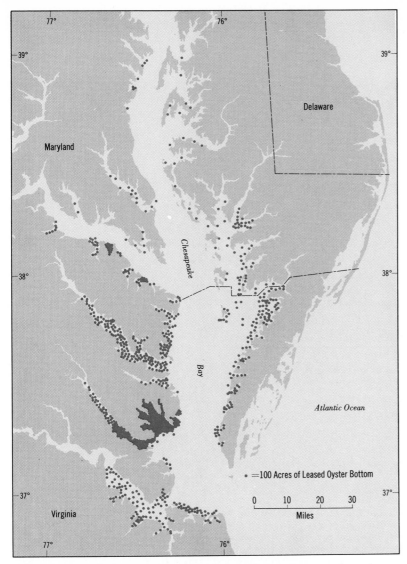

Figure 10-13 Oyster grounds in Chesapeake Bay   Oysters are boundary dwellers. They live in salt water but need the protection and nutrients of a shoreline. A zone of estuaries and deltas with deep interfingering of land and water offers the best environment for them. (John J. Alford, "The Role of Management in Chesapeake Oyster Production," *The Geographical Review,* vol. 63, no. 1, January, 1973, fig. 2, p. 48, copyrighted by the American Geographical Society of New York.)

districts surrounding it. One interesting example suggested by these ideas is in the North Beach area of San Francisco (Figure 10–14).

This area, which is directly west of the Barbary Coast of nineteenth century fame, before World War II included an Italian community

North Beach (Italian)

Telegraph Hill

The Embarcadero

San Francisco Bay

Powell

Columbus

Russian Hill

Steamship Docks

Pacific

Old Barbary Coast

Grant

Chinatown

Financial
District

California

Nob Hill

Market

Union Square

Counterculture

Reclaimed Land

Figure 10-14 The North Beach and Chinatown areas of San Francisco
Boundaries of ethnic districts in urban areas may provide an environment
for boundary dwellers in society. The zone between the tightly knit ethnic
communities of Chinatown (Chinese) and North Beach (Italian) was the
location of a series of counterculture developments in the 1950s and 1960s.

*Human
Geography:
Spatial
Design
in World
Society*

218

in North Beach, particularly along Columbus
and Grant Avenues, and the well-known
Chinatown to the south. In the years following
the war the Chinese community held firm in
its traditional location, but little by little buildings on the Italian edge of Chinatown were
given up by their original tenants. By the early
1950s this boundary zone between the two
ethnic communities had become the seedbed
for the earliest beginnings of what was later

to be known as the counterculture. Bohemians,
who were later to be followed by beatniks,
hippies, and flower children, began frequent-
ing bars and eating places such as the famous
hungry i. Small shops offering handicrafts and
organic foods first appeared there, and until
commercialization made the area a tourist
mecca, people dropping out of the system and
seeking a place to live often went there. Later,
the developing elements of the counterculture

moved westward to the Haight-Ashbury district, which flourished for a short time. Again the area sought out was in a sense a boundary zone. This time, low-cost rooms and stores were located between an expanding black district to the north and east and a contracting middle-class Jewish neighborhood to the south. The immediate presence of Golden Gate Park was an added inducement for street people and others to frequent the district.

Oysters, craft shops, and urban blight all can be described in terms of the special boundary environments or domains which help sustain them. In this way boundaries become a special class of regions in themselves. Where indentations and promontories are few in number—that is, where the contact zones are smooth and perhaps straight—transitions are usually abrupt, gradients steep, and zones almost linear in nature. Deep embayments very often create broad zones with shallow gradients.

Industrial Regions of the United States

Let us use some of our techniques for regionalization to find the industrial core of the United States. As we might expect, the distribution of manufacturing activities in America has a definite spatial expression. Knowledge that production is located in a few geographically limited regions provides useful insight into the spatial organization of not only America but the entire world.

How can we define a useful set of criteria with which to delimit such regions? Certainly the number of workers employed in industry should give some notion of where manufacturing takes place. We already know that few commuters travel more than an hour each way to and from work. Fifty miles, about the distance traveled in one hour on a busy highway, easily constitutes the outer limit that most people are willing to travel every day. The majority of workers travel somewhat less. If we locate the major centers of industry in terms of the numbers of employees and give each center a hinterland with a radius of 50 miles, we can define a region or regions based on industrial employment. But workers are

only part of the total picture of industry. Certainly, the difference between the value of raw materials delivered to a factory and the price of the finished products coming out the other end will be a good measure of the importance of the industrial center under consideration. Such a measure is called the *value added*. We would expect a close correlation between sites where many workers are employed and those places where the greatest value is added during the process of changing raw materials to finished goods. The automobile industry is an example of this. In other places, particularly in those industries which are highly automated, such as petroleum refining, and others where the end product is extremely valuable yet produced by a relatively small number of highly skilled craftsmen, such as tool and die making, we might expect value added to outstrip the absolute number of workers. Conversely, some industries pay relatively low wages, employ large numbers of workers, and produce relatively bulky goods of moderate

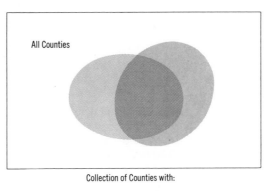

Collection of Counties with:

Over 10,000 Manufacturing Employees

Over $100,000,000 Value
Added by Manufacture per Year

Figure 10-15 Venn diagram of criteria defining manufacturing regions A Venn diagram represents sets of elements which share one or more attributes. In this instance, the elements are counties and the number of manufacturing employees and the value added by manufacturing are the attributes of interest. That subset of counties which exceed given levels in both attributes are chosen as the basic units of the manufacturing regions being sought.

Dividing Space Around and Within Cities: Regional Analysis

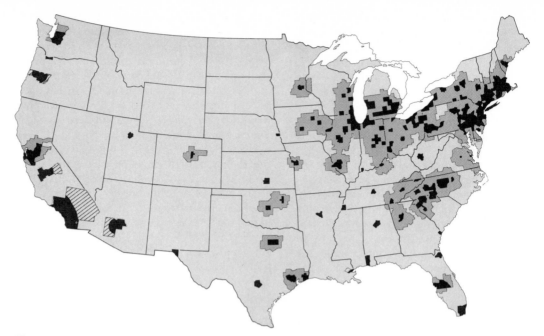

Figure 10-16 United States manufacturing regions The manufacturing regions shown are defined to include counties with over 10,000 annual average production workers and over $100 million value added by manufacturing (darker tone) and in addition, those counties whose centers of population are within fifty miles of a county of the type defined in part *A* and whose areas also adjoin one or more similarly defined areas (lighter tone). Portions of large Western counties which are beyond fifty miles of the county's population center are excluded from the region. (Compiled from data in *County and City Data Book 1967,* U.S. Bureau of the Census, Wash., D.C.)

value. The textile and garment industries fall within this category.

Which measure should we use, number of workers or value added? We can resolve this choice with a simple Venn diagram. Figure 10–15 shows value added and the number of employees in manufacturing as two overlapping sets. On the one side can be found all those instances where workers are a determining factor; on the other, all the cases where value added is most significant. The area common to both is less likely to occur and therefore is somewhat more narrowly defined than any other part of the universal set. Certainly any area sharing both characteristics can be thought worthy of inclusion in a core industrial region, so let us use both criteria in combination.

The next problem is a choice of scale. Data for the two measures we have chosen have been compiled by the census on a national, state, county, and city basis. States provide too coarse a filter to show much useful detail, although using them we might see indications of the general location of industry. Also, anomolies like the poverty-stricken Appalachian region penetrating the well-developed Northeastern states cannot be shown at a state-sized scale. Cities, on the other hand, appear as points on the maps of the United States small enough to be used in this book. This leaves counties as the most useful unit recording the data we wish to use. County units shown in the 1967 *United States Census of Manufacturing* as having more than 10,000 employed industrial workers *and* in which more than 100 million dollars in value is added by manufacturing are shown in Figure 10-16. While clusters of counties thus defined appear with some regularity in the Northeast, many units are isolated from their neighbors. This leaves us with too many regions which are too small for a good understanding of the national distribution of industry.

This is where the epsilon measure of a 50-mile commuting radius serves us well. We simply roll an epsilon circle with a suitable radius around all the clusters of counties. Any county so close to its neighbors that the circle cannot pass between it and others nearby is included inside an industrial region. On the other hand, so too are nonmanufacturing counties found within the line. Empty spaces inside a region thus defined are also fitted with the same epsilon measure. Areas untouched by the inside epsilon fall within the region but are too far from industrial counties to be included in the classification. In other words, our regions can have holes in them. Finally, we add two additional rules to neaten up our presentation. First, since regionalization is putting things together, we will not include as a region any single industrial county so far from a neighboring industrial county that it stands completely alone. Second, we will carefully observe a rule that keeps our epsilon circle within 50 miles of the center of population in each unit. With small counties this will make little or no difference as to the final appearance of our regions. Very large counties, such as Riverside and San Bernardino in southern California, which have large empty tracts as well as densely settled areas will be subdivided by this procedure, and part excluded, part included.

The resulting map showing the location of industry in the United States (Figure 10-16) resembles previous maps of value added and manufacturing workers (Figure 10-17). However, it also provides some surprises and new insights. The industrial Northeast shows up very clearly. This region still dominates American industry with 58.2 percent of the workers and 61.6 percent of the value added for the entire United States. But unlike earlier pre-

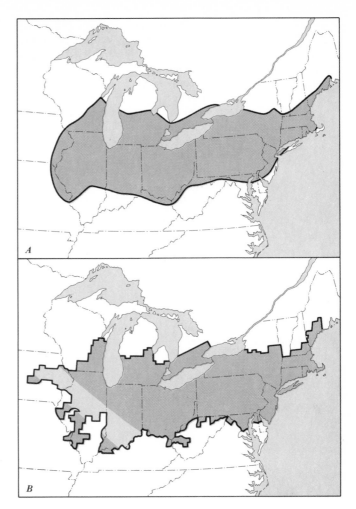

Figure 10-17 The manufacturing belt (*A*) 1919 (After de Geer), (*B*) 1958. Compare the Northeastern manufacturing belt as defined in two earlier figures with the one shown in Figure 10-16. They show nearly the same pattern. Noteworthy variations occur in southern Indiana and Ohio and in northern Pennsylvania, which are excluded from the areas defined in Figure 10-16. (Allen Pred, "The Concentration of High-Value-Added Manufacturing," *Economic Geography,* vol. 41, no. 2, April, 1965, p. 111)

sentations, the epsilon technique has clearly defined a large hole within the region in northern Pennsylvania. Also significant is the southward extension of another manufacturing region along the Carolina Piedmont into Georgia. This second region accounts for 7.1 percent of the workers and 4.7 percent of the value added in the United States and cannot be overlooked. Finally, significant islands of industry are scattered in the Midwest, in the South and along the Gulf Coast, and in the Pacific states. These account for 12.6 and 15.5 percent of the American totals and indicate the expansion of population and capital out of the Northeast into the West and South. All in all, however, the historic pattern of development in the United States remains the same.

We hope that two messages in particular are made clear in this chapter. First, the infinitely complicated world can be ordered by intuition or analytical techniques into intellectual constructs called *regions*. Second, our regionalization of industrial production indicates a significant core area in eastern North America. The two chapters that follow discuss a theory of agricultural location which in its broadest application relates urban land uses to those of rural areas besides showing how the industrial core areas of the world act, in part, as focal points of human spatial organization on a global scale.

11 | THE MARKET AND THE FARM: AGRICULTURAL LOCATION THEORY

A pilot flying over the cities of the North China Plain would see each settlement surrounded by a ring of green fields. The circles shade from bright green nearest the cities to more yellow hues and finally merge with browns and russets of the open farmlands far away from any urban place. This is called *green ring effect* and results from the use of human fertilizer on lands adjacent to the settlements. Soil nutrients concentrated in agricultural products are shipped to the cities, passed through human consumers, and returned in part to the fields as human waste, called *night soil,* which is collected and spread back on the land. Transportation costs are high for night soil, and it cannot be shipped long distances. Thus, the rapidly diminishing ring of green vegetation reflects the friction of distance on the return flow of nutrients to China's land.

You're on your way west. Interstate 80 stretches 2,000 miles ahead of you to San Francisco. You and your friend are driving shifts, and the road peels away steadily behind you. The suburbs of Chicago with their plumes and fumes disappear, and tall corn rises to the right and left as Illinois swings past. You started late, and as night comes down you are still moving through the green fields of Iowa. Morning comes up behind you and you stop to walk around a rest stop, stretching and looking. Western Nebraska now. Wheat fields. Dry

and getting drier. Grasslands ahead with *Danger: Livestock on Road* signs whipping by. The farms turn to ranches with windmills set back against the hills, and then you reach the Continental Divide with little towns hot under the high sun and sheep like pillows far off where pines begin. . . .

Chinese cities or American landscapes, the great earth stretches on; band upon band of different crops, different uses for the land; each region shading into the next. Is it chance the way farm activities are distributed? Does nature alone dictate that corn grows in one place and wheat in another? Why corn, then wheat, then cattle, then sheep? What structures the country as it is? In this chapter we discuss how geographic theory helps to explain the distribution and location of different types of agriculture. In the following chapter we suggest ways in which world land use as a whole is organized. More specifically, in both chapters we will be talking about a well-known body of thought referred to as *agricultural location theory.* Such theory was formalized by Johann von Thünen in the nineteenth century. Thünen's ideas present an opportunity to show the relationship between nodal or hierarchically organized regions and homogeneous, multifactor regions. In the next chapter we try to place the city in the context of its total environment on a worldwide scale.

The Areal Basis of Farming

Mankind ultimately depends on farming the land. Over many thousands of years a complex relationship has developed between humans on the one hand and their domesticated plants and animals on the other. This relationship is symbiotic; that is, it is a two-way street. Good farmers and a wise society give back to nature what they take. Soil is fertilized and mulched to replace nutrients and minerals removed by harvesting. Plants and animals, in turn, depend upon the people who eat them for their survival in competition with undomesticated nature. Corn, more correctly referred to as Indian corn or maize, was originally a tiny wild plant far different in form from today's tall, tasseled giants. In the wild state it could reproduce itself annually with no help. Thousands of years of selective breeding at the hands of man have changed all that. Maize must now be harvested, and the kernels must be removed from the cob and stored and then carefully planted the following spring in well-prepared ground. If man were to disappear and maize left to reseed itself, the domesticated species would be unable to do so and would disappear within a season or two following our own demise. We eat the plant, but in turn, we nurture it and help it to survive. In fact, though some domesticated plants and animals might survive in some form without man's help, their relationship to us is symbiotic. Without man their numbers and areal extent would be vastly reduced.

Almost all domesticated plants are heliophytes, or sun lovers. Sunlight is an areal phenomenon, and as we have said before, plants must spread over an area in order to obtain enough solar energy to prosper. At very large scales, within tiny areas, we can view plants as transportation systems. Leaves spread out to catch sunlight in order to form chlorophyll; roots bring water from below. The entire system maintains the plant in equilibrium with its environment through evaporation and transpiration. If we step back a bit and view plants at local scales incorporating slightly larger areas, we are dealing with point

-area relationships: plants spread as points across fields of sun-warmed soil. This same distribution when viewed at neighborhood scales creates small homogeneous areas easily identified as corn fields, wheat fields, pastures, and so on. At a regional scale farms can be viewed as nodally organized collections of fields. The farmhouse and buildings serve as a focal point for the activities of the farmer, who makes frequent trips outward from his own shelter to tend his crops. At harvest time, the sun's energy and soil's nutrients are brought from the fields in the form of produce, which is temporarily stored near the farm's focal point before being sent cityward. If we consider the point, line, and area relationships involved at several of these levels in the scale of operations, we can see collections of plants defining fields, which in turn are nodally organized around the farmhouse and farm buildings. Collections or sets of farms make up farm regions and are joined to farm communities and local markets by roads and telephones along which messages and produce move back and forth. Agricultural regions in turn serve urban concentrations of population which in most cases are still small enough to be shown as points on world maps. Thus, at some scales the system linking the land to the city can be seen as nodally organized into functional regions; at other scales homogeneous regions of particular crops or farm types can be identified.

The geographic significance of food processing

Communication and transportation links join points and areas in all possible combinations. Messages and energy move through the system as much as produce does. At the same time, the system concentrates and alters the resources which it transports. Food processing increases the value of produce in proportion to its weight or volume. This is done by removing excess water and waste material. The result, in each case, is a more transportable commodity. Every grocery store and household cupboard is full of examples. Jam is concentrated fruit. A steak is simply a cow with its hide, horns, and viscera removed. The pound of sugar in the jar on your breakfast table is refined from 11 pounds of sugar cane taken from the field.

Perishability is also important. Fresh grapes can be shipped only with great difficulty and expense. Raisins are less perishable and more easily transported than grapes. Wines are more valuable, and properly handled, nearly as transportable as raisins. But here we must distinguish between *concentration* and *preservation*, although one usually implies the other. Preservation of foodstuffs makes them available at other times than the harvest. Large populations are thus able to sustain themselves through the lean and hungry months of winter and spring. Concentration also is crucial to the development of civilization and urban lifestyles because it allows food to be transferred at lower cost to places where consumption far surpasses the ability of the local land to provide produce.

Storage and preservation of food represent a transfer through time from one season to another. *Concentration and transportation of food represent a spatial transfer* from areas of surplus to areas of need. Incidental to these processes are changes in flavor and texture, sometimes producing new foods even more desirable than the original fresh produce. In either case, concentration and preservation play important roles in the transportation and transfer systems which help to create agricultural regions.

The regionalization of farm types

When we speak of agricultural regions, we necessarily deal with abstractions born of our own imaginations. Nevertheless, we divide the world around us into homogeneous areas for convenience in classifying and understanding it. We speak casually of the *Corn Belt* or the *Cotton Belt*. We write learned papers about the types of agriculture, their numbers and spatial distribution. Even a simplified map of world agriculture identifies nine types of farming scattered across the globe (Figure 11–1).

The most interesting thing, however, is not the number or complexity of the regions we perceive, but rather the homogeneity within them and the singleness of choice which their farmers exercise. Farm numbers are limited by the availability of land, and within broad limits by the character of the physical world. A conservative estimate gives us more than 280 million individual farms throughout the world, with at least 2 million in the United States. If we were to examine these farms in more detail than shown in Figure 11–1, in order to acknowledge the variety we observe around us we might increase the number of farm types to 100 or more. The possibility of 280 million farmers choosing from over 100 types of farming leads to astronomical combinations, but similar farms are found clustered together. There is a distinct regional effect which creates the Corn Belt in the United States, the Rice Bowl of China, the dairy districts of Scandinavia, and the cattle region of Argentina, to name but a few.

Why do people making independent choices end up making the same one? Why does one farmer in Iowa decide to raise maize and soybeans and to fatten hogs, and his neighbor decide in favor of the same combination, and his neighbor, and his? These are important questions, for if the nature of farm decision making is understood, then changes in systems of agriculture can be brought about more easily.

Variables Determining Farm Production

The reasons for the choices farmers make can be subdivided into four categories. These are (1) site characteristics, (2) cultural preferences and perception, (3) available technology and organization, and (4) geographic situation or relative position. Let us briefly survey the first three of these before considering the fourth in greater detail.

Site characteristics

Site characteristics are the *in place* attributes of a particular area viewed at large, local, or

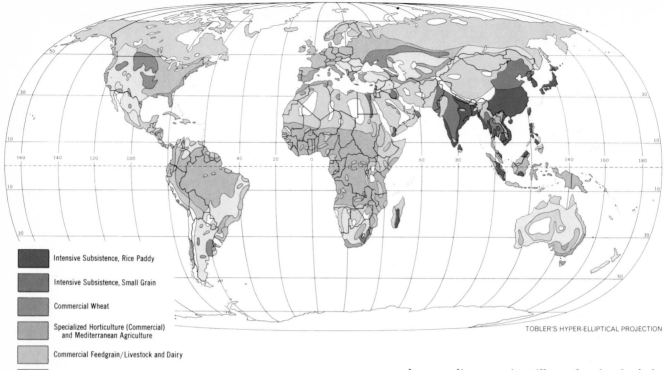

Intensive Subsistence, Rice Paddy

Intensive Subsistence, Small Grain

Commercial Wheat

Specialized Horticulture (Commercial) and Mediterranean Agriculture

Commercial Feedgrain/Livestock and Dairy

Tropical Export Crops, Plantation/Small Holders

Tropical Subsistence

Stock Raising

Nomadic Herding, Hunting, Fishing, Collecting, Forestry

Little or No Economic Activity

TOBLER'S HYPER-ELLIPTICAL PROJECTION

Figure 11-1 World agriculture

*Human
Geography:
Spatial
Design
in World
Society*

226

neighborhood scales. Thus, the amount of rainfall and average annual temperature of an area are considered important site characteristics. Soil type and fertility, slope, drainage, and exposure to sun and wind are also used to characterize the physical geography of each and every site. These things all relate to the amount of energy available in the physical system within which the location is incorporated. Other site characteristics could include the number of insect species, their populations, and their potential for destroying crops. The same is true for plant, animal, and human diseases. At still another level of abstraction, the human population density of an area can be considered one of the characteristics helping to determine the qualities of site. The type and intensity of pollution, the amount of built-up area, and the nature of land ownership and property fragmentation could be included in this category.

Cultural preference and perception

Perhaps the least known and possibly the most important of all the conditions which help to determine the type of agricultural activity which takes place at a given site are the cultural, psychological, and emotional characteristics of the people involved. For example, we do not eat everything which is available; sometimes people starve rather than consume perfectly edible but taboo food. Muslims abhor pork; certain Hindus abstain from eating all meat, but particularly beef; many Africans will not eat chickens or their eggs. The Chinese and some other peoples of East and Southeast Asia refuse to drink milk or eat milk products.

Figure 11–2 shows the areal extent of some of these food prejudices.

The refusal to eat certain foods places real constraints upon the agricultural systems possible within an area. Maize is scarcely considered human food in much of Europe, and therefore its production is restricted to animal fodder in all but a few places. Americans consume large quantities of meat despite its expense. A diet with greater emphasis upon vegetables and cereal grains would be just as healthful and would certainly cost much less. Most nationalities can be characterized in part, at least by their food preferences and prejudices. Think of the variety of ethnic restaurants which add to the allure of any large city.

The way we perceive the resources around us is also important. For example, the European settlement of North America was largely from the northeast to the west. The firstcomers were Anglo-Saxons and other Europeans accustomed to a moist, mild climate and a tree-covered landscape. Those yeoman farmers equated trees with fertility. To them, land to be suitable for farming should, in its wild state, have a cover of trees. New England and the East Coast met their expectations when they settled there. But as subsequent waves of migrants pushed west to the edge of the central prairies and Great Plains, they en-

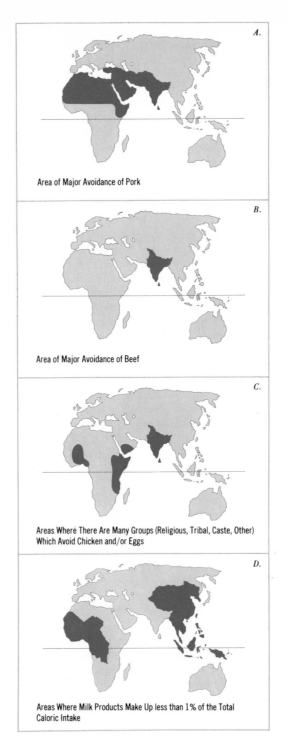

A.

Area of Major Avoidance of Pork

B.

Area of Major Avoidance of Beef

C.

Areas Where There Are Many Groups (Religious, Tribal, Caste, Other) Which Avoid Chicken and/or Eggs

D.

Areas Where Milk Products Make Up less than 1% of the Total Caloric Intake

Figure 11-2 Four food avoidance areas These represent very general regions of food avoidance; within them are subgroups with entirely different preferences and avoidances. We could also show the United States with major avoidances of nutritious meats which could be or are readily available: horsemeat, dogmeat, guinea pig meat, etc. These, as well as iguana, monkey, camel, and others, are relished by some peoples and totally rejected by others. Prejudices and sanctions for and against eating of animal foods are generally much stronger than those concerned with use of grain, fruit, and vegetable foods. Nevertheless, custom and preference have been found to play a major role in the use of all foods. (Maps adapted from several figures and references in Frederick J. Simoons, *Eat Not This Flesh,* University of Wisconsin Press, Madison, Wisc., 1961; average milk product consumption 1959–1961 from *The World Food Budget 1970,* Foreign Agricultural Report No. 19, U.S. Dept of Agriculture, Economic Research Service, Foreign Regional Analysis Division, Table 1, p. 4)

countered treeless, grass-covered areas. This lack of trees failed to meet their definition of truly fertile land. They referred to this area as the Great American Desert—which according to some people began at the Mississippi River—and pushed across it to the valleys along the Pacific Coast. There again they had to clear the land of timber before farming it, but they were satisfied. Those early farmers failed to see in the grasslands the latent fertility of what was to become the Great American Breadbasket. It took a later generation of migrants, this time people from the steppelands of Eastern Europe, to take advantage of the rich, grass-covered soils of Nebraska and Kansas. Thus, the way in which those immigrant groups perceived the environments which they encountered colored their subsequent use of the resources available to them. Many other factors influenced the pattern of settlement on the Great Plains. Certainly technological developments such as the moldboard plow and barbed wire fencing also were important. However, it is not our purpose in this section to explore these topics in great detail. We want, rather, only to identify some of the important elements which complicate reality and make simple explanations so difficult. As part of this we should not overlook intangible but significant human interpretations of the environment.

Available technology and organization

Since the end of World War II and the subsequent creation of international development programs, whole libraries have been written about technology and organization in agriculture. It is convenient to summarize this general category by describing two types of farms and farmers located at opposite ends of the developmental spectrum. Modern commercial agriculture as it is practiced in the United States might be one case; subsistence-level farming in an emerging economy would be the other.

Modern commercial farming The modern commercial farm is characterized by the large amount of capital necessary for its operation. We describe this as *capital-intensive*. Farms substituting human labor in place of all the conveniences and mechanical aids that money can buy are called *labor-intensive*. The investment necessary to operate a viable, capital-intensive farm unit in the United States is impressive. The average value of the property and buildings on "first class" American farms in 1959 was 135,000 dollars. Table 11−1 shows the average size of and the amount of capital invested in a variety of American farms in 1963. When we compare the capital invested with gross farm income for the same properties, it is easy to see why farmers prefer to leave the countryside and take jobs in urban areas. Remember, the gross farm income must compensate the farmer for his annual investment of labor as well as capital.

Modern farming is energy intensive. Mechanized agriculture utilizes energy not only to run its machines and to transport its crops to market but also to produce fertilizer and pesticides for its fields, to acquire irrigation water, and to carry out essential management functions. Fossil fuels are used for all these activities, and the growing energy crisis promises to influence modern farming everywhere in the world. We have already seen in the preceeding chapter how one characteristic of "developed" nations is their use of very large amounts of energy. For example, the United States in 1970 accounted for more than one-third of the energy consumed in the world, while only about 6 percent of the earth's people lived there.

All this is reflected in conditions on modern American farms. From 1950 to 1971 the number of farm tractors increased 86 percent from 2.4 million to 4.5 million. Fuel consumption rose accordingly by 4.3 billion gallons between 1940 and 1969 to a total of 7.6 billion gallons in the later year. In the case of corn, actual fuel use by farm machinery increased from 15 gallons per acre in 1945 to an estimated 22 gallons per acre in 1970. Table 11−2 shows the energy equivalents required for all the other tasks and items associated with corn production. Altogether, in 1945 kilocalories equal to the amount contained in 26 gallons

Table 11-1 Size, Investment, and Returns by Type of Farm, United States, 1963

Type of Farm* and Location	Size of Farm in No. of Units	Total Farm Capital, 1/1/63	Gross Farm Income†
Dairy, Central Northeast	32.2 cows	$ 43,400	$ 14,475
Dairy, western Wisconsin	23.8 cows	37,410	10,267
Hog and beef fattening, Corn Belt	153 acres	98,920	31,024
Cash grain, Corn Belt	246 acres	137,020	24,581
Cotton, southern Piedmont	101 acres	30,750	7,153
Cotton (nonirrigated), Texas, High Plains	445 acres	84,950	19,584
Cotton-specialty crops (irrigated), San Joaquin Valley, Calif.	329 acres	305,450	112,987
Tobacco, North Carolina Coastal Plain	47 acres	27,640	12,581
Spring wheat, small grain, livestock, northern Plains	588 acres	57,540	12,384
Winter wheat, sorghum, southern Plains	684 acres	125,910	16,632
Cattle ranches, intermountain region	149.5 cows	95,550	17,460

*All except cotton farms in California are family-operated.
†Includes both income from farming and government payments.
Source: *Farm Cost and Returns Commercial Farms by Type, Size and Location*, Agricultural Information Bulletin 230, Economic Research Service, U.S. Department of Agriculture, June 1964, p. 4.

of gasoline were used to produce one acre of corn, while in 1970 the equivalent amount of gasoline was 80 gallons. There was a compensating increase per acre in corn yields from 34 bushels per acre in 1945 to 81 bushels in 1970. However, energy inputs increased 3.1 times, while the yield per acre in corn food calories increased only 2.4 times. This was a decrease of 24 percent in the production of corn calories per kilocalorie input of fuel.

As long as fossil fuel is plentiful and inexpensive, such figures can be justified. But there are many indications that the lavish use of fossil fuel for farming cannot continue indefinitely. In 1970 it took about 112 gallons of gasoline per person to feed the population of the United States. If similar technology were used to feed a world population of 4 billion at the American nutritional level, 488 billion gallons of fuel would be required each year. One estimate of known world petroleum reserves is 546 billion barrels—which, if used only for farm-oriented activities, would last an estimated twenty-nine years given present conditions.

Another way of viewing modern agricultural production is to contrast the cost of producing 1,000 kilocalories of plant product in America and in India. In the former, the cost is about 38 dollars; in the latter, about 10 dollars. However, it is not our purpose here to suggest alternatives to the dilemma implied above. The point we wish to make is that modern farming requires very large amounts of energy and that energy is becoming increasingly expensive. The implications of all this give considerable food for thought, if little else.

Modern farming is quick to change under the necessity to return profits on such sizable investments of money, material, and energy.

Table 11-2 Energy Inputs (kilocalories) in Corn Production

Year / Input	1945	1959	1970
Labor	12,500	7,600	4,900
Machinery	180,000	350,000	420,000
Gasoline	543,400	724,500	797,000
Nitrogen	58,800	344,400	940,800
Phosphorus	10,600	24,300	47,100
Potassium	5,200	60,400	68,000
Seeds for Planting	34,000	36,500	63,000
Irrigation	19,000	31,000	34,000
Insecticides	0	3,300	11,000
Herbicides	0	1,100	11,000
Drying	10,000	100,000	120,000
Electricity	32,000	140,000	310,000
Transportation	20,000	60,000	70,000
Total Inputs	925,500	1,889,000	2,896,000
Corn Yield (output)	3,427,200	5,443,200	8,164,800
Kcal return/Input Kcal	3.70	2.88	2.82

Source: David Pimentel, et al., "Food Production and the Energy Crisis," *Science*, vol. 182, No. 4111, pp. 443–449. The above data are drawn from Table 2, page 445; a complete explanation of the values and their derivation can be found in footnotes to that table and to Table 1, page 444, as well as in the text of the article.

Fluctuations in the market are watched closely by farmers, and for example, the number of animals they raise varies dramatically from season to season. Figure 11–3 illustrates the rapid fluctuation in the number of hogs butchered over a 19-year period. The enormous variation from year to year reflects the uncertainty of farmers' efforts to anticipate market demands and shifting wholesale prices. Animal types also change rapidly. American hogs were once fat porkers heavy with lard. Consumer tastes changed rapidly in favor of lean bacon and ham at the same time that vegetable oils provided a cheap substitute for cooking fats. Innovation plays its role here, as well. Now pigs being fattened for market are sometimes fed from raised troughs which they must reach by standing on their hind legs, thus producing lean, well-developed hams.

Not only does the market fluctuate widely, but new markets for new crops bring about abrupt changes in farming. Hybrid corn and soybeans have both made dramatic entries into American farming in recent years. Figure 11–4 illustrates the nearly geometric increase of the area devoted to soybean production. In the period between 1960 and 1965 alone, more than 10 million additional acres were sown in this crop. Changes result not only from market fluctuations but also from competition with new sources and substitute products. Rubber was originally produced from trees growing wild in South American jungles. By 1920, 90 percent of all rubber came from trees grown in orderly plantations halfway around the world in Southeast Asia. World War II reduced all production of rubber trees, both wild and plantation-grown, to only 16 percent of the total. In the decades that followed, synthetic rubber was less important, but in every case, wild rubber production remained an insignificant proportion of the total (Figure 11–5).

The modern farmer's qualities match the demands of the system within which he operates. He must be an agronomist able to assess the physical requirements of crops both new and old. He must be receptive and able

*Human
Geography:
Spatial
Design
in World
Society*

230

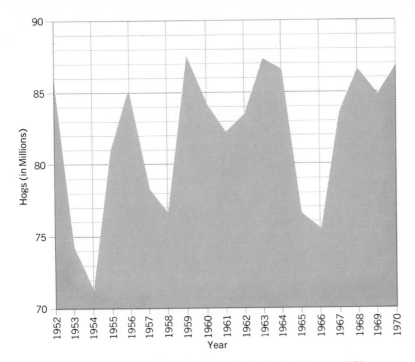

Figure 11-3 Number of hogs slaughtered in the United States, 1952–1970 The number of hogs slaughtered in the United States varies greatly from year to year. From this record, it appears to take a few years to recover from a decline, which can be as much as 20 percent lower than the previous peak year. The fluctuations are due, in large part, to uncertainty regarding future price and the fact that a farmer must start his production cycles months ahead of when he plans to market the products. (Data from *Historical Statistics of the U.S. Colonial Times to 1957: Continued to 1962 and Revisions; Statistical Abstract of the U.S. 1963–1971,* U.S. Dept. of Commerce, Bureau of the Census, Wash., D.C.)

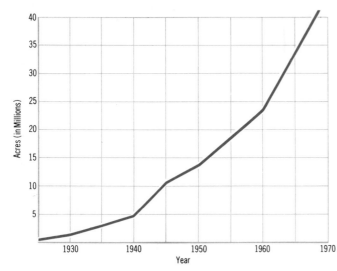

Figure 11-4 Introduction of soybeans in the United States Soybeans, a source of vegetabls oils and proteins, have become a major crop in the United States in recent decades. The consumer has shifted to vegetable oils for cooking and in margarine and has preferred leaner meats. These changes in market demand have encouraged farmers to switch from corn to soybeans, which are processed directly into foodstuff as well as providing protein supplements for animal feed. (Op. cit., Figure 11.3, and *Bulletin #951,* Dept. of Commerce, Bureau of the Census, Wash., D.C.)

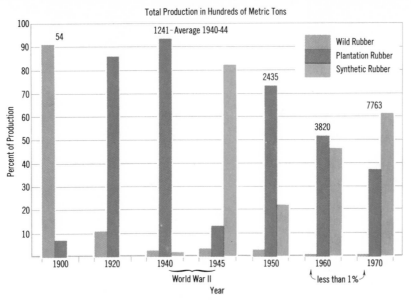

Total Production in Hundreds of Metric Tons

Figure 11-5 Percent of world rubber production in wild, plantation and synthetic rubber, 1900–1970 (Data from: Rubber Study Group, *Commodity Year Book 1956 and 1971;* wild rubber percentages, Jones and Darkenwald, *Economic Geography,* Macmillan, New York, 1954, and Jean le Bras, trans., *Introduction to Rubber,* Hart, New York, 1969)

to understand and accept the advice given by the Department of Agriculture's county agents as well as that from state university experimental farms and from seed, chemical, and machinery salesmen. He also must be able to think like a market economist. If his evaluation of the market is wrong, he will be left with an unsalable surplus of crops or animals. To avoid this he must utilize every source of information available. City people would be surprised if they listened to the farm programs broadcast in the early morning over many stations. Market futures are given regularly, as are the number of animals delivered, bought, and butchered at major stockyards. The farmer listens to all this and more and must decide for himself how to operate his enterprise. At the same time, the commodities produced on modern farms travel long distances, sometimes to the other side of the world, to reach the consumer. This means that the farmer must follow not only the fortunes and activities of his neighbors but also those of farmers producing similar crops in distant states or other countries.

All these activities require financing, and the farmer must know something of the money market. Acquiring loans and mortgages is an everyday part of the farmer's life. Again, he must know where money is available and at what rates of interest. He must decide whether he should get by on what he has, or take out a short-term loan, or perhaps operate with long-term mortgages. He must be able to anticipate whether interest rates will diminish or climb, and time his requests for money accordingly, that is, if the needs imposed on him by nature and his creditors allow him the luxury of choice.

In the same way, he must be a lawyer and politician of some ability. If his farm is near an expanding city or in the path of an advancing highway, he must be able to defend himself against unfair invasions without adequate payment for land appropriated by the government or damages caused by industry and housing developments. In other cases he must struggle to defend his rights to the use of water for his crops and animals. Legal conflicts over water are particularly characteristic of drier regions. In the same way, increasing government manipulation of farming makes it vital that the farmer be able to advise his congressman and senator at both the state and national levels. Simultaneously, he must help elect representatives who will best serve his interests.

All in all the modern commercial farmer must be a superb manager if he is to survive. He must assess and juggle all the things described above and many more while balancing his decisions against a capricious and often uncooperative Mother Nature. To do this he has a variety of information sources available: radio and television, farm journals and magazines, special newspapers and stock market reports, government farm agents, and advisors sent by private industry. At the same time, his aspirations are almost the same as those of urban dwellers. He wants the same conveniences, the same family transportation, the same schools for his children, and the same high level of living. In the final analysis, the modern farmer in all ways resembles his city cousins much more closely than he does subsistence-level farmers in emerging economies.

Subsistence-level farming By subsistence-level farming we mean agriculture which provides food, shelter, and the basic necessities for its participants but which allows little or no surplus with which to enter the commercial market system. It would be difficult to find a completely self-sufficient farm anywhere in the world today. Here, however, we present a description of such a system in order to clarify the traditional characteristics which in various combinations with those of modern farming go to make up the middle and lower range of the agricultural spectrum. For our present purposes we will use the terms *subsistence-level* and *traditional* agriculture interchangeably.

The traditional farmer fortunate enough to

Sugar beet harvest in California. American agriculture is capital intensive; that is, great use is made of equipment, chemicals, and high-quality but expensive breeds and seeds. This results in high labor productivity but at the cost of great energy inputs. Such a system is not easily exported to less developed countries, where the economy may not be able to supply the financial and industrial services required. We are also becoming increasingly aware of undesirable ecological results from capital intensive agriculture.

own the property he tills nevertheless works the land with his own labor and without the use of modern machines. *Labor-intensive* agriculture requires that he and his family toil long hours in order to farm fewer acres of ground than his modern counterpart. It is difficult to make direct comparisons between these two types of farming, for virtually no data exist which show the capitalization of subsistence-level farms. We can, however, make some qualitative comparisons. The Near Eastern farmer, for example, may own one or two oxen which he uses to pull a wooden plow or solid-wheeled cart. In some cases fodder is so scarce, because of the extreme scarcity of irrigation water, that only the very richest farmers can afford to feed draft animals. Lacking animal power, the farmers must spade their fields by hand. Similar conditions exist in South and Southeast Asia, where more fortunate farmers rely on oxen or water buffalo while the poor depend on the sweat

The Market and the Farm: Agricultural Location Theory

Subsistence agriculture. This man is cultivating maize with a hoe on a steep mountain slope in Colombia, South America. His farming methods are labor intensive; that is, most of the value he applies to the land is his own labor. He buys little or no mechanical equipment or chemicals. As a consequence, his inanimate energy and financial inputs are modest to nil. However, production is also low, perhaps not even enough to feed his whole family throughout the year. From an ecological point of view the evidence is mixed. Some subsistence agriculture is clearly destructive of the long-run food producing capacity of the environment; others seem nicely balanced with nature.

of their own brows. The picture is repeated again in Latin America, while in much of Africa sleeping sickness and rinderpest disease have kept the horse and cattle population at a minimum, unavailable even to those farmers who might afford them. Particularly in Africa, *hoe culture* is common, with humans using those tools in place of plows pulled by animals.

In some parts of the emerging world absentee landlords living in the cities may own hundreds of villages. In these cases, the landlord may provide seed, equipment, land, and water, while the tenant farmer invests only his own labor. The harvest, however poor, is divided into five portions; each part is allocated to one of the five subdivisions just mentioned, with the landlord receiving four-fifths and the tenant one-fifth of the produce.

All these conditions are reflected in the low per capita incomes found in the predominantly agricultural nations of the world. Figure 1–3 shows the world distribution of income. It is no coincidence that the distribution of predominantly rural populations shown in Figure 3–16 matches that of the low per capita income countries.

Subsistence-level farming with its lack of cash or surplus crops presents few opportunities for experiment and change. We should not consider this as completely bad, though, for subsistence-level agriculture throughout the world is remarkably resilient and able to survive all manner of disasters. We should not ask the question, "Why are traditional farmers so inefficient?" but rather, "How have such impoverished methods of farming survived thousands of years of drought and flood, heat, cold and storms, unfair taxation, war, pillage, and looting? Indeed, why does traditional agriculture continue to resist the well-intentioned, well-financed, and highly trained technicians who have tried to change it in recent years?"

The answer can be summed up in a short sentence: *Tradition is wise.* Subsistence-level or traditional agricultural systems lack the flow of information so necessary for rapid change. Poor education and ignorance of modern farm methods are everywhere apparent in the emerging nations. But we should not think that the participants in these systems are either stupid or lazy. Lacking capital, outside information, and scientific methodology, the farmers have learned farming strategies by trial-and-error methods over hundreds and hundreds of years. Their inherited culture, which provides them with techniques and attitudes necessary for survival, is their most valuable asset. For example, wooden needle-nosed plows without moldboards are used everywhere in arid regions by subsistence-level farmers. While they are seemingly far less efficient than our own moldboard metal plows, which turn a deep furrow, thereby exposing the soil to sun and air, needle plows stir the earth without severely disturbing the surface. By not exposing the underlayers, valuable soil moisture is preserved for subsequent plant use. The simple needle plow is also less expensive, and can be made and repaired from local materials. When modern farm technicians first attempted to introduce the iron moldboard plow into the Near East, it was not readily accepted by local farmers, who knew more of their own environment and pocketbooks than did their would-be helpers. Similarly, when tractors were used to replace oxen in some areas, a major conflict arose. Plowing was easier and the timing of crop planting was improved, but the departure of the oxen deprived the villagers of their major source of fuel. In those treeless areas, dried dung mixed with straw was in many settlements the only material available for the cooking fires. The tractors were an improvement but necessitated an additional investment in kerosene cookstoves. In the words of one enlightened developmental technician, "There's no fuel like an old fuel." Thus farmers in the emerging world are slow to change their ways for fear of overtaxing themselves, their pocketbooks, and their resources. Given enough slack and the opportunity to change, they are as willing to accept new developments as are our own farmers. It is simply because they already have a system that works reasonably well that they are cautious about experimenting with irreplaceable materials and money. Tradition tells them what will succeed and how to survive, albeit at a low economic level. In other words, don't rock the boat.

In summary, the traditional and the modern farmer *viewed as stereotypes* have contrasting characteristics and skills. The modern farmer is a specialist in technology, money matters, and management. The traditional farmer is able to provide himself and his dependents with food, shelter, clothing, and equipment made with his own hands. He is at a disadvantage in the modern market system but could probably survive a major catastrophe like war as well as or better than his modern counterpart. This is particularly true when we consider the elaborate supply system which provides the modern farmer with necessities. If his communication lines were cut, he would soon run out of fuel, spare parts, store-bought foods, and clothing purchased off the rack.

Traditional communities, on the other hand, depending on the outside world for fewer things, would miss it far less if cut off from central places ranked above them in the settlement hierarchy.

Geographic situation or relative position

The emphasis placed upon communication and organization in the above section brings us to the central point of this chapter. Wherever the movement of energy, goods, and information is important, so too will be the friction of distance and the relative location of the farms in question. We have already described three sets of variables which help to determine the form that agricultural land use will take. Let us now consider our fourth set, relative location expressed particularly in terms of distance. To do this, we must resort to our method of holding all other variables constant in a greatly simplified model of the world. By controlling variation in site characteristics we return to the homogeneous plain used in earlier chapters. If we assume no variation from place to place in the cultural preferences and perception of the actors involved in our drama, we eliminate, for the moment, the vexing questions which those things raise. The same is true for available technology and organization. If everyone behaves exactly the same, we have created a homogeneous cultural as well as physical space. This makes a perfect medium within which to let our farm systems grow uncluttered by any but spatial considerations. This model world can be our petri dish; let us start simply and see what develops.

Johann Heinrich von Thünen

Relative position is important in agriculture at all scales from world patterns to patterns of production surrounding a single settlement. The analytical principles underlying this statement were first demonstrated in 1826 by Johann Heinrich von Thünen, a north German landowner and farmer who wrote on the economics of production. Thünen had observed that various types of farming occurred with surprising regularity in circular bands or rings around his own settlement. The pattern was not always clear, but in his book, *The Isolated State*, he presented a logical scheme which explained what he had observed. The importance of Thünen's work, however, lies not in his explanation of the world in which he lived but rather in the fact that *his methods may be applied to other situations with other sets of data, with results differing from what he observed but consistent with the geographic theory which he outlined.*

Thünen's ideas are of particular interest to geographers because they deal with geographic rather than nominal locations. In the words of Michael Chisholm:

His argument started from the premise that the areal distribution of crops and livestock and of types of farming depends upon competition between products and farming systems for the use of any particular plot of land. On any specified piece of land, the enterprise which yields the highest net return will be conducted and competing enterprises will be relegated to other plots where it is they which yield the highest return. Thünen was, then concerned with two points in particular: 1. The monetary return over and above the monetary expenses incurred by different types of agriculture; 2. Such net returns pertaining to a unit area of land and not to a unit of product. For example, if a comparison is being made between potatoes and wheat, we will not be concerned with the financial return obtained per ton of produce but with the return which may be expected from a hectare of land in either crop. Thus, at certain locations wheat may be less profitable than potatoes because, although the return per ton on wheat is higher than on potatoes, the latter yield perhaps three times the weight of crop to a hectare of land. In this case, potatoes will occupy the land.[1]

Rentals and economic rent

In our discussion of agricultural land use we are assuming that each type of activity, each

[1]Michael Chisholm, *Rural Settlement and Land Use*, Hutchinson, London, 1962, pp. 21–22.

crop raised, will give a certain monetary return to the farmer. If we take the total value of production for a given farm and subtract from it the total costs involved in bringing forth the product, we will have the net return on the farm. This divided by the number of units of land the farm incorporates (acres, hectares, etc.) will give the net return per unit area, for example, dollars per acre. Economists call this the *economic rent* of the activity; we prefer the term *location rent*. If we imagine two pieces of land both being used for the production of wheat, one piece so poor and/or far removed from market that it is at the absolute margin of production and another which has the highest, best, and most lucrative wheat yields possible, the difference in profits between the two will again constitute the economic rent of the more fertile, nearby piece.

We frequently hear the term *rent* used in a different way, meaning the amount paid by a tenant for the right to occupy and use a certain property. The use of the same term for two such different concepts is confusing. In the first case the word refers to the value of production at a given site; the second term really refers to one of the costs of production which must be subtracted before net profit or economic rent accrues. For this reason we will follow the lead of Paul Samuelson and use the term *rental* for the second, reserving the term *rent* for use in place of the longer term *location rent*. One further point should be made. Rentals rarely match the absolute productive value or rent for a given piece of land. Sometimes they are far lower. Rental controls in the Netherlands and England allow some farmers the use of property at a fraction of its true worth. We have all heard stories about a village rented for the price of one red rose delivered yearly from a maiden's hand. Conversely, rentals may sometimes exceed the true worth of the property and their collection can thus force bankruptcy and rapid turnover in businesses. This is particularly true for commercial properties near campuses which are valued at unreasonably high rates by their owners, thus leading to a succession of restaurants and shops being established and failing one after another. This discussion will refer only to the economic *rent* of land, not to its rental.

Characteristics of the isolated state

In order to explain the world in which he lived, Thünen had to simplify and restrict the conditions describing his model of farm production. To do this he assumed six characteristics for his agricultural region. (1) At the center of the area was a single, isolated market town. No links connected it to other settlements or to the outside world in general. Movement was only to and from this one place, with its population being the only urban one and all other people being rural farmers. (2) The area in question was a homogeneous plain having equal fertility in all its parts and neither hill nor valley to vary its surface. (3) All labor costs were everywhere equal on this plain. Nowhere were there fewer laborers or more skilled workers. No cost differential could occur as a result of competition for employees. (4) Transportation costs were the same everywhere and in every direction. This required an initial roadless condition, since roads of any kind would focus transportation into a radial pattern centered on the town. The result in that case would resemble the star-shaped diagrams discussed in Chapter 3. Thus, he assumed that all carts could go to the central market by the most direct route. (5) Within this region there existed a static economy. The entire system was in equilibrium, with no long-range trends leading inevitably to lower or higher prices, nor were there sudden shocks within the system such as depressions or inflations. (6) Finally, he assumed that the market price of any commodity was fixed for any single farmer and that farmers could not form combines or cooperatives in order to manipulate the market by holding back crops to raise prices or by dumping them to ruin their competitors.

The isolated state as an energy system

Thünen showed a city and its hinterland in an isolated and very stable condition. His model, however, cannot be considered an isolated

system.[2] Although he did not consider his isolated state in modern systems terminology, it may be convenient for us to view it in that way. Energy in the form of sunlight constantly entered the area with which he dealt. Foodstuffs were shipped to the central settlement and were reduced there to waste materials and heat. The waste in turn might further decompose, releasing more heat; some of the waste would be returned to the fields. (In this latter case Thünen concerned himself only with the return of horse manure as fertilizer to the land. In the early nineteenth century the major form of power for urban transportation was horses, which required large amounts of fodder and produced equally important quantities of manure as a by-product.) Eventually, the energy which had entered the system as sunlight would escape from it as some form of reradiation back to the heavens. This kind of system, which exchanges energy but no mass with its surroundings, is called a *closed system*.

It was this flow of energy through the system which helped organize its many parts into a recognizable structure. Much as logs floating on a stream become aligned with each other as a result of the flowing water, so too do all man−environment systems reflect the particular characteristics of the energy flows which they utilize and in turn help to create. Just as a steady stream of water maintains the logs in a given orientation, so too does a steady flow of energy in the form of farm products through Thünen's model maintain it in a *steady state* or single form without change. If new conditions are introduced into the model, adjustments leading to steady states will result. In the following sections we will discuss and demonstrate the Thünen model as it was originally proposed. In the next chapter we will introduce basic changes in transportation and fertility and see what happens.

Unit commodity concepts

Before we examine Thünen's model for its areal characteristics, we should define some of

[2]In systems terminology, an *isolated* system exchanges neither mass nor energy with the environment that contains it.

its basic terms. These deal with unit measures of commodities such as bushels of corn or hundredweights (cwt) of milk, liters of wine, and kilograms of butter. We also need to introduce the notation which will be used to indicate other elements such as distance. As soon as our definitions are clear, we will transform our thinking into its areal form.

Let us begin, for example, with milk. It has a market price we can call p. That would be the per unit price for any commodity, in this case, a hundred pounds (cwt) of milk. Land and labor and the cost of cows, barns, and fodder are all investments of capital that must be repaid. The total expenses necessary to produce our cwt of milk must be subtracted from the market price. Market price p minus production costs c leaves a net return r, that is, the profit for each unit of produce, in this case milk (Figure 11-6).

The above relationship assumes that the market is located at the production site. This might be true if we lived next door to a dairy and could buy our milk by leaning out the window, but in most cases the produce has to be shipped some distance d to market. This can be measured in miles or kilometers. Milk is perishable, and the glass-lined, chilled tank trucks, sanitary milksheds, and everything else that it takes to get the milk from the cow to you contribute to transportation costs.

Now let us consider another commodity with different shipping characteristics. Bulk corn is much easier and cheaper to move from farm to mill or market. It can be shoveled or sucked up with vacuum hoses. It will not spoil if it is kept dry. High temperatures within the normal range will not damage it. Thus, the cost of transporting corn will be much less than the cost of moving fresh milk to market. Large or small, the cost of transporting a unit commodity a given distance (one bushel or cwt per mile) is called the *transport rate* and is given the symbol t.

Let us assume that we ship a hundredweight of milk and a hundredweight of corn 10 miles. For each mile that the commodities are shipped we must add one increment of transport cost t, but each commodity will have a different value for t depending upon its perishability and general transportability. This rate times the distance shipped gives the total transportation cost td. The lines in Figure 11-7 representing the costs of shipping milk and corn have different slopes, a steep one for milk and a more gentle one for corn.

We can put the terms p, c, and td together in order to see their interrelationship when the point of production is not located at the marketplace. This relationship is stated: The net return on a unit of a commodity is equal to the price at the market less the cost of production less the transport cost. It is written thus:

$$r = p - c - dt$$

We can graph this relationship for the crop being considered. Figure 11-8 shows the unit commodity price p at the marketplace. This price is extended across the graph (line $P—P'$) to suggest the *market price* which any farmer would receive once he got his goods to the market. Line $C—C'$ represents the production costs for a commodity unit; the difference between p and c illustrates the net return r. However, this presentation shows the value of r as being everywhere the same and does not take the cost of transportation td into account. We know that transportation costs increase in direct proportion to the distance from market and must be subtracted from the net return. To show this in Figure 11-8 we

Figure 11-6 Price and cost condition at market
The market price p of a commodity at the market less the production cost c equals the net return r; that is: $p - c = r$.

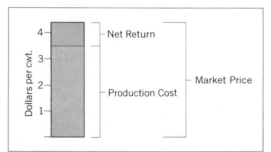

have taken the transportation costs off the top of the net return. If production occurred directly at the market, the distance between market and farm would be 0 and therefore the value td would equal 0. At point A the distance would be 10 and td would be $10t$. When this is subtracted off the top of the net return r, a new value r_A results.

If the sloping transport cost line is projected outward from the market, it will eventually intersect the production cost line C—C' at point X. At that intersection, the cost of transportation will equal the original net return r. In other words, all the profit earned if the market and the farm were in the same place will have been eaten up by transportation costs. Beyond that distance from market there would be no more profit, and production would stop.

Areal concepts

As geographers we are interested in giving spatial dimensions to our ideas whenever possible. Unit commodity concepts deal with *items* of production but do not relate them to the *areas* from which they come. Three basic concepts relating agriculture to area are *the intensity of inputs per unit area*; the *yield*, or production per unit area; and the *rent*, or net return per unit area. In order to understand the competition for land which exists between different types of activities we must have some notion of their rent-paying abilities.

To change our comments on unit commodities into ideas incorporating space we must multiply all the elements in the basic equation $r = p - c - dt$ by the *yield* Y or output per unit area. For example, instead of talking about bushels of wheat we must now discuss bushels of wheat per acre. We must convert measures like gallons of milk into gallons per acre. Since milk will be produced every day on a dairy farm and, on the other hand, wheat is harvested but once a year, we also need to consider production over some reasonable period of time, usually 12 months. Multiplying our original expression by yield Y we obtain:

$$Yr = Y(p - c) - Ydt$$

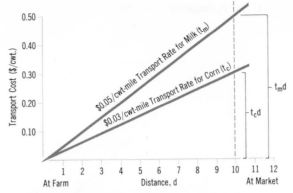

Figure 11-7 Transport rate per mile and transport cost related to distance from market The transport cost for delivering a commodity to the market is the product of the distance to the market and the transport rate per mile.

We can simplify this by substituting single capital letters in place of subgroups in the above equation. Let $P = Y(p - c)$; that is, P equals the *market margin* or profit on the amount of a crop produced per acre. For example, if farmland can produce 20 bushels of

Figure 11-8 Net return relative to distance from market Net return is market price p minus production costs c minus transport costs td. Beyond distance x from the market, transport costs exceed the market margin (price minus production costs), and net return is negative. Farmers located this far away have no incentive to enter the market. In this diagram, transport rates and cost are exaggerated relative to production costs in order to show the relationship clearly. Today milk is often shipped over 100 miles to market.

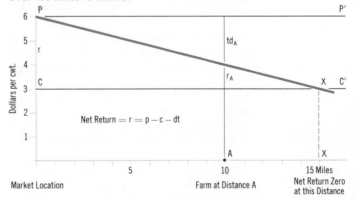

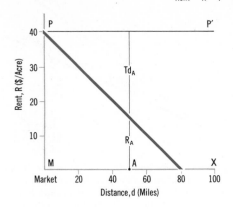

A. Rent and Transport Cost per Acre of Crop

$$\text{Rent} = R = P - Td$$

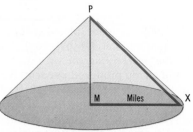

B. Rent Surface and Limit of Marketable Crop

Limit of Commercial Agriculture

Figure 11-9 Bid rent as a function of distance from the market (*A*) Rent and transport cost per acre of crop. Rent is the net return of a commodity per unit area, e.g., $/acre. In order that the rent equation be in the proper units, one must think of the transport rate as the cost of moving an acre's worth of crop a unit distance. (*B*) Rent surface and limit of marketable crop.

wheat per acre, then the profit per acre f.o.b. the farm is 20 times the market price of 1 bushel less 20 times the cost of producing 1 bushel.

Let $T = Yt$, in other words, the transportation rate on the amount of crop produced on 1 acre of land. If it costs 1 dollar to ship 1 bushel of wheat 1 mile, then in our example T will equal 20 dollars.

After we have made these substitutions, it remains for us to use R in place of Yr. In this case, R represents the net return per unit area,

or the rent. This is all expressed by a new equation very similar to our first one:

$$R = P - Td$$

Note carefully that distance d does not change.

We may now redraw the graph in Figure 11–8 in a simpler form showing the relationship between the market margin P, transportation costs T, distance d, and rent R. This is shown in Figure 11–9*A*. Again, if the farm is located at the market, distance and transportation costs are reduced to 0. This means that the market margin P and the rent R on a unit of land are the same. (Be sure to note that we have now included production costs in a single expression with the market price, and have eliminated the cost line c—c' from our second diagram.) The point x where the sloping transportation rate line intersects the line of 0 profit marks the distance from market beyond which production of the crop will not be found. If we take this sloping line and rotate it around its vertical axis, the distance between m and a becomes the radius of a circle with the market at its center (Figure 11–9*B*). This is the areal extent of crop production.

We can now draw our first two conclusions from Thünen's work. First, we see that *rent R and transport costs Td are inversely related.* As transportation costs increase, land rent decreases. Second, *given a single market taken as a point on a homogeneous plain, there will be a limit to commercial farming.* No one beyond the radius where transport costs completely eat up profit will want to try to enter the market. Thus, an agricultural region with definite limits will be formed around the city.

Agricultural interdependencies

What happens when farmers have more than one activity from which to choose? Let us return for a moment to the two commodities shown in Figure 11–7, milk and corn. We are already familiar with the steeply sloping line representing shipping costs for milk. We also have seen how that line's intersection with the 0 rent value defines a distance beyond which milk will not be produced. When we consider this in terms of yield, that distance becomes the radius of the milk-producing region around the city. Now let us superpose the sloping line indicating the costs of shipping corn onto the same diagram (Figure 11–10.) Corn commands a lower price in the market, but its transportation costs accumulate at a slower rate than do those for milk. The corn line as a result extends beyond that of the milk line. Imagine these two lines as cross sections of intersecting cones; next, imagine the two cones seen from above. Near and at the market the higher cone belonging to milk will hide that of corn. But farther from the market the situation will be reversed and the lower cone representing corn will not only extend farther from the market than that of milk but also cover or obscure the one representing milk for some distance outward from the intersection M_2. In terms of rent this means that where the milk line is highest, the greatest profit can be made in the market from dairy products. Where the corn line predominates, maize will be more profitable.

What *adjustments* occur when a second commodity, like corn, is added to a one-product system? In the original diagram milk production extended from the central market to point M_1. When corn is added, the superior profits for milk end at point M_2. Under the competition from corn the milk-producing area will be forced to shrink inward from its original boundaries (Figure 11–10). If we add a third crop, let us say wheat, the boundaries of the agricultural regions again adjust under the impetus of competition among unequal rent paying abilities of the different crops (Figure 11–11A). The amount of wheat grown on an acre has the lowest price in the market but is least expensive to ship. It will be found growing farthest from the marketplace because of the slow rate at which its transportation costs use up available profits. Now it is corn's turn to draw in its boundaries from c_1 to c_2 which mark the intersection of the corn and wheat transportation slopes. When things have settled down, wheat will be found growing from line c_2 as far out as line w_1 beyond which no

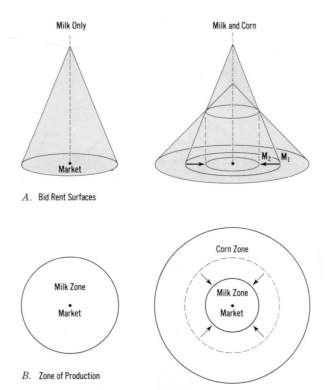

A. Bid Rent Surfaces

B. Zone of Production

Figure 11-10 Two-crop system (*A*) Bid rent surfaces. (*B*) Zones of production. The effect of adding an additional crop to the commercial agricultural system can be seen in the diagram. Corn has a lower bid rent near the market, but because this bid rent falls off more slowly with distance than the bid rent of milk, beyond a certain distance farmers receive more for corn than for milk. They will switch to corn production, and additional farmers beyond the limit of milk production will enter the market. There will then be a reduction in the size of the milk zone, with the result that less milk will reach the market. Milk prices will rise, and the market boundary will adjust outward somewhat. See Figure 11-14 for more details.

profits can be made by milk, corn, or wheat. We come, with this observation, to the third conclusion provided us by Thünen's analysis. *At any given distance from market the crop with the highest rent paying ability is chosen and agricultural land use forms rings of homogeneous activity around the market.* This is illustrated in Figure 11–11B for a three-crop system.

The Market and the Farm: Agricultural Location Theory

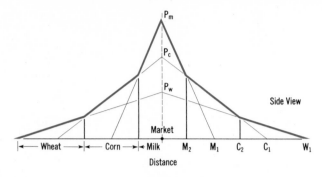

A. Bid Rent Surfaces for a Three Crop System

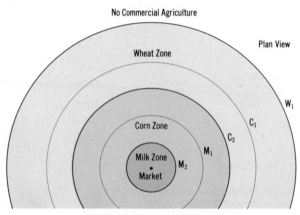

B. Agricultural Land Use Rings

Figure 11-11 Three-crop system (A) Bid rent surface for a three-crop system. (B) Agricultural land use rings. Adding additional crops to the system will cause market boundaries to adjust according to which crop has the highest rent-paying ability. Individual and independent farmers with profit motives for farming will come to the same crop decisions, depending upon their relative distance from the market, and land use rings centered on the market will form.

Figure 11–12 shows the land use surrounding Thünen's original central place. Once we have seen the pattern, it is a simple exercise to reconstruct the relative value of crop types in the market and their varying degrees of transportability. Notice that the distribution of land use types in Thünen's day was somewhat different from our own. We again turn

to Michael Chisholm for his commentary on this circumstance:

A point which many writers have seized upon is the fact that Thünen put forestry as the land use occupying the zone second from the central city, whereas certain types of agriculture were put at greater distances. This arrangement accords so ill with the reality of location patterns in the developed parts of the world in the mid-twentieth century that people are often tempted to reject the whole analysis. A few explanatory words are therefore in place. At the time Thünen wrote, forest products were in great demand for building and, more particularly, for fuel. Large quantities of timber were required for these purposes, and consumers were not willing to pay high prices. A hectare of land produced a very large quantity of lumber, even though few inputs were applied; the bulky material incurred high transport costs. Thus, the advantages of proximity to the market were such that all other types of agricultural use, except the innermost zone of intensive production, were displaced by forestry; it produced a higher Economic Rent than any other product in the second zone. For the time at which he wrote, this arrangement was entirely logical. Since then, technical conditions have changed and forestry has been ousted from much of the land near the urban centres. This does not undermine the method by which von Thünen arrived at his circles.[3]

Thünen proposed a static model in which changes would occur instantaneously. If a system were filled with short-range uncertainties, such as the rapid variation in the price of hogs we mentioned earlier, farmers in the transition zones such as the one between milk and corn would have imperfect knowledge and always be trying to outguess the market. Thus, some would be raising cows while others would be trying grain. The two kinds of farms would be found side by side, and an interfingered boundary zone like those mentioned in Chapter 10 would result. In this

[3]Michael Chisholm, op. cit., p. 30.

case we might say that *tradition would no longer be wise*, for changes in the market, miles beyond the ken and knowledge of the farmers, would affect their lives. A farmer could make all the right decisions just as his grandfather had, but because he is a member of a market economy, forces beyond his control could change the price of his crop so much that he might find himself facing bankruptcy. In the case of market economies, we come to our fourth conclusion based on Thünen: *Agricultural industries (crop types) are interdependent.* If you change one part of the system, you will affect all its parts.

Intensity of land use

In much the same vein we may add a fifth and final conclusion: *Intensity of agriculture increases toward the market.* We have seen that a crop to be competitive must pay a high rent or profit per acre. This means that centrally located land with a subsequent transportation advantage will be high-priced. People will compete for property near the center to avoid high transportation costs. The actual price of land (in this case a *rental,* not a *rent*) may be bid up and up until any advantage given to it by its centrality may all but disappear. If land becomes high-priced, it will then pay the farmer to shift more and more of this total investment from actual land to other factors of production. (By *factors of production* economists mean the three basic elements which in various combinations make farming possible: land, labor, and capital.) He must increase his yields, and to do so he must invest in more and more fertilizer, greater care by men and machines, better seeds or livestock, and dozens of other improvements. This will result in higher intensities of land use in areas nearest the market. Conversely, farms on the periphery of things will utilize more and more land with

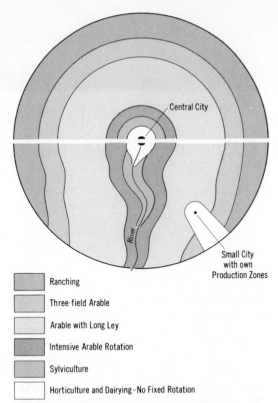

Ranching

Three-field Arable

Arable with Long Ley

Intensive Arable Rotation

Sylviculture

Horticulture and Dairying - No Fixed Rotation

Figure 11-12 Thünen's original diagram showing land use rings Half of the diagram shows the effects of lower transport costs along a navigable river and Thünen's ideas concerning the effects of a satellite city in the region. (Michael Chisholm, *Rural Settlement and Land Use,* Hutchinson, London, 1962, p. 29)

less and less investment per acre. At the same time, perishable goods will be limited in space to locations near the market unless some way can be found to make them more durable and cheaper to ship. We have already commented on the roles played by *concentration* and *preservation*, and in the examples in the next chapter these factors will again become important.

The Market and the Farm: Agricultural Location Theory

12 | THE URBAN WORLD AND ITS HINTERLAND: LAND USE THEORY

The preceding chapter has presented a neat theoretical scheme with which to find order in the seemingly unordered world. But does it all work? The six basic assumptions underlying Thünen's initial theory restrict his model's correspondence with reality. Is there any evidence that agricultural activities really do increase in intensity toward the central point and that rent on land is greatest near the market?

Real Agricultural Locations at Village Scales

Chisholm describes various studies carried out in Finland and Sicily on the relation between distance and agricultural inputs and outputs. He discusses the land use pattern around the Sicilian settlement of Canicatti, an agricultural town of 30,000 in the central part of the island. A variety of agricultural pursuits are practiced by the townspeople. Vegetable gardens, citrus orchards, vineyards, and olive trees, as well as almonds, hazelnuts, and pistachios, dry farming (grains), and pasture and woodlots, are all ranged around the town. The pattern is at first confusing (Figure 12–1), but order can be brought from seeming chaos by drawing a series of concentric rings 1 kilometer (0.6 mile) in width around the settlement and counting the amount of land given

over to a particular activity in each zone. Table 12–1 summarizes Chisholm's findings. Looking only at the percentage of land area by distance and crop type gives us some notion of the ordering of activities. What we really need, though, is a further measure of intensity.

If you have ever gardened or worked on a farm, you know that some tasks take much more time than others. This is particularly true if we consider the inputs of labor on a per acre basis (or in this case a per hectare basis). Weeding a vegetable garden which is only $1/10$ of an acre may take longer than plowing the "south forty" with a powerful tractor. The National Institute of Agricultural Economics in Rome provided Chisholm with figures indicating the number of man-hours per hectare required for each of the several agricultural activities on his list. He then weighted the number of hectares allocated to each activity in each ring by the number of hours of work they require. Thereafter, he summed up all the hours for all the jobs on all the land in each zone. The resulting average number of man-days per hectare in each distance zone is shown at the right in Table 12–1. If we consider the investment of labor in agriculture a good measure of its intensity, the case is well made for the increase of intensity as we approach Canicatti, the center of the market-farm system in question.

Now let us consider whether such increasing investments are repaid by corresponding increases in rent. In this case, we will examine another example cited by Chisholm and derived from a number of Finnish farms. Here the measure of production is in net output. This would be the end value of the yield per hectare minus the costs of production and transportation to some central point like a town or village. In this case, three separate studies were made of the rent in money terms for farms located $1/10$, $1/2$, 1, $1\frac{1}{2}$, 2, 3, 4, and 5 kilometers from some central point (Table 12–2). The net profit per acre at the very center of each of the three study areas was considered to represent 100 percent of the possible rent to be earned from any plot. Table 12–2 shows that in the first case a hectare of land in the second ring from the center (0.5 kilometer) earned only 78 percent of the amount obtained in rent from a central hectare. In the second case, rent in the second ring was only 67 percent of that at the center for equal-sized units of land. A slightly higher value (83 percent) was true for similar properties in the third example. In every case, rent as a percentage of the profit earned on a central hectare grows progressively smaller with each step outward from the center. In this Finnish study it is safe to assume that more intense agriculture was practiced near the center of each study area and that higher returns made such an investment worthwhile.

Relaxing the Basic Assumptions

Two assumptions underlying Thünen's thinking were the equal fertility of his area and equal ease of transportation in all directions in all its parts. What would happen if we introduced areas of high and low fertility into his model and also some special route, such as a navigable river, which would lower the cost of transportation in one spatial sector? Thünen anticipated these questions and commented on the most likely results.

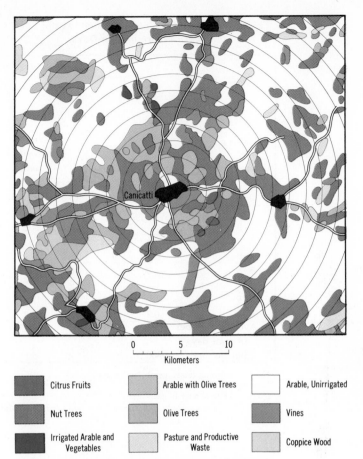

	Citrus Fruits		Arable with Olive Trees		Arable, Unirrigated
	Nut Trees		Olive Trees		Vines
	Irrigated Arable and Vegetables		Pasture and Productive Waste		Coppice Wood

Figure 12-1 Land use pattern around Canicatti, Sicily.

Differences in fertility

Imagine an area with a two-crop system much as we have been considering. But in this case there is a large, infertile swamp located astride the boundary between the two crops (Figure 12–2). If the swamp remains unreclaimed, there is a hole in the productive area and the rings of production will have expanded to make up the difference by adding land at the outer edge of each crop ring. Now suppose that the swamp is reclaimed and that the costs of reclamation are charged directly against the rent which will be derived from the newly productive land. In this case, recla-

The Urban World and Its Hinterland: Land Use Theory

245

Table 12-1 Canicatti, Sicily: Percentage of Land Area in Various Uses and Labor Requirements per Hectare in Man-Days

| Distance from Canicatti, km | Percentage of Land Area | | | | | | | | | | Average Number of Man-Days per Hectare in Each Distance Zone |
	Urban	Irrigated Arable and Vegetables	Citrus Fruits	Vines	Arable with Trees	Olive	Trees*	Arable, Unirrigated	Pasture and Productive Waste†	Coppice Wood	
0–1	44.7			15.8			19.7	19.7			52
1–2				18.0	16.7	8.4	41.0	15.9			50
2–3			2.6	2.3	21.8	14.4	35.4	23.6			46
3–4			2.1	13.3	18.7	0.6	47.2	18.1			50
4–5				5.1	19.2	2.4	28.4	43.4	1.4		42
5–6		1.0		6.3	4.7	1.6	17.6	64.1	4.7		41
6–7	1.3	0.7		3.3	6.7		18.3	68.7	0.9		40
7–8				4.0	7.7		23.6	62.4	0.8	1.6	39
Total‡	1.0	0.3	0.4	6.1	11.1	2.2	26.3	50.8	1.4	0.4	
Average number of man-days per hectare		300	150	90	50	45	40	35	5	5	42

*Mainly almond, hazel, carob, and pistachio.
†Sometimes sown.
‡Percent of total area in each activity.
Source: Michael Chisholm, *Rural Settlement and Land Use*, Hutchinson, London, 1962, p. 63.

Table 12-2 Finland: Relation of Production per Hectare and Distance to Farm Plots

| Distance km* | Wiiala | | Virri | | Suomela |
	Gross Output	Net Output	Gross Output	Net Output	Net Output
0–0.1	100	100	100	100	100
0.5	92	78	89	67	83
1.0	84	56	80	50	68
1.5	77	34	73	40	56
2.0	69	13	67	33	46
3.0			57	25	32
4.0			50	20	
5.0			44	17	

*0–0.1 km equals 100
Source: Michael Chisholm, *Rural Settlement and Land Use*, Hutchinson, London, 1962, p. 55.

mation will constitute an additional cost to be added to all the other ones already taken into consideration in the basic equation: $R = P - Td - C_r$, where C_r is the cost of reclamation. This is the same as raising the cost floor shown as line $c—c'$ in Figure 11–8. If we follow the slope of decreasing rent for each crop, we find that they bump into the newly elevated cost floor, and beyond that point production cannot take place (Figure 12–3). It can be seen that the land nearer the market can be reclaimed at a profit but that swampland on the outer edge cannot meet the added costs.

Now let us suppose that the costs of reclamation will be borne by all the farmers in the entire region in the form of a fixed property tax. Since rents, intensity, and land value all increase toward the center even though the tax rate is fixed, farmers near the center will pay more money in absolute terms than those on the edge because their land will be worth more. This taxation represents an added production cost that must be charged against profits, and is shown in Figure 12–4 as an added layer on the cost floor. This will mean lower rent or profits for farmers everywhere, and since costs such as these are often passed on to the consumer, prices may go up, with temporary inflation resulting. At the same time, if the entire swamp has been reclaimed (which is possible since costs are being charged against everybody and not just against the reclaimed farmland), more land nearer the market has become available and the outer boundaries of both types of production will shrink inward. In this way consumers may experience long-range benefits as better transportation patterns form with shorter supply lines.

This simple example can be endlessly complicated in reality. The results can be good or bad, depending upon a multitude of other factors important in each individual case. One example where society as a whole has accepted the costs of reclamation and undoubtedly has benefited is the Zuider Zee reclamation project in the Netherlands (Figure 12–5). In this case valuable land adjacent

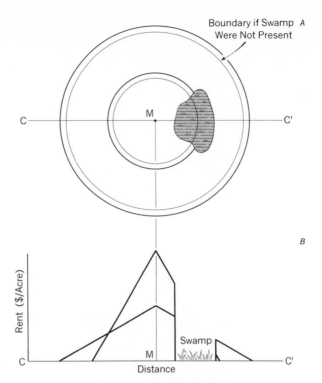

Figure 12-2 Neighboring swampland variation in the Thünen model (A) Two-crop system with a swamp existing near the market *m*. (B) Rent surface along cross section C–C'. Swampland has no value.

to the Randstadt, the Dutch equivalent of Megalopolis, has been brought into production. At the same time, internal transportation routes have been shortened in Holland. It makes good sense to reclaim lands which because of their relative location can repay the costs of putting them into production. Even if the tax burden is distributed among all the taxpayers, there will be a variety of indirect savings compensating everybody.

The opposite may be true in the United States, where Western irrigation projects sometimes reclaim arid land at tremendous investment costs. In this case, the government may provide low-cost loans to farmers within newly opened irrigation districts, or unrealistically low rates will be charged for irrigation water. Since the low rates charged some of

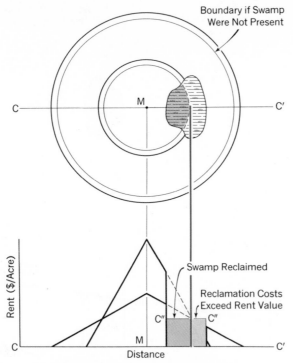

Figure 12-3 Reclamation of swampland
Reclamation costs C″–C″ added to basic production cost line C–C′. Rent-paying ability of crops justified reclaiming only swampland nearest to the market. The assumption is that the people reclaiming the swamp bear the entire cost of the reclamation.

our government pays farmers *not to produce* crops on much of their land (through the soil bank and crop quotas), and many of our reclamation projects seem even more fantastic. In this way it is possible to gain some practical insights into land use and the money allocated for it. A good knowledge of Thünen's principles can enhance your decision making at the polls. Now let us see what differences improved transportation can make in our basic model.

Figure 12-4 General land tax pays for reclamation of a swampland   Tax is proportionate to land value. (Entire swamp is reclaimed.) After the project is paid for, rings contract to an ideal circular pattern. The assumption is that the entire society accepts the expense of the reclamation. For an agricultural society, this would probably mean a land tax, for that is where most of the wealth exists. The public benefit justifying such a policy would derive from the more ideally arranged land use at the end of the payment period.

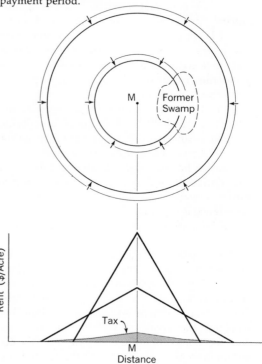

the farmers can never hope to repay the costs of development, the difference above and beyond water sales and total costs must be subsidized by taxpayers everywhere in the country. But consider the relative location of such projects (Figure 12–6). They are often far beyond the periphery of the industrial and densely settled regions of the United States. Because of this, land rents are low and cannot compensate for the initial investments in irrigation facilities. At the same time, the remote location of the new production areas means transportation costs will be great and represent another cost that will be passed on to the consumer. Add to this the fact that

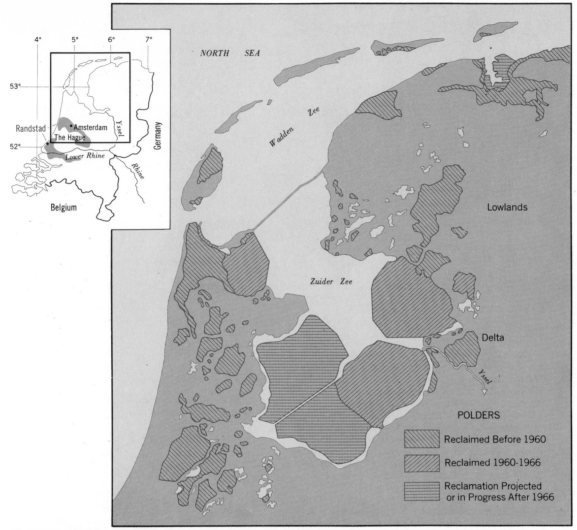

Figure 12-5 Polders of the Netherlands Polders are Dutch lands reclaimed from the sea. They now represent a significant portion of the total land area of the Netherlands.

Differences in transportation

If we consider the nature of reality and compare it with Thünen's isotropic plain, one of the first contradictions between them will be differences in the ease of travel. We have already discussed the relationship between distance and direction and have seen how geographic circles transform space into new map patterns. Where travel costs are high in terms of time, effort, or money, the distances people travel will shrink; where a good road or navigable river makes transportation easier, trips and connectivity of all kinds will increase.

Thünen recognized this and added a river

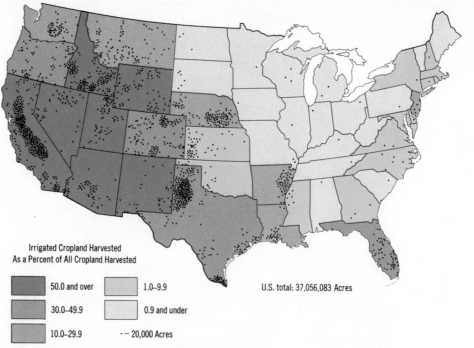

Irrigated Cropland Harvested
As a Percent of All Cropland Harvested

▮ 50.0 and over		▮ 1.0–9.9	
▮ 30.0–49.9		▯ 0.9 and under	
▮ 10.0–29.9		· – 20,000 Acres	

U.S. total: 37,056,083 Acres

**Figure 12-6 Irrigated land in farms in the United
States, 1964** Most of the irrigated land in the
United States is in the Western half of the nation,
far away from the major Eastern market. The
Bureau of Reclamation, the federal agency
responsible for most federally financed irrigation
projects, has authority to propose and support only
projects which are located west of the Mississippi
River. A government program to promote intensive
agriculture far from the densest population areas
would tend to increase long-haul shipment of
food and add to the total transport burden. (*The
National Atlas of the United States of America,* Dept.
of the Interior Geological Survey 1970, plate 168;
compiled from Census of Agriculture 1964, vol. 1)

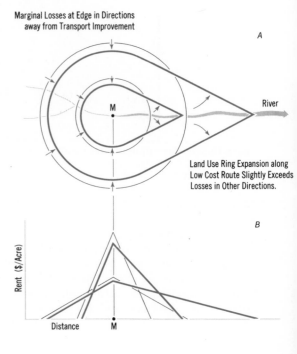

Marginal Losses at Edge in Directions
away from Transport Improvement

A

River

Land Use Ring Expansion along
Low Cost Route Slightly Exceeds
Losses in Other Directions.

B

Rent ($/Acre)

Distance   M

**Figure 12-7 Directional improvement in
transport** (*A*) Effects on land use pattern
of a decrease in transport cost in one direction (a navigable river route). (*B*) Adjustment
in rent surface along a low-cost route. Land
use margins expand in the direction of transport improvement and contract in directions
away from transport improvement; prices
fall; and the total volume of a product reaching the market increases.

*Human
Geography:
Spatial
Design
In World
Society*

250

to his landscape (Figure 11–12). The stream passes directly through his market town and has the head of navigation just at the town. This is a common condition in the real world. The tidewater settlements of colonial America were located at or near navigation headwaters on rivers flowing from the Appalachian Mountains to the sea. This led to some interesting geographic conditions, which we will soon discuss. In Thünen's case, the use of the river downstream from the market allows farmers to move goods more quickly and cheaply from points along its banks into the central settlement. The relative differences in transportation costs for a two-crop system are shown in Figure 12–7. Note how the downstream side of the cost cone is elongated. This means that additional land along the river can be used for producing the more valuable crop of the innermost ring. The same thing is true for the other zone of production. At the same time that new land comes into production downstream, farmers within a particular zone who are using land on the very periphery find they cannot compete with the newer areas of production. The boundary of the inner-ring crop will draw inward toward the center. Farmers on the edges will have to switch crops in order to stay in business. Less lucky farmers located away from the river on the outer edge of the second ring will experience the same loss from competition with new lands, but they will have no alternative crop and will have to give up commercial farming.

Spatial discontinuities

Another important variation results from different costs in unlike transportation domains. Figure 12–8 shows a hypothetical situation in which a central market is supplied in part by land continuous with it and in part by an overseas area. The crop supplied by the innermost ring is unaffected by the presence of low-cost marine transportation. Its transportation costs are so great that any possible profit would be eaten up long before its zone of production had reached the coast. On the

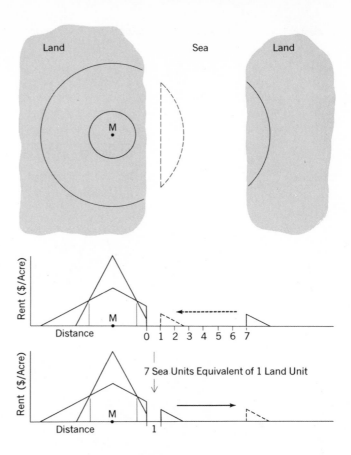

Figure 12-8 Effects of difference in transport rates in different travel domains In a region where land areas are separated by navigable seas, two transport domains exist. Sea travel is much cheaper than land travel, and distant shore areas may be able to enter the market before marginally distant land areas. It can be seen that the distant shore land is within marketing range if the sea distance is reduced by the ratio of sea-to-land transport costs. Some empty territory would exist in the ideal market ring, which implies that costs would be slightly higher for a market located in the position shown, compared with a market in the flat, homogeneous plane of the original Thünen formulation. This abstract argument helps to explain why distant places with access to ocean transport have been able to enter world commerce since the development of modern ocean travel.

The Urban World and Its Hinterland: Land Use Theory

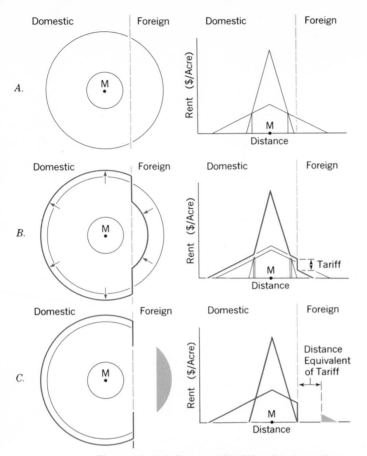

Figure 12-9 Influence of tariff on land use rings

Two-crop system. (*A*) No tariff, ideal ring pattern, (*B*) Tariff on second crop. Rent falls and rings are reduced in foreign supply area; prices rise and marginal domestic producers enter the market. (*C*) Distance equivalent of force of tariff. A tariff has an effect much like that of an additional transport charge at a national border. In part *A* an ideal two-crop system exists, with a national boundary running through the region. With no tariff there is no effect on land use pattern. In part *B* a tariff is imposed and can be seen on the profile of the rent cone as an additional depression of the rent-paying ability of crops at the border and beyond into the foreign land. The foreign marginal farmer goes out of business, and, because of less product in the market, prices rise and marginal domestic producers are able to enter the commercial system. The distance equivalent of the tariff can be estimated as shown in part C in a manner similar to the difference in transport domain shown in Figure 12-8. The effect of the tariff then is to raise prices and allow marginal domestic producers to exist in the marketing system.

*Human
Geography:
Spatial
Design
In World
Society*

252

other hand, the second crop has not only a lower transportation rate on land but an even less costly one at sea. This would be true of many bulk goods such as wheat. The combined costs of transportation by sea and land are still low enough to allow some production on the other side of the water. (In this example we have averaged special terminal costs into the average transportation rate.) If we project the transportation cost slope outward and downward from the market, we can estimate where production would end if land rather than sea existed to the east of the market. If we slide the fractional part of the transportation cost cone back toward the central market until it just fits inside the cost cone projected on the basis of land transportation alone, we can get some notion of the relative effects of land and sea transportation. In this case, seven sea units are seen to be the equivalent of one unit of distance by land transportation.

Various conditions bring about *spatial discontinuities* in production similar to the one just described. Tariff barriers have the opposite effect on production areas, as does low-cost sea transportation. Two countries with a common land boundary may raise the same crops for a single market (Figure 12-9). With no customs barrier at the border the area of production for each of two crops would remain symmetrically arrayed around the central settlement. But suppose that a protectionist policy places heavy duties on crop imports. This will mean that imported produce will cost more than domestic produce, and in order to remain competitive foreign farmers must take less of a profit. At the same time, marginal farms in foreign areas will become impractical since their low profits will be consumed by a combination of transportation costs and tariffs. As they fail and go out of production, the supply in the market will diminish; prices will rise; and marginal domestic farm areas will be able to enter the market at the expense of foreign farmers. These *before* and *after* conditions are shown in Figure 12-9A and B. It is also possible to assign a distance which would be the equivalent of the tariff involved. We use the same technique as in the previous case for ocean transportation. This is illustrated in Figure 12–9C.

Real Agricultural Locations at Regional, National, and Global Scales

Here, then, are several variations on the original theme proposed by Thünen. We have already seen real life examples at the village and small town level; let us see what these ideas can tell us about the way the world is organized at regional, national, and global scales.

Demon rum, distance, and the Whiskey Rebellion

If an insight is a good one, it should apply in many places, to different cultures, and at different times in history. It should also work at different scales of analysis or observation. This is true of Thünen's analysis of the localization of production. We have already seen how farms and farm villages in Sicily and Finland follow orderly spatial production patterns. Now let us go back in time to the eighteenth century and a newly emerged United States to find still another example of the role played by distance and transportation costs in determining farm activities. Our example concerns the drinking habits of colonial America and is told on a regional scale.

Drink, for better or worse, has always been a part of exploration and settlement. Few frontier societies have lived without it in some form. The settling of North America by Europeans was no exception, and the drinking habits of Americans have long figured in the country's history. George Stewart, in his superb book *American Ways of Life*, gives the background to the colonists' drinking habits. With a bow in the direction of the master storyteller let us summarize a few of his ideas and add one or two geographic observations of our own.

Americans in those early days imbibed four basic types of spirits: brandy, gin, rum, and whiskey. We must skip the details about the first two kinds, which were of consider-

ably less importance to Americans than rum and whiskey. Brandy was a gentlemen's drink, introduced by the French and difficult to make out of local materials. Gin never seemed to catch on with the American taste. Although it could be made from fermented grains grown locally rather than grapes, which were, at that time, unavailable along the Atlantic coast, the ravages it wreaked among the English poor were not repeated in the colonies. This story belongs rather to rum and whiskey, both of which are rich with geographic lore.

Rum came first. The need for locally manufactured products in the New England colonies, combined with a dearth of good farmlands and an ambitious, hard-working group of colonists, created an active if small center of industry and manufacturing in the northern colonies. Other English, French, and Dutch settlers had colonized the warmer, more fertile Atlantic shores from Maryland south to Georgia as well as the islands of the Caribbean. These latter colonists specialized in agricultural products grown on plantations which very soon were worked almost exclusively by slaves brought from Africa. While New England was becoming self-sufficient in manufacturing, the South and the islands depended upon the export of produce and the import of everything from shoes and glassware to tools from either England or the Northern colonies. In the West Indies the production of sugar from cane became so dominant that even foodstuffs such as grains and fish also had to be brought from overseas.

New England merchants soon found out that high profits were theirs for the taking through various kinds of *triangular trade*. A skipper, sailing a fine ship built in Massachusetts or Rhode Island from local timber, might take a load of dried New England cod, lumber, and some cereals to the West Indies in exchange for a shipful of sugar. This sugar would bring a high price in England and could be converted into English goods which commanded high prices in the colonies. Another, and vile, form of triangular trade also developed. Large amounts of molasses were produced during the refining of sugar in the

West Indies. This syrup was taken by New England skippers back to their home ports, where it was turned into rum. Rum was cheaper than brandy and soon became the popular drink of the people all up and down the colonies from Maine to Georgia. But more rum was produced than could be locally used, and the remainder found its way in Yankee bottoms to the Ivory, Gold, and Slave Coasts of West Africa, where it was traded for black slaves. Those unfortunates were taken under hellish conditions back to the Indies and the Southern colonies, where they were exchanged for more molasses and also for silver and gold. Many different kinds of trade patterns developed as a result of the *complementarity* and *transportability* of these trade items (Figure 12–10). There were other developments as well. Viewed over a long time scale, the importation of black slaves and their subsequent victory in their struggle for freedom enriched the culture of the United States in numberless ways unforeseen at that time. In the short run, as we have said, low-priced rum became available to the colonists all along the Atlantic seaboard. In fact, rum became so much a part of American life that even today we use its name to signify all kinds of alcoholic drinks when we speak of *rum runners* and *demon rum*.

Overland transportation in those early days was difficult. The sea provided the easiest means of movement north and south along the Atlantic coast, while sailing ships, because of the relatively shallow streams, unloaded their goods only a few miles inland from the coast. Rum, like many other goods, was plentiful near tidewater, but as the frontier moved farther and farther west, transportation costs soon made it a rare and expensive drink. Scotch-Irish frontier farmers from Ulster were soon making their own brand of whiskey. Back in the old country they had made their Scotch and Irish whiskey from barley, but in America they chose rye grains, thus creating the rye whiskey so famous in folk songs. Beyond the Allegheny Mountains still another grain came

into use. Indian corn grew well in the hills of Kentucky, and Bourbon County in that state soon gave its name to another kind of whiskey, one which was uniquely American.

Not only had the inland farmers found a new drink; they also had solved an important economic problem which faced them. The major centers of population and major markets in colonial America were located close along the Atlantic shore. New farmlands were increasingly distant from those markets, and the costs of transporting farm products long distances overland hampered the frontiersmen. Nearest to the seaboard were located dairy farms which supplied milk and milk products to the growing cities. Beyond them woodlots supplied fuel and lumber needs just as they did in Thünen's original north German settlements. Beyond the woodlots grain fields ripened. Each of these commodities with a progressively lower rent paying ability was matched by increasing ease of transportation. Milk was perishable; firewood was necessary but heavy; grains cost less in the market but could be bagged and barged or brought on horseback down muddy mountain roads. These relationships are shown in terms of the Thünen model in Figure 12–11. Beyond the point where grain no longer could turn a profit for its farmers, cattle and hogs provided some livelihood and cash. Their advantage was that they were their own transportation. Droves of animals were walked to market from remote farms and butchered at the marketplace. Thus, meat-producing areas were found beyond the grains. But even then the advancing wave of farmers soon found themselves beyond the range of the market.

At this point whiskey became important to them. They could take the grain from an entire field and after distillation have a highly transportable product in a few kegs that could be lashed to the back of a pack animal for shipment to Eastern markets. American whiskey had established itself as rum's competitor. In George Stewart's words:

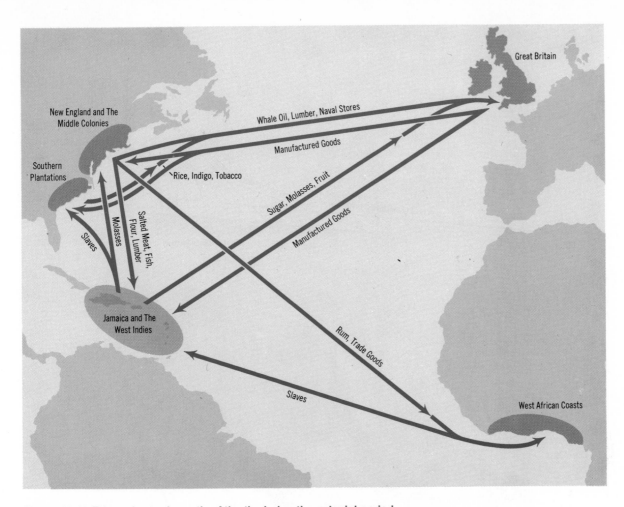

Figure 12-10 Triangular trade on the Atlantic during the colonial period.

In the middle seventeen hundreds there was a country of rum along the seacoast and a country of whiskey farther inland, but the whiskey gradually encroached upon the rum. The frontiersmen had to come down to the tidewater towns once a year anyway to get their supplies of salt, ammunition, and ironware, and they found that for those supplies they could barter whiskey as well as beaverskins. Then, the seven years' war of the Revolution must have had a great effect. The British held the sea and many of the seaports, and rum was hard to come by. War, also, is a great spreader of new ideas and new customs. Many an Ephraim Potter or Eben Stubbs of the Marblehead Regiment must have had his first taste of whiskey when he took the proffered flask from some Patrick Wilson or Archy Loughry of the Pennsylvania Line. Moreover, the country of rum could not grow except by colonizing the oyster beds, and the country of whiskey was on the frontier and had all the West open to it.[1]

The frontiersmen of western Pennsylvania were satisfied with their market arrangements

[1]George R. Stewart, *American Ways of Life*, Doubleday, Garden City, N.Y., 1954, p. 120.

The Urban World and Its Hinterland: Land Use Theory

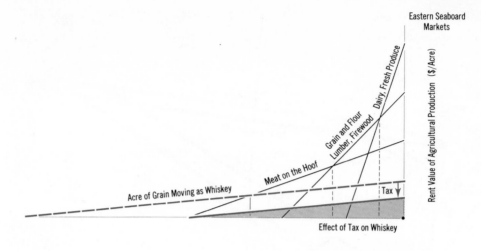

Eastern Seaboard Markets

Rent Value of Agricultural Production ($/Acre)

Dairy, Fresh Produce

Grain and Flour
Lumber, Firewood

Meat on the Hoof

Acre of Grain Moving as Whiskey

Tax

Effect of Tax on Whiskey

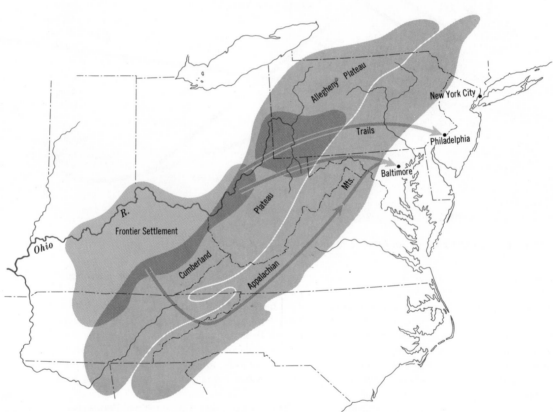

Allegheny Plateau

New York City

Trails

Philadelphia

Baltimore

Plateau

Mts.

R.

Frontier Settlement

Ohio

Cumberland

Appalachian

until President Washington with the help of the New Congress placed a heavy excise tax on whiskey in order to help pay the expenses of the new government. This had a similar effect on the marketing of whiskey as would a tariff. A new cost floor was added, and the margin of profit was reduced. Transportation costs could claim less than before, and the frontier Pennsylvania farmers lost their source of income as the ring of profitable farm production shrank eastward toward the coastal markets. Rioting began in western Pennsylvania in 1794, and courtrooms were disrupted and tax collectors and local law enforcement officers intimidated. Washington called out the militia and sent 12,000 men to put down the rebels. His force was so overwhelming—it was larger than any he had commanded during the Revolutionary War—that peace was quickly restored along the frontier. Happily, the tax was repealed during Jefferson's administration and the issue was short-lived.

This Whiskey Rebellion is often described as a test of power between the newly constituted government of the United States and local groups. While that interpretation may well be true, it tells us little about the causes of the trouble or of the real solutions to the problem.

The nation and its agriculture

The above discussion of the Whiskey Rebellion illustrates the application of geographic theory at a regional scale. We return now to modern times and the United States as a whole in order to see how the same basic principles apply to modern agriculture and land use. The sequence of American land use with which Chapter 11 began took us from urban landscapes, through fields of corn, to wheat ranches, and finally to open range where sheep and cattle grazed. A moment's reflection on this sequence of land uses will suggest Thünen's rings to us again. The central city with its market; high-priced but perishable corn; cheaper, more transportable wheat; and finally cattle grazing on acres and acres of unimproved range are similar to other sequences of land use already described. (We should be careful to note that the cattle referred to here are not the sleek, corn-fattened beasts kept in feedlots and destined for immediate butchering. These are, instead, yearling steers getting their first growth on cheap grass before being shipped cityward for final conditioning on special diets. Range cattle are called *stockers* and provide new stock for city-oriented feedlots, where they became *feeders* before becoming steaks and hamburgers.)

Given the concentration of industry and urban markets in the northeastern United States, we would expect that area to be the focal point for a Thünen model conceived on a national scale. Adjacent to this core area we should find perishable, high-value commodities raised for city use such as dairy products and fresh fruits and vegetables. Next we might expect high-yielding field crops, followed by less and less intensive uses of the land. Corn, wheat, and rangeland for grazing match our expectations there. Thus a completely theoretical United States would look like the map pattern in Figure 12-12. Another way of putting all this would

Figure 12-11 The geography of the Whiskey Rebellion, 1794 The key to entering the Eastern commercial markets in the early days of trans-Appalachian settlement was to lower the transport cost on products crossing the mountains. Hogs and cattle could walk to market, but grain had to be carried. Moving grain as whiskey concentrated the value of an acre of crop into smaller loads. A tax on the trans-Appalachian whiskey reduced the rent-paying ability of grain crops to zero and the Western farmers rebelled. The face that Eastern seaboard interests could import rum by sea in competition with the inland whiskey was important in creating the political problem, a division of interests which still exists in many contexts between the seaboard and inland regions of the country.

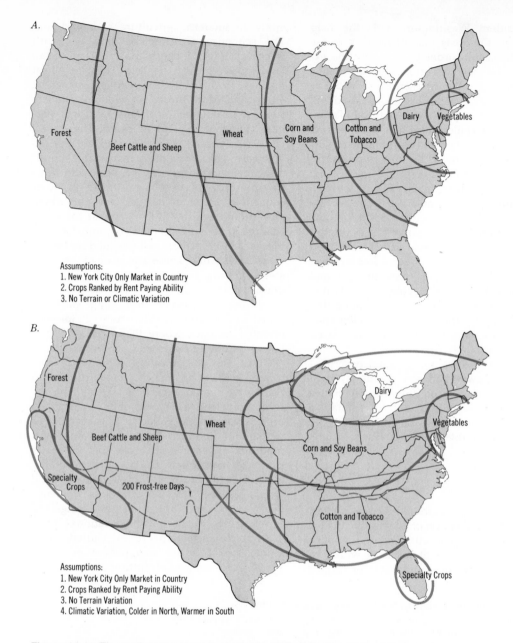

A.

Forest

Beef Cattle and Sheep

Wheat

Corn and
Soy Beans

Cotton and
Tobacco

Dairy

Vegetables

Assumptions:
1. New York City Only Market in Country
2. Crops Ranked by Rent Paying Ability
3. No Terrain or Climatic Variation

B.

Forest

Beef Cattle and Sheep

Wheat

Corn and Soy Beans

Dairy

Vegetables

Specialty
Crops

200 Frost-free Days

Cotton and Tobacco

Specialty Crops

Assumptions:
1. New York City Only Market in Country
2. Crops Ranked by Rent Paying Ability
3. No Terrain Variation
4. Climatic Variation, Colder in North, Warmer in South

Figure 12-12 Theoretical land use rings in the United States   Theoretical land use rings in part *A* become more realistic by recognizing North/South temperature variation as shown in part *B*. Rings shift around because different crops respond differently to temperature variation. Pasture for dairying can grow in short, cool seasons; corn and soybeans require 150 frost-free days and a hot summer. Cotton cannot grow north of the 200-frost-free-day line. Specialty crops exist in regions with mild winters. Adopting other assumptions, such as accounting for soil and terrain differences, would result in a more complex and realistic pattern.

be in terms of the rent paid by various land uses. Urban and industrial rents are unquestionably highest; beyond them we would expect land uses, whatever they might be, to provide less and less profit the farther we traveled from urban centers. Now let us look at the actual distribution of crops and rent earned by agricultural activities in the United States.

We should not expect reality to match the smooth rings, neat homogeneous areas, and abrupt transitions allowed us by the models we build. This becomes evident when we look at the maps in Figures 12–13 and 12–14. The first of these maps shows the average value per acre in dollars derived from all types of agricultural activity excluding livestock and poultry production. The two letters inside each state indicate the two leading money-earning crops in order of their importance. The pattern shown here is interesting both for the way in which it meets our theoretical expectations and also for the several exceptions for which Thünen's theory of land rent does not prepare us. As we expected, the highest returns per acre of agricultural land come from that part of Megalopolis between Boston and New York City. New York State itself has lower values, since the shape of the state means that most of its area is farther removed from its major city than areas of New Jersey, Connecticut, Rhode Island, and Massachusetts. Farm values fall off regularly to the west away from the urbanized Atlantic seaboard. In West Virginia and Pennsylvania the effect of the Appalachian Mountains and Appalachia can be seen in lower values that pick up again as Illinois with the major urban focus of Chicago is approached. Going south along the Atlantic coast from New York City we encounter a ridge of high rents which runs inland from the Carolinas to Kentucky. This matches the southern Piedmont and is easily explained by the presence of tobacco. Another high point over Louisiana comes as more of a surprise, although rice and sugar cane account for this rise in the topography of rents. Viewed as a whole, the United States shows a steady, if slightly irregular, decline in rents west-

Irrigation agriculture. Irrigation agriculture has dramatic results. Contrast the natural sagebrush cover in the foreground with the orchards and irrigated fields in the middle and background. Perhaps this is why irrigation projects have received generous public support. This picture is of a lateral canal along the edge of the Snake River Valley in Idaho. The water is taken from the river upstream and brought along the edge of the valley in canals, from which it can be diverted into the orchards and fields using gravity feed.

ward across the Great Plains to the Rocky Mountains.

Let us note in passing that our theory of land rent works at another, more localized scale. Figure 12–14 shows county-by-county returns from agriculture for the state of Illinois. Remember that although Illinois shows an average value of only 83 dollars per acre, we are dealing here with an average for the entire state. We would expect to find high agricultural land values near Chicago. We would also expect to see them regularly tapering off to the south and west, just as shown in the figure. Thus, while Illinois as a whole has a lower place on the rent surface of the United States than does New Jersey, at a local scale Chicago's urbanization pulls values up to over 150 dollars per acre.

Idaho, Washington, Arizona, and California all seem much too high compared with expected values. Irrigation plays a significant part in raising land rents. As we have already noted, major inputs of capital have reclaimed

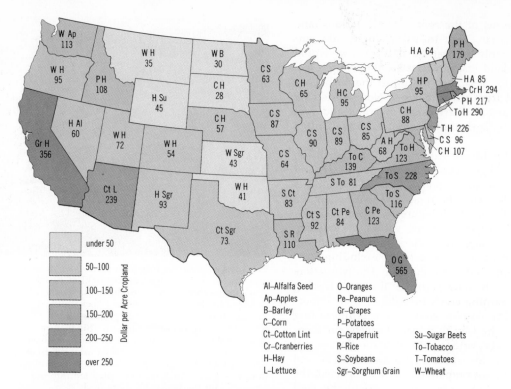

Figure 12-13 Average value ($) per acre of cropland derived from all types of agriculture, excluding livestock and poultry, 1970 (Compiled from *Statistical Abstract of the United States, 1972,* U.S. Dept. of Commerce Table 1011., "Principal Crops")

Figure 12-14 Return from agriculture in Illinois (George F. Jenks and Fred C. Caspall, "Error on Choroplethic Maps: Definition, Measurement, Reduction," reproduced by permission from the *Annals* of the Association of American Geographers, vol. 61, June 1971, p. 236)

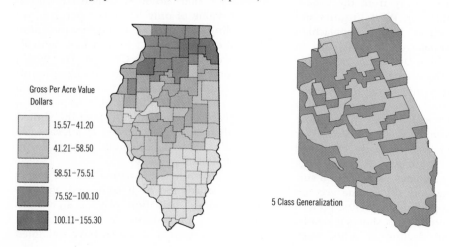

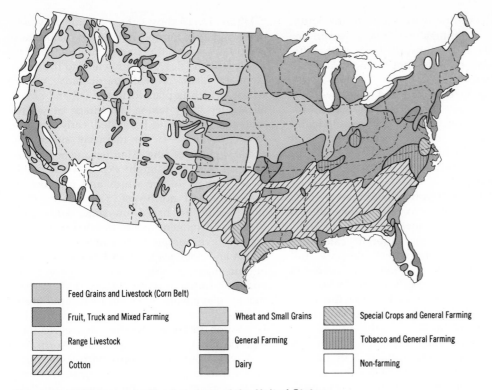

Figure 12-15 Major agricultural regions of the United States

large tracts of dry land in our Western states. In the Southwest mild winters combined with irrigation water help to produce bumper crops of cotton, fruit, nuts, and vegetables. Those conditions are enhanced by modern transportation developments with refrigerated freight trains and diesel trucks which carry fresh produce to the Northeastern states. The high value in Florida also represents areas of special crops such as citrus which are possible in the subtropical climate of the area. Wheat from the rich hills of the Palouse country in eastern Washington and Idaho potatoes raise returns in the Northwest. At the same time, the mild winters and green, rain-drenched pastures of western Oregon and Washington create conditions favorable for dairy farming although the immediate market for fresh milk is very small by national standards. This problem is solved by turning fresh milk into condensed milk, cheese, and

butter for shipment to the East and Southern California.

If we regionalize production by crop type for the country as a whole (Figure 12–15) and compare this map with the idealized one in Figure 12–12, we see that the general pattern is the same. However, dairy products dominate across parts of New England, northern New York State, and the upper Midwest. This is because these areas have poor soils and are north of the 90-day frost-free growing season. As a result, they are better suited for the production of hay for fodder. But even if we consider only the price structure for milk, we find our general expectations for the United States are fulfilled. Wholesale buying prices for fresh milk diminish steadily from New York State west to Minnesota in the Northeastern dairy region. Since these prices do not include transportation costs, dealers must pay less for milk the farther they

The Urban
World and
Its Hinterland:
Land Use
Theory

261

are from the central market area. In the South, where high temperatures make caring for dairy herds and producing fresh milk difficult, demand exceeds supply and prices are again higher.

Returning to our idealized map, we find exceptions where high-yielding cotton, tobacco, and peanuts tend to force out corn. The same is true for the specialty crops (Figure 12-12) which provide alternate choices for farmers distant from the major markets of the Northeast.

Perhaps the best way to summarize these several descriptions is to turn to the maps in Figure 12-16 which show the actual distribution of production for different categories of dairy products, corn, wheat, livestock, and specialty crops. The myriad dots scattered like confetti across these maps could be confusing, but we hope that by now the basic processes underlying their distribution have become clear. Naturally, one theory and one approach cannot fully explain anything as complex as agricultural production in a country as large as the United States, but a geographic point of view can help. We also hope that the next time you drive across the country, your trip will be enriched when you see and understand the sequence of crop production and other activities.

Europe and the world

If our purpose were solely to describe the theory and technique proposed by Thünen, it would be repetitive to seek additional examples, but geography has two major purposes. One is to describe world patterns; the other is to help explain the processes underlying the observed distributions. Thus we present maps of selected agricultural yields in Europe partly as description and partly as confirmation of the ideas we have already outlined.

Figure 12-17 shows the variation in yields of two major European crops. Potatoes are important across the colder, moister reaches of the British Isles, Scandinavia, and the north German plain. Wheat—particularly winter wheat, which is planted in the fall and grows all winter long, taking advantage of winter moisture until it is harvested early the following summer—is the mainstay among the cereal grains of the Mediterranean region. Because of this we might expect wheat yields to be highest in the south and potatoes in the north and northwest. Such an expectation would be based on some knowledge of the environment alone. In what way could we improve our prediction of yields of both wheat and potatoes in all of Europe? A glance at our maps of urbanization (Figure 3-16) and per capita income (Figure 1-3) reveals that even at a world scale northwestern Europe is a focal point for world organization. This is enough to let us theorize that agriculture will be most intensive near the North Sea and will diminish outward with some regularity. The map pattern once again confirms what agricultural location theory predicts. With a few exceptions such as Switzerland and northern Italy (no real surprise in either place) the bulls-eye pattern of high agricultural rents is focused on the nations adjoining the North Sea.

If we choose a smaller-scale map covering the entire world (Figure 12-18), we can put both Europe and the United States in global perspective. Here we see the average caloric yield from both small grains (wheat, corn, barley, rye, etc.) and potatoes. Pounds and bushels per acre are converted to a more universal caloric value in order to overcome the problem of comparing unlike crops. The results of our analysis confirm what we have already anticipated. The bulls-eye pattern of intensive agricultural production centers now on the North Atlantic. Some details have

Figure 12-16 Distribution of selected farm products in the United States (Compiled from *Statistical Abstract of the United States, 1971,* Dept. of Commerce, Wash., D.C., Tables 968, 970, 977, and 989; *Annual Crop Summary,* Crop Reporting Board, SRS, Dept. of Agriculture, Wash., D.C., January, 1972)

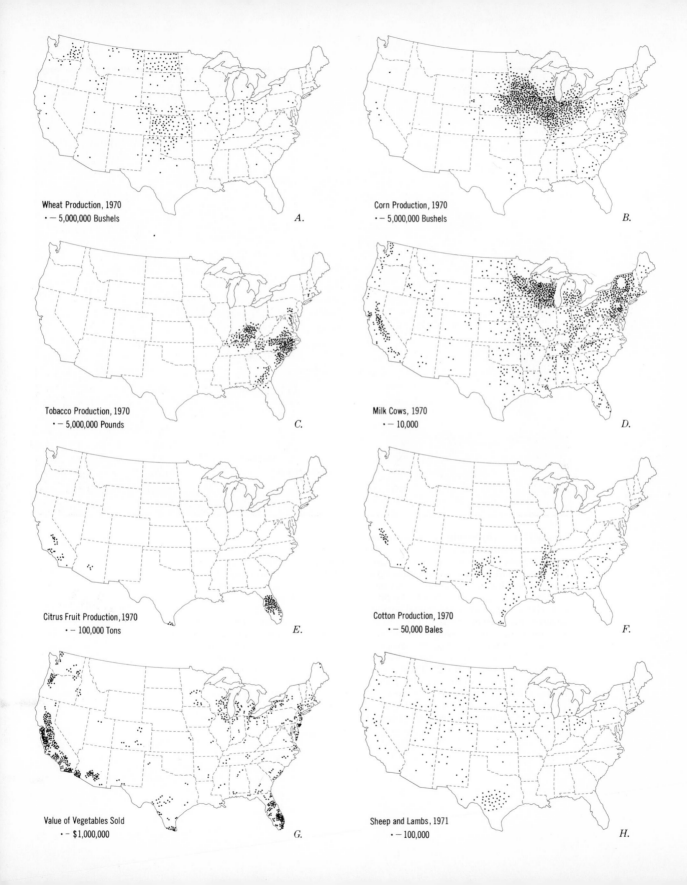

Wheat Production, 1970
• — 5,000,000 Bushels
A.

Corn Production, 1970
• — 5,000,000 Bushels
B.

Tobacco Production, 1970
• — 5,000,000 Pounds
C.

Milk Cows, 1970
• — 10,000
D.

Citrus Fruit Production, 1970
• — 100,000 Tons
E.

Cotton Production, 1970
• — 50,000 Bales
F.

Value of Vegetables Sold
• — $1,000,000
G.

Sheep and Lambs, 1971
• — 100,000
H.

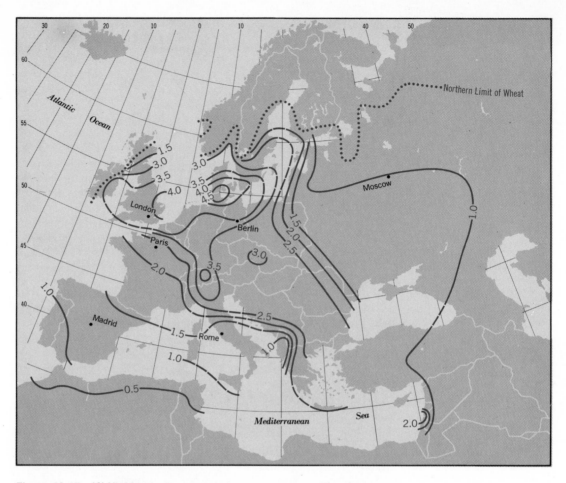

Figure 12-17 *(A)* **Yields of wheat in metric tons/hectare**   The abstract
Thünen agricultural model predicts a fall in intensity of cropping with
distance from the market. In reality, many factors influence crop choice, not
the least of which is climate. Notice, however, that the maximum yield for
wheat in northwestern Europe is not far from the northern limit of where
the crop can be grown at all. On the other hand, the high population density
and relatively affluent commercial society of northwestern Europe exert
considerable pressure on land users to be efficient in the returns they obtain
from the land. This fits well with the Thünen model. The pattern of yields in
potatoes, another staple crop in Europe, also supports this view. (*Agricultural
Regions on the European Economic Community*, 1960 Series Documentation in
Agriculture and Food No. 27, Paris, Organization for European Economic
Cooperation and the European Productivity Agency; *Annual Abstract of
Statistics*, United Kingdom, 1970, London, Her Majesty's Stationary Office,
Central Statistical Office; Tarımsal Yapı ve Üretim (*Agricultural Structure and
Production*), Ankara, Turkish State Institute of Statistics Publication No. 564,
1968)

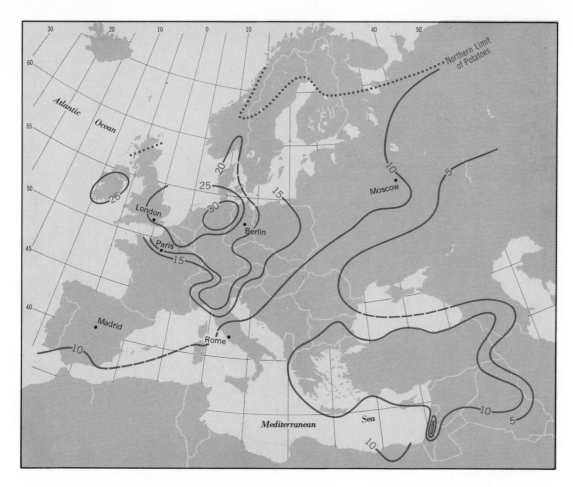

Figure 12-17 *(B)* Yields of potatoes in metric tons/hectare

been lost—for example, in the Soviet Union and America—but the general pattern of distribution focuses upon the *have* nations of the world. Outliers do exist in Argentina, South Africa, Australia, and Japan, but those places are all industrial and commercial centers which have grown up at the opposite end of the major sea routes which supply Europe.

Thünen and the Geography of Transportation

A pattern of world development emerges in terms of the rent-paying ability of various activities and of the competition among them for the lands they occupy. The pattern is skewed by culture and nature, and yet the amazing thing is the spatial orderliness which certain kinds of human activity display. It is possible now to see in simple geographic terms the connection between urbanization and agriculture as well as the association between the rich nations and the poor.

If industry forms the core of the contemporary world, and if certain kinds of urbanization go hand in hand with such activities, we have defined the focal points for centers of several bulls-eyes around which agricultural activities are ordered. Such foci can be thought of as great magnets pulling the people, pro-

The Urban World and Its Hinterland: Land Use Theory

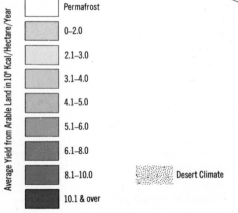

Average Yield from Arable Land in 10⁶ Kcal/Hectare/Year

	Permafrost
	0–2.0
	2.1–3.0
	3.1–4.0
	4.1–5.0
	5.1–6.0
	6.1–8.0
	8.1–10.0
	10.1 & over

Desert Climate

Figure 12-18 Average caloric yield from arable land as measured by yields from small grains and potatoes   The crops included in the survey were wheat, rice (milled weight), rye, barley, oats, maize, and potatoes. Bananas and casava, staple foods in the tropics, have been left out of the figures because of difficulty in establishing a unit area yield figure. Individual plants yield very high caloric values, although no protein values; but since they are normally grown in very small garden plots surrounded by unproductive land, areal measures are meaningless. Also, data are poor or lacking concerning variation in returns. The azimuthal projection centered on Europe facilitates comparing the real distribution with a worldwide Thünen agricultural model centered on Europe. (Op. cit. Figure 12-17 and materials from the Foreign Market Information Division, Foreign Agricultural Service, USDA; *Production Yearbook 1968*, FAO of the UN, Statistics Division, 1969; *Statistisk Arbog 1970* vol. 74, Copenhagen; *Statistisk Arsbok 1970*, vol. 57, Stockholm)

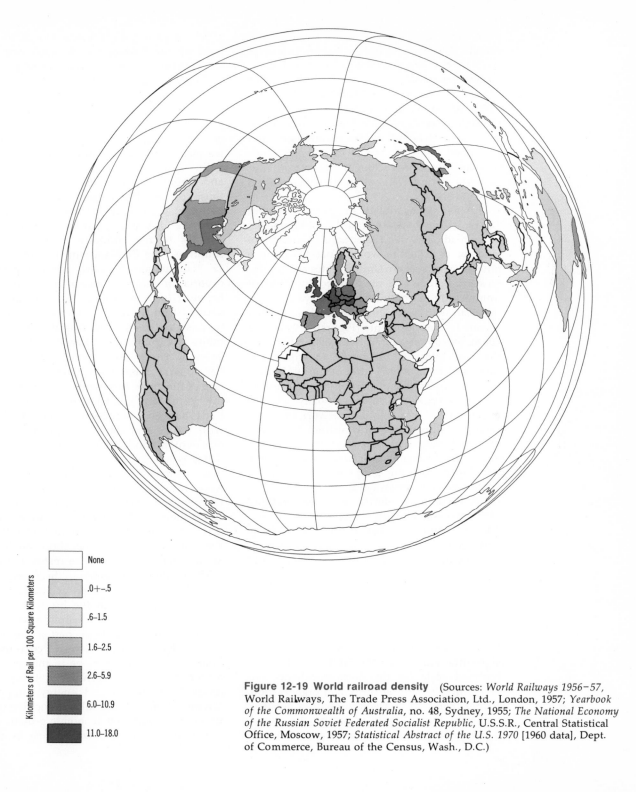

Kilometers of Rail per 100 Square Kilometers

None

.0+–.5

.6–1.5

1.6–2.5

2.6–5.9

6.0–10.9

11.0–18.0

Figure 12-19 World railroad density   (Sources: *World Railways 1956–57*, World Railways, The Trade Press Association, Ltd., London, 1957; *Yearbook of the Commonwealth of Australia*, no. 48, Sydney, 1955; *The National Economy of the Russian Soviet Federated Socialist Republic*, U.S.S.R., Central Statistical Office, Moscow, 1957; *Statistical Abstract of the U.S. 1970* [1960 data], Dept. of Commerce, Bureau of the Census, Wash., D.C.)

duce, and ideas of the world toward their centers. This fanciful notion has an important truth in it. Huge quantities of raw and semi-finished materials from the farthest reaches of the earth move by land and sea to the urban cores. All kinds of resources find their way through systems of concentration into a few select spots where they are manipulated and consumed and from which their waste products are dispersed. Thus transportation becomes a critical element in the organization of world society.

This is demonstrated in part by Figure 12–19, which shows the number of kilometers of railroad lines per 100 square kilometers of land for each of the world's nations. Notice how the Northeastern United States and Northwestern Europe are surrounded by rings of diminishing railroad intensity. If we compare this map with those showing levels of general economic development (Figures 10–7 and 10–8), we can see a direct relationship between the availability of transportation within nations and their overall level of living. But internal transport is only part of the picture. The world is organized internationally as well as nationally by a complex network of roads, railroads, ship routes, and airlines by means of which raw materials and manufactured goods are exchanged between nations. We have seen how the geographic ordering of space creates different land use regions. When regional complementarity and transferability exist, exchanges of all kinds will take place. The subsequent pattern of international trade and commerce is one good measure of the organization and connectivity of world society.

Spatial design in world society

Just as a geographic point of view offers insight into human behavior at a local or neighborhood scale, so too does it enhance our global understanding of human organization. Rather than end this volume with a detailed, region-by-region description of the world, let us take a parting look at the spatial organization of society in terms of one of its basic patterns, the flow of wealth across the entire world measured in terms of natural resources and manufactured goods.

Figure 12–20 shows the movement of exports—excluding petroleum, coal, and natural gas—from all over the world to the two predominant centers of industrial power, northwestern Europe and the United States. The paths shown on the map indicate the value and origin of goods and materials reaching those places. The largest flows are actually between European nations and between Europe and America, but the entire earth contributes to the affluence of a few favored countries. The diagram which follows (Figure 12–21) illustrates the flow of both imports and exports in terms of major connecting links between individual nations and/or groups of nations throughout the world. This diagram reveals even more regarding the relative centrality and importance of each world area. The dominance of an area is indicated by the number of links it has with other places and the size of the circle representing it. In the case of the European countries the circle includes trade between European nations as well as with the rest of the world and exceeds any other international flow, although the United States is not far behind. (We should also note that if interstate traffic in the United States were included, the relative magnitudes of Europe and America would be reversed.) Other nations and groups show fewer connections. In fact, the Communist countries of Asia at the present time show no links of similar magnitude with the rest of the world.

The evidence presented in these two figures should not be interpreted as indicating any inherent superiorty in the life-styles or peoples inhabiting those central places. Their good fortune is in large part a function of relative location and historical circumstance. That is, they happen to be in the right place at the right time. Conversely, the growing crises in resources and energy supplies is forcing all of us to rethink the doctrine of continual and unlimited economic growth which the wealthy nations have so long espoused.

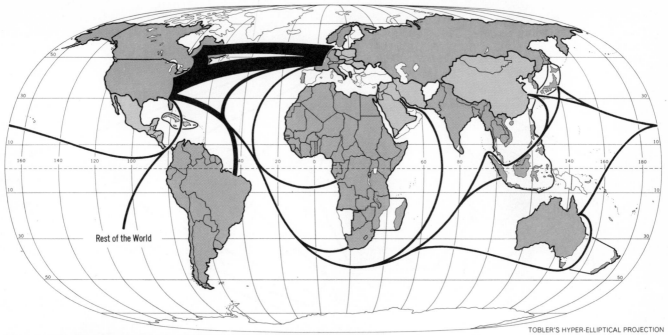

TOBLER'S HYPER-ELLIPTICAL PROJECTION

Figure 12-20 World trade patterns, 1969 Lines show exports in excess of 100 million dollars per year in either direction, petroleum and petroleum products, coal, and natural gas are excluded. Data are compiled for groups of nations. Nations left uncolored have been included from the flow lines. (Data: *Yearbook of International Trade Statistics,* 1969, Department of economic and Social Affairs, Statistical Office of the United Nations)

Europe and America are rapidly depleting their own resources and are becoming more dependent upon the rest of the world. Vows of self-sufficiency notwithstanding, we will depend more and more on raw materials provided by the remoter corners of the earth. In fact, even now we are as dependent upon the developing nations for supplies of critical raw materials as they are upon our factories, banks, and laboratories. Our final map (Figure 12–22) clearly illustrates this point. No industrial nation can long survive without ample sources of energy, and few nations have enough reserves within their borders to ignore the international flow of resources, including fossil fuels. Nuclear reactors and hydrogen fusion processes may someday relieve growing demands for energy in the industrialized nations, but many years will pass before they do.

Meanwhile, Europe and Japan are tied to Middle Eastern sources of petroleum, just as Canada, South America, and, to a lesser extent, the Middle East will remain vital sources of energy for America. As the resource-rich developing nations become increasingly able to control their own destinies, and, as a result, the prices they charge for their exported raw materials, the demands of their crowded poor for a higher level of living will become more forceful. The world's population will more an more share a single destiny, just as earth itself is more and more becoming a single, complexly interconnected home for humankind.

Postscript

We began our investigation of a geographic

The Urban World and Its Hinterland: Land Use Theory

269

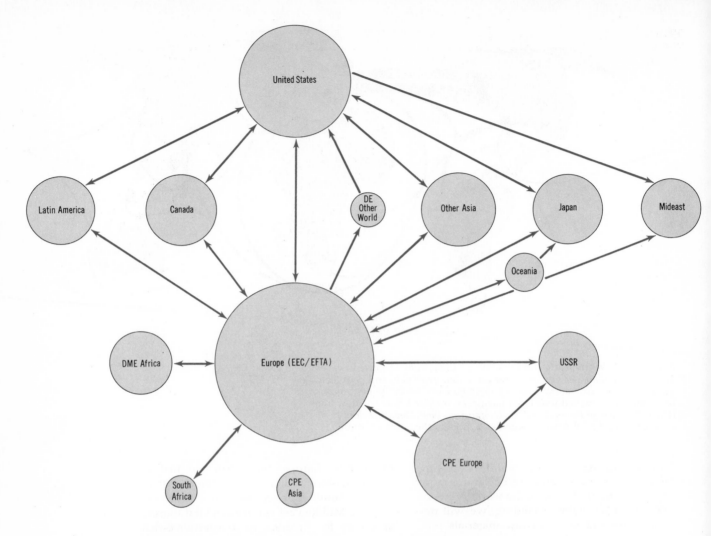

Figure 12-21 Import/export links between world trade blocks The abbreviations refer to: DE (Developing Economies), CPE (Centrally Planned Economies), EEC/EFTA (European Economic Community/European Free Trade Association), DAE (Developing African Economies). Circles are proportional to the volume of export trade of each nation or group of nations. Arrows indicate direction of movement in excess of 100 million dollars per year. Note that the Centrally Planned Economies of Asia have no such links. (op. cit. Figure 12-20)

Human
Geography:
Spatial
Design
In World
Society

270

point of view by considering the importance of scale in human affairs. Our first examples were largely drawn from within the limits of cities. In this final chapter, global space has occupied our thought. In either case, we hope that the geographic point of view we have presented will help you understand the unity of the one world we all must share. We recognize that our discussion of the spatial organization of world society has emphasized human

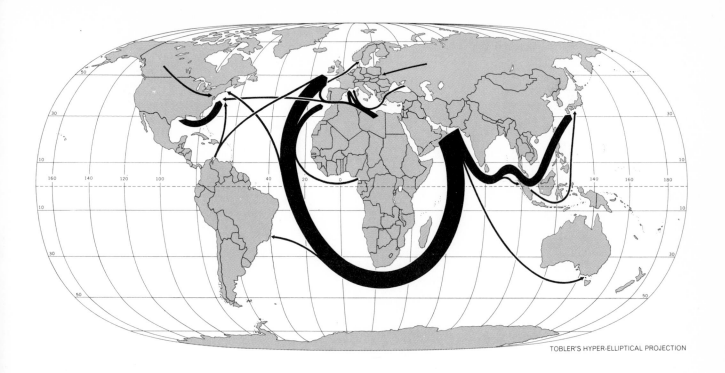

TOBLER'S HYPER-ELLIPTICAL PROJECTION

**Figure 12-22 International trade in petroleum and petroleum products—
1969** Source: Department of Economic and Social Affairs, Statistical Office
of the United Nations.

spatial systems and that the natural environment and the systems which constitute it have received far less attention. Our purpose in this volume, however, has been to make you, the reader, more aware of the human uses of geographic space. We hope that we have succeeded and that you will now go on to learn more about the spatial relationships and spatial processes that inextricably link man and nature into a single human ecosystem.

*The Urban
World and
Its Hinterland:
Land Use
Theory*

271

INDEX